The Ambivalence of Gay Liberation

The Ambivalence of Gay Liberation

Male Homosexual Politics in 1970s West Germany

CRAIG GRIFFITHS

OXFORD
UNIVERSITY PRESS

OXFORD
UNIVERSITY PRESS

Great Clarendon Street, Oxford, OX2 6DP,
United Kingdom

Oxford University Press is a department of the University of Oxford.
It furthers the University's objective of excellence in research, scholarship,
and education by publishing worldwide. Oxford is a registered trade mark of
Oxford University Press in the UK and in certain other countries

First Edition published in 2021

Impression: 2

Published in the United States of America by Oxford University Press
198 Madison Avenue, New York, NY 10016, United States of America

British Library Cataloguing in Publication Data
Data available

Library of Congress Control Number: 2020946226

ISBN 978-0-19-886896-5

DOI: 10.1093/oso/9780198868965.001.0001

Printed and bound by
CPI Group (UK) Ltd, Croydon, CR0 4YY

To my parents, and in loving memory of my father

Acknowledgements

This book has been a long time in the making, and I have accrued a lot of debts along the way. Firstly, I would like to thank the staff and volunteers of the *Schwules Museum* archive in Berlin, especially Jens Dobler. I am also grateful to archivists from the WDR archive and *Centrum Schwule Geschichte*, both in Cologne; the APO and Social Movements archive at the Free University Berlin; the *Spinnboden Lesbenarchiv*, also in Berlin; the Hall-Carpenter archives at the LSE; the LGBT Community Center National History Archive in New York; and the Manuscript and Archives division of New York Public Library. I am grateful to Detlef Mücke for allowing me access to his private archival collection, and to Michael Holy, whose collection is available at the *Schwules Museum*. I would also like to thank Michael for his advice and for the stimulus provided by his scholarship. Similarly, I am grateful to those who agreed to be interviewed for this project.

In carrying out the research for this book, I was fortunate to be able to draw upon support provided by the Arts and Humanities Research Council, the German Academic Exchange Service, the German History Society, the German Historical Institute in Washington, DC, and the History Research Centre of Manchester Metropolitan University. I benefitted greatly from the feedback provided by organizers and participants of numerous seminars and conferences, which helped clarify and sharpen my thinking. This book would not have been possible without the wonderful support and expertise of my doctoral supervisor, Christina von Hodenberg. Also at Queen Mary, University of London, I would like to thank Julian Jackson, Rhodri Hayward, and Miri Rubin. I am grateful to my PhD examiners, Bernhard Rieger and Chris Waters. The genesis of this work dates back to my undergraduate and MA programmes; thank you to Lars Fischer, Philipp Müller, Robert Gillett, and Godela Weiss-Sussex.

My heartfelt thanks to those who have read proposals and chapter drafts, offered advice, and tolerated my ramblings about this manuscript. Your encouragement and support has kept me going; your constructive criticism has also considerably improved the book. This includes several colleagues at Manchester Metropolitan University; Mercedes Peñalba-Sotorrío, Jonathan Spangler, Mark Fenemore, Ros Oates, and Melanie Tebbutt. From the University of Manchester, my thanks to Charlotte Faucher, Laure Humbert and Max Jones. Further afield, I am grateful to Chris Waters, Bernhard Rieger, Christina von Hodenberg, and Nikos Papadogiannis. Beyond the specifics of this book, I am deeply indebted to friends and colleagues in queer history, whose generosity of spirit has made me feel part of a community; thank you especially to Chris Waters and to Benno Gammerl, and Justin Bengry, Rebecca Jennings, Dan Callwood, Robert Mills and Matt Cook. In this vein, I would also like to thank all my fellow convenors of the History of Sexuality seminar at the IHR in London, as well as colleagues at Manchester Metropolitan University.

For their support, attention to detail, and guidance, thank you to series editors Neil Gregor and Len Scales, and to Cathryn Steele and Katie Bishop at Oxford University Press. I am also grateful to the anonymous peer reviewers; your generous feedback and thoughtful criticism has greatly improved the manuscript. Thank you to Gregor Wind, Kristine Schmidt, Peter Hedenstöm, Rolf Fischer, and Egmont Fassbinder for help with photo permissions. Not only in relation to the book, I am deeply grateful to Martin Gill and Diane Turner.

Finally, I would like to place on record the tremendous debt I owe to my friends and family, whose moral support has helped me navigate academic life—and beyond. Thank you to Joe, Sara, Mercedes, Laure, Jonathan, Lisa, Ariane, Mandy, Sol, Adrian, Molly, Nick, Jenny, Kathryn and Katie. Particular thanks are due to Charlotte, not only for reading all of the manuscript, but for her unstinting support, kindness and friendship. Lastly, thanks to my family; to James, Amanda and Thomas, to my grandparents, to Mum, and to Dad.

Manchester, 2020.

Contents

List of Figures

List of Abbreviations

APO	Extra-Parliamentary Opposition
ARD	First Channel (public television broadcaster)
CSU	Christian Social Union
DKP	German Communist Party
FAZ	*Frankfurter Allgemeine Zeitung*
FDP	Free Democratic Party
KBW	Communist League of West Germany
KPD	Communist Party of Germany
SDS	Socialist German Student League
SPD	Social Democratic Party of Germany
VVN	Association of those Persecuted by the Nazi Regime
WDR	Public television broadcaster based in North-Rhine Westphalia; largest constituent member of the ARD consortium
ZDF	Second Channel (public television broadcaster)

Homosexual groups

AHA	General Homosexual Action Alliance (West Berlin)
AHB	Action Group Homosexuality Bonn
DAH	German Action Alliance Homosexuality (umbrella group)
DHO	German Homophile Organization
FHAR	Homosexual Revolutionary Action Front (Paris)
fuori!	United Front of Italian Revolutionary Homosexuals
GLF	Gay Liberation Front (New York, San Francisco, London)
glf-Köln	GLF Cologne
GSR	Society for Sexual Reform (Aachen)
HAB	Homosexual Action Bremen
HAG	Homosexual Action Group (Bochum)
HAH	Homosexual Action Hamburg
HAK	Homosexual Action Kassel
HAKI	Homosexual Action Kiel
HAM	Homosexual Action Munich
HAN	Homosexual Action Nuremberg
HAS	Homosexual Action Saarbrücken
HAW	Homosexual Action West Berlin
HSM	Homophile Student Group Münster/Student Action Group Homosexuality
IDH	Interest Association of German Homophiles (Wiesbaden)
IHB	Initiative Group Homosexuality Bielefeld
IHS	Initiative Group Homosexuality Stuttgart
IHT	Initiative Group Homosexuality Tübingen

IHWO   International Homophile World Organization (Hamburg)
LAZ   Lesbian Action Centre (West Berlin)
NARGS   National Working Group Repression against Gays
Rotzschwul *Rote Zelle Schwul*—Red Cell Gay (Frankfurt)
SAK   Gay Action Cologne
SMB   *Schwules Museum Berlin* (Gay Museum)
VSG   Association for Sexual Equal Rights (Munich)
WüHsT   Würzburg Homosexual Action

Introduction

In the opinion of the Editor, Germany is now the best place in Europe for a gay person to live. [. . .] The Germans are quick to exploit and advance their homosexual freedom, and especially in the bigger cities, almost anything goes. Old inhibitions are dying quickly, and gay life is swinging.

– Spartacus International Gay Guide, 1974.[1]

Today we wear the Pink Triangle again in order to show that we perceive this society as a new concentration camp.

– Homosexual Action Munich, 1975.[2]

Until September 1969, male homosexuality in West Germany remained criminal, subject to the Nazi-era version of Paragraph 175, the sodomy law originally dating from the unification of Germany in 1871. Almost 25,000 guilty verdicts were passed down in the 1960s alone and more men were prosecuted in the period 1953–1965 than in the 12 years of National Socialist rule.[3] In 1979, after what one prominent gay publicist called the 'decade of homosexual emancipation', activists invited the 'gays of the world' to Frankfurt, to celebrate *Homolulu*, a week-long 'dance of the gays on the volcano,' a volcano which would bury 'hetero-chauvinism' under its queer lava.[4] The misery of illegality had given way to sexual abandon. Furtive, restrained campaigning behind the scenes, characteristic of the 1950s and 1960s, had been transformed into unabashed celebrations of same-sex desire, loud and proud. This apparent transformation has allowed a certain story to be told about gay liberation, whether in West Germany or elsewhere in the Western world. This story imagines the 1970s as the decade when the closet doors

---

[1] *Spartacus International Gay Guide* (Amsterdam, 1974), 145.

[2] HAM, 'Wir tragen den Rosa Winkel', in *Der Rosa Winkel*, ed. by HAW (1975), 16. *Schwules Museum Berlin* archive [hereafter, SMB archive]. Unless otherwise stated, all translations are my own.

[3] The highest number of convictions in a calendar year was 3267 (in 1961). In 1969 there were 894 convictions. These figures include Paragraph 175b, which related to bestiality. *Statistisches Jahrbuch für die Bundesrepublik Deutschland* (Wiesbaden [published annually]). On the comparison to the Third Reich, see Robert Moeller 'The Homosexual Man Is a "Man", the Homosexual Woman Is a "Woman": Sex, Society, and the Law in Postwar West Germany', *Journal of the History of Sexuality* 4 (1994), 395–429 (427).

[4] For the publicist's remark, see Alexander Ziegler, 'Das letzte Wort', *du&ich* 12 (1979), 52. On *Homolulu*, see 'Aufruf zur Reise nach Tunix'. SMB archive, box Rosa Winkel Verlag.

The Ambivalence of Gay Liberation: Male Homosexual Politics in 1970s West Germany. Craig Griffiths, Oxford University Press (2021). © Craig Griffiths.
DOI: 10.1093/oso/9780198868965.003.0001

were ripped off their hinges, when gays and lesbians threw off decades of shame and oppression and strode proudly into a golden future of visibility and sexual equality.

In this book, I give a different account of homosexual emancipation in the 1970s. Gay liberation was never some utopian, radical, hedonistic interlude, an assumption held by both its supporters and detractors. West German gays aggressively challenged representations of homosexuality as deviant, as abnormal, even as they remained perpetually divided over which representations should be offered up for public consumption instead. Was society prepared to tolerate and accept homosexuals, if only they would be, well, less queer and act like everybody else? Or was it rather a case of society being in need of change, and if so, should that change be incremental or revolutionary? Younger gay activists lambasted older homosexuals for their supposed conformism and reactionary outlook, just as they scorned those politically apathetic men who spent their time furtively cruising for sex in the scene. Yet nowhere did the politics of confrontation totally eclipse the politics of recognition. Shame was not vanquished by pride. The pushes of revolt and resistance sat uneasily alongside the pulls of convention and the desire to be accepted. Gay men's ambivalence about themselves, their desires and the society in which they lived is placed at the heart of this book.[5]

In part, gay liberation heralded a dizzying sense of the possible, with same-sex desire breaking free from the chains of homophobia and sexual conservatism. This is evidenced both by the rapid expansion and diversification of the gay scene, and the emergence of various forms of homosexual organizing, first of a largely liberal and moderate tendency and then with a more militant hue. If in 1969 there was not a single group in West Germany providing help and support for homosexuals, nor agitating for gay rights, by 1980 some 53 towns and cities in the Federal Republic were home to such groups, and there were several hundred in total.[6] Divided Berlin, Frankfurt, and Hamburg were important. But quite unlike the situation in the United States, dominated by San Francisco and Los Angeles on the West Coast and New York on the East Coast, or in France and Britain, dominated by Paris and London respectively, gay liberation in West Germany played out in places as varied as Stuttgart, Münster, Bremen, Munich, and Aachen. This period, book-ended by homosexual law reform in 1969 and the arrival of the HIV/AIDS crisis in the early 1980s, also saw the face of homosexual print culture utterly transformed, with a multitude of mimeographed activist zines (Infos) jostling alongside a new breed of glossy gay magazines. The British editor of the

---

[5] For reasons I explain below, this book focuses on gay male politics only, as opposed to conducting an equal analysis of gay liberation and lesbian feminism. Similarly, this book focuses on West Germany only, though the relationship between West and East German activists will be discussed in Chapter 1. On East Germany, see Josie McLellan, 'Glad to Be Gay Behind the Wall: Gay and Lesbian Activism in 1970s East Germany', *History Workshop Journal* 74 (2012), 105–30.

[6] According to an annual list kept updated by the Action Group Homosexuality in Bonn (AHB). *Addressen zur Schwulenemanzipation* (May 1980). SMB archive.

Spartacus International Gay Guide waxed lyrical in 1974 that 'Germany is now the best place in Europe for a gay person to live', adding 'old inhibitions are dying quickly, and gay life is swinging'.[7]

Yet for all their energy and hopeful longings, closer inspection reveals that gay men equally encountered the frustration of feeling *verklemmt*—inhibited. This oscillation between affirmation and inhibition was never only sexual, but always also political. This book therefore addresses a wider story about the ambivalence of a political culture—that of mainstream West German society but also that of the alternative left which developed after 1968. Rather than seeing homosexual law reform as but further evidence of the Federal Republic's successful shedding of the Nazi past, the liberalization of Paragraph 175 in 1969 offered gay men only a precarious foothold in society, one that they could never take for granted.[8] The Nazi version of the sodomy statute was no longer in force, but another legacy of the Third Reich was to make a very visible impact. The symbol of the pink triangle, developed by the Nazis to categorize homosexual concentration camp prisoners, was 'rediscovered' in the 1970s and subsequently became a prominent feature of gay rights activism in the decade. The Homosexual Action Munich (HAM) declared in 1975, 'Today we wear the Pink Triangle again in order to show that we perceive this society as a new concentration camp', only the most drastic iteration of an influential discourse emerging from the gay left.[9] In homosexual emancipation, the tendency to invoke the fascist past ran deep. In the 1970s, it was not sexual liberation, nor anti-authoritarianism, but instead reference to oppression that would prove to be the most reliable means by which gay men could win some purchase in the wider public sphere, and especially in the alternative left. If contemporaries were caught between an atmosphere of upheaval and a sense of crisis, between an *Aufbruchstimmung* and a *Krisengefühl*,[10] then gay liberation was both the beneficiary and casualty of this ambivalent situation.

The German History of Homosexual Emancipation

Before delving into the queer idiosyncrasies of gay liberation, allow me a few words about earlier forms of homosexual emancipation. German history and the German language provide a rich legacy in this regard. It was in German that the

---

[7] *Spartacus International Gay Guide* (Amsterdam, 1974), 145. The guide's editor was John Stamford.

[8] The 1969 reform set the age of consent for male homosexual activity at 21. A further reform to Paragraph 175 in 1973 reduced this to 18. This diluted version of Paragraph 175 remained in force until 1994, when the measure was repealed altogether.

[9] HAM, 'Wir tragen den Rosa Winkel', in *Der Rosa Winkel*, ed. by HAW (1975), 16. SMB archive.

[10] Konrad Jarausch, 'Verkannter Strukturwandel: Die siebziger Jahre als Vorgeschichte der Probleme der Gegenwart', in *Das Ende der Zuversicht? Die siebziger Jahre als Geschichte* (Göttingen, 2008), 10–26 (10).

word 'homosexual' was first used, in a letter written by Karl Maria Kertbeny to Karl Heinrich Ulrichs in May 1868.[11] Though he did not himself use the language of homosexuality, Ulrichs played a key role in disseminating the idea that same-sex sexual acts were the congenital feature of a specific class of persons. He suggested the terms *Urninge* and *Urninden* for same-sex desiring men and women respectively. According to Ulrichs, same-sex desiring men constituted a 'third sex', characterized by a feminine soul trapped inside a male body. Ulrichs, a lawyer from Hanover, contended that same-sex love was an in-born, natural condition, and as such should not be criminalized. He argued his case in a series of pamphlets in the 1860s, unsuccessfully seeking to prevent the Prussian criminalization of sodomy being rolled out across Germany upon unification in 1871—including in states like Hanover and Bavaria, where sodomy, under the influence of the Napoleonic code, had not been illegal. Ulrichs stoutly defended his publications against confiscation by officials in Leipzig: 'My writings are the voice of a socially oppressed minority that now claims its rights to be heard.'[12]

Building on these foundations, the world's first homosexual emancipation movement can be dated to 1897, when sexologist Magnus Hirschfeld founded the Scientific-Humanitarian Committee in Berlin. Hirschfeld did not at first use 'homosexual' in his work (preferring terms like 'third sex', 'Urning', or 'invert'), and never referred to his own same-sex sexuality in print.[13] A rich historiography on sexology and its impact on early homosexual rights activism has developed.[14] All this work recognizes the pivotal role played by German-language sexology and psychiatry. Alongside Hirschfeld, Albert Moll, Iwan Bloch, Carl Westphal, and especially Richard von Krafft-Ebing were all important, even if what became homosexuality was for most of them a form of perversion or degeneration. Profitable historiographical debate continues to rage over the exact relationship between sexological discourse and subject formation, or the manner in which a homosexual category was gradually and incompletely transformed into a

---

[11] For a facsimile of the letter, with an introduction by Manfred Herzer, see 'Ein Brief von Kertbeny in Hannover an Ulrichs in Würzburg', *Capri: Zeitschrift für schwule Geschichte* 1 (1987), 26–35.

[12] Robert Beachy, *Gay Berlin: Birthplace of a Modern Identity* (New York, 2014), 21.

[13] Ibid., 86; Laurie Marhoefer, *Sex and the Weimar Republic: German Homosexual Emancipation and the Rise of the Nazis* (Toronto, 2015), 124.

[14] This builds on the theoretical impetus bequeathed by Michel Foucault, and the pioneering work of James Steakley, *The Homosexual Emancipation Movement in Germany* (New York, 1975). Among recent work, see Beachy, *Gay Berlin*; Marhoefer, *Sex and the Weimar Republic*; Robert Deam Tobin, *Peripheral Desires: The German Discovery of Sex* (Philadelphia, 2015); and Marti Lybeck, *Desiring Emancipation: New Women and Homosexuality in Germany, 1890–1933* (New York, 2014). On the contribution of psychoanalysis, see Katie Sutton, *Sex between Body and Mind: Psychoanalysis and Sexology in the German-speaking World, 1890s-1930s* (Ann Arbor, MI, 2019). For an introductory overview, see Clayton Whisnant, *Queer Identities and Politics in Germany: A History, 1880–1945* (New York, 2016), 14–40.

homosexual identity (if only for a minority of subjects, normally upper or middle-class and male).[15]

The German homosexual rights movement continued to grow after the First World War, deploying 'a rhetoric of citizenship invigorated by the war'.[16] Hirschfeld founded the Institute for Sexual Science in Berlin in 1919, seeking to put the Scientific-Humanitarian Committee's motto into practice ('justice through science'). As censorship was loosened, that same year saw the arrival of *Die Freundschaft* (Friendship), the world's first homosexual paper to be placed on public sale. Over the course of the Weimar Republic, 30 such periodicals were published.[17] The Scientific-Humanitarian Committee had only a small membership, but the new *Bund für Menschenrecht* (League for Human Rights) recruited up to 100,000 members. Homosexual rights in the Weimar Republic, according to both Laurie Marhoefer and Robert Beachy, became a mass movement.[18] The German centrality to early homosexual emancipation is further demonstrated by the fact that the first homosexual rights group in the United States was directly modelled on German organizations. Henry Gerber had encountered the aforementioned 'League for Human Rights' during his post-war service in Germany with the US military, and then set up the short-lived 'Society for Human Rights' upon his return to Chicago in 1924.[19]

Already before the First World War, there had been competing paths to emancipation in the German homosexual rights movement. Hirschfeld focused on the promises of science and sought to build links with the German women's movement, whereas Benedict Friedlaender and Adolf Brand rejected any notion of a 'third sex', and instead insisted on the hyper-virile, masculine nature of homosexual men. Their 'masculinist' vision of homosexual emancipation was given organizational shape in the *Gemeinschaft der Eigenen* ('Community of the Special'), which they co-founded with another activist, Wilhelm Jansen, in 1903.[20] The masculinist cause received a boost through the First World War, because some same-sex desiring servicemen were able to use their wartime experience to appropriate 'militarized, nationalistic ideals of comradeship', in order to counter the idea that they were 'effeminate social outsiders'.[21] The war was also the context that animated the influential concept of the *Männerbund*, the all-male association. Its most well-known adherent, Hans Blüher, argued that

---

[15] Marti Lybeck recognizes that sexological discourse was 'indispensable to the development of middle-class homosexual identity', but shows how the women in her account did not merely 'passively accept the claims of doctors and experts'. *Desiring Emancipation*, 194. Despite the many criticisms of Foucault, the field remains indebted to his notion of discourse and reverse discourse. Foucault, *The History of Sexuality. Volume One: An Introduction* (London, 1990 [1976]), 100–1.

[16] Marhoefer, *Sex and the Weimar Republic*, 22. [17] Beachy, *Gay Berlin*, 164.

[18] Marhoefer, *Sex and the Weimar Republic*, 40–1; Beachy, *Gay Berlin*, 221.

[19] Marc Stein, *Rethinking the Gay and Lesbian Movement* (New York, 2012), 37–40.

[20] Beachy, *Gay Berlin*, 103.

[21] Jason Crouthamel, '"We Need Real Men". The Impact of the Front Experience on Homosexual Front Soldiers', in *An Intimate History of the Front* (New York, 2014), 121–46 (122).

erotic bonds between men constituted a necessary bedrock for the German state. The distinctly authoritarian, misogynistic, and anti-Semitic bent to Blüher's vision provided a bridge for some homosexual men to engage with National Socialism, in which, for a short period, they had a poster-boy in the shape of Ernst Röhm, the homosexual leader of the SA (*Sturmabteilung*, stormtroopers).[22]

Any hopes of an accommodation between fascism and homosexual emancipation were soon dashed, not least by Röhm's murder in 1934, and then by the sharpening of Paragraph 175 in 1935, which made it much easier to secure convictions. Immediately upon coming to power, the Nazis smashed the homosexual scene and closed the Institute for Sexual Science. Its library was ransacked and its books were burned. Homosexual men, wearing the pink triangle on their uniforms, were made into a distinct category of prisoner in the concentration camp system. At least 10,000 such men ended up in the concentration camps, where more than half of them died.[23]

After 1945, it proved exceedingly difficult to re-establish the movement, not least because most of the key activists, including Hirschfeld, were dead. Upon German division in 1949, the Nazified version of Paragraph 175 remained in force in the Federal Republic, unlike the German Democratic Republic, which returned to the milder 1871 version of the law. Nevertheless, the early 1950s did see the establishment of several homosexual journals in West Germany, which were the main means of communication for the groups that were founded alongside them, including the Association for a Humanitarian Way of Life in Frankfurt and the International Friendship Lodge in Bremen.[24]

The caution and discretion of these groups and journals can be seen through their choice of terminology. In West Germany, just as elsewhere in the Western world, 'homophile' was the term generally used by the homosexual emancipation movement in the 1940s, 1950s, and 1960s, a label designed to avoid drawing attention to the *sexual* in homosexual. As we will see at the start of Chapter 2, the extremely hostile social environment in the early Federal Republic put paid to the hopes of these groups of emulating the Weimar-era movement. Torn asunder by

---

[22] On Blüher, see Beachy, *Gay Berlin*, 140–59 and Claudia Bruns, 'Der homosexuelle Staatsfreund: Von der Konstruktion des erotischen Männerbunds bei Hans Blüher', in *Homosexualität und Staatsräson: Männlichkeit, Homophobie und Politik in Deutschland 1900–45*, ed. by Susanne zur Nieden (Frankfurt a.M., 2005), 100–17. On homoeroticism in the SA, see Marhoefer, *Sex and the Weimar Republic*, 146–73 and Andrew Wackerfuss, *Stormtrooper Families: Homosexuality and Community in the Early Nazi Movement* (New York, 2015).

[23] On the Third Reich, see further Chapter 4. On the Institute for Sexual Science and its destruction, see Heike Bauer, *The Hirschfeld Archives: Violence, Death and Modern Queer Culture* (Philadelphia, PA, 2017), 78–101.

[24] On the West German homophile movement, see Clayton Whisnant, *Male Homosexuality in West Germany: Between Persecution and Freedom 1945–1969* (New York, 2012), especially 64–111; Andreas Pretzel and Volker Weiß (eds), *Ohnmacht und Aufbegehren: Homosexuelle Männer in der frühen Bundesrepublik* (Hamburg, 2010); and Burkhardt Riechers, 'Freundschaft und Anständigkeit. Leitbilder im Selbtsverständnis männlicher Homosexueller in der frühen Bundesrepublik', *Invertito: Jahrbuch für die Geschichte der Homosexualitäten* 1 (1999), 12–46.

the impact of the 1953 'Law on the Dissemination of Youth-Endangering Texts', all of these homophile organizations and journals collapsed. There was to be no German version of the French *Arcadie*, the Dutch COC (Centre for Culture and Recreation), or the American Mattachine Society.[25] In terms of print culture, only *Der Kreis* (published from Zurich, with sections in French and in English) and *Der Weg* (published from Hamburg) managed to achieve any longevity whatsoever, before ceasing publication in 1967 and 1970 respectively, before the onset of gay liberation.

Writing Gay Liberation

The first wave of historiography on gay liberation was overwhelmingly the product of activists or former activists from the very movements now made into the object of historical enquiry. These pioneers generally proceeded from the perspective that homosexuality had always been 'hidden from history' and saw it as their political and intellectual duty to enhance the visibility of gays and lesbians, making good on the historical marginalization of same-sex love by creating affirmative narratives that could help stabilize gay identity in the present.[26] Indeed, this was the foundational mission of the whole field of gay and lesbian history. My work does not seek to denigrate this mission, and I do not claim to be unaffected by it.

The corpus of work produced by activists-turned-historians has been of immense importance in the German context. Activists produced not only the first wave of scholarship but in 1985 also set up the *Schwules Museum* (Gay Museum) in Berlin, the archive of which has proved indispensable to this and many other projects.[27] So vital to subsequent historical research, we should not forget the significance of pioneering collecting and archiving work, nor the costs involved. One such prominent activist-turned-historian, Michael Holy, reflects on how his 15-year mission to collect and order sources on the gay movement

[25] See further Julian Jackson, *Living in Arcadia: Homosexuality, Politics and Morality in France from the Liberation to AIDS* (Chicago, 2009); Meeker, *Contacts Desired: Gay and Lesbian Communications and Community, 1940s–1970s* (Chicago, 2006); John D'Emilio, *Sexual Politics, Sexual Communities. The Making of a Homosexual Minority in the United States, 1940–1970* (Chicago, 1983).

[26] 'For many, gay history helps constitute the gay community by giving it a tradition, helps women and men validate and understand who they are by showing them who they have been.' George Chauncey, Martin Bauml Duberman, and Martha Vicinus (eds), *Hidden From History: Reclaiming the Gay and Lesbian Past* (New York, 1989), 12.

[27] In this vein, I would like to acknowledge the work of Andreas Salmen, Albert Eckert, and especially Michael Holy. See for example Salmen and Eckert, *20 Jahre bundesdeutsche Schwulenbewegung 1969–1989* (Cologne, 1989) and Holy, 'Jenseits von Stonewall – Rückblicke auf die Schwulenbewegung in der BRD 1969–1980,' in *Rosa Radikale: Die Schwulenbewegung der 1970er Jahre*, ed. by Andreas Pretzel and Volker Weiß (Hamburg, 2012), 39–79.

ultimately derailed his doctoral study.[28] The German historical profession has been slower than its counterparts in Britain and the United States to open its doors to historical enquiry into homosexuality, and therefore the pioneers of gay and lesbian history have not entered the academy to the same extent as elsewhere.[29] As Rüdiger Lautmann states, at the conclusion of his volume dedicated to the prolific activist-turned-historian Manfred Herzer, 'without the ideas and findings of the professional outsiders, homo history would be virtually a blank page'.[30]

At the same time, this early work has set rather a one-dimensional framework for conceptualizing gay liberation. Kristina Schulz, in her study of the West German and French women's movements of the 1970s, has argued that the movements' first historians were so preoccupied by the desire to establish an activist continuity with feminist organizations from earlier in the twentieth century that they could not successfully apprehend what was specific about the new women's movements.[31] For the West German gay movement, rather the opposite is the case. Convinced of having witnessed—of having themselves ushered in—a dramatic departure from earlier forms of homosexual organizing, historians were able to stress the 'new' and the 'specific' of gay liberation, but continuities were elided. This has led to the introduction into accounts of homosexual politics of the structural dichotomy 'radical/integrationist'.[32] These early historians essentially argued that there were on the one hand those who sought radical change to society, and on the other, those who sought to integrate themselves into existing society, but this dichotomy did not capture the complexities inherent in gay liberation—and in individual queer lives.

For these reasons, while this book began life as a social movement study of the West German gay movement in the 1970s, it has become a much wider history of homosexual politics: ways of thinking, feeling, and talking about homosexuality. I adapt this description from Julian Jackson's important work on homosexuality in modern France, in which he reassesses the role of the French homophile

---

[28] Holy, 'Bewegungsgeschichte und Sammelleidenschaft: Zur Entstehung der "Sammlung Holy"', in *Politiken in Bewegung: Die Emanzipation Homosexueller im 20. Jahrhundert*, ed. by Andreas Pretzel and Volker Weiss (Hamburg, 2017), 193–245 (200).

[29] Recent developments suggest that this may be changing. The best-known German-language historical conference, the *Historikertag*, held its first panel on the history of homosexuality in 2014, while the German Historical Museum—in collaboration with the *Schwules Museum*—curated its first exhibition on the theme in 2015, '*HOMOSEXUALITÄT_EN*'.

[30] Lautmann (ed.), *Capricen: Momente schwuler Geschichte* (Hamburg, 2014), 276. Lautmann is something of an exception to the rule, as he was awarded a professorship as early as 1971 (in Sociology and in Law rather than in History).

[31] Schulz, *Der lange Atem der Provokation: Die Frauenbewegung in der Bundesrepublik und in Frankreich 1968–1976* (Frankfurt a.M., 2002), 19.

[32] Michael Holy, 'Historischer Abriß'; Salmen and Eckert, *20 Jahre bundesdeutsche Schwulenbewegung*; Elmar Kraushaar, '"Nebenwidersprüche". Die neue Linke und die Schwulenfrage in der Bundesrepublik der siebziger und achtziger Jahre', in *Die Linke und das Laster: Schwule Emanzipation und linke Vorurteile*, ed. by Detlef Grumbach (Hamburg, 1995), 142–78.

movement.³³ Jackson shows how the politics and ways of life of French homo-philes were misunderstood and widely mocked by younger gay liberationists who arrived on the scene in the early 1970s. Drawing on E. P. Thompson's phrase, Jackson seeks to rescue 'homophilia' from 'the enormous condescension of pos-terity': interrogating the assumption that the end goal of homosexual history is the pride, visibility, and sexual fulfilment associated with gay liberation. Accordingly, he writes that we need to 'liberate ourselves from gay liberation'. However, we do not advance our understanding by following Jackson's conceptualization that the 'radicalism of the 1970s' represents a parenthesis rather than a departure in homosexual history.³⁴ It was neither. I am interested neither in lionizing nor deprecating the 1970s, but in escaping an exceptionalist reading of that decade. What we need to liberate ourselves from is not gay liberation, but a tendency to treat the period as an interregnum, a brief moment either of unfulfilled promise or melodramatic theatrics, depending on one's perspective. Following Laurie Marhoefer, in her work on the Weimar Republic, we need to consider 'the complexity and ugliness of homosexual emancipation' in order to arrive at a more productive relationship with the queer past.³⁵

This book therefore complicates the standard narrative of gay liberation in two main ways. Firstly, by foregrounding the ambivalence of gay liberation, I disturb a well-told story of shame giving way to pride, subjugation transforming into freedom, and fear blossoming into hope. Ambivalence, the simultaneous attach-ment to conflicting feelings and attitudes, draws attention to how gay liberation was structured by oscillations between irreconcilable poles. These will be discussed more fully below, but three main tensions, or axes of ambivalence, were pride/shame, normal/different and hope/fear. Secondly, this book is not structured around breaks and ruptures. In particular, I challenge the traditional chronology of 1968/69 marking a sharp historical divide. The major culprit here is Stonewall. Beginning in the early hours of Saturday, 28 June 1969, when patrons of the Stonewall Inn on Christopher Street, New York City, defended themselves against a police raid, the Stonewall riots are often credited as the spark that set gay liberation alight.³⁶ American gay and lesbian activists marked the first anniversary of the Stonewall riots in 1970 with a large demonstration. This event became annual and was subsequently exported around the world, not least to Germany, where annual CSD (Christopher Street Day) parades continue to take place in most major cities each June.³⁷

³³ Jackson's usage is 'ways of thinking and talking about being homosexual.' *Living in Arcadia*, 15.
³⁴ Ibid., 13, 248.   ³⁵ Marhoefer, *Sex and the Weimar Republic*, 217.
³⁶ As Marc Stein notes, the riots are often understood, incorrectly, as the first 'first act of lesbian and gay resistance *ever*.' See his *City of Sisterly and Brotherly Loves: Lesbian and Gay Philadelphia, 1945–1972* (Chicago, 2000), 289. Emphasis in the original.
³⁷ The first such event in Germany took place in Bremen, Stuttgart, Cologne, and West Berlin on 30 June 1979, to mark the tenth anniversary of the Stonewall riots. 'Zehn Jahre Stonewall Day', *Emanzipation* 5 (1979), 28–31. See further Craig Griffiths, 'The International Effects of the Stonewall

The Stonewall riots were not the first example of gay and lesbian public protest, but the first example to be successfully commemorated. In this light, the 'Stonewall story is thus better viewed as an *achievement* of gay liberation rather than as a literal account of its origins.'[38] Elizabeth Kennedy argues that by periodizing lesbian and gay life as 'pre-' and 'post-Stonewall', the historian creates a metanarrative, 'an overarching story' of lesbian and gay history that relegates everything that came before to the mere prehistory of gay liberation—not only homophile movements but also the working-class lesbian bar communities researched by Kennedy.[39] The Stonewall metanarrative has spatial as well as temporal characteristics, privileging the American national context over others. For same-sex desiring men in West Germany, the most significant development to occur in 1969 was not Stonewall, but homosexual law reform. Consider also 1968, the student movement and the wave of protest and activism that it unleashed. Certainly, 1968/69 was an important historical moment, whether we look at New York or closer to home in the Federal Republic. Yet none of these events gave rise to a linear shift from 'cautious' to 'radical,' from 'closeted' to 'visible,' or from 'shame' to 'pride'. By viewing the 1970s primarily as the period when this dramatic transformation took place, we end up in a historiographical straitjacket.

As part of this same approach, I have chosen to define 'gay liberation' in deliberately capacious terms. This book is not just a study on the gay left, but about the tremendous dynamism and ambivalence with which homosexuality was thought, felt, and discussed in the 1970s. By 'gay left', I mean those groups which emerged on the scene in the early 1970s and generally linked homosexual oppression to the capitalist system, declaring their solidarity with other oppressed groups. Yet liberation, *Befreiung* in German, was a term used widely not only in the gay left, but also by more moderate or liberal-minded homosexual rights organizations, as well as in the commercial gay press. It had a purchase that went far beyond those groups which actually included the term in their names.

Were this book about the Anglo-American context, it would be possible to define gay liberation in narrower terms: as a movement based organizationally in the Gay Liberation Front (GLF).[40] The first GLF was founded in New York in July 1969, shortly after the Stonewall Riots. The Liberation Front designation was inspired by liberation struggles in Algeria and Vietnam.[41] Describing itself as 'a

---

Riots', in *Global Encyclopedia of Lesbian, Gay, Bisexual, Transgender, and Queer History*, ed. by Howard Chiang et al. (Farmington Hills, MI, 2019), 1549–55.

[38] Emphasis added. Elizabeth Armstrong and Suzanna Crage, 'Movements and Memory: The Making of the Stonewall Myth', *American Sociological Review* 71 (2006), 724–51 (725).

[39] Kennedy, 'Telling Tales: Oral History and the Construction of Pre-Stonewall Lesbian History', *Radical History Review* 62 (1995), 58–79 (73).

[40] For more on either broad or narrow definitions of gay liberation, see Stein, *Rethinking the Gay and Lesbian Movement*, 90–1.

[41] Martin Duberman, *Stonewall* (New York, 1994), 217.

revolutionary homosexual group of women and men formed with the realization that complete sexual liberation for all peoples cannot come about unless existing social institutions are abolished', the GLF defined itself sharply against existing homophile organizations, including the Mattachine Society.[42] Local and regional Gay Liberation Fronts sprang up elsewhere in the United States, either as new groups, or as radicalized versions of existing organizations. For example, in San Francisco, the Committee for Homosexual Freedom, founded in February 1969, was renamed the GLF in August 1969. In 1970, the first Gay Liberation Front outside of the United States was founded, in London.[43]

There was no GLF in West Germany, if we translate the term directly into *Schwule Befreiungsfront*. This name was proposed by one caucus within the Homosexual Action West Berlin (HAW) in 1973, but the proposed change of name did not come to fruition.[44] The closest direct comparison to GLF organizations in the West German context would be homosexual 'action groups' (*Aktionsgruppen*). This explains the idiosyncratic plethora of initialisms and acronyms beginning with 'HA', such as the two groups already mentioned, the HAW in West Berlin and the HAM in Munich, alongside scores of others, including the Homosexual Action Kiel (HAKI) and the Homosexual Action Bremen (HAB). While 'gay' (*schwul*) was certainly the term preferred internally, and often in public-facing activist literature, these action groups nevertheless stuck with 'Homosexual' in their names. There were only a few exceptions, including the *Schwule Aktion Münster* (Gay Action Münster—SAM) and, based in Frankfurt, *Rotzschwul* (*Rote Zelle Schwul*—Red Cell Gay). Collectively, I refer to these groups as the gay left, but this was but one current within gay liberation.

There *was* a GLF in West Germany, if we include the *glf-Köln* (GLF Cologne), which used the English-language abbreviation in lower-case. According to an article in the group's newsletter, the name was inspired by the GLF in London, but it seems to have been intended as something of a discreet signifier, as 'glf' was not translated into German.[45] The group declined to participate in public actions, which ran the risk of increasing popular aversion to 'our minority'.[46] A faction broke away from *glf-Köln* in 1976, and this group *did* translate 'gay' into German, becoming the *Schwule Aktion Köln* (Gay Action Cologne: SAK). A member of the larger, original group made sure to explicitly differentiate his organization from 'extremist and militant' groups which dreamed of creating 'heaven on earth for homosexuals' by radical social change.[47]

---

[42] Gay Liberation Front, untitled editorial, *Come Out: A Liberation Forum of the Gay Community* 1, no. 3 (1970), 2. LGBT Community Center National History Archive, New York City.

[43] Emily Hobson, *Lavender and Red: Liberation and Solidarity in the Gay and Lesbian Left* (Oakland, CA, 2016), 26; Lucy Robinson, *Gay Men and the Left in Post-War Britain* (Manchester, 2007), 66.

[44] HAW Feministengruppe, 'Feministenpapier' (October 1973). SMB archive.

[45] Dieter Beheng, '2 Jahre GLF! Versuch einer Bilanz', *glf Journal* 5 (1973), 1–4 (1).

[46] *du&ich* 6 (1976), 43.   [47] *du&ich* 5 (1976), 45; Beheng, '2 Jahre GLF!', 2.

Despite the transnational reach the English-language term was subsequently to achieve later in the twentieth century, 'gay' was not always understood by Germans in the 1970s. Present at the first anniversary celebration of the Stonewall Riots in New York in late June 1970, Alexander Ziegler pondered how one would translate 'Gay Liberation Front' into German for a subsequent article in the gay magazine *du&ich*. Spectacularly missing the point about the reclamation of 'gay', Ziegler failed to recognize that gay in this context was akin to *schwul*, instead of his suggestion of *fröhlich* (i.e. cheery, happy, gay).[48] Strange as it may seem, the early 1970s saw a certain acceptance of the English-language 'gay', even where its German equivalent, *schwul*, was roundly rejected. For example, the editors of the short-lived *gay-journal* would explain the English-language title of their magazine through the term's perceived reference to 'the homosexual consciousness'. They bemoaned what they saw as a lack of equivalent in German, criticizing both the overly scientific (*homosexuell, homophil*) and the vulgar (*schwul, warm*).[49]

Even were it possible, for reasons of language, to restrict this study to groups calling themselves GLFs or individuals calling themselves 'gay liberationists', this would come at a cost. I do not wish to erase the important differences between disparate actors in gay liberation, in thinking, feeling, and talking about homosexuality: the gay left, more moderate liberal-minded organizations, and the commercial gay press, to name just three broad currents. However, adopting neat categorizations that this group or constituency was part of gay liberation, while this group or constituency was not, negates a more holistic story of homosexual emancipation in the 1970s: crucially, one which recognizes its ambivalence.

In the American context, Marc Stein distinguishes between 'radical gay liberation' and 'reformist gay and lesbian liberalism', with liberation gradually giving way to liberalism in the course of the 1970s. Yet what is 'radical' and what is 'reformist' depends both on the historical context and individual perspective, and the differences between liberalism and a 'broader leftist agenda of freedom, justice and equality' cannot always be easily drawn.[50] For example, if we were to insist on commitment to multi-dimensional solidarity being a defining feature of gay liberation, then we might posit the end of gay liberation almost as soon as it began, with the Gay Activists' Alliance breaking away from the New York GLF in 1970, due to the latter's declaration of support for the Black Panther Party.[51]

---

[48] 'Liebe auf den Straßen', *du&ich* 11 (1970), 2. This mistranslation of GLF was no one-off; the last issue of the homophile journal *Der Weg* carried a report on an action in San Francisco, following the arrest of several gay activists. Again, the translation *fröhlich* was given rather than *schwul*. 'Homosexuellen stürmten Rathaus', *Der Weg* 228 (1970), 43.

[49] *gay-journal: Das Blatt homophiler Emanzipation* 2 (May 1972), 2. In German, *schwul* is etymologically related to *schwül*, meaning humid or sticky: hence the homophobic slur 'warmer Bruder', 'warm brother'.

[50] Stein, *Rethinking the Gay and Lesbian Movement*, 12, 82.

[51] Hobson, *Lavender and Red*, 30.

Moreover, categorizations between the 'radicals' and the 'leftists' on the one side, and the 'liberals', 'reformists' or 'integrationists' on the other, suggest we are still too indebted to the idiom of the period, with its furious debates and reciprocal denigrations between this and that wing of gay liberation. We can only escape this idiom by departing from narrower social movement studies, recognizing that gay liberation became a much broader cultural phenomenon than the group that originally spawned its name.[52]

Reflecting my capacious definition of gay liberation, the source base for this book both builds on and goes beyond what might be more narrowly defined as 'social movement material'. I pay close attention to activist paraphernalia including local, regional, and national magazines, correspondence between group members, the minutes of organizing meetings and leaflets or posters designed for public consumption. These were supplemented by ten oral history interviews with former gay (and in one case, lesbian) activists, conducted between 2012 and 2014. Yet these sources, valuable as they are, cannot be seen in isolation from other material which offers an insight into how homosexuality was thought, felt, and spoken about in the 1970s. These range from material produced by and for homosexuals, including gay travel guides, works of literature, and the two largest commercial gay magazines (*him* and *du&ich*), to the coverage of gay liberation in both the left-alternative and the mainstream press, the representation of homosexuality on television, audience correspondence received by broadcasters about these films and documentaries, set against parliamentary proceedings, prosecution records, opinion polls, sex education manuals, and contemporary sociological data.

Homosexual, Queer, Gay, Lesbian

The various approaches to writing the history of gay liberation set out above come from different, if overlapping, methodological practices. The contribution of queer theory to historical research on same-sex desire has been significant, even if the differences between 'queer history' and 'gay and lesbian history' are not always easy to pin down. If early gay historians aimed to 'reclaim' the gay and lesbian past, queer historians are more sceptical about the desirability and very possibility of this restitutive mission. Rather than there existing an essential gay identity, stretching throughout time, just waiting to be discovered and recovered by the historian, queer history underscores the 'unknowability and indeterminacy of the

---

[52] Dan Callwood makes a similar point in 'Anxiety and Desire in France's Gay Pornographic Film Boom, 1974–1983', *Journal of the History of Sexuality* 26 1 (2017), 26–52 (27).

sexual past'.[53] Instead of starting from our present-day understanding of sexual categories, queer historians attempt to step outside these constructed, contingent identities. According to Jennifer Evans, 'To queer the past is to view it sceptically, to pull apart its constitutive pieces and analyse them from a variety of perspectives, taking nothing for granted.'[54] Queer theory, for Laura Doan, has 'blasted to smithereens' the possibility of fixed identities, stable meanings, and knowable truths.[55]

Early gay and lesbian historians were sometimes guilty of unthinkingly applying modern identity categories to past societies. More reflective work quickly reassessed this tendency, showing that sexual categories are socially constructed and historically specific, rather than being biological or 'natural', existing throughout time, as if written on stone. This evolved into the 'essentialist' versus 'social constructionist' debate, which predates the emergence of what became known as queer theory. That the 'homosexual' is an invention of the modern world is an insight regularly attributed to Michel Foucault,[56] although historians such as Jeffrey Weeks, drawing on the work of Mary McIntosh, were making similar arguments at the same time.[57] Where some works of queer history go further than the 'social constructionist' analysis is in their rejection of identity altogether as a useful category of analysis.[58] However, complicating terminological matters further, 'queer' is often used by historians not in a methodological but in an ontological sense. In fact, this is probably the predominant use of queer: as an umbrella term, a convenient shorthand for various types of people and desires, more differentiated than 'homosexual' or 'gay' or 'lesbian', but a group nevertheless somehow united by their shared challenge to the 'normal', to normative sexual and gender identity. Used in this way, 'queer' is something of a synonym for 'same-sex desiring', with the possibility of referring both to self-defined homosexuals, gays, and lesbians and to those who did not understand their desires in these categories. In Laura Doan's typology, this is 'queerness-as-being', rather than the more productive 'queerness-as-method.'[59]

---

[53] Laura Doan, *Disturbing Practices: History, Sexuality and Women's Experience of Modern War* (Chicago, 2013), 61.

[54] Evans, 'Why Queer German History?,' *German History* 34, 3 (2016), 371–84 (371).

[55] Doan, *Disturbing Practices*, 27.

[56] 'Homosexuality appeared as one of the forms of sexuality when it was transposed from the practice of sodomy onto a kind of interior androgyny, a hermaphrodism of the soul. The sodomite had been a temporary aberration; the homosexual was now a species.' Foucault, *The History of Sexuality*, 43.

[57] Jeffrey Weeks, *Coming Out: Homosexual Politics in Britain from the Nineteenth Century to the Present* (London, 1990 [1977]); Mary McIntosh, 'The Homosexual Role,' *Social Problems*, 16 (1968), 182–92. See further Chris Waters, 'The Homosexual as a Social Being in Britain, 1945–1968', *Journal of British Studies*, 51:3 (2012), 685–710 (709).

[58] Chris Waters, 'Distance and Desire in the New British Queer History', *GLQ: A Journal of Lesbian and Gay Studies* 14 (2008), 139–55 (141).

[59] Doan, *Disturbing Practices*, viii.

In contrast to earlier historical periods, I am writing about a decade in which the sexual categories 'homosexual' and 'gay' were in widespread use, and therefore these are not a scholarly imposition. Throughout the book, I seek to respect contemporary usages. I do not subsume the different vocabularies of 'homosexual', 'homophile', or 'gay' into a singular 'queer', because this would elide important debates about nomenclature, especially in the early part of the 1970s. To refer to those men who desired other men, but did not claim any of these identity categories—or those whose identifications are not present in the historical record—I use the adjectives 'same-sex desiring', or, to avoid repetition, queer. While this book does foreground a sexual category—namely, homosexuality—I do not proceed from the assumption that there was a stable homosexual population in 1970s West Germany, a constituency which historians can unproblematically identify and define as a type of people through reference to their same-sex sexuality. This means respecting the fluidity of desire, and paying close attention to the multi-directional form of individuals' political and emotional attachments. Homosexual politics, ways of thinking, feeling, and talking about homosexuality, was by no means the work of self-defined homosexuals alone. Moreover, those self-defined 'homosexuals' had very different ideas about what homosexuality was and how it should be lived. As will be seen in Chapter 5, for example, there was no hard and fast distinction in gay liberation between 'sexual orientation' on the one hand and 'gender identity' on the other. In other words, this book will include manifestations that another historian might include under the label 'transgender', a term not yet in use by the 1970s.

This book pertains to male homosexual politics only, as opposed to a more equal analysis of gay liberation and lesbian feminism. Some gay action groups, especially at the start of the decade, had both male and female membership. The HAW, for example, had a women's section for three years, before this section formally split from the rest of the group in early 1975, renaming themselves the Lesbian Action Centre (LAZ).[60] In the course of the 1970s, lesbians tended to organize much more closely with and in the women's movement than with gay men. Some lesbian groups were sections of larger women's organizations from the very start. For other activists, the experience of homosociality and same-sex affection within the women's movement facilitated their lesbian self-understanding.[61] In the context of the 1970s, then, it would be erroneous to talk of a gay *and* lesbian left: these were two different movements.[62]

---

[60] Gabriele Dennert, Christiane Leidinger, and Franziska Rauchut (eds), *In Bewegung bleiben: 100 Jahre Politik, Kultur und Geschichte von Lesben* (Berlin, 2007), 47. See further section 'The Sexual Politics of 1968' in Chapter 3.

[61] Ursula Linhoff, *Weibliche Homosexualität: Zwischen Anpassung und Emanzipation* (Cologne, 1976), 125.

[62] According to Magdalena Beljan, a common gay and lesbian movement did not exist until the 1990s. Beljan, *Rosa Zeiten? Eine Geschichte der Subjektivierung männlicher Homosexualität in den 1970er und 1980er Jahren der BRD* (Bielefeld, 2014), 19.

Not only is the history of criminalization (and therefore of decriminalization) very different for male and female homosexuality, but so are patterns of commerce, sociability, and print culture. Female homosexuality was not subject to prosecution in the Federal Republic, and indeed had never been criminalized in German history, including in the Third Reich. The pink triangle, one of the most important symbols of gay liberation, had been used in the concentration camps by the Nazis only in reference to male, not female, homosexuals: as such, the 'rediscovery' of this history, catalysed by the publication in 1972 of Heinz Heger's *The Men with the Pink Triangle*, did not hold the same significance for lesbians.[63] Commercial gay magazines such as *him* and *du&ich*, which arrived on the West German market immediately following homosexual law reform in September 1969, briefly had small sections for lesbian readers, but were overwhelmingly male-dominated, both in their textual and photographic content. Given differences of disposal income and access to public space, the gay scene which I introduce in Chapter 1 was really a gay *male* scene. Guides which sought to document that scene were written for a specifically male audience: for example, in 1979, the editors of the annually produced *Spartacus International Gay Guide* did away with what few lesbian listings there were in what was by then a 600 page book.[64]

Ambivalence

Heather Love has contended that the most problematic aspect of gay and lesbian historiography to date has not been 'its attachment to identity', but rather 'its consistently affirmative bias'. In her analysis of four modernist texts, she aims to resist this affirmative approach and instead 'feels backward', focusing especially on 'nostalgia, regret, shame, despair, *ressentiment*, passivity, escapism, self-hatred, withdrawal, bitterness, defeatism, and loneliness'.[65] Researching this book, I have encountered most of these feeling-states in archival material. At times, this has been a jarring experience, because these emotional expressions cannot be easily accommodated within the standard narrative on gay liberation. This well-told story runs something like the following. A young, radical generation of gays and lesbians inaugurated a totally new phase in the history of homosexual emancipation. With the riots on Christopher Street in New York in June 1969, a new spirit of defiance was born, which soon spread around the world. The old politics of respectability and conformism, of waiting behind the scenes for piecemeal reform and relying on plaintive appeals to sympathetic doctors and politicians, was over.

---

[63] Heinz Heger (pseudonym), *Die Männer mit dem Rosa Winkel* (Hamburg, 1989 [1972]).
[64] *Spartacus International Gay Guide* (Amsterdam, 1979), 8.
[65] Love, *Feeling Backward: Loss and the Politics of Queer History* (Cambridge, MA, 2007), 45 and 4.

It was dramatically eclipsed by the politics of confrontation, as angry gays and lesbians came together, came out, overcame their shame, and waged war on anti-homosexual society.

This assessment is not wrong, but it is incomplete. It locates 'backward' emotions or attitudes as phenomena that can be vanquished, neatly replaced by their foils: for shame, think pride; for fear, think hope; for conformism, think confrontation. Activists-turned-historians tended to associate the 'backward' emotions and attitudes with the preceding homophile movement, a movement whose leaders had supposedly so internalized mainstream society's values that they hid their desire behind 'homophile', a label designed to avoid the sexual in homosexual. Certainly, post-war homophile movements fare badly when reduced merely to the dusty antechamber of gay liberation. Counter-intuitively, though, the 1970s do little better, in terms of arriving at a balanced historicization of homosexual politics. For if homosexual life in the 1950s and 1960s is seen as closeted, conservative, and shame-filled, it follows that gay life in the 1970s, the other side of that 'mythical queer historical marker', the Stonewall Riots in 1969,[66] must appear as characterized by visibility, radical politics, and pride. This does not do justice to the ambivalence of gay liberation. In this section, I set out what I mean by that ambivalence, the prism through which I have made sense of the tensions and complexities of gay liberation.

In her *Epistemology of the Closet*, Eve Sedgwick argues that issues of homosexual/heterosexual definition are structured 'not by the supersession of one model and the consequent withering away of another, but instead by the relations enabled by the unrationalized coexistence' of those models. That is, to be gay or 'potentially classifiable as gay' is to come under 'the radically overlapping aegises of an universalizing discourse of acts or bonds and at the same time of a minoritizing discourse of kinds of persons'.[67] It is not the 'correctness or prevalence of one or the other side' of this 'enduring deadlock' but rather the 'persistence of the deadlock itself' that is of analytic significance. Sedgwick convincingly challenges a 'unidirectional narrative of supersession' when it comes to homo/hetero definition.[68] Through my attention to ambivalence, I seek to do the same with the emotional politics of homosexual emancipation. This approach is in keeping with recent work which embraces multiple chronologies, 'chronologies that defy the temptation to order narratives around crises, breaks, and ruptures'.[69] It recognizes that shifts and transformations are never fully formed, that emerging

---

[66] Horacio N. Roque Ramírez, 'Sharing Queer Authorities: Collaborating for Transgender Latina and Gay Latino Historical Meanings', in *Bodies of Evidence: The Practice of Queer Oral History*, ed. by Nan Alamilla Boyd and Horacio N. Roque Ramírez (Oxford, 2012), 184–201 (194).

[67] Sedgwick, *Epistemology of the Closet* (Berkeley, 2008 [1990]), 47 and 54. She prefers 'minoritizing' and 'universalizing' to the more common 'constructivist' and 'essentialist'.

[68] Ibid., 91 and 44.

[69] Helmut Puff, 'After the History of (Male) Homosexuality', in *After the History of Sexuality*, ed. by Scott Spector, Helmut Puff and Dagmar Herzog (New York, 2012), 17–30 (21).

ways of thinking do not simply replace, but instead jostle with residual discourses.[70] With respect to attitudes towards the HIV/AIDS crisis in Britain, Matt Cook has argued that 'Residues of the past remain as part of the complex layering of opinions, ideas and feelings.'[71] Heather Love concurs, tackling the politics of gay pride: 'We can turn shame into pride, but we cannot do so once and for all: shame lives on in pride, and pride can easily turn back into shame.'[72]

A psychoanalytic term originally coined by Eugen Bleuler, ambivalence can be defined as 'The simultaneous existence of contradictory tendencies, attitudes or feelings in the relationship to a single object – especially the coexistence of love and hate.'[73] That 'single object' could be oneself, or parts of oneself, another individual, the society in which one lives, a smaller group of which one may be a member, or alternatively a concept, movement or idea. An example: Freud is said to have noted, perhaps disguising some jealousy on his part, that it was only natural for his fellow analyst Bleuler to have coined ambivalence, 'given his alternating hostility and devotion to psychoanalysis'.[74] Ambivalence has also been used by other disciplines. Sociologist Zygmunt Bauman discusses the 'extreme assimilatory pressures' faced by Jews in interwar Germany, arguing that the 'bait of assimilation', offered up in contrast to the prevailing 'stigma of otherness', ended up luring German Jews 'into a state of chronic ambivalence'.[75] Bauman's usage of the 'internalization of ambivalence' is not convincing to a psychoanalytic frame of mind, because in this view ambivalence is not something external, waiting 'out there' to exert its social force on groups and individuals.[76] Rather, psychoanalytically speaking, ambivalence is a psychic conflict, which operates on a partly unconscious level, the parameters of which are set in childhood development. Here, I understand ambivalence as a window into the juncture between the psychic and the social, in that while the individual psychic conflict is significant, the individual is more or less susceptible to ambivalence depending on their social situation.[77] This recognizes that gays and lesbians, and other stigmatized groups, may be especially prone to the pushes and pulls of ambivalence.

[70] On residual and emergent discourses in the history of sexuality, see especially Doan, *Disturbing Practices*, 164–93.
[71] Cook, 'AIDS, Mass Observation, and the Fate of the Permissive Turn', *Journal of the History of Sexuality* 26:2 (2017), 239–72 (271).
[72] Love, *Feeling Backward*, 28.
[73] Jean Laplache and Jean-Bertrand Pontalis, *The Language of Psycho-Analysis* (London, 1973), 26.
[74] Cited in Robert Merton and Elinor Barber, 'Sociological Ambivalence', in *Sociological Ambivalence and Other Essays*, ed. by Robert Merton (New York, 1976), 3–31 (3).
[75] Bauman, *Modernity and Ambivalence* (Ithaca, 1991), 128 and 102.   [76] Ibid., 128.
[77] Joanna Bourke, focusing on fear, talks about the 'bruising encounter between individual subjectivity and social norms'. Bourke, *Fear: A Cultural History* (London, 2005), 9. On combining psychoanalytic and sociological approaches, see further the work of Deborah Gould, which has been influential in my own understanding of ambivalence. Gould, *Moving Politics: Emotion and ACT UP's Fight against AIDS* (Chicago, 2009), 12–13. Merton and Barber also seek to develop a 'psycho-social' theory of ambivalence. See their 'Sociological Ambivalence', 5.

The context in which male homosexuality could be lived was transformed in 1969, following homosexual law reform. With reduced fear of arrest and social ostracization, men who loved or desired other men now had greater possibilities for claiming a public identity, for coming to terms with their desire, and for coming together and organizing with others who shared their sexual or political orientation. Yet this was no easy task. The ambivalence felt by gay men about themselves, their desires and the society in which they lived proved especially pronounced in this historical moment. Because this ambivalence is central to the book, I elucidate the concept here through three examples, which I call axes of ambivalence: pride/shame, normal/different and hope/fear. These are only three of several such axes, tensions, or contradictions in gay liberation. Some others would include affirmation/inhibition, visible/hidden and confrontation/conformism. Crucially, none of these are polarized binaries: both/and as opposed to either/or. Recall Sedgwick: it is not the 'correctness or prevalence of one or the other side' of the 'enduring deadlock' between minoritizing and universalizing discourses but rather the 'persistence of the deadlock itself' that matters.[78] That is, I am less interested in calculating whether same-sex desiring men primarily stressed the 'difference' or essential 'normality' of homosexuality, whether they were subject to proportionately greater levels of pride or of shame, or whether gay liberation was characterized more by utopian thinking or by perceptions of crisis. Rather, these poles formed deadlocks that structured the course of gay liberation.

Pride/Shame

Drawing on Eve Sedgwick's definition of shame as revolving around the pain of non-recognition, Deborah Gould has argued that a desire for relief from this condition can 'create a pull toward social conformity, and specifically toward adoption of mainstream political norms'.[79] This might be one way to explain periods of conformism within homosexual politics, most often associated with the homophile movement. Martin Dannecker, one of the key figures in the West German gay left in the 1970s, has contended that homophiles were driven by an insatiable desire for recognition. Eager to appear as normal as possible, homophiles sought to refute defamatory stereotypes but in so doing ended up enmeshed in homophobia themselves: 'shame, convention and decency, in the name of

---

[78] Sedgwick, *Epistemology of the Closet*, 91.
[79] Gould, 'The Shame of Gay Pride in Early AIDS Activism', in *Gay Shame*, ed. by David Halperin and Valerie Traub (Chicago, 2009), 221–55 (224). See further Eve Sedgwick, *Touching Feeling: Affect, Pedagogy, Performativity* (Durham, NC, 2003), 35–7. Sedgwick, in turn, was heavily influenced by the work of psychologist Silvan Tomkins, who conceptualizes shame as a 'specific inhibitor of continuing interest and enjoyment'. Tomkins, 'Shame-Humiliation and Contempt-Disgust,' *Shame and its Sisters: A Silvan Tomkins Reader*, ed. by Eve Sedgwick and Adam Frank (Durham, NC, 1995), 133–78 (134).

which homosexuals were denigrated and marginalised, were for most of them positive categories'.[80]

In contrast, gay liberation has been viewed almost exclusively through the optics of gay pride. According to Dannecker, gay activists in the 1970s made a radical break with the politics of recognition. Rather than attempting to refute the perception of homosexuals as perverse and abnormal, activists sought instead to seemingly *confirm* these perceptions through the manner of their actions, paroles and theories.[81] In his influential contemporary work, Australian activist Dennis Altman posited that the very essence of gay liberation was self-affirmation.[82] The archetypal expression of this self-affirmation in West Germany came with Rosa von Praunheim's provocative film *It Is Not the Homosexual Who Is Perverse, but the Society in Which He Lives*, co-written with the aforementioned Martin Dannecker. First screened in 1971, and broadcast on national television in January 1973, the film was a key factor in the expansion of gay liberation, as we will see in Chapter 2. The film concluded with footage of a commune of naked gay men, alongside calls directly aimed at homosexuals: 'out of the toilets and into the streets!' and 'be proud of your homosexuality!'[83]

Accounts that stress the formation and significance of pride are not exactly wrong, but gay pride is perhaps best analysed alongside its unwanted sibling, gay shame. David Halperin and Valerie Traub, for example, seek to move beyond what they call the 'increasingly exhausted and restrictive ethos of gay pride' by recognizing the 'transformative energies that spring from experiences of shame'.[84] Considering West German gay liberation, one is struck by the coexistence of pride and shame. There were certainly striking elements of self-affirmation, but this was not accompanied by a no-holds-barred acceptance and celebration of same-sex desire. Activists, alongside other gay men, remained ill-at-ease with aspects of their homosexuality. The very denomination 'homophile' was intended to downplay the centrality of the sexual to homosexuality. That this manoeuvre was rejected by men who preferred to use *schwul* (gay) does not mean that those men can therefore be described as having celebrated all aspects of gay desire. In fact, a rather censorious tendency can be observed in gay liberation. *Not the Homosexual* was a case in point. The film was intended as an attack on several aspects of homosexual life and was consciously provocative. Yet the three-fold

---

[80] Dannecker, 'Der glühende Wunsch nach Anerkennung und die Affirmation der Differenz. Von den Homophilen der Nachkriegszeit zur Schwulenbewegung der 1970er Jahre', in *Ohnmacht und Aufbegehren: Homosexuelle Männer in der frühen Bundesrepublik*, ed. by Andreas Pretzel and Volker Weiß (Hamburg, 2010), 231–41 (237).

[81] Ibid., 240.   [82] Altman, *Homosexual: Oppression and Liberation* (London, 1974), 188.

[83] *Nicht der Homosexuelle ist pervers, sondern die Situation in der er lebt* (Bavaria Atelier, 1971).

[84] Halperin and Traub (eds), *Gay Shame*, 5 and 44. Elspeth Probyn also views shame as a productive phenomenon: 'Denying or eradicating shame, whether by an individual or a community, seems futile to me. It is also a waste of an important resource in thinking about what it means to be human.' Probyn, *Blush: Faces of Shame* (Minneapolis, 2005), xiii.

description of homosexuals as 'whores' and language such as 'park fuckers' and 'urinal gays' (*Pissbudenschwule*) speaks also of a distinctly judgemental tone, which may have been influenced by shame about gay sexual practices.

In his analysis of the Swiss homophile journal, Hubert Kennedy has argued that *Der Kreis* propagated a vision of 'the ideal gay man': he who followed a code of conduct that stressed responsibility, gender normative behaviour and respectability.[85] Gay liberation, too, had its own rules and regulations, its own tacit code of conduct. One of the more infamous lines in *Not the Homosexual* came towards the end of the film, with the narrator screeching 'Let us be more gay! The false half-gays must find the courage to become whole gays.' According to the filmmakers, the 'whole gay' of gay liberation, its 'ideal gay man', was to be politically conscious, should reject sentimentality and apathetic consumerism, and show solidarity with fellow gay men facing discrimination, and other oppressed groups.[86] But he must also display responsibility and discipline. Rather than visiting parks, public toilets, saunas and bars, gay men should boycott these establishments. Gays should try to 'screw more freely' but this abandon was twinned with obligation, too: 'We must become erotically free and socially responsible.' The latter message was picked up by activists from the Homosexual Action Hamburg (HAH), who argued that society forced roles onto homosexuals, leaving gay men with no opportunity for what was described as 'self-conscious' and 'self-responsible' behaviour.[87] Indeed, concerns over responsibility and respectability were never far from the surface in gay liberation.

Normal/Different

That homosexuals were just the same as the rest of the population, save for one insignificant difference, was a key tenet in homophile activism and the campaign for homosexual law reform. This approach depended on stressing the normality and harmlessness of homosexuals, in contrast to discourses which emphasized sickness, menace, or criminality. Such has been its success that this outlook continues to shape contemporary gay and lesbian politics. As Deborah Gould has argued, the struggle for gay marriage requires no acknowledgement of gay sexuality whatsoever: in the quest for *resemblance*, the mainstream movement has 'repudiated gay sexual difference'.[88] Indeed, the history of homosexual emancipation is not least the history of homosexuals frantically disavowing that which 'at

---

[85] Kennedy, *The Ideal Gay Man: The Story of Der Kreis* (Binghampton, NY, 1999).
[86] The narrator specifically cited the black power and women's liberation movements.
[87] HAH, 'Gedanken zum Film'. SMB archive, IHWO box one.
[88] Gould, 'The Shame of Gay Pride', 221.

least partly define[s], distinguish[es], and constitute[s] the group in the first place'.[89]

Very much in line with his activism during the 1970s, Martin Dannecker has written that 'being gay means insisting on the difference that accrues from love between men'.[90] This is one article of faith that failed to chime with many other same-sex desiring men, among them the prolific film-maker Rainer Werner Fassbinder. At the height of his fame in the mid to late 1970s, and his sexual relationships with other men no secret, Fassbinder kept his distance from the gay movement.[91] Gay activists would especially criticize his 1975 film *Fox and His Friends*, which portrays the story of the working-class Franz 'Fox' Bieberkopf (played by Fassbinder himself), who after winning the lottery is taken in by a male lover from a bourgeois background, exploited for his wealth, and unceremoniously discarded when no longer useful.[92] Interpretations of the film were unanimous in viewing the depiction of homosexuality as far from idealistic, but split over whether that should be judged a merit or a flaw: instead of homosexuality, it is in fact class that appears as the central theme in the film.[93] In this sense, the film marked a significant departure from other films in the German homosexual canon, including the ground-breaking *Anders als die Andern* (Different from the Others) from 1919 and *Anders als Du und Ich* (Different from You and I) from 1957. Playing on these famous titles, one reviewer of *Fox and his Friends* penned his review under the heading 'Die Anderen sind nicht anders', translating as 'The others are not different.'[94] Fassbinder explained the negative response to his film from gay groups thus: the film 'shows that homosexual life is not that much different from so-called normal life, and that shocked them. They see themselves as something special. If you are gay, you are something particular.'[95]

Rather than reaching any firm conclusions, gay men remained perpetually divided over whether their sexuality was something that set them apart, or instead something rather inconsequential, or at any rate a matter about which not to make too much of a fuss. This was not unrelated to the attitudes of wider society. Consider the response of one of the several million readers of *Stern* in October

---

[89] David Halperin, *How to Be Gay* (Cambridge, MA, 2012), 73.

[90] Dannecker, 'Der unstillbare Wunsch', 43.

[91] Ronald Gregg, 'Fassbinder's Fox and His Friends and Gay Politics in the 1970s' and Randall Halle, 'Rainer, Rosa, and Werner: New Gay Film as Counter-Public', both in *A Companion to Rainer Werner Fassbinder*, ed. by Brigitte Peucker (Oxford, 2012), 542–63 and 564–78 respectively.

[92] *Faustrecht der Freiheit*, dir. by Rainer Werner Fassbinder (1975).

[93] For responses from gay activists, see Walter Weber, 'Faustrecht der Freiheit: oder, stellt Fassbinder die Klassenfrage', *Schwuchtel* 1 (1975), 15 and Peter Krämer, 'Faustrecht der Freiheit', *glf-journal* (December 1975), 10. A review in the *Süddeutsche Zeitung* criticized the film for depicting homosexuals as exotic creatures, as 'flesh-eating plants'. Hans-Günther Pflaum, 'Wie fleischfressende Pflanzen: Rainer Werner Fassbinders neuer Film Faustrecht der Freiheit' (14 June 1975). A review in *Die Zeit*, meanwhile, praised Fassbinder for his uninhibited, open, and honest portrayal of the gay scene. Hans C. Blumenberg, 'Der Rest sind Tränen' (13 June 1975).

[94] Hans Fröhlich, 'Die Anderen sind nicht anders,' *Stuttgarter Nachrichten* (6 June 1975), 4.

[95] Cited from an interview in *Blueboy*, an American gay magazine. Gregg, 'Fassbinder's Fox', 572.

1978, after 682 men had declared their homosexuality in a front-page special the previous week.[96] Oskar, from Heidelberg, reported that he and his wife were of the opinion that there 'really are some very nice homosexuals', but that mostly 'they're just kind of different' (*aber meistens sind sie ja doch irgendwie anders*).[97] *Anders* can mean both 'different' and 'other': it was precisely to counter othering portrayals of their desires and characters that many of the 682 men agreed to take part in this collective self-presentation. Yet there was no unanimity over what, precisely, should be offered up for public consumption. One activist bemoaned the association between homosexuality and gender transgression: 'when the "normals" talk about homosexuals, they always mean the queens, swanning around with eyeliner. That we're completely normal doesn't register with them.' Another concluded, 'Heterosexuals need to learn that homosexuals are just as perverse and normal as themselves. Homosexuality is nothing other than a sexual variant.' A third declared 'the public needs to learn to deal with us gays and to accept our difference [*Anderssein*]. We have a right to openly live out our homosexuality.'[98]

Ambivalence over the 'normality' or 'difference' of homosexuality was closely linked to the question of minority, a concept whose importance to this study warrants its introduction here. The conception that homosexuals might constitute a particular kind of persons dates back to nineteenth-century German-language legal and sexological discourse. In the 1860s, Karl Heinrich Ulrichs used the term 'minority' when defending his pamphlets on same-sex desiring men ('Urnings') against confiscation.[99] Although the language of minority rights was already used by parts of the German homosexual emancipation movement in Imperial Germany and in the Weimar Republic, it took until the post-Second World War period for the associated idea to gain widespread traction: that homosexuals formed a discrete minority in need of protection from discrimination. This built on the framework provided by the analysis of race relations in Britain and, in the United States, by the inspiration offered to the homophile movement by African-American civil rights.[100] As Clayton Whisnant argues, this language became popular with West German homophile activists because it chimed with human rights discourse, anchoring the protection of minorities, and with the parallel to anti-Semitism and the need to defend the Jewish minority from persecution.[101] However, Whisnant neglects a crucial part of the story in claiming that the 'redefinition of homosexuals as a minority that required legal protection' was

---

[96] 'Wir sind schwul' - 682 Männer bekennen', *Stern* 41 (1978).   [97] *Stern* 42 (1978), 9.
[98] *Stern* 41 (1978), 106–7.   [99] Beachy, *Gay Berlin*, 21.
[100] Chris Waters, 'The Homosexual as a Social Being', 698. In the United States, the publication in 1951 of Edward Sagarin's *The Homosexual in America* was a key development (published under the pseudonym Donald Webster Cory). See further David K Johnson, *The Lavender Scare: The Cold War Persecution of Gays and Lesbians in the Federal Government* (Chicago, 2004), 182.
[101] Whisnant, *Male Homosexuality in West Germany*, 104.

subsequently 'widely embraced by the gay liberation movement of the 1970s', eventually resulting 'in antidiscrimination laws in the 1990s'.[102]

In fact, whether or not homosexuals constituted a minority was to prove highly controversial within gay liberation. Lothar Meier, an activist from the Initiative Group Homosexuality Stuttgart (IHS), argued forcefully in 1975 that comparisons between homosexuals and ethnic minorities were misplaced, because homosexuals had been *made into* a minority though criminalization and oppression. Tackling the causes of discrimination meant at the same time that the gay 'minority' must overturn this errant conceptualization of belonging to a delineated group. Continuing, Meier underlined that gay liberation would end in a dead end if activists sought only to win freedom for four per cent of the population.[103] Similarly, an activist from Munich, describing the pink triangle, declared that the symbol was not about a 'minority' begging for 'tolerance', and not a symbol of specifically gay oppression, but instead a symbol of sexual oppression more widely.[104]

The antipathy of some activists towards the concept of 'minority' has led scholars to essentially argue that gay liberation was *defined* by its opposition to an ethnic- or an interest-group model.[105] Stephen Valocchi describes gay liberation as a 'brief interlude' that lasted between 1969 and 1973, characterized by its calling into question of 'minority group understandings'.[106] Valocchi is persuasive in his later argument that efforts to stabilize gay identity represent 'a project that will always involve smoothing over differences, excluding some interests, and shaming some desires'.[107] Yet, I do not wish to retain gay liberation as a placeholder for a period of homosexual politics in which a minority group understanding had not yet taken hold or was rejected, or for a period when the affirmation of difference successfully supplanted normalizing impulses. Rather, it seems that many gay men just could not make up their minds. Even those in the gay left who poked fun at the idea of belonging to a homosexual minority, indeed those who candidly celebrated their difference and departure from the heterosexual norm, at times became fixated on demonstrating their *resemblance* to heterosexual

---

[102]   Ibid., 208.
[103]   Meier, 'Homosexuelle – eine Minderheit?', *ihs info: Informationen der Initiativegruppe Homosexualität Stuttgart* 2 (1975), 3–4 (3). The 4% alludes to the number of men posited to be exclusively homosexual by the Kinsey Report, which explains the frequent proposition put forward in the gay press that there were between two and three million homosexuals amongst the West German population. According to the May 1970 census, the West German population was 60.65 million. *Statistisches Jahrbuch für die Bundesrepublik Deutschland* 1974 (Wiesbaden, 1974), 82.
[104]   Violet, 'Warum tragen wir den Rosa Winkel?', *Carlo Sponti* 16–17 (1975), 10.
[105]   Mary Bernstein, 'The Strategic Uses of Identity by the Lesbian and Gay Movement', in *The Social Movements Reader: Cases and Concepts*, ed. by Jeff Goodwin and James M Jasper (Oxford, 2003), 234–48 (244).
[106]   Valocchi, 'The Class-Inflected Nature of Gay Identity', *Social Problems* 46 (1999), 207–24 (217).
[107]   Valocchi, '"Where Did Gender Go?" Same-Sex Desire and the Persistence of Gender in Gay Male Historiography', *GLQ: A Journal of Lesbian and Gay Studies* 18 (2012), 453–79 (466).

leftist activists, whether in their activist behaviour or in their political analysis. One activist in the Homosexual Action West Berlin bemoaned in 1976 that the 'pink HAW norm' was damaging the gay movement, since it excluded all those who did not exhibit the 'correct' consciousness, along with those who liked to wear leather, suits or indeed anyone who just came across as conformist.[108] Attending to ambivalence, then, recognizes that normativity is not so easily escaped.

Hope/Fear

Gay liberation often appears as a brief moment of utopianism, when dreams of a better world for queer people were earnestly held and put into action. One is struck by the hope, energy, and playfulness that pervades much gay liberation material: winged phalluses flying around the marginalia of journals are a regular discovery in the archives. Equally, one becomes aware of a deep-seated pessimism, an antipathy to 'progress' and fear of an oppressive society. This was especially the case within the gay left, that tendency within gay liberation most influenced by '1968', itself a moment that is at times associated only with the utopianism and high spirits of anti-authoritarian protest, as opposed to its more sober side. Anxiety about the state of West German society and a loss of optimism in what the future held was not, however, limited to leftist activists, gay or otherwise. A key date in this regard was 1973, when the first oil price shock hit. Exceptional economic growth had come to be taken for granted before 1973, with the current state of affairs extrapolated into the future. A programmatic document published that year by the governing Social Democrats (SPD) blithely assumed an annual growth rate of 4.5 per cent until 1985.[109] The Bretton Woods system had already collapsed in 1971, but the oil price shock hastened the end of an era of full employment, as the cheap prices upon which economic growth was dependent quadrupled in 1973.[110]

The Federal Republic weathered this storm far better than many of its European neighbours, but unemployment still rose from 0.7 per cent in 1970 to 5.4 per cent in 1975.[111] The reform programme of the SPD came to an abrupt end. Confidence in the inexorability of progress evaporated as optimism gave way to crisis management, symbolized by the replacement of Willy Brandt by Helmut Schmidt as Chancellor in 1974.[112] This is borne out by opinion polls, which posit a massive

---

[108] Claire, 'Zur SM-Diskussion: Thesen zur Funny', *HAW Info* 22 (1976), 18–19.

[109] The SPD's *Orientierungsrahmen '85*. Evidently, the authors of that document had taken little notice of the Club of Rome's *The Limits to Growth* report, published a year earlier. Ralph Jessen, 'Bewältigte Vergangenheit – blockierte Zukunft? Ein prospektiver Blick auf die bundesrepublikanische Gesellschaft am Ende der Nachkriegszeit', in *Das Ende der Zuversicht?*, ed. by Jarausch, 177–95 (185).

[110] Anselm Doering-Manteuffel and Lutz Raphael, *Nach dem Boom: Perspektiven auf die Zeitgeschichte seit 1970* (Göttingen, 2010 [2008]), 48–53.

[111] Ibid., 48.   [112] Jarausch, 'Verkannter Strukturwandel', 10.

shift from 'hope' to 'fear' in 1973. Carried out annually by the Allensbach Institute, respondents were asked whether they met the coming year with hope, with fear or with scepticism. Surveyed in December 1972, fully 60 per cent selected hope and only 13 per cent fear. A year later, just 30 per cent indicated hope, with this number exceeded by those who indicated fear (34 per cent).[113]

Subsequent surveys suggest 'hope' returned to 1972 levels. Polled in December 1977, the number indicating hope was back to 60 per cent.[114] Perhaps this was down to the reduced prominence of terrorism in public discourse, after this had reached its height with the 'German autumn' a few months previously.[115] The upswing in public mood was not to last. Soon, a period of détente in cold war tensions came to a close, with the NATO 'double-track decision' of 1979, under which Pershing and Cruise missiles were ultimately stationed on West German soil. This was presumably responsible for a subsequent decline in confidence by the decade's end: in December 1979 only 34 per cent expressed that they met the coming year with hope, while 27 per cent indicated fear.[116] Rather than representing a precise empirical barometer of shifting emotions, the significance of these undulations in hope and fear lies in contextualizing the climate in which gay men moved. Gay liberation did not take place on a blank canvas: its movers and shakers were part of West German society and not immune to the real and imagined impact of socio-economic and political developments.

Indeed, that which may have alleviated fear amongst the general population may have *increased* anxiety among certain parts of gay liberation.[117] As will be explored in Chapters 3 and 4, the state's response to terrorism and to political protest more generally formed a central plank of the gay left's understanding of the prevalence and nature of gay oppression. Through their analysis of what was seen as the pervasive and structural role of fear in capitalism, alternative leftists created an 'emotional regime', which not only reflected how activists felt, but told them how they *should* feel—namely, afraid and lonely.[118] Frank Biess identifies the

[113] Based on a representative sample size of 2000. *Jahrbuch der öffentlichen Meinung 1968–1973* (Allensbach, 1974), 602.

[114] *Allensbacher Jahrbuch der Demoskopie 1978–1983* (Munich, 1983), 675.

[115] The 'German autumn' symbolically ended on 18 October 1977, with the presumed suicides of the imprisoned RAF members Andreas Baader, Gudrun Ensslin and Jan-Carl Raspe, the storming of the hijacked Lufthansa Flight 181 in Mogadishu, and the murder of Hanns Martin Schleyer by his RAF captors. On the RAF (Red Army Faction), see amongst many others Petra Terhoeven, *Deutscher Herbst in Europa. Der Linksterrorismus der siebziger Jahre als transnationales Phänomen* (Munich, 2014).

[116] *Allensbacher Jahrbuch der Demoskopie 1978–1983* (Munich, 1983), 675.

[117] 'According to most commentators', writes Joanna Bourke, 'the word "fear" is used to refer to an immediate, objective threat, while anxiety refers to an anticipated, subjective threat.' Bourke, *Fear: A Cultural History*, 189. Nevertheless, I follow Bourke in not positing a clear analytic distinction between fear and anxiety. This is all the more important in German, as the word *Angst* can be translated into either English term.

[118] Joachim C Häberlen and Jake Smith, 'Struggling for Feelings: The Politics of Emotions in the Radical New Left in West Germany, c.1968–84', *Contemporary European History* 23 (2014), 615–37 (617 and 620). See further Häberlen, *The Emotional Politics of the Alternative Left: West Germany, 1968–1984* (Cambridge, 2018), 123–35.

development of fear-ridden subjectivity in the 1970s, and contrasts that decade's 'culture of fear' (*Angstkultur*) with the optimism of 1968.[119] However, as Häberlen and Smith state, this description of the 1970s may be somewhat totalizing, not least because the leftist discourse on fear also included the formulation of strategies to overcome it.[120] An example is *Homolulu*, through which one can observe a growing problematization of the almost constant invocation of 'oppression', and instead a renewed focus on gay subjectivities and community-building efforts. The English-language invitation to the week-long festival promised, 'Here it will be fun to be gay. Free of the constraints forced on us by hetero-terror: we plan to stage theatre performances, sing, love, work, dance, celebrate and discuss with each other.'[121] Reported on widely (and largely positively) by the mainstream press, several journalists noted the exuberance, colour and theatricality of the large demonstration that took place at the end of the festival.[122]

While not disregarding manifestations such as *Homolulu*, I resist the temptation to portray this exuberance and theatricality as representative of the decade. Perhaps one might expect to find more unequivocal evidence of fun-filled hopeful experimentation following the partial legalization of homosexuality in 1969. That would belie the ambivalence of gay liberation. If what one publicist called the 'fear of the brown paragraph' reduced in 1969, when the Nazi version of Paragraph 175 was finally set aside, this did not erase all prevailing anxieties.[123] Just because it was less likely to end you up in prison did not mean that gay sex was therefore always experienced in a liberating manner. The editors of *Medicine for Gay Men*, a manual on gay sexual health and practice first published in 1978, stated that their motivation was to provide sorely-needed information on sexually transmitted infections, but more importantly to help dispel the fear of their own bodies and its illnesses that was held by many gay men.[124] There was evidently a demand for the manual, since by 1982 the publication was already in its fourth edition. Attending to ambivalence does not imply suggesting that all same-sex desiring men suffered under some blanket fear of their bodies and its illnesses. Indeed, there was plenty of queer fun-filled frolicking in the 1970s. The *Homolulu* organizers included a handy trilingual glossary of terms that might come in useful

---

[119] Biess, 'Die Sensibilisierung des Subjekts: Angst und "Neue Subjektivität" in den 1970er Jahren', *Werkstatt Geschichte* 49 (2008), 51–71 (54).

[120] Häberlen and Smith, 'Struggling for Feelings', 623.

[121] Trilingual flyer, untitled. SMB archive, NARGS box two, folder NARGS 79.

[122] According to the *Frankfurter Allgemeine Zeitung*, some passers-by mistook the demonstration as a promotion for a local circus. Attendance was placed in the region of 1000–2000. 'Farbenfrohe Demonstration und schließlich eine Resolution', *FAZ* (30 July 1979). See also 'In Homolulu suchten Männer ihre Märchenprinzen', *Die Welt am Sonntag* (29 July 1979) and 'Ungewöhnliches Festival gegen Vorurteile', *Süddeutsche Zeitung* (30 July 1979).

[123] Karl August Schrey, 'Köpfe sind rar', *du&ich* 1 (1969), 3.

[124] Autorengruppe schwule Medizinstudenten, *Sumpf Fieber: Medizin für schwule Männer* (Berlin, 1978), unpaginated foreword. The guide was produced by a collective of gay medical students, three of whom were also members of the HAW.

for festival participants: yes, the pink triangle was inevitably listed, but most entries were sex-based, including *abgrabbeln* (translated into English for participants as 'to touch somebody up'), *auf die Klappe gehen* ('cottaging'), *abspritzen* ('to come, to shoot one's load') and *durchficken* ('to screw s.o. silly').[125] Attending to ambivalence does, however, recognize that the fear generated by the HIV/AIDS crisis in the 1980s played out on somewhat fertile ground.[126]

Prosecution, including possible imprisonment and financial ruin, was less likely after 1969, but this meant the possibilities of claiming a public identity were suddenly all the more realistic, a development at least as sobering as it was appealing. According to an early account from the commercial gay press, 'every one of us is afraid of being discovered, because everyone is afraid to stand up and say: *I am gay*'.[127] Undoubtedly, gay liberation allowed some same-sex desiring men to take this step: in so doing, at least to some extent, overcoming their fear. Yet the emphasis on 'coming out' meant different things to different people. If some same-sex desiring men experienced this as liberating, others found it deeply threatening.[128] There was never a simple injunction to 'come out'. How, where, to what extent, in which style of attire, and to whom were all questions that continued throughout the 1970s. Indeed, the problem of visibility and the public sphere was a central driving force of gay liberation.

Activists and publicists had to reckon not only with their own fear, but the anxieties of wider society. Consider Udo Erlenhardt, who as chief editor of *du&ich* and then *him* in 1970 was caught between going on the offensive and reassuring heterosexual interlocutors that they had nothing to fear. In an open letter to the Federal Chancellor Willy Brandt, he stated that homophiles wanted nothing more than tolerance, certainly not a 'homosexualization' of the Federal Republic.[129] Others, especially later in the decade, were less circumspect in their language, demanding social transformation rather than tolerance. But for all sides, the hope accrued through successes and advances—however these were divergently defined—summoned forth the fear, all of a sudden, of actually having something to lose. Hard-won progress, winning a proverbial seat at the table; for some activists, this was not altogether desirable in the first place, for others, any progress

---

[125] *Homolulu: Schwule Tageszeitung* 0 (23 July 1979), 4. SMB archive, NARGS box two, folder NARGS 79. The third language was French.

[126] The 1982 edition of *Medicine for Gay Men* included a short section on Kaposi's Sarcoma and a deadly cancer that seemed to be particularly prevalent among young gay men: this was soon to become codified as HIV/AIDS. 'Das Karposi-Syndrom', in *Sumpf Fieber: Medizin für schwule Männer*, ed. by Die schwulen Medizinmänner (Berlin, 1982), 155–7. The authors noted panic already present in the gay scene and 'sensationalist reports in the heterosexual press'. This foreshadowed the infamous front-page story in *Der Spiegel* in June 1983, which declared that the 'homosexual plague' had now reached Europe. AIDS: Eine Epidemie, die erst beginnt', *Der Spiegel*, 23 (1983), 144–63. For more on fear and HIV/AIDS, see Bourke, *Fear: A Cultural History*, 306–12.

[127] Emphasis in the original. Hanno Müller-Kittnau, 'Gesellschaften haben sich noch nie von selbst verändert,' *him* 7 (1971), 52.

[128] Jackson, *Living in Arcadia*, 13.   [129] *him* (July 1970), 40.

brought with it the fear of the rug being pulled out from under their feet just as soon as they thought it was safe to sit down.

~   ~

This book is organized as follows. Chapter 1 focuses on the most immediate consequences of homosexual law reform in 1969: the emergence of the commercial gay press and the development of a larger and more open gay scene. These were important contexts for the emergence of gay liberation, which is the story told by Chapter 2.

The debate between 'homophiles' and 'gays' is placed at the centre of this chapter, which analyses a cluster of news reports, documentaries, and films featuring homosexuality that appeared in the early 1970s. I do this not only to supplement the textual source base of much of my book, but also because it was precisely over these television programmes, and their respective portrayals of homosexuality, that the debate between homophiles and gays was most clear (and given the wide audience, when the stakes were at their highest).

Chapter 3 explores the connection between gay liberation and the alternative left. Following women's liberation, gay liberation was at once both a product of and response to the sexual politics of the student movement and the wave of protest and activism associated with '1968'. This chapter provides a detailed reading of those sexual politics, before exploring the gay movement's struggles to gain recognition from sought-after leftist partners, which culminated in gays characterizing themselves as victims of fascism.

Chapter 4 proceeds to examine the 'rediscovery' of the Nazi persecution of homosexuals, catalysed by the publication in 1972 of Heinz Heger's *The Men with the Pink Triangle*. I explore how memory of this persecution, combined with the experience of contemporary discrimination, produced a profound alienation on the part of left-wing gay men from the West German state. Although the pink triangle, as a gay liberation symbol, was used most widely in the gay left, the theme of Nazi persecution was never confined to that political trajectory. In the shape of demanding compensation for surviving homosexual victims of the concentration camps, the politics of restitution became a key feature of homosexual politics, an effective mechanism for gaining traction in the public sphere.

Chapter 5 provides an important example of how gay liberation was never a 'free-for-all', by focusing on debates over gender presentation and sex. Gay liberation opened up the space to allow some gay male activists to embrace effeminacy for political reasons. Yet this tactic of 'gender fuck' was rejected by others, who accused its adherents of 'unpolitical' behaviour and for endangering the already fragile level of left-wing support. Turning to how sex featured in gay liberation, I show how a shared antipathy to the gay scene, and sites of sexual activity, especially cruising grounds, resembled an important point of connection between gay action groups and more moderate homosexual organizations. These contestations therefore highlight that the politics of 'respectability' proved to be remarkably tenacious in this period of transition, from 'homophile' to 'gay'. This chapter then explores how activists and publicists confronted and managed psychological distress in homosexual life. Here, I set the rise of consciousness-raising and self-help groups, of the first telephone crisis helplines, against changing medical and psychoanalytic attitudes towards homosexuality. In a concluding chapter, I discuss the memory of gay liberation, and how we might better integrate the 1970s into a longer history of homosexual emancipation in German history.

The axes of ambivalence set out in this introduction, pride/shame, normal/different and hope/fear, will run through every chapter that follows. In psychoanalytic theory, ambivalence is understood as a painful condition: in its earliest formulation, it was particularly associated with schizophrenia.[130] I do not doubt the psychic difficulty of bearing ambivalence, but I suggest in this book that we might also conceptualize ambivalence as a historically *productive* tension. It was precisely the ambivalence generated by possibilities of pride coming up against the inescapability of shame, by the desire to be 'normal' clashing with the affirmation of difference, by hope meeting fear, that lent gay liberation its power and dynamism. The 1970s was a period of intense and considerable change, but was also shot through with ambiguities and ambivalence. Gay liberation was characterized by a thoroughly unstable blend of competing conceptions and feelings about what being gay meant and involved, alongside contrasting analyses of what liberation stood for and how this might be reached. Yet, upon closer inspection, it is precisely the coexistence of a range of divergent understandings, contradictory feelings and competing visions that lay at the heart of gay liberation.

---

[130] Eugen Bleuler, 'Die Ambivalenz', in *Beiträge zur Schizophrenielehre der Züricher Psychiatrischen Universitätsklinik Burghölzli (1902–1971)*, ed. by Manfred Bleuler (Darmstadt, 1979), 85–97.

1

The West German Gay World after Homosexual Law Reform

Gay liberation was a struggle for space, language, and communication: for a public. Gay liberation expanded the possibilities of conceptualizing, talking about, and living same-sex desire, but did not do so on a blank canvas. A critical mass of student or former student activists could not have come together to form the gay left had they not benefited from an era of expansion to higher education, which in turn was dependent on a period of sustained economic growth.[1] Gay liberation could not have emerged without the greater connectivity fostered by the advent of the commercial gay press, which was made possible by legal reform, in the shape of the liberalization of Paragraph 175 of the West German penal code in 1969. This reform, in turn, was dependent not only on the entry of the Social Democrats into government in 1966 and their control over the Justice ministry, but also on a rapid and fundamental 'process of liberalisation and change in sexual morality'.[2]

This chapter therefore 'sets the scene' for gay liberation by focusing on the liberalization of Paragraph 175 in 1969, before analysing two interconnected phenomena that the legal reform gave rise to: firstly, the commercial gay press, glossy monthly magazines including *du&ich* and *him* that immediately appeared on West German newspaper stands; and secondly the larger and more diversified gay scene, referring to the various locations where same-sex desiring men met each other for the purposes of leisure, sociability, and sex. This exposition is necessary to comprehend the third main consequence of homosexual law reform: the emergence of various forms of homosexual organizing, which will be examined in the next chapter.

Make no mistake, these forms of homosexual organizing were the consequence, not the cause of homosexual law reform. The homophile movement of the 1940s and 1950s was essentially moribund by the early 1960s. While the quiet lobbying of homosexual individuals was important, there was no significant grassroots

---

[1] Schulz, *Der lange Atem*, 36.
[2] Michael Kandora, 'Homosexualität und Sittengesetz', in *Wandlungsprozesse in Westdeutschland: Belastung, Integration, Liberalisierung 1945–1980*, ed. by Ulrich Herbert (Göttingen, 2002), 379–401 (400). Between December 1966 and October 1969, the SPD was the junior partner in a coalition with the CDU/CSU, the Christian Democrats.

The Ambivalence of Gay Liberation: Male Homosexual Politics in 1970s West Germany. Craig Griffiths,
Oxford University Press (2021). © Craig Griffiths.
DOI: 10.1093/oso/9780198868965.003.0002

agitation, forcing the government to act.[3] These three main consequences of homosexual law reform—the gay press, the larger gay scene, and homosexual organizing—all constituted crucial contexts for homosexual politics in the 1970s. Gay liberation cannot be seen in isolation from them. In this vein, historians should rightly interrogate what Benno Gammerl has called the 'gay success story', a narrative that paints gay activists in a heroic light and credits gay liberation with rescuing homosexuals from their shame-filled existence. This narrative not only neglects the efforts of the homophile movement of the 1950s, but also fails to give due weight to the changed social context in which gay activists found themselves.[4] Equally, I show in the first part of this chapter that gay liberation was never the inevitable outcome of structural changes to society. Indeed, there is the danger of another 'success story' lurking around, namely accounts that portray the Federal Republic as a success story of democratization and liberalization, to the exclusion of troubling continuities and the pronounced limits of that liberalization. For while gay liberation was indeed indebted to preceding developments, the political and social context for gay activism in the 1970s was not as auspicious as it may seem.

Homosexual Law Reform and the Limits of Liberalization

In September 1969, a liberalized version of Paragraph 175 came into effect, thus finally putting an end to the version of the law introduced by the National Socialists in 1935. This reform set the age of consent for male homosexual activity at 21. A further reform in 1973 reduced this to 18, and also replaced the language of sodomy (*Unzucht*) with the more neutral 'homosexual acts'.[5] In seeking to persuade the government of the need to overhaul the criminal code, the critical views of prominent lawyers, doctors and academics were significant, not least those compiled in the collection of essays *Sexuality and Crime*, published in 1963 and co-edited by Fritz Bauer, the Attorney General of the Federal State of Hesse.[6]

---

[3] See further Whisnant, *Male Homosexuality*, 166–203.

[4] Gammerl, 'Mit von der Partie oder auf Abstand? Biografische Perspektiven schwuler Männer und lesbischer Frauen auf die Emanzipationsbewegungen der 1970er Jahre', in *Rosa Radikale: Die Schwulenbewegung der 1970er Jahre*, ed. by Andreas Pretzel and Volker Weiß (Hamburg, 2012), 160–76 (160).

[5] The 1969 reform removed Paragraph 175a, introduced by the Nazis in 1935, which allowed for a harsher sentence of penal servitude to be imposed rather than imprisonment. Two of the measures contained within 175a were absorbed into the revised Paragraph 175: special sanctions regarding male prostitution and abuse of a relationship of dependency. These were both dropped in the 1973 reform. For the 1935 version, see *Strafgesetzbuch* (Munich, 1966), 79–80. 1969 version: *Strafgesetzbuch* (Munich, 1970), 92; 1973 version *Bundesgesetzblatt: Teil 1*, 98 (Bonn, 1973), 1725.

[6] Fritz Bauer, Hans Bürger-Prinz, Hans Giese and Herbert Jäger (eds), *Sexualität und Verbrechen: Beiträge zur Strafrechtsreform* (Frankfurt a.M., 1963). Hans Giese, a sexologist and psychologist, himself homosexual, testified to the Federal Constitutional Court in 1957, in support of the effort to have Paragraph 175 declared unconstitutional. In so doing, he differentiated between socially

In 1968, the writer Rolf Italiaander solicited a series of short statements from politicians and intellectuals who were sympathetic to homosexual law reform, including Theodor Adorno, Max Brod, Ossip K Flechtheim, Ulrike Meinhof, Gustav Heinemann, and Richard von Weizsäcker.[7] These statements were then sent to every member of the *Bundestag*. After the law was changed they were published in book form as *Neither Sickness nor Crime: Plea for a Minority*.[8]

Despite these efforts, the 1969 reform was not primarily the result of pressure from below. For example, there was no West German equivalent to the Homosexual Law Reform Society, founded in 1958 to campaign for the implementation of the Wolfenden Report, which had recommended partially decriminalizing male homosexuality in the United Kingdom.[9] The British case was important, not only because the Wolfenden Report was translated and copies sent to West German parliamentarians, but also because the delayed implementation of the Report in 1967—in England and Wales only, not in Scotland or Northern Ireland—put further pressure on the West German government to act, since by that point the Federal Republic had become increasingly out of step with its European neighbours.[10]

In *Neither Sickness nor Crime*, Italiaander particularly praised the example set by recent legal reform not only in England and Wales but also in Denmark and in the Netherlands.[11] Indeed, by 1969 the legal situation facing male homosexuals in West Germany was worse than that not just in those countries, but also in Belgium, Switzerland, France, Italy, Sweden, and Norway.[12] Greater embarrassment to the Federal government was caused by legal reform on the other side of the German–German border: the German Democratic Republic (GDR) repealed

---

productive long-term homosexual relationships and 'perverse' forms of homosexuality, including promiscuity, prostitution, and seduction. *Entscheidungen des Bundesverfassungsgerichts* (Tübingen, 1957), 403–6. See further Dannecker, 'Der unstillbare Wunsch nach Anerkennung' and Whisnant, *Male Homosexuality*, 71–80.

[7] Heinemann played a key role in initiating reform as the Justice Minister (SPD) between 1966 and 1969 and in March 1969 he was elected Federal President. Von Weizsäcker (CDU) was voted Federal President in 1984 and in 1985 he became the first German head of state to officially acknowledge that homosexuals had been persecuted by the Nazis. See further Chapter 4.

[8] Rolf Italiaander (ed.), *Weder Krankheit noch Verbrechen: Plädoyer für eine Minderheit* (Hamburg, 1969).

[9] See further, Weeks, *Coming Out*, 168–82.

[10] Whisnant, *Male Homosexuality*, 185. See also Katharina Ebner, *Religion im Parlament: Homosexualität als Gegenstand parlamentarischer Debatten im Vereinigten Königreich und in der Bundesrepublik Deutschland (1945–1990)* (Göttingen, 2018), especially 112–41.

[11] Italiaander, *Weder Krankheit noch Verbrechen*, 28.

[12] Stephan Heichel and Adrian Rinscheid, 'Ein klassischer Fall von Inkrementalismus: Die Liberalisierung der Regulierung von Homosexualität', in *Moralpolitik in Deutschland: Staatliche Regulierung gesellschaftlicher Wertekonflikte im historischen und internationalen Vergleich*, ed. by Christoph Knill et al. (Wiesbaden, 2015), 127–46 (131).

Paragraph 175 in 1968.[13] As the reform to Paragraph 175 was making its way through the West German parliament, Social Democrat Justice Minister Horst Ehmke invoked two international examples in support of homosexual law reform. One was from the other side of the Atlantic. Ehmke quoted Canadian Prime Minister Pierre Trudeau ('The government has no business in the bedrooms of the nation'), which was met with applause in the *Bundestag*. His other example was much closer to home. Ehmke added another reason for modernizing the criminal code—the fact that the GDR had already done so.[14]

According to Ulrich Herbert, liberalization is best understood as a 'learning process', the core phase of which took place from 1959 to 1973/1974.[15] Chronologically, homosexual law reform in 1969 and in 1973 might appear as one of the final acts of this process. Herbert's account and the scholarship that it has helped generate are in many ways persuasive. Certainly, there is no denying that fundamental change took place in the Federal Republic, so much so that the situation at the start of the 1970s bears little resemblance to West German society in the period immediately following the Cold War division of Germany in 1949. This holds broadly true whether our focus is placed on 'liberalization', 'modernization', 'westernization', or 'democratization'.[16]

The sheer speed of this process is striking. To take homosexual law reform as an example, the 1969 liberalization was not the result of a gradual long-term change but instead a reaction against a bill proposed by the governing Christian Democrats in 1962.[17] That bill would have not only maintained criminalization but would have also explicitly legitimized a 'moral-making' role for the law in bolstering a 'dam' against the 'depraved drive' of male homosexuality.[18] The Christian Democrats were emboldened by the decision of the Federal Constitutional Court five years earlier, which refused the bid by two homosexuals, Günther R. and Oskar K., to have their convictions against Paragraph 175 declared unconstitutional. The judges ruled that neither Article 2 nor 3 of the Basic Law, promising the free development of the personality and equality before

---

[13]   Paragraph 175 was replaced by a new law, Paragraph 151, which set the age of consent for same-sex sexuality at 18. *Strafgesetzbuch der DDR* (Berlin, 1981), 43.

[14]   'Plenarprotokoll 5/230', *Deutscher Bundestag—5. Wahlperiode* (7 May 1969), 12715–16. <http://dipbt.bundestag.de/doc/btp/05/05230.pdf> [accessed 8 December 2018]. Ebner cites the first but not the second example. Ebner, *Religion im Parlament*, 135.

[15]   Herbert defines liberalization as a 'concept of political culture referring to values and acts, dealing above all with mentalities and models of perception, action and reaction, and therefore with social structures of disposition from those of the family to those of the government'. Herbert, *Wandlungsprozesse in Westdeutschland*, 13.

[16]   Bernhard Rieger and Friedrich Kießling (eds), *Mit dem Wandel leben: Neuorientierung und Tradition in der Bundesrepublik der 1950er und 60er Jahre* (Cologne, 2011), 9.

[17]   Kandora, 'Homosexualität', 401.

[18]   The full text of the bill is included as an appendix to Fritz Bauer et al., *Sexualität und Verbrechen*, 405–12. Here, 411. See further Dagmar Herzog, *Sex after Fascism: Memory and Morality in Twentieth-Century Germany* (Princeton, 2005), 129–34.

the law, were sufficient grounds to overturn Paragraph 175, since male homosexuality in their view clearly infringed moral law.[19]

Seeking to historicize liberalization, Herbert argues that less value came to be placed on inherited conservative moral and political values. Pessimistic prophecies predicting the downfall of culture and society had not come true, economic security had increased, and Cold War tensions were on the wane. It was therefore no longer necessary to cling to what functioned as a prop in the context of an uncertain socio-economic situation.[20] The 'containment' or 'diking' of modernity had been frequently used metaphors in the 1950s, which explains the Christian Democrats' intention to erect a 'dam' against homosexuality.[21] By the 1970s, according to Herbert, 'firm and sharply sanctioned bonds to marriage and heterosexuality, to a specific, narrow model of gender roles, to sharply defined notions of normality and authority, [had] turned out to be ballasts and were thrown overboard'.[22] Certainly, there were moves towards greater pluralism, depletion of authoritarian structures, and a more flexible popular conception of gender roles. To deny this altogether would mean to fall into the idiom of the 1970s gay left and activists' symptomatic antipathy to the very idea of liberalization, or their construction of a straight line of oppression, linking Nazi Germany with the contemporary Federal Republic. This line of thinking will be explored in Chapters 3 and 4.

Nevertheless, historians should exercise caution when generalizing from wider liberalizing trends. It is true that on the federal level, after two decades of uninterrupted rule from 1949 to 1969, the Christian Democrats (CDU/CSU) found themselves in opposition for the duration of the 1970s. Following the 1969 election, the liberal Free Democrats (FDP) joined the Social Democrats (SPD) as the minority partner in a social–liberal coalition which would be re-elected in 1972, 1976, and 1980. On the left of the social–liberal coalition, a plethora of countercultural groups, cadre parties, loose collectives, social movements, and alternative milieu proliferated. Some parts of this left–alternative spectrum would eventually find parliamentary expression in the Greens, the 'anti-party party' founded in 1980 and which entered the *Bundestag* in 1983.[23]

This does not mean that the 1970s are best characterized as a 'red' or as a 'social-democratic' decade.[24] The Christian Democrats retained much influence

---

[19] *Entscheidungen des Bundesverfassungsgerichts* (Tübingen, 1957), 389–443.

[20] Herbert, *Wandlungsprozesse*, 48.

[21] Ibid., 24. On the association between homosexuality and modernity in 1950s West Germany see Whisnant, *Male Homosexuality*, 59–60.

[22] Herbert, *Wandlungsprozesse*, 48.

[23] On the Greens, see for example Andrei Markovits and Philip Gorski, *The German Left: Red, Green and Beyond* (Cambridge, 1993).

[24] A point made by Axel Schildt in reference to Gerd Koenen's 'red decade' and Bernd Faulenbach's 'social-democratic decade'. Schildt, '"Die Kräfte der Gegenreform sind auf breiter Front angetreten": Zur konservativen Tendenzwende in den Siebzigerjahren', *Archiv für Sozialgeschichte* 44 (2004), 449–79 (449). See further Gerd Koenen, *Das rote Jahrzehnt: Unsere kleine deutsche Kulturrevolution,*

through the upper house of parliament (*Bundesrat*) and through state governments. The federal election result in 1972, when the SPD out-polled the CDU/
CSU for the first time, was not repeated in 1976 or in 1980. Indeed, while the early
1970s was a period of crisis for the CDU, the decade subsequently became a time
of renewal, with more new members joining the party each year than the SPD, an
average of 70,000.[25] Much has been made of individualization and secularization,
but the numbers of those leaving the Protestant and Catholic Churches had
reached their height by the early 1970s, reducing thereafter.[26] In February 1975,
the Federal Constitutional Court annulled the government's recently-passed liberalization of abortion law.[27] Later that year, the Catholic Church put paid to any
hopes of reform raised by the Second Vatican Council by issuing its '*Persona
Humana*: Declaration on Certain Questions Concerning Sexual Ethics'. According
to the document, one of the most serious indications of the contemporary
'corruption of morals' was the 'unbridled exaltation of sex'. Sexuality belonged
to the sphere of marriage alone, and therefore homosexual acts were 'intrinsically
disordered and can in no case be approved of'.[28]

Focusing on homosexuality, one is confronted by the limits of liberalization.
Firstly, homosexual law reform came later in West Germany's liberal democracy
than in the state socialist German Democratic Republic. Unlike in the West, the
GDR never enforced the 1935 Nazi version of the law upon the division of
Germany in 1949, and repealed it altogether in 1968.[29] Secondly, even if we can
posit liberalized attitudes on the part of lawyers, medical practitioners, journalists,
and politicians in the Federal Republic, these did not necessarily entail a more
widespread acceptance of these attitudes on the part of the wider West German
population. An opinion poll in December 1968 suggested that a clear majority
rejected the impending decriminalization of homosexuality.[30] It is also necessary

---

1967–1977 (Cologne, 2001) and Bernd Faulenbach, *Das sozialdemokratische Jahrzehnt. Von der
Reformeuphorie zur neuen Unübersichtlichkeit. Die SPD 1969–1982* (Bonn, 2011).

[25] Frank Bösch, 'Die Krise als Chance: Die Neuformierung der Christdemokraten in den siebziger
Jahren', in *Das Ende der Zuversicht?*, ed. by Jarausch, 296–312 (300).
[26] Bösch, 'Die Krise als Chance', 298; Karl Gabriel, 'Entkirchlichung und (neue) Religion', in *Auf
dem Weg in eine neue Moderne? Die Bundesrepublik Deutschland in den siebziger und achtziger Jahren*,
ed. by Thomas Raithel, Andreas Rödder and Andreas Wirsching (Munich, 2009), 99–111 (100).
[27] The law permitted abortion within the first trimester of pregnancy, and was passed by parliament
in April 1974. Due to come into effect in June of that year, the law was first put on hold by the
Constitutional Court and then nullified the following year. In June 1976, a revised reform came into
effect, which maintained criminalization but allowed for abortions in case of medical, eugenic, social, or
ethical indications. See further Schulz, *Der lange Atem*, 106–73.
[28] Issued by the Congregation for the Doctrine of the Faith; confirmed and published by Pope
Paul VI. <http://www.vatican.va/roman_curia/congregations/cfaith/documents/rc_con_cfaith_doc_
19751229_persona-humana_en.html > [accessed 25 June 2018]. Not paginated.
[29] Jennifer Evans, 'Decriminalization, Seduction, and "Unnatural Desire" in East Germany',
Feminist Studies 36 (2010), 553–77 (560).
[30] Based on a representative sample of 2000. 38% of those polled supported legal reform, with 45%
opposed. *Jahrbuch der öffentlichen Meinung 1968–1973* (Allensbach, 1974), 244.

to interrogate what exactly is understood by liberalized attitudes. Polls can only ever give an approximation of popular opinion, but evidence suggests that under-standings of homosexuality underwent a significant shift between the 1960s and the 1970s. According to the Christian Democrats' draft bill in 1962, the illegality of homosexuality was justified because 'in easily the most predominant opinion of the German population, sexual relationships between men are to be regarded as contemptible aberrations, which tend to ruin character and destroy moral feel-ing'.[31] Based on a representative sample of 1000 people in September 1963, the Allensbach Institute found that 45 per cent of men and 46 per cent of women understood homosexuality as a vice (Laster), 37 per cent and 43 per cent as a sickness, 16 per cent and 11 per cent as a habit, and only 5 per cent and 3 per cent as a 'natural thing'. These were almost identical results to a poll with exactly the same wording from 1949.[32] The poll was repeated in 1977, and these results suggested that the percentage of those who judged homosexuality to be a vice had drastically fallen to 25 per cent of men and 20 per cent of women. The number of those indicating they understood homosexuality as a 'natural thing' had risen to 13 per cent of men and 20 per cent of women.[33] However, the perception of homosexuality as a crime seems to have been displaced also by an understanding relating to sickness. The poll suggests that the percentage of the public which perceived homosexuality as an illness significantly increased: fully 49 per cent of the men and 46 per cent of the women surveyed selected this option.[34]

In a victory for American gay activists, homosexuality was removed from the *Diagnostic and Statistical Manual of Mental Disorders* (DSM) in 1973.[35] It con-tinued to be cited, however, in the *International Classification of Diseases* (ICD), which was used more widely in Europe.[36] In this context, medical interventions seeking explicitly or implicitly to cure homosexual behaviour continued to achieve a certain prominence. An article in the liberal weekly *Die Zeit* in April 1969 reported on the stereotactic brain surgery performed on three homosexuals by

---

[31] Appendix, *Sexualität und Verbrechen*, ed. by Bauer et al., 405–12. Here, p. 407.

[32] *Jahrbuch der öffentlichen Meinung 1958–64* (Allensbach, 1965), 591. The percentages add up to 104 for men and 106 for women. For the 1949 poll, see *Allensbacher Jahrbuch der Demoskopie 1976–1977* (Allensbach, 1977), 144. The sample size in 1949 was also 1000, but only men were surveyed.

[33] *Allensbacher Jahrbuch der Demoskopie 1976–1977*, 144. The sample for the latter poll was not representative: those polled were restricted to 332 married women and 325 married men between the ages of 18 and 70.

[34] Ibid., 144. 13% of men and 20% of women understood homosexuality as a habit.

[35] Compiled by the American Psychiatric Association. The decision to remove homosexuality as a mental disorder was taken by the Association's Board of Directors in 1973 and ratified by the membership in 1974. See Ronald Bayer, *Homosexuality and American Psychiatry: The Politics of Diagnosis* (Princeton, 1987 [1981]), 101–54.

[36] In a reply to a query by SPD *Bundestag* representative Hans-Joachim Hoffmann, the West German government recognized in 1980 that homosexuality was not an illness 'in the conventional sense' and pledged to consider whether it might support efforts to have it removed from the ICD. *Emanzipation* 5 (1980), 12–13.

Fritz Douglas Roeder. One of the men had undertaken long-term psychotherapy but this had failed to resolve what was referred to as his 'perversion'. Seeking to avoid coming into conflict with the law, the man had sought surgery, but this had only reduced the force rather than change the orientation of his desire. Were he to live in a country which tolerated homophilia, the man stated, he would immediately give in to his homosexual inclinations, but thanks to the operation he could better control his tendencies at home in Germany. Rather than suggesting that in this context perhaps greater tolerance of same-sex desire might be desirable, *Die Zeit* noted that stereotactic brain surgery was a better option than psychotherapy or castration, especially since the latter would preclude a future marriage for those whose orientation was successfully changed.[37] *Der Spiegel* was similarly uncritical about the prospects raised by the research of Günter Dörner, an East German endocrinologist. Based on experiments on rats, Dörner suggested in 1969 that homosexuality arose from an early hormonal imbalance, which might be corrected via injections into the womb during pregnancy, especially in cases where there was a family history of homosexuality. The *Spiegel* article concluded with Dörner's consideration that he might in the future also be able to treat adult homosexuals, whether through hormonal injections or surgical interventions.[38] In the same year as homosexuality was decriminalized, the debate over how best to cure the affliction was evidently alive and kicking.

If the notion that homosexuality constituted an illness enjoyed much currency during the 1970s, it was accompanied by the conception that homosexuality posed a danger, and especially a danger to youth. Michael Kandora states that Paragraph 175, as a result of the 1969 and 1973 reforms, was refashioned into a 'purely youth-protection paragraph', as if that were straightforwardly a benign development. According to Kandora, 'All homosexual acts which did not fall into the narrow sphere of the protection of youth were in the future not to be subject to prosecution.'[39] In the event, the sphere of the protection of youth proved *not* to be all that narrow. Over a thousand men were convicted of homosexual offences in between the two parliamentary reforms. Even after 1973 hundreds of guilty verdicts were still passed down each year.[40]

Between 1969 and 1973, young same-sex desiring men were placed in a particularly invidious position. Because the age of consent was 21, but the age of

[37] Wolfgang Schmidbauer, 'Vom Trieb befreit durch Operation', *Die Zeit* (4 April 1969). In the piece, 'homosexual', 'paedophile', and 'homophile' were used in an interchangeable fashion.
[38] 'Gesteuerte Lust', *Der Spiegel* 10 (1969), 152. See further Florian G. Mildenberger, 'Socialist Eugenics and Homosexuality in the GDR: The Case of Günter Dörner', in *After the History of Sexuality*, ed. by Spector, Puff, and Herzog, 216–30.
[39] Kandora, 'Homosexualität', 384 and 400.
[40] *Statistisches Jahrbuch für die Bundesrepublik Deutschland* (Wiesbaden [published annually]). In 1970 there were 340 convictions against Paragraph 175; 372 in 1971; and 362 in 1972. In 1974, after the age of consent was reduced to 18, there were 235 convictions; by the decade's end, in 1979, 148. In 1993, the last calendar year before Paragraph 175 was eventually repealed altogether, there were 76 convictions.

criminal responsibility was 18, male adolescents could legally sleep with each other, but as soon as one partner turned 18, this sexual relationship became subject to criminal prosecution.[41] Moreover, by legalizing adult male homosexuality, but setting a different age of consent for homosexual and heterosexual acts (21 and 16 respectively; from 1973, 18 and 14 respectively), the pre-existing notion that homosexuality *was* a danger to youth, and one from which boys and young men needed to be protected, was codified in law. In 1972, when the relevant commission reported to the *Bundestag*, recommending a reduction in the age of consent for male homosexuality from 21 to 18, this was expressly predicated upon the assumption that the heterosexual orientation of men aged between 18 and 21 was already set and that this would immunize them against any homosexual influence. Moreover, commission members rejected the path set by the Netherlands in setting the age of consent at 16, since in their opinion it could not be ruled out that 16 and 17 year-olds would be more significantly influenced by homosexual encounters.[42]

That homosexuality continued to be treated as a threat to youth relativizes Sybille Steinbacher's claim that in West Germany by the 1960s sexuality was 'definitively' no longer interpreted as a social threat. It also calls into question Steinbacher's contentions that the reforms to the sexual criminal code in 1969 and 1973 marked 'a deep socio-cultural caesura' and that sexual morality was no longer considered a matter for state regulation.[43] These generalizations simply do not hold water when one focuses on homosexuality. In 1974, the secondary school teacher Reiner Koepp and the Church youth worker Klaus Kindel both lost their jobs on account of living openly as homosexuals. The gay left would present these cases as *Berufsverbote,* 'bans on careers', part of an attempt to banish 'extremists' and 'radicals' from the civil service.[44] The language used in a ruling upholding Koepp's dismissal was particularly revealing. According to the court, the issue at stake was not homosexuality per se, since what people did in private was the business of nobody else, but that Koepp had sought to make his 'aberrant' way of life the centre of attention in the school, creeping 'from behind, as it were' into the teaching profession as an 'agent of homosexuality'. Continuing, the court decreed that teachers had a particular responsibility to ensure that their behaviour

---

[41] This state of affairs was deplored by Rolf Italiaander, whose book was published just after the reform to Paragraph 175 came into effect: Italiaander (ed.), *Weder Krankheit noch Verbrechen*, 224.

[42] 'Schriftlicher Bericht des Sonderausschusses für die Strafrechtsreform', *Deutscher Bundestag—6. Wahlperiode* (14 June 1972), 30 and 31. <http://dipbt.bundestag.de/doc/btd/06/035/0603521.pdf> [accessed 25 June 2018].

[43] Steinbacher, *Wie der Sex nach Deutschland kam: Der Kampf um Sittlichkeit und Anstand in der frühen Bundesrepublik* (Munich, 2011), 358 and 357.

[44] Referencing the *Extremistenbeschluß*, the 'Extremists' Resolution'. More commonly referred to as the *Radikalenerlass* (radicals' decree) and dubbed the *Berufsverbot* by its opponents, the measure was introduced in 1972. See further Gerard Braunthal, *Political Loyalty and Public Service in West Germany: The 1972 Degree against Radicals and its Consequences* (Massachusetts, 1990).

did not infringe the 'unwritten laws of honour, convention and decency'.[45] While the ruling stopped short of accusing Koepp himself of engaging in relations with his pupils, his presentation of homosexuality was blamed for contributing to the reduction of psychological inhibitions in children, thus making them liable to be seduced into homosexual acts.[46]

The 'unwritten laws' infringed by Koepp proved remarkably resilient, which meant that homosexual law reform offered homosexuals no direct and automatic route into public discourse. Indeed, the notion that homosexuality was youth-endangering provided the justification for regular attempts to police the public sphere.[47] Reading the Christian Democrats' draft 1962 bill, one is struck by the anxiety expressed about the potentially disastrous consequences for public life were homosexuality to be legalized. Even with Paragraph 175, the bill's authors worried, homosexuals still came together in the larger cities and were developing propaganda through their publications and sociable events, furthering their goal of advancement in public life through mutual support.[48] This deplorable situation would be worsened by decriminalization, since nothing would stand in the way of the 'promotional activity of homosexual groups'. Moreover, the increased levels of homosexual promotion and activity in the public sphere would prove especially captivating to youth.[49] These concerns did not disappear even after the decision had been taken to liberalize Paragraph 175. The Society for Sexual Reform (GSR), one of West Germany's most discreetly named gay action groups, was refused permission to hold an information stall and distribute leaflets by the city of Aachen in 1973. The initial decision cited the importance of upholding public order, which included 'good morals and public decency'.[50]

Defending the decision, the Cologne *Regierungspräsident* agreed that the planned information stall would have contravened public order, since passers-by were to be confronted by homosexuality in an 'intrusive' form—'intrusive' because homosexuals themselves were to refer to their homosexuality in public.[51] Not without some justification, gay activists later in the decade were to interpret

---

[45] Full text of verdict printed as 'Im Namen des Volkes', in *Schwule sich emanzipieren lernen: Materialien zur Ausstellung*, ed. by Peter Hedenström (Berlin, 1976), 16–18.

[46] Ibid., 18.

[47] I follow the broad definition of 'public sphere' provided by Christina von Hodenberg: 'a structure of many co-existing forums in which a society selects topics for debate and negotiates patterns of interpretation, values and conflicting interests'. Hodenberg, 'Mass Media and the Generation of Conflict: West Germany's Long Sixties and the Formation of a Critical Public Sphere', *Contemporary European History* 15 (2006), 367–95 (369). Some of these 'co-existing forums' will be analysed in Chapter 3, which discusses the left-alternative concept of a *Gegenöffentlichkeit*, a 'counterpublic'.

[48] Appendix, *Sexualität und Verbrechen*, ed. by Bauer et al., 405–12 (407).

[49] Ibid., 409 and 410.

[50] *Oberstadtdirektor*, Stadt Aachen to GSR, 5 June 1973. SMB archive, NARGS box one, folder 'Dokumentation Aachener Info-Tisch-Fall' [hereafter 'Dokumentation'].

[51] *Regierungspräsident* to GSR, 8 November 1973. SMB archive, folder 'Dokumentation'.

the logic of this decision as 'only an invisible homosexual is a good homosexual'.[52] Though GSR members were initially successful in their appeal, the North-Rhine Westphalian Higher Administrative Court ruled in 1976 that the initial rejection of their request had been legal, and refused the group permission to appeal. The court's verdict acknowledged that the configuration of the 'intimate sphere' had been greatly liberalized, but ruled that the state was nevertheless permitted to banish matters of this 'intimate sphere' from the public arena. The verdict decreed that nonconformist behaviours, and opinions expressed about these behaviours, if aired in public, could harm the interests of the general population, and especially threaten youth and the 'undisturbed development of their sexual sphere'.[53] Acknowledging the 1969 and 1973 reforms to Paragraph 175, the court nevertheless cited the Federal Constitutional Court decision from 1957, arguing that the recent legal changes had not nullified the earlier judgement that male homosexuality infringed moral law.[54]

In 1967, the Federal Minister for Health, Family and Youth, Käte Ströbel (SPD) commissioned *Helga*, the first West German film to document childbirth live on screen. Two years later, her department published its 'sex education atlas', distributed to schools around the country. Aiming to liberate sex education from 'ideological prejudices', the book offered matter-of-fact information on masturbation, conception, childbirth and sexually transmitted infections—including an image of a penis displaying symptoms of primary syphilis for good measure.[55] Such developments would have been unthinkable until very recently, the result not only of the entry to government of the Social Democrats but of the impact of the 'sexual revolution': the commercialization, liberalization and politicization of sex.[56] Radical leftists would criticize the sex education atlas for not going far enough, either in its suggestion that sexuality begins only after the onset of puberty, or in its almost complete restriction of sexuality to its reproductive role alone.[57] For queers growing up in the late 1960s, the atlas offered precisely nothing—no possibility whatsoever of recognizing their desire within its pages. The word 'homosexuality' appeared once in the entire publication, and only then in the page with suggestions for further reading.[58]

---

[52] National Working Group Repression against Gays press release (10 December 1978). SMB archive, NARGS box one, folder 1979/1.
[53] Verdict of the NRW *Oberverwaltungsgericht*, 15 March 1976. SMB archive, folder 'Dokumentation'.
[54] Ibid.
[55] *Sexualkunde-Atlas: Biologische Informationen zur Sexualität des Menschen* (Opladen: CW Leske, 1969), preface and p. 43.
[56] Herzog, *Sex after Fascism*, 141.
[57] Zentralrat der sozialistischen Kinderläden (ed.), *Für die Befreiung der kindlichen Sexualität* (Berlin, 1969); Reimut Reiche, 'Zeugung ist Ordnung', *Der Spiegel* 28 (1969), 115.
[58] The text cited in this regard is Hubert Bacia, *Themen zur Sexualität* (Bochum, 1969 [2nd edition]). *Sexualkunde-Atlas*, 47.

Käte Ströbel may have taken on the conservative establishment in pushing through the publicly-funded sex education atlas, but her liberalizing impulses did not stretch to homosexuality. Indeed, in 1970, she attempted to have *him* placed on the index of 'youth-endangering materials', because the gay magazine's 'sexual-ethical misorientation' (*Fehlorientierung*) supposedly posed a danger to youth.[59] In particular, Ströbel took exception to dating ads placed by those younger than 21, a pull-out poster displaying a young man wearing just a loincloth, and an advert for a sex toy.[60] Being indexed would have banished the publication from the public sphere. Indexed materials could not be placed on public display and instead had to rely on subscriptions or under-the-counter sales alone, exactly the situation faced by *him*'s homophile journal predecessors in the 1950s and 1960s.

Placing homosexuality at the centre of attention therefore reveals not only the limits of liberalization in West Germany in the late 1960s and 1970s, but the limits of liberalism. The rise of legal liberalism had been a crucial factor in homosexual law reform, especially in attacking the claim of the Christian Democrats that there should be a 'moral-making' role for the law in bolstering a 'dam' against male homosexuality.[61] Yet legal liberalism did not offer an especially promising framework for gay activism. Tenets of this liberalism—that it was not the role of the state to intervene in citizens' private lives, and that what happened between two people within four walls was no business of anybody else—provided a compelling narrative for decriminalization, but not for political agitation. Indeed, while various forms of homosexual organizing could not have expanded without this liberalism having taking hold, gay liberation was also a reaction *against* this relegation of sexuality to the private sphere.[62]

The Gay Press: Between 'an Ethics of Homophilia' and a 'Parade of Cocks'

The efforts of Kate Ströbel notwithstanding, the commercial gay press became a durable part of the West German media landscape in the 1970s. The appearance in newspaper stands of gay magazines was the most immediate, and most visible, consequence of homosexual law reform: the first on the market, *du&ich* ('You and I'), adopted the subtitle 'the post-September magazine', acknowledging its debt to the liberalization of Paragraph 175, which had come into effect in

---

[59] *him* 6 (1970), 14–18.   [60] Ibid., 14.

[61] See especially the collection of essays in Bauer et al. (eds), *Sexualität und Verbrechen*.

[62] Clayton Whisnant argues that proponents of legal liberalism saw the need to couple this liberalism with 'a much stricter attitude towards the public expression of sexuality'. Whisnant, *Male Homosexuality*, 183. Jeffrey Weeks makes a similar point in relation to homosexual law reform in England and Wales: Weeks, *Coming Out*, 176.

September 1969.[63] *him* followed in May 1970. Both magazines sold for 5DM per monthly issue, rising to 8DM by the end of the decade. This was substantially more than the activist gay press, which will be discussed in Chapter 3. Individual gay groups produced their own hastily-compiled information sheets and zines, which were generally disseminated internally, free of charge. The first two activist journals to be released nationally, both in 1975, were *Emanzipation* and *Schwuchtel* ('Fag'): these titles sold for 2DM each. *him*, with its editorial office based in Hamburg's red light district on the *Reeperbahn*, was owned by Helmut Rosenberg, whose *St Pauli Verlag* also published a number of popular (heterosexual) pornographic magazines.[64] In 1980, to mark the publication's tenth anniversary, *him* editors formed a collective to buy out Rosenberg. In their words, this meant that 'for the first time, one of the most important homosexual magazines in Europe will belong to the persons concerned', bringing with it freedom from exploitation by heterosexual publishers.[65] (That freedom was short-lived, since *him* ceased publication within a year.)

The two most influential and longest-lasting commercial titles, *him* and *du&ich* offered their readers very similar packages: a smorgasbord featuring glossy photos of adolescents and men in various states of undress; news stories relating to homosexuality; gossip columns; cultural coverage of literature, television and theatre; advice and information about discrimination, crime and sexually transmitted infections; updates on various types of homosexual organizations; contact ads, which functioned as a type of dating agency; a smattering of erotic stories; and finally reports on the gay scene both domestically and internationally.[66] Celebrity interviews included the likes of Christopher Isherwood, Jean Genet, and even Muhammad Ali.[67] Much of the content of these magazines was not 'political' in a narrow sense, yet their significance for homosexual politics was profound. The last remaining journal of the post-war homophile movement, *Der Weg* ('The Path'), written in a dense literary style and produced in smaller A5 format, survived only until early 1970, financially hamstrung by being available only to a small number of subscribers. On sale in newspaper stands around the country, *du&ich* and *him* were unprecedented sources of information, connectivity and erotic fulfilment for same-sex desiring men. Crucially, these magazines offered a forum for exchange,

---

[63] *du&ich* published its first two issues in late 1969, before beginning monthly instalments in 1970. For clarity, I will use *du&ich* throughout, though the title appeared in various forms (including du+ich, Du&Ich and DU&ICH). *du&ich* ceased publication in 2014.

[64] These included *Deutsche Sex-Illustrierte* and *St Pauli Nachrichten*. Cited from *him* 10 (1974).

[65] *him applaus* (May/June 1980), 10; Hans-Peter Reichelt, untitled editorial, *him applaus* (July/August 1980), 2. The magazine changed its name to *him applaus* in October 1976: for clarity, I will use *him* throughout.

[66] The other gay monthly was *Don*, established initially under the name *Sunny* in May 1970. Both *du&ich* and *him*, briefly, had small sections for lesbian readers. Neither magazine provided information about their circulation figures, but the first issue of *du&ich* had a print run of 10,000, which was doubled for the second issue. 'Schöne Aufgabe', *Der Spiegel* 50 (1969), 212.

[67] *him* (January 1974), 41–3; *du&ich* 4 (1976), 25–8 and 45–8; *du&ich* 3 (1972), 5–7.

with two pages of readers' letters each issue. According to Martin Meeker, communication has been the most stubborn problem facing homosexuals in the twentieth century. He argues that the increased dissemination of texts and images relating to homosexuality was a prerequisite for overcoming isolation and forming a group identity.[68] Seen in this light, the likes of *du&ich* and *him* were a leap forward, a founding stone of gay liberation in West Germany.

In their earliest phases, those involved with commercial gay magazines would not have recognized their publications as 'gay'. The chief editor of *du&ich*, Udo Erlenhardt, fulminated in a 1970 editorial that homosexuals who called themselves 'gay' (*schwul*) were 'degrading themselves'. For Erlenhardt, society's image of the homosexual remained characterized by the 'gay swine', buying or selling himself at the train station.[69] Homophiles needed to challenge this image: 'we will be understood and accepted by society according to the manner in which we present ourselves'. Erlenhardt's position was unequivocal: 'I say it hereby loud and clear: I don't belong to the gays.'[70] Erlenhardt soon departed, but the magazine's stance, for the time being, remained the same. In an editorial in December 1970, readers were reminded that *du&ich* was a homophile, not a homosexual magazine.[71] In no other arena was the visual transformation from the homophile era so marked, yet continuities remained. In 1972, the short-lived magazine *unter uns* would remove its initial subtitle, 'for men who like men'. This was explained as stating the obvious, but editors were evidently also concerned by the impression such a message would give, with its foregrounding of homoerotic desire. They chose instead 'For Friendship and Tolerance', exactly the same subtitle used by the long-running homophile journal *Der Weg*.[72]

The more influential *du&ich*, meanwhile, opted in September 1970 for 'A magazine for cultivated people in an enlightened age'.[73] Nevertheless, both *du&ich* and *him* were evidently unsure as to exactly how cultivated their readers were or how enlightened West German society actually was. The chief editor of *him*, Dieter Michael Specht, complained in 1971 about the levels of self-aggrandizement in homosexual circles and bemoaned the lack of an 'ethics of homophilia'.[74] The same author argued later that year that the aim of gay publications should not be to integrate homosexuals into existing society, but to change that society to the extent that an integration would no longer be necessary. Yet he saw himself as hamstrung by on the one hand demands from a militant minority for demonstrations and actionism, which he chastized as 'intellectual

---

[68] Meeker, *Contacts Desired*, 1.   [69] 'Die schwule Sau', *du&ich* 1 (1970), 4.   [70] Ibid., 4.
[71] *du&ich* 12 (1970), 10–11.
[72] *unter uns* 4 (1972). The magazine ran for only five issues in 1972, returning briefly in 1977, and then again in 1978, under the new name of *Adam International*.
[73] *du&ich* 9 (1970).
[74] 'Trauerspiel des Idealisten im Sandkästchen deutscher Homophilen-Verbände', *him* 2 (1971), 6–9 (6).

hokum', and on the other by the 'reactionary way of thinking' of most of his readership.[75]

Irritated by the style of the two first issues, Wilfried R. wrote to *du&ich* in 1970, criticizing the attempts made to justify and legitimate homosexuality: 'I and certainly the majority of the readers of *du+ich* just do not have the desire to explain ourselves. I'm rather proud of being homosexual.'[76] The very first issue of *him* carried an evocative double-page spread depicting a naked young man emerging from the shadows, striking a valiant pose, above the large text *ICH BIN HOMO* ('I'm a homo'). This image of a proud, youthful, healthy homosexuality was not an inclusive one. In the accompanying text, the reader learns that 'I'm a homo' meant 'therefore different to' three manifestations that were all disavowed in the strongest possible terms: effeminate 'queens' (*Tunten*); gossipy 'gentlemen from tea parties'; and rent boys, for 'a real homo' could not do the job performed by these 'inhibited, complex-laden, cowed, cowardly, sanctimonious specimens'.[77]

Then again, in the same issue, Uwe Conrad admitted that the gay scene was not to everyone's taste, but warned against adopting a *spießbürgerlich* (bourgeois, philistine) understanding of homosexuality. Those who belong to an oppressed minority would betray themselves if they, of all people, were to adopt the way of life of the 'upstanding citizens.'[78] While the commercial gay press sought to police the self-presentation of homosexuals, its ire was often directed at wider society, too. An angry article in an early issue of *du&ich* took aim at the hypocrisy of those who attacked the GDR as a political dictatorship while tolerating or rearing a 'moral dictatorship' in the Federal Republic. While East German citizens were imprisoned by barbed wire and a wall through Berlin, on 'this side of the iron curtain' homosexuals were confined in a 'psychological ghetto' caused by spite and a misinterpretation of Christian ethics, and were forced to suffer under a morality that made life torturous and had driven thousands to their deaths.[79]

No figure so captures the ambivalence of the early 1970s as Udo Erlenhardt. Erlenhardt has the rare distinction of having been the chief editor of both *du&ich* and *him*, though he lasted only two issues at the former and four at the latter.[80] Dubbed the 'homo pope' by *Der Spiegel*, due to his background as a seminarian, Erlenhardt was not one to shun the limelight, leading to the charge from his editorial team at *du&ich* that he was more concerned with developing his own

---

[75] 'Die dritte Lernphase für deutsche Homosexuelle', *him* 7 (1971), 2.   [76] *du&ich* 1 (1970), 3.
[77] Günther Raab, 'Ich bin Homo', *him* (May 1970), 20–1. The German usage is not exactly equivalent to the English 'homo', being somewhat closer to the meaning of 'gay'. The informal and non-pejorative shorthand currently used for 'gay marriage', for example, is *Homo-Ehe*.
[78] 'Außenseiter der Gesellschaft?', *him* (May 1970), 46.
[79] J.U., 'Fragen an "gewisse" Mitbürger', *du&ich* 2 (1970), 1.
[80] Erlenhardt edited the second issue of *du&ich* in 1969 and the first issue of 1970. After he was sacked, he was appointed the chief editor of *him*, where he remained until September 1970.

image than that of the magazine.[81] Though he thoroughly rejected the use of 'gay', he was explicit that homosexuals must *bekennen*—must avow their homosexuality, come out.[82] Erlenhardt was certainly prepared to practice what he preached, and took to announcing his homosexuality though a microphone in Central Hamburg. This was in defence of *him*, and in opposition to the attempt of Käte Ströbel to have it placed on the index of 'youth-endangering materials'.[83]

In an impressive performance addressing the indexing board, Erlenhardt pointed out that, due to the age of consent for male homosexuality, the 19 or 20 year-old was legally allowed to vote, marry, have children and serve in the military, but apparently unable to decide whether he was homophile. Moreover, he continued, the ostensibly youth-endangering photos in *him* paled in comparison in terms of naked flesh to other magazines on the market aimed at a heterosexual audience.[84] Emboldened by this experience, Erlenhardt struck a markedly militant tone in a subsequent issue: 'If homophiles fail to struggle for their equal position in society through public actions, they will always feel like a rejected minority. [...] The next step leads to communication, in the streets, in parliament. The public must be confronted with realities.'[85] Recorded and broadcast on national television in a sympathetic ten-minute segment on the current affairs programme *Monitor*, Erlenhardt's actions foreshadowed the activism of gay liberation, but took place before a single gay action group existed in the Federal Republic.[86]

While Erlenhardt may have wanted to confront the public 'with realities', he was nevertheless anxious to reassure his audience that they had nothing to fear. Using his microphone, he underlined that homophiles wanted nothing other than equality before the law, and certainly not a 'homoeroticization' of society. In part, these were the terms on which Erlenhardt and other editors thought they could best secure a modicum of public support, thereby defending their own newfound and precarious presence in the public sphere. Their limited demands were crucial in maintaining a space which could be exploited more forcefully by others in gay liberation later in the decade. Yet this was never just a question of tactical approaches, but also of deep-seated ambivalence, with editors caught between the commercial need to satisfy their readers' emotional and erotic demands, and

[81] 'Thema Eins', *Der Spiegel* 32 (1970), 32–46 (33); 'Pardon, Frater Andreas, wir distanzieren uns', *du&ich* 2 (1970), 5.
[82] *du&ich* 1 (1970), 5.   [83] *him* (June 1970), 14–18.
[84] He cited *twen, spontan* and *konkret. Monitor* current affairs programme, ARD (broadcast 9 July 1970). A copy is held at the SMB archive.
[85] 'Freiheit für Homos erst ab 21?', *him* (August 1970), 14–21 (17). Though *him* was not indexed on this occasion, it faced the same predicament two years later, when the Bavarian Ministry for Labour and Social Order submitted its own indexing request. The indexing board ruled this time that the magazine was youth-endangering, but nevertheless did not place the publication on the list of indexed materials, so the ruling had little practical consequence. '*him* ist jugendgefährdend! Dennoch keine Indizierung', *ihs-info* 1 (1973), 3 and 6.
[86] *Monitor* was produced by the WDR and broadcast on the first channel, the ARD. 9 July 1970.

their efforts to present a sanitized vision of homosexuality for public consumption.

In his editorial opposing the word 'gay', Udo Erlenhardt had placed the blame for the continuing ostracization of homosexuals exclusively at homosexuals' doors.[87] If Käte Ströbel was the villain, so were the queens, prostitutes, and gays giving all right-thinking homophiles a bad name. One can observe a similar ambivalence on the part of those responsible for the *Monitor* television coverage. Initially, the narrator left no doubt as to where his allegiances lay. Right at the top of the footage, the general population were described as stubborn and obstinate in their prejudice against homosexuals and the authorities seeking to index *him* were characterized as 'guardians of a morality that has preached persecution for centuries.' Yet queers were not let off the hook, either. The narrator continued that homophiles needed to convince society of the facts that homosexuality was not a vice, not a bad habit, not a sickness and not a perversion. Homosexuals needed to come out, but that would not suffice: they were told to correct the view that homosexuals were either work-shy or effeminate, to make clear that homophiles had absolutely nothing to do with 'outgrowths' in transvestite bars or train station toilets, and to prove that the homosexual was not 'an animal whose everyday life consists of one long sexual orgy'.[88]

Other commentators were also concerned about sexual propriety. A self-defined 'good old-school German' would denounce *du&ich* in 1970 in the following way: 'Some of the photos are disgusting and obscene. Sex is of course very nice, but it must remain normal. Otherwise where will we end up in Germany. We should leave this dirtiness to the French and the Italians. Germany must remain clean, including in the sexual sphere.'[89] The individual had evidently taken the trouble to look past the front cover, suggesting that their own sexual desire may not have so neatly fitted into the realm of the 'normal' and the 'clean'. However, of greater interest than the existence of abusive correspondence is the fact that such language was not rejected wholesale by gay publicists themselves. In December 1970, *du&ich* editors informed their readers that they did not want to underline the sexual component of 'homophilia', but to instead give expression to homophile feeling and disposition. Anything else could damage the reputation of homophiles in the wider public. It was therefore crucial that the magazine proved its 'cleanliness', a quality so sorely lacking in the so-called 'sex papers of "normal" character'.[90]

him badly misjudged the inclination of its readers in early 1973, when editors described the publication so far as a 'good product in poor packaging'. In the future, there were to be fewer nude photos, to make way for extended editorial

---

[87] 'Die schwule Sau', *du&ich* 1 (1970), 4.
[88] *Monitor* (ARD, 9 July 1970). My transcription from the footage.   [89] *du&ich* 2 (1970), 4.
[90] *du&ich* 12 (1970), 10–11.

content seeking to raise homosexual consciousness.[91] As a sign of what to expect, there followed a lengthy report on human rights abuses in Vietnam.[92] Two months later, *him* had received almost 2,000 letters on this shift in content, and editors were forced to admit they had underestimated the importance of images to their readers.[93] One reader, Walter S., suggested a compromise, whereby images of clothed models would replace nudes: '*him* tries to make clear to heterosexuals and homosexuals alike that the homosexual is first and foremost a human being, that he is not "gay by trade", that he doesn't only fuck, but also thinks, feels, loves, suffers and works'.[94]

The vast majority, however, demanded a return to semi-nude or nude representations of the male body, and saw reportage in the vein of the Vietnam article as a poor substitute. Michael H. argued that there was nothing immoral about erotic photography, and continued 'if we want to emancipate ourselves, then only under the condition that one accepts us as we are – and nude photos belong to *our* sexuality too!'[95] Another reader emphasized that erotic images were all the more important for the lonely, the old, and those who live in rural areas far away from any gay bar. For these constituencies, images served as a 'modest substitute for that which is unfortunately unattainable'.[96] Perhaps it was these negative reactions which prompted chief editor Dieter Michael Specht to complain to *Der Spiegel*, when interviewed in 1973, that 'one cock photo less = 5000 customers lost'.[97]

du&ich faced the same balancing act as *him*. One reader wrote to the magazine praising the second issue and calling for further moves towards the ideal of a 'homophile *Spiegel*'.[98] Others were evidently less interested in international coverage and investigative journalism than in titillating images. According to the magazine's own analysis of 759 letters received in early November 1972, over 40 per cent criticized the magazine's choice of photos, the most common complaint being that there were insufficient images of 'young or very young' models.[99] Minority voices could be found, with one man complaining not about the lack or style of erotic images, but about their excessive presence in the magazine: 'Have you really failed to notice that you are gradually degenerating to a lousy porno?'[100] In early 1973, a disappointed subscriber lamented that the magazine's photos were degenerating into a 'monotonous parade of cocks'. This reader did not seek a less graphic or more academic publication, but rather more images of 'beautiful arses' instead.[101] Most of *du&ich*'s photos portrayed nearly nude models, but it seems

---

[91] 'Gute Ware in schlechter Verpackung', *him* 3 (1973), 7.
[92] Le Bouc, '120 Jahren Verbrechen am Volk von Vietnam', *him* 3 (1973), 8–11.
[93] 'Briefschwemme', *him* 5 (1973), 5.   [94] Ibid., 7.
[95] Ibid., 6. Emphasis in the original.   [96] Ibid., 7.
[97] 'Bekennt, daß ihr anders seid', *Der Spiegel* 11 (1973), 46–62 (58).   [98] *du&ich* 1 (1970), 3.
[99] *du&ich* 1 (1973), 16. These made up 273, or 36% of the total. I have written about the portrayal of adolescents and intergenerational desire elsewhere: Craig Griffiths, 'Sex, Shame and West German Gay Liberation', *German History* 34 (2016), 445–67, especially 449–51.
[100] *du&ich* 1 (1973), 16.   [101] *du&ich* 1 (1973), 9.

they were not as explicit as readers would have liked. After a reform to Paragraph 184 of the penal code came into effect in 1975, many readers expected that they would now be able to enjoy images of erect penises: editors were forced to disappoint them, stating that were this change to be made the magazine could only be sold in sex shops rather than from newspaper stands.[102]

Even after the gay press had established and defended itself, one does not find an unequivocal recognition of erotic desire and sex acts in its pages. Throughout the decade, publicists kept up a running theme of disavowing ostensibly opprobrious aspects of gay sexuality while at the same time visually depicting and emboldening those same aspects. This saying one thing and doing another was not just an indication of the competing priorities facing publicists. It was also indicative of an ambivalence that the editors, writers, and photographers of the gay press were no more immune to than their magazines' readers.[103] In 1977, the chief editor of *du&ich*, Alexander Ziegler, was forced to defend himself after criticism following comments he had made at a podium event, to the effect that most of the blame for discrimination should be placed at the door of those minority of homosexuals who insisted on frequenting cruising grounds, toilets and 'seedy dives'.[104] According to Ziegler, when the mainstream press wrote about homosexuality, this caused associations to rent boys, 'arse-fuckers', blackmail, train station toilets and make-up: 'outgrowths' that represented 'no more than 2 per cent of our minority'.[105] This was a clear example of continuity rather than rupture in homosexual politics, since the journals of the early post-war homophile movement were fond of invoking the same scapegoats, especially prostitution and effeminacy.[106]

Ziegler clearly found anal sex problematic too: he suggested here that less than 2 per cent of homosexuals practised the behaviour. He had evidently forgotten research published in his own magazine a few years previously. A survey of 5000 *du&ich* readers had revealed that 34 per cent of 18–25 year-olds regularly practised anal sex, with almost 85 per cent of those 40 years or older doing so.[107] In its front-cover special on homosexuality in 1973, *Der Spiegel* expressed extreme scepticism about the claim that those who enjoyed anal sex were but 'a minority in the minority'.[108] The liberal weekly instead featured a sociological study of 789

---

[102] *du&ich* 2 (1975), 13. See further Peter Rehberg, 'Männer wie Du und Ich': Gay Magazines from the National to the Transnational', *German History* 34, 3 (2016), 468–85, especially 471–4.

[103] On the erotic photography of Herbert Tobias, which was featured in *him* from the mid-1970s, see further Jennifer Evans, 'Seeing Subjectivity: Erotic Photography and the Optics of Desire', *American Historical Review* 18:2 (2013), 430–62.

[104] *du&ich* 6 (1977), 11.

[105] Ibid., 11. On the train station as a site of prostitution, see Jennifer Evans, 'Bahnhof Boys: Policing Male Prostitution in Post-Nazi Berlin', *Journal of the History of Sexuality*, 12 (2003), 605–36.

[106] Riechers, 'Freundschaft und Anständigkeit'.

[107] Ferenz Bauer, 'Wie liebt der homosexuelle Mann?', *du&ich* 10 (1974), 8–11 (9).

[108] 'Bekennt, daß ihr anders seid', *Der Spiegel* 11 (1973), 46–62 (52). Like Ziegler, *Der Spiegel* editors had a short memory. Their previous front-cover special from May 1969 had described the association

male homosexuals, *The Ordinary Homosexual*, co-written by gay activist Martin Dannecker and leading student movement theorist Reimut Reiche.[109] According to the statistic cited by *Der Spiegel*, an estimated 64 per cent had practised active anal sex at least once in the previous 12 months (mid-1970 to mid-1971) and 52 per cent had practised passive anal sex.[110] Other findings from the study also cast doubt on Ziegler's claim that only a tiny minority cruised for sex. The 789 respondents were asked where they had met their sexual partners in the previous 12 months: 74 per cent had met at least one sexual partner through gay bars or clubs; 55 per cent at private parties; 45 per cent in parks; 41 per cent in public toilets; 39 per cent on the street; 37 per cent in saunas; 30 per cent at home, when friends came to visit and brought acquaintances; 25 per cent at indoor or outdoor swimming pools; 22 per cent through bars and discos that catered predominately to heterosexuals; 15 per cent through cultural events such as theatre; 15 per cent in the workplace and 15 per cent through contact ads placed in gay magazines.[111] Ironically, back in 1970, *him* had urged its readers to take part in Dannecker's and Reiche's study, arguing that the prospective publication would offer the chance to dispel prevailing prejudice against homosexuals.[112] Five years later, a *him* columnist would castigate the study's authors for ostensibly *confirming* harmful stereotypes, especially the contention that homosexuals were promiscuous.[113]

The Gay Scene

Ziegler's denigration of cruising grounds, public toilets and 'seedy dives' is but one example of the ambivalent position of the gay scene in homosexual politics. I use 'gay scene' to refer to the various locations where same-sex desiring men (and not

---

of homosexuality with anal sex as a 'stubborn prejudice'. According to that earlier article, only about 8% of male homosexuals practiced anal sex, about the same figure as for heterosexuals. 'Späte Milde', *Der Spiegel* 20 (1969), 55–76 (70).

[109] The study was featured by *Der Spiegel* before its publication a year later. Dannecker and Reiche, *Der gewöhnliche Homosexuelle: eine soziologische Untersuchung über männliche Homosexuelle in der Bundesrepublik* (Frankfurt a.M., 1974). Reiche had been a key student movement leader and remained the left's perhaps most well-known spokesperson on sexuality, having authored *Sexuality and Class Struggle* in 1968. Reiche, *Sexualität und Klassenkampf : Zur Abwehr repressiver Entsublimierung* (Frankfurt a.M., 1968).

[110] Dannecker and Reiche, *Der gewöhnliche Homosexuelle*, 204. The authors stated that their study should not be considered properly representative, but did point to the large sample size. While previous studies had often been reliant on specific groups of homosexuals, such as those imprisoned or those seeking medical treatment, Dannecker and Reiche deployed a 'snowball' system, in which participants were found from the overlapping but diverse contact networks of 139 initial respondents, individuals who were carefully selected so that neither 'subculture hyenas', 'career homosexuals' nor 'leftist students' predominated. Ibid., 17.

[111] Dannecker and Reiche, *Der gewöhnliche Homosexuelle*, 103.

[112] 'Homosexualität in Deutschland: zur Vorbereitung einer Studie', *him* (December 1970).

[113] Joachim Hohmann, 'Der glückliche Schwule – unauffindbar?', *him* (October 1975), 20–3 (22).

just homosexuals) met each other for the purposes of leisure, sociability, and sex. The term includes first and foremost gay bars and clubs, but also cruising sites (primarily saunas, public parks, and public toilets—*Klappen*, to use the idiom of the period). Clayton Whisnant draws attention to the local specificities of the gay scene, whose physical contours were ever-changing: bars would close down, move location, change ownership, develop a new atmosphere, cater to a different crowd. Due to violence or police presence, the popularity of certain parks or public toilets as cruising opportunities would rise and fall.[114] Nevertheless, the scene was less a collection of fixed locales than 'an abstract space constructed by the knowledge of its participants'.[115] Christopher Bollas argues that what he calls the 'homosexual arena', rather than being 'characterized by the aesthetics of space', more properly 'exists in the cruiser's frame of mind'. 'A cinema for one homosexual', Bollas continues, 'is a place to watch the film; for another it is the arena'.[116] Indeed, the gay scene was meaningful to all same-sex desiring men, regardless of whether they were regular participants. According to Bollas, 'for many homosexuals the arena may be a place of some exciting yet dreadful existence, whether frequented or not. It remains a point of anxious reference. As the airplane may haunt a person whose fear of flying results in total abstention from taking to the skies, the arena may still worry some gay men.'[117]

Activists of all political hues variously railed against the scene, seeking to exploit it as a recruiting ground, and attempting—and mostly failing—to inaugurate non-commercial alternatives. While the scene was a crucial platform for gay liberation, activists were often uncomfortable with its somewhat subterranean nature, hidden from public view. This understanding informed a popular activist refrain of the decade, 'come out of your hiding places!' (*Raus aus euren Löchern!*). In 1974, *Rotzschwul* activists launched what they referred to as Frankfurt's first 'gay commune', as part of the *Häuserkampf*, a struggle waged by various leftist groups and local residents over housing conditions in the city. The banner hung outside their squatted building included the slogan *Raus aus euren Löchern!*, and in a leaflet distributed after they were evicted by police, activists defined these hiding places as including gay bars, cruising grounds, and living arrangements in which homosexuals could not be open about their sexuality.[118] According to the short-lived communards, their project had offered a route out of isolation and 'permanent self-denial'. Until then, they had only known the 'brief fuck in the park', 'superficial conversations in the bar' or the 'retreat to the idyllic

---

[114] Whisnant, *Male Homosexuality*, 6.   [115] Ibid., 6. Whisnant uses 'gay scenes' in the plural.
[116] Bollas, 'Cruising in the Homosexual Arena', in *Being a Character: Psychoanalysis and Self Experience* (London, 1994), 144–64 (164). Bollas focuses only on men cruising for sex, and not on other aspects of the gay scene.
[117] Ibid., 158.
[118] 'Wir sind geräumt!' [undated but 1974]. Printed as appendix to Barbara Wackernagel, *Die Gruppe Rotzschwul: Eine Analyse homosexueller Subkultur* (Unpublished *Diplomarbeit*: Saarbrücken, 1975).

monogamous relationship'. While not renouncing these elements of gay life, they demanded more: 'We no longer want to be part-time gays!'[119]

For some men who desired sociability or intimacy with other men, tentative forays into the scene were a form of emancipation. For others, gay liberation meant reminding wider society of that which it would rather ignore, liberating gay life from its oppressive restriction to the scene, or the 'subculture' as it was often called at the time. Gay activists regularly expressed their desire to leave the 'ghetto' of the gay scene behind, principally through the means of the gay action group.[120] For an activist in the Aachen-based GSR, the gay bar offered a mere illusion of togetherness, and was tolerated by wider society only because it was a mechanism through which to control homosexuals.[121] In their position paper on the homosexual 'subculture', Martin Dannecker and fellow Rotzschwul activists called not for the destruction but the transformation of the scene, noting that its spaces offered the only guarantee for homosexuals to live their sexuality and even— perhaps—to experience it as something positive.[122] In their understanding, the scene was not just a temporary haven from the hostility of wider society, but constituted a permanent retreat from the required engagement with that society. The subculture was therefore described as an 'instrument of conformism of the worst kind'.[123]

Unsurprisingly, this kind of perspective rarely went down well with the owners of gay bars. Following the broadcast of his film Not the Homosexual in 1973, Rosa von Praunheim was thrown out of the Trocadero bar in West Berlin, and members of the Homosexual Action West Berlin (HAW) were banned from entry. Activists used this to good effect, distributing a flyer stylizing themselves as a thorn in the side of commercial bar owners, and calling on patrons to realize that they were being financially exploited throughout the 'false brothel atmosphere' of the gay scene.[124] Nevertheless, bars did sometimes act as the recruiting grounds for activists. For example, Erwin Kirchner's first encounter with the gay movement came when he witnessed an impromptu gathering by HAW activists in the bar he was in at the time: he turned up to their regular meetings the very next week.[125]

The early 1970s saw a significant expansion and diversification of the gay scene, a direct result of homosexual law reform. According to berlin-report, a slender guidebook to the gay scene in the city, there were at least 41 bars of interest by December 1972. In addition, five saunas, three beaches, three hotels, seven parks

---

[119] Ibid.   [120] HAW Info 3 (1972), 14.
[121] Ewald, 'Rotes Licht und weicher Samt', GSR Information 3 (1974), 1.
[122] 'Die homosexuelle Subkultur', 1. SMB archive, folder Frankfurt.   [123] Ibid., 6.
[124] 'Randalierer?' (undated). Printed as appendix to Andreas Pareik, 'Kampf um eine Identität. Entwicklung, Probleme, Perspektiven der neuen Homosexuellen-Emanzipationsbewegung am Beispiel der Homosexuellen Aktion Westberlin' (unpublished Diplomarbeit: Berlin, 1977), 288.
[125] Oral history interview (28 August 2012). Pseudonym used.

and 27 public toilets were listed.[126] Two years later, the guide included a small section on East Berlin, which was said to have eight bars, two swimming baths, three parks and 12 toilets to offer.[127] The copy of this edition that I have consulted offers an intriguing glimpse into how this kind of material was used. Using a pen, the names of bars and other locations have been added, and eight of the 30 toilets have been ticked off, most of them clustered around a small geographical area near the Zoologischer Garten in central West Berlin (at the Zoo train station, near Savignyplatz, at the Ku'Damm underground station, in the KaDeWe department store).[128] Whether these ticks denote the accuracy of the listings, or offer a record of where the individual in question visited (or even enjoyed), remains elusive.

Gay guides such as *berlin-report* were generally small-scale enterprises and had existed in one form or another since at least the 1950s. One of the first was *Le Guide Gris* (The Grey Guide), which was assembled by American activist Bruce Baird because he lacked information on local scenes during his European travels.[129] The *Spartacus International Gay Guide*, still in publication today, was launched in 1970. The first two issues in 1970 and 1972 were in English only and published from Brighton, but from 1973 the guide included text in French and German too.[130] West Germany was the only country other than the UK to merit an article of its own in the first edition, and listings were provided for 33 German cities.[131] By 1973, this had grown to 74 cities, and, as we saw in the introduction, in 1974 the editor opined that Germany was 'the best place in Europe for a gay person to live'. In 1978, West Germany was described as standing 'head and shoulders above the entire flock', with the rural gay scene especially praised in comparison to other European countries. One learns that West German gay bars had excellent hygiene and service, and the eulogizing did not stop there: 'Add to this the natural German demand for the best of everything, and a booming economy and you have a really superb gay scene'.[132] (Spare a thought for the unfortunate exceptions: according to the guide, Bonn was 'the most dull and dreary capital in Europe. Not worth a visit. Its gay scene is almost dead' and Frankfurt counted among 'the most unpleasant cities in Germany. "Rent" and worse, abounds, VD is rife, and it is a city to avoid if possible at all costs'.)[133]

---

[126] *berlin-report* (Berlin, 1973). SMB archive.

[127] *berlin-report für Freunde* (Berlin, 1975). SMB archive.   [128] Ibid., 20.

[129] One source Baird did come across were brief listings in the German homophile journal *Der neue Ring*. *Le Guide Gris* included information on the gay scene in most Western countries, but not the United States, and was first published in 1959. Meeker, *Contacts Desired*, 205.

[130] By which point the guide had moved to Amsterdam. *Spartacus International Gay Guide* (Amsterdam, 1973). Swedish was added in 1976, and Spanish in 1977. The guide was edited by John D. Stamford.

[131] *Spartacus International Gay Guide* (Brighton, 1970), 22–9.

[132] *Spartacus International Gay Guide* (Amsterdam, 1978), 28.

[133] Ibid., 221 and *Spartacus International Gay Guide* (Brighton, 1972), 33. 'Rent' refers to prostitution and VD to venereal disease.

Based on their findings in *The Ordinary Homosexual*, Dannecker and Reiche stated that homosexuals displayed an 'astonishing mobility', citing not only their frequent change of occupations and of sexual partners but also their travel habits.[134] According to a study of 4588 West German men between the ages of 20 and 65 conducted in 1970, 51 per cent had travelled on holiday in the previous 12 months. Among single men, this was slightly higher, at 58 per cent.[135] In contrast, fully 86 per cent of the homosexuals surveyed in Dannecker and Reiche's study had travelled in the previous year, and unlike the male population as a whole, this figure barely changed when educational qualifications or income were taken into account.[136] 39 per cent of those surveyed had been to Amsterdam within the last two years; 23 per cent to Sylt, a North Sea island off the Schleswig-Holstein coast; and 11 per cent to Torremolinos.[137] According to Lucas Hilderbrand, gay tourism in the 1970s marked a transition between 'the long history of privileged men seeking out erotic colonial adventures and the more industrialized version of gay travel that exists today.'[138] Those erotic colonial adventures, according to several articles in *du&ich*, were still to be had in Morocco, even though destinations in North Africa became less feted as the decade wore on.[139] As air travel became somewhat cheaper, other locations were discovered as gay destinations. *Gay Journal* declared Kenya a 'gay paradise' in 1972, blithely asserting that the country knew no discrimination against homosexuals, and alluding to the aesthetic and erotic opportunities on offer.[140]

Soon, South-East Asia was added to the mix. In 1976, a *Spartacus* correspondent waxed lyrical about the Philippines: 'it is true that you find a lover within a few minutes of your plane touching down [...] within a few days I had 30–40 boys calling me every day to offer themselves.'[141] Four years later, the publication would rather hypocritically bemoan that 'a huge army of sex-hungry gays' had since invaded the country, one example of 'the rape of the developing nations by gay pirates'. Apparently, 'beautiful, happy, innocent youths were turned into nasty, avaricious, dangerous drop-outs by stupid Europeans, mainly (but not only) affluent and arrogant Germans, who gave too much money for sex, who promised a life of luxury in Frankfurt, Berlin, Cannes or Stockholm. Paradise lost.'[142] As Christopher Ewing has shown, these kind of travel reports, whether in gay guides or gay magazines, 'reinforced and rearticulated long-standing racial

---

[134] Dannecker and Reiche, *Der gewöhnliche Homosexuelle*, 136.   [135] Ibid., 136.
[136] Ibid.,136–8.   [137] Ibid., 138.
[138] Lucas Hilderbrand, 'A Suitcase Full of Vaseline, or Travels in the 1970s Gay World', *Journal of the History of Sexuality* 22 (2013), 373–402 (395).
[139] See for example *du&ich* 3 (1970), 18–20 and 11 (1974), 40. Christopher Ewing, ' "Toward a Better World for Gays": Race, Tourism, and the Internationalization of The West German Gay Rights Movement, 1969–1983', *Bulletin of the German Historical Institute* 61 (2017), 109–34 (110).
[140] 'Afrikas Gay Paradies: Für Sie offen', *gay journal* 2 (1972), 6.
[141] *Spartacus International Gay Guide* (Amsterdam, 1976), 481–7 (481).
[142] *Spartacus International Gay Guide* (Amsterdam, 1980), 7 and 8.

stereotypes'. If any of these places were 'gay paradises', they were paradises whose construction was 'dependent on Orientalist perceptions of the primitiveness of the men who lived there'.[143] The 'ethnic fetishization' that Hilderbrand identifies in his analysis of the American *Ciao!* magazine therefore applies equally to the West German gay press, even if we heed his caveat that one might charitably read into this fetishization a diverse and inclusive conception of what was considered attractive.[144] Certainly, gay magazines attempted to erotically cater for all, though this was rarely expressed so bluntly as in 1978 in *unter uns,* when editors announced a new format: 'We want nothing more and nothing less than for you to relax and enjoy: the race and class boys, the men, the youths and the guys. A bit of sex. A bit erotic. Much excitement...a lot of lust...no problems.'[145] Nevertheless, this kind of mission statement and the regularly offensive depiction of non-white men give the lie to the fanciful claim made in a *du&ich* editorial in 1970 that the homosexual community knew no racial or class prejudice.[146]

Even though the 'gay world' of West German same-sex desiring men was becoming increasingly global, there was a glaring blind-spot, much closer to home. It is striking just how rarely references to East Germany appear in either the West German gay press, or in gay activist material. Similarly, in a pioneering book-length collection of interviews with 14 East German gay men from the 1980s, 'the other German state' is referred to precisely once.[147] This mutual detachment can only be explained by the lack of a common framework for understanding. In the GDR, political activity not in the remit of the state (or to a lesser extent, under the umbrella of the Church) was inherently difficult, and there was no commercial gay press. Information on developments in West Germany and elsewhere in the world was limited, though Rosa von Praunheim's *Not the Homosexual* was available to those with access to a television in East Berlin, and copies of gay magazines such as *him* could be smuggled across the border.[148]

Despite these difficulties, the Homosexual Interest Group Berlin (HIB) was set up in 1973, an organization that Josie McLellan describes as Eastern Europe's first gay liberation group. Focusing on the gay left, McLellan shows how a 'shared language, a shared sexuality and a shared commitment to socialist principles gave Eastern and Western activists a degree of common ground', but this was not

---

[143] Ewing, 'Toward a Better World for Gays', 109 and 110.

[144] Hilderbrand, 'A Suitcase full of Vaseline', 380.

[145] *unter uns/Adam international* 15 (1978), 3.

[146] *du&ich* 3 (1970), 1. *du&ich,* indeed, was the worst offender. See for example 'Verstehen Neger wirklich mehr von der Liebe?', *du&ich* 7 (1974), 12–13; Peter Jacob, 'Vive la Négritude. Oder: Warum ich Schwarzafrikaner liebe', *du&ich* 7 (1977), 2–4; the front cover of *du&ich* 3 (1979). See further Christopher Ewing, '"Color Him Black"': Erotic Representations and the Politics of Race in West German Homosexual Magazines, 1949–1974', *Sexuality and Culture* 21 (2017), 382–403.

[147] Jürgen Lemke (ed.), *Gay Voices from East Germany* (Bloomington, IN, 1991), 190. Originally published as *Ganz normal anders* in 1989, the interviews were conducted between 1979 and 1987.

[148] Josie McLellan, 'Glad to be Gay Behind the Wall', 109.

enough to facilitate any meaningful cooperation between Eastern and Western activists, even in divided Berlin.[149] The socialism of the GDR was not the socialism of the West German alternative left (with the exception of the German Communist Party, the DKP, which was in part funded by the East German regime). Gerd Koenen, reflecting on his own experience as a member of the Communist League of West Germany (KBW), has recalled how the existence of the GDR represented a 'twofold embarrassment' for leftist activists in their engagement with the working class, since it was not the vision of socialism they wished to convey, and moreover provoked questions of German nationalism that they sought to avoid.[150] More generally, West German gay men were not immune to prevailing stereotypes of East Germany as grey, uninspired, and characterized by repression. In any case, this was the view espoused by the editors of the *Spartacus International Gay Guide*, who were positively gushing about the gay scene in West Germany, but had this to say about gay life in the GDR: 'All bars are state-owned, thus, luxury, décor, and atmosphere rarely can be found. [...] There is an air of gloom and despair which contrasts sharply with West Berlin. [...] All drinks taste like soapy water.'[151]

~ ~

The popularization of gay guidebooks played a role in constructing what Martin Meeker has termed a 'homosexual geography', which allowed gay men 'to see how and where they fit[ted] into the gay world'.[152] To be sure, this was not a disinterested exercise, notwithstanding the protestation of *Spartacus* editors, who maintained that 'making money is purely the slave of our ambitions and not the master' and described their guide as 'one of the many gifts of love which we try to create for the gay world'.[153] As will be seen, the commercial basis of the gay scene and the gay press was one factor in making gay activists so suspicious of the whole enterprise. But from a historical perspective, it appears that the *function* of gay activism actually had much in common with more commercial activities. It, too, provided a way for gay men 'to see how and where they fit[ted] into the gay world.' It is to the different models of homosexual organizing that emerged after homosexual law reform in 1969 that we now turn.

---

[149] Ibid., 105 and 126.   [150] Koenen, *Das rote Jahrzehnt*, 223.
[151] *Spartacus International Gay Guide* (Amsterdam, 1973), 109. In this issue, the GDR had two pages of listings; the FRG had 40. In the 1975 edition, East German gays and lesbians were described as living 'trapped in this vast, nation-wide prison.' *Spartacus International Gay Guide* (Amsterdam, 1975), 4.
[152] Meeker, *Contacts Desired*, 224 and 223.
[153] *Spartacus International Gay Guide* (Amsterdam, 1976), 3.

2

'It Is Not the Homosexual Who Is Perverse'

The Emergence of Gay Liberation

The die is cast – for Germany. We thank all those who played their part, openly or in private, including our MPs. We thank the Grand Coalition, which brought about the change of mind in the CDU [. . .]. We thank fate, time, providence, God, which taught us patience and perseverance. We thank ourselves, those who found the strength to wait in silence, in isolation, in the ghetto, or even in prison. The bad years are over: humanity has prevailed. We are satisfied with this partial success.

– Jack Argo [Johannes Werres], *Der Weg*, 1969.[1]

For many same-sex desiring men, homosexual law reform, in the shape of the liberalization of Paragraph 175 in 1969, came as an enormous relief. Since liberalization did not mean full decriminalization, the fear of blackmail and arrest remained, but in strongly diminished form. Some homosexuals saw the reform as the overdue culmination of efforts dating back over seventy years, to the founding of Magnus Hirschfeld's Scientific-Humanitarian Committee and its subsequent parliamentary petition to repeal the law.[2] Johannes Werres, who had written and worked for various homophile publications for the best part of two decades, understood the reform as delayed reward for his activism, alongside evidence of divine providence. Others took a rather different view. In the same publication as Werres, Harry Stein argued that homosexuals should show no gratitude whatsoever to the government, since their new-found freedom remained only incomplete. Moreover, the plaudits for this partial freedom should go instead to progressive scientists and academics, foreign organizations and not least to student protesters, who had brought about the 'sexual explosion' which left parliament with no other choice.[3] All actors involved in homosexual politics—whether

---

[1] 'Die Würfel sind gefallen', *Der Weg* 224 (1969–1970), 227–8 (227). The 'grand coalition' refers to the coalition government between 1966 and 1969 of the two largest parties, the SPD and the CDU/CSU.
[2] The petition came close to success in 1929, when a parliamentary committee narrowly voted in favour of abolishing Paragraph 175. It would have been replaced by a new paragraph, 297, to penalize more harshly male prostitution. In the event, in the throes of the Great Depression, the *Reichstag* did not adopt the committee's recommendation. Marhoefer, *Sex and the Weimar Republic*, 112–45.
[3] Harry Stein [pseudonym], 'Ein politisches Wort', *Der Weg* 221 (1969), 145–6.

The Ambivalence of Gay Liberation: Male Homosexual Politics in 1970s West Germany. Craig Griffiths, Oxford University Press (2021). © Craig Griffiths.
DOI: 10.1093/oso/9780198868965.003.0003

they preferred the vocabulary 'homosexual', 'homophile' or 'gay'—recognized that further reform was needed: at the very least, to reduce the age of consent to 18. Activism towards this aim was to constitute one of the few areas of cooperation between 'homophiles' and 'gays'. These efforts played their part in the passage of a further liberalization of Paragraph 175 in November 1973, which set the age of consent at 18.

This chapter focuses on the debates between 'gays' and 'homophiles' between 1969 and 1973, between the two reforms of Paragraph 175, which found expression in contrasting forms of organizing and activism, with restrained, civic-minded homophile interest groups and associations on the one hand lining up against more militant gay action groups on the other. Activists in those action groups often imagined that they were standing before a blank canvas as they set about building their movement. In 1974, four activists from the Homosexual Action West Berlin (HAW) blithely asserted that, in Berlin at the start of the decade, the gay movement had been re-established 'after forty years' interruption', thereby drawing a straight line between the 1930s and the 1970s, consigning the homophile movement of the 1940s, 1950s and 1960s to the historical dustbin.[4] Their contention also unduly privileged the role of Berlin, since the HAW was not founded until late 1971: the Federal Republic's first gay action groups had been formed not in major cities such as West Berlin, Munich, Cologne or Frankfurt but at the universities of Bochum and Münster, in December 1970 and May 1971 respectively. The role of Münster, a strongly Catholic city with a population of just over 200,000 in 1969, was cemented in April 1972, when it hosted Germany's first demonstration by gays and lesbians.[5] Attended by activists from dozens of action groups from around the country, the demonstration was accompanied by energetic slogans including 'down with capitalism!' and 'being gay is fun!'[6]

Homophile politics did not die out in September 1969, the month when homosexual law reform came into effect. The first organizations founded after this date were not gay action groups, indeed not 'gay' at all, but groups that labelled themselves 'homophile', such as the Hamburg-based International Homophile World Organization (IHWO), which took its name from a Danish umbrella group. The world of the IHWO, which rejected taking part in protests, at times used the formal *Sie* to address its members, and had hobby groups for chess, card games, and stamp collecting,[7] was in many ways far removed from the milieu of the gay left: that is, the dominant political current in gay action groups, which

---

[4] Helmut Ahrens et al., 'Die Homosexualität in uns', in *Tuntenstreit: Theoriediskussion der Homosexuellen Aktion Westberlin* (Berlin, 1975), 5–34 (5).

[5] The population in June 1969 was 203,300. By way of comparison, West Berlin had a population of 2.14 million, Munich 1.3 million, Cologne 861,000 and Frankfurt 662,000. *Statistisches Jahrbuch für die Bundesrepublik Deutschland* (Wiesbaden, 1971), 32–3.

[6] *him* 7 (1972), 6; 'Bekennt, daß ihr anders seid', *Der Spiegel* 11 (1973), 46–62 (49).

[7] Cited from *IHWO Rundbrief* 1 (1973). SMB archive.

was characterized more by revolutionary verve than polite discussions and philately.

Nevertheless, I show in this chapter that we cannot map onto the linguistic shift from *homophil* to *schwul*, from homophile to gay, a whole set of other transformations, whether from 'caution' to 'radical', 'closeted' to 'visible' or from 'shame' to 'pride'. Alongside the newsletters, zines, and internal correspondence of various groups, and coverage in the gay and mainstream press, the material that animates this story is a cluster of news reports, documentaries, and television films featuring homosexuality. We have already seen how publicist Udo Erlenhardt was filmed on national television announcing his homosexuality to passers-by in Hamburg in 1970. The broadcaster responsible for that footage, the WDR, raised the stakes significantly higher the following year, by producing Rosa von Praunheim's iconoclastic film *It Is Not the Homosexual Who Is Perverse, but the Society in Which He Lives*.

The cinematic spark which ignited a wave of action groups in West Germany, the planned broadcast of *Not the Homosexual* on national television in 1972 was delayed by a year after complaints by the Bavarian state broadcaster, in which time the leaders of the IHWO took legal action seeking to prevent the film ever reaching the country's television screens. Yet it would be simplistic to characterize the struggle over the film as a tale of young, radical gays winning out against a hostile establishment, taking on the authoritarian-minded public and those older homosexuals who sought to placate them in the process. Homosexual politics, especially in this early period of gay liberation, between 1969 and 1973, were exceedingly fraught, as partial decriminalization opened up welcome yet daunting possibilities. The ambivalence engendered by this moment cannot be used to demarcate 'gays' from 'homophiles', or 'radicals' from 'liberals', or one generation from another. Rather, this ambivalence ran through the very heart of organizations, publications, and individuals themselves. Neither was it entirely a homosexual affair. The debates between 'homophiles' and 'gays' were not just about what homosexuals thought and felt about wider society, but were informed by what that society thought and felt about them. Through the case study of *Not the Homosexual*, this chapter therefore also reveals the ambivalence of the wider public and the liberal media to the early claims of gay liberation.

Homophile Politics Before and After 1969

The rise and fall of the homophile movement in West Germany presents a unique case. As John D'Emilio has argued, gay liberation could only spring up so quickly in the United States in the late 1960s because of the preceding community-building efforts of homophile organizations such as the Mattachine

Society, founded in 1950.[8] Similarly, organizations such as the French *Arcadie*, founded in 1954, and the Dutch *Cultuur en Ontspanningscentrum* (Centre for Culture and Recreation, COC), founded in 1946, were organizing homosexuals and challenging discrimination decades before gay liberation, and did not dissolve once it had arrived.[9] Yet all three of these organizations shared a longevity completely without parallel in the West German homophile movement. In the Federal Republic not one single organization or publication straddled the 1960s and 1970s, the periods pre- and post- homosexual law reform.[10]

The early 1950s had seen the establishment of a wide array of homophile journals, including *Der Weg, Die Freunde, Die Insel, Die Gefährten, Der Ring* and *Humanitas*. Concomitantly, groups bearing discreet names such as the Society for Human Rights (GfM—Hamburg), the Society for the Reform of the Sexual Criminal Code (GfRdS—West Berlin), the Association for a Humanitarian Way of Life (VhL—Frankfurt) and the International Friendship Lodge (IFLO—Bremen) attempted to counsel homosexuals and to press for legal reform.[11] Frankfurt hosted the second annual meeting of the International Committee for Sexual Equality (ICSE), an umbrella group set up by the COC.[12] Willhart Schlegel and Hans Giese, homosexual scientists associated with the movement, both gave testimony to the Federal Constitutional Court in 1957, in support of the unsuccessful bid by Günther R. and Oskar K. to have their convictions against Paragraph 175 declared unconstitutional.[13] Moreover, the late 1940s and early 1950s saw a cautious but steady expansion of the homosexual scene.[14]

What may have blossomed into a wider and more visible movement was smashed by the 1953 'Law on the Dissemination of Youth-Endangering Texts'. This set up a federal indexing board which could ban any publication judged to be youth-endangering from public view (for example, on newspaper stands or in public libraries). Often referred to as the 'filth and trash' law, mail-order erotica firms such as Beate Uhse could mitigate the impact of the measure through

---

[8] D'Emilio, *Sexual Politics, Sexual Communities*.

[9] The COC still exists. *Arcadie* was dissolved as late as 1982. On *Arcadie*, see Jackson, *Living in Arcadia*.

[10] In Britain, too, there was no long-standing homophile organization to rival the Mattachine Society, *Arcadie* or the COC. However, unlike in West Germany, there did exist a pressure-group calling for a change in the law, the Homosexual Law Reform Society, founded in 1958. The North-West branch of this group would become the Committee for Homosexual Equality (later the Campaign for Homosexual Equality), which remains in existence today. See further Weeks, *Coming Out*, 168–82; and Charles Smith, 'The Evolution of the Gay Male Public Sphere in England and Wales, 1967–c.1983' (unpublished doctoral dissertation, Loughborough University, 2015), 101–26.

[11] On the West German homophile movement, see Whisnant, *Male Homosexuality*, especially 64–111; Pretzel and Weiß (eds), *Ohnmacht und Aufbegehren*; and Riechers, 'Freundschaft und Anständigkeit.'

[12] On the ICSE, see Leila Rupp, 'The Persistence of Transnational Organizing: The Case of the Homophile Movement', *American Historical Review* 116 (2011), 1014–39.

[13] *Entscheidungen des Bundesverfassungsgerichts* (Tübingen, 1957), 389–443 (398 and 403–6).

[14] See further Whisnant, *Male Homosexuality*, 112–65.

innovative PR techniques and extensive legal teams, but homophile journals had no such resources.[15] Publicists were forced to play a game of cat and mouse with the authorities, with journals being confiscated, banned, and often appearing elsewhere under a slightly different name. Even the ability to distribute magazines to subscribers through the post was impaired, depending on the Post Office's definition of what counted as 'visible content'. The editors of *Die Freunde* were forced to fight a costly and lengthy legal battle over precisely this issue, and then had to face obscenity charges from Hamburg state prosecutors.[16]

In this inhospitable climate, only *Der Kreis* (published from Zurich) and *Der Weg* managed to achieve any longevity whatsoever, before ceasing publication in 1967 and 1970 respectively. Deprived of their major means of communication, all the aforementioned organizations had been dissolved by 1961.[17] So rather than a context of a movement growing in size and confidence, accompanied by a militant turn in homophile organizing, the 1960s in West Germany saw an involuntary retreat by homophile activists. There was no West German counterpart to the picket of the White House in 1964. There was no reclamation of 'gay' *before* gay liberation, as in the United States.[18] The particularity of the West German case is that the style of politics that went by the name homophile—and which gay activists came into contact with and reacted against—was espoused by activists and organizations who were themselves new on the scene.

Alongside the IHWO, several other organizations using the moniker homophile were founded in 1969 and 1970. These included the Association for the Protection of German Homophiles (SDH—West Berlin), the Interest Association of German Homophiles (IDH—Wiesbaden) and the German Homophile Organization (DHO—West Berlin).[19] Looking abroad for inspiration, the Dutch COC was the most important frame of reference for these organizations: the IDH invited the general secretary of the COC to their inaugural meeting, and the IHWO welcomed COC representatives to Hamburg in 1971.[20] The IDH, in particular, was successful in attracting press coverage, with the group's first public meeting in August 1970 covered not only by *Der Spiegel* but also the centre-right broadsheet *Frankfurter Allgemeine Zeitung* (*FAZ*). The leader of the IDH, Horst Bohrmann, claimed to represent over 200 members, but only twenty turned

---

[15] Elizabeth Heineman, *Before Porn was Legal: The Erotica Empire of Beate Uhse* (Chicago, 2011); Steinbacher, *Wie der Sex nach Deutschland kam*, especially 242–66.

[16] Whisnant, *Male Homosexuality*, 85.

[17] Andreas Pretzel, 'Aufbruch und Resignation: Zur Geschichte der Berliner "Gesellschaft für Reform des Sexualrechts e.V." 1948–1960' in *NS-Opfer unter Vorbehalt: Homosexuelle Männer in Berlin nach 1945*, ed. by Andreas Pretzel (Münster, 2002), 287–343 (331–3).

[18] In August 1968 the North American Conference of Homophile Associations chose 'gay is good' as its official slogan. Frank Kameny, 'Gay is good', in *The Same Sex: An Appraisal of Homosexuality*, ed. by Ralph Weltge (Philadelphia, 1969), 129–45 (145).

[19] See Wolfert, *Gegen Einsamkeit und 'Einsiedelei'*, 77–80.

[20] 'Das Manifest vom Neroberg', *du&ich* 6 (1970), 8; Wolfert, *Gegen Einsamkeit und 'Einsiedelei'*, 119.

up to hear a lecture and subsequent discussion on the social problems facing homosexuals.[21] Foreshadowing similar complaints by gay activists, Bohrmann bemoaned this lack of participation, suggesting that many German homophiles did not see the need for organizations such as his now that homosexual law reform had been achieved.[22] Bohrmann had ambitious plans. His first priority was to offer legal advice to IDH members, but he also wanted to set up a network of clubs, saunas and advice centres around the country. The IDH stated its intention to confront society with 'the homophile theme', although this confrontation was to be achieved primarily through the means of a lecture series (for which the organization did not yet have the requisite number of 'experts' on board).[23]

The IDH may have been foremost in the mind of a du&ich columnist in February 1971, in his acerbic criticism of the state of homosexual politics: 'Bombastic, as only queens can be, every few months some little society or other announces a homophile "world congress", to which only thirty put in an appearance.'[24] Of the various organizations founded in the period immediately following homosexual law reform, only the IHWO successfully established itself, not least due to the limited but significant coverage it received in the gay press. From November 1971, the IHWO was given its own page in him to set out its position directly to readers, along with the HSM (Homophile Student Group Münster—of which more below). In the first of these accounts, IHWO leaders stated that there were between two and four million homophiles in Germany, yet only 200 members organized in the IHWO. The organization wished to emulate the model of a trade union, seeking to organize homosexuals in a similar way to organizing labour, and exerting a comparable influence on social and political change.[25]

Advertising itself to the readers of du&ich in 1973, the IHWO listed its activities as counselling homosexuals in need, tackling prejudice by engaging with the media, offering spiritual guidance, and informing the 'opinion-forming classes' in science, politics, and education.[26] By this time, the IHWO had adopted the more sincere subtitle 'Association for Sexual Equal Rights': to be sure, the German International Homophile World Organization was neither an 'international' nor a 'world' organization. It was originally envisioned as the Hamburg chapter of the Danish IHWO, which dated back to the 1950s but had become defunct by 1970.[27] Nevertheless, the (Hamburg-based) IHWO went on to establish several regional groups throughout the Federal Republic, and would reach a combined

---

[21] 'Die Eingeladenen blieben vorerst aus', FAZ (25 August 1970); 'Nicht wundern', Der Spiegel 37 (1970).
[22] 'Für den Abbau der Vorurteile: Versammlung der Interessenvereinigung Deutscher Homophiler', FAZ (30 December 1970).
[23] Ibid.; 'Das Manifest vom Neroberg', du&ich 6 (1970), 8.
[24] 'Zur Lage der Verbände', du&ich 2 (1971), 54–5 (54).   [25] 'IHWO', him 11 (1971), 49.
[26] du&ich 6 (1973), 42.
[27] The German chapter of the Danish IHWO dates to Autumn 1969; formal independence followed in October 1970. Wolfert, Gegen Einsamkeit, 82 and 98.

membership of around 600.[28] No other West German organization would come close to this figure throughout the decade. Membership dues and donations were the IHWO's only source of funding. The group opened its first 'club-centre' in July 1971 in Hamburg, but this did not prove to be a source of income, and in fact chronically destabilized the organization's finances.[29]

Other than its focus on same-sex love, the IHWO was a classically liberal organization, *bürgerlich* (bourgeois, middle-class, established) in manner, aims, and methods. Too great an intrusion into the public sphere was considered dangerous. The organization not only objected to socialist iconography such as a clenched fist, but the notion of distributing leaflets to passers-by.[30] Discussions with the 'man on the street' should be avoided; instead, homosexuals should engage with institutions such as political parties, churches, and schools. Activism must be patient and tenacious, based on objective information, not on provocation.[31] One such provocation was perceived as establishing a youth group, a course which the IHWO rejected, citing the need to avoid all 'moments of suspicion.'[32] The organization welcomed the arrival of gay action groups, and sought limited co-operation: yet in the same breath noted that in so doing one must expect a 'considerable amount of youthful abandon' and 'extensive ideological convulsion'.[33] IHWO activists did not deny that West German society was in need of change, but contended that as this change would not happen overnight, practical actions needed to be taken to help homosexuals in the here and now. Since this necessitated working in and with wider society, agitation and provocation were hazardous: 'Should we give the public even more cause to be against "gays"?'[34]

The scare quotes were not incidental: the IHWO thoroughly rejected the use of 'gay'. For this reason, it is difficult to categorize the organization as part of what contemporaries called the *Schwulenbewegung*, the gay movement. In his sympathetic and detailed account of the IHWO, Raimund Wolfert clearly states that the IHWO was not part of the gay movement that emerged in 1971–1972.[35] As he points out, however, while IHWO figures may have had few links or little in common with gay action groups, neither did they with homophile organizations of the 1950s. While their organizational name shows a terminological continuity

---

[28] Calculated from *IHWO Rundbrief* 1 (1973). Not paginated.

[29] Wolfert, *Gegen Einsamkeit*, 106.   [30] 'Weg mit $175', *IHWO Report* 6 (1973), 7.

[31] Ibid., 7.   [32] Wolfert, *Gegen Einsamkeit*, 101.

[33] 'DAH Treffen in Münster', *IHWO Report* 6 (1973), 4–6 (5). This attitude can be compared to the stance of the French *Arcadie* and its leader, André Baudry. In 1971, *Arcadie* set up a youth group, but this group was expelled by Baudry in 1973 when it proposed a stunt at a Paris courthouse, during a trial concerning homosexuality. Jackson, *Living in Arcadia*, 194.

[34] Article in *Gay-Journal* 4 (1972). Cited from Wolfert, *Gegen Einsamkeit*, 143.

[35] Wolfert, *Gegen Einsamkeit*, 8. In his book on gay emancipation in the 1970s, Patrick Henze mentions the IHWO only in passing, instead focusing entirely on action groups and particularly the HAW. Henze, *Schwule Emanzipation und ihre Konflikte: Zur westdeutschen Schwulenbewegung der 1970er Jahre* (Berlin, 2019).

from the 1950s and 1960s, 'homophile' was rarely used by IHWO members internally: 'homosexual' was more common.[36] They were hardly alone in calling themselves one thing in private and another in public: gay action groups did exactly the same, rarely incorporating 'gay' into their group names.

Notwithstanding their choice of vocabulary, leading figures from the IHWO would appear on national television to promote their cause. Similarly, the IDH leader Horst Bohrmann was more than happy to affirm his sexuality, having his name and photo printed in *Der Spiegel* and telling the magazine 'Of course I'm homosexual.'[37] Crucially, the presence and activities of groups such as the IHWO provided an explicit challenge to those who had a different understanding of homosexual politics, but had not yet articulated their position.[38] Moreover, the early influence of the IHWO did not end with its ignominious collapse in 1974, amid financial ruin: several of its regional chapters became independent groups in their own right.[39] This included the AHA in West Berlin. In a semantic bridge to gay action groups, the AHA, initially called the General Homosexual Committee (*Allgemeine Homosexuelle Arbeitsgemeinschaft*), changed its name later in the decade to the General Homosexual Action Alliance (*Allgemeine Homosexuelle Aktionsgemeinschaft*).[40] Of the erstwhile regional chapters of the IHWO, especially the AHA and the Association for Sexual Equal Rights (VSG—Munich) numbered among the largest and most significant gay groups for the rest of the decade.

Early Steps: On Television and in Universities

Udo Erlenhardt was not the only figure to acknowledge his homosexuality on national television in July 1970. This was on the first channel, the ARD, on an episode of the current affairs show *Monitor*, which focused on Käte Ströbel's request to have the gay magazine *him* placed on the index of 'youth-endangering materials'. Though neither their names nor affiliation were given, the ten-minute segment also featured the two leading members of the IHWO executive, Claus Fischdick and Carl Stoewahs. It was a big moment for the couple, since they used the occasion to inform Stoewahs' mother about the nature of their relationship.[41] The broadcast was also a chance to put forward their vision of homosexuality.

---

[36] Ibid., 9 and 81.   [37] 'Nicht wundern', *Der Spiegel* 37 (1970), 84–6 (84).
[38] Michael Holy, 'Lange hieß es, Homosexualität sei gegen die Ordnung. Die westdeutsche Schwulenbewegung (1969-1980)', in *Dokumentation einer Vortragsreihe in der Akademie der Künste: 100 Jahre Schwulenbewegung*, ed. by Manfred Herzer (Berlin, 1998), 83–109 (89).
[39] Detailed in *IHWO Report* 8 (1973). Inordinately high costs on stationary material seem to have been the straw that broke the camel's back.
[40] Salmen and Eckert, *20 Jahre bundesdeutsche Schwulenbewegung*, 77. The new name is indicated in *AHA INFO Intern* 1 (November 1978).
[41] Wolfert, *Gegen Einsamkeit*, 94.

Fischdick assured viewers that he and Stoewahs knew many couples who lived in marriage-like situations and had an 'orderly' sex life, without coming to any excesses such as sex orgies. Continuing, Fischdick underlined that he and his partner both held down decent, 'orderly' jobs. He was of the opinion that one could not recognize them as homosexual at first glance, and explicitly distanced himself from the misconception that all homosexuals were feminine. According to Fischdick, 'The homosexual, or rather the homophile, is a person like any other, neither sick nor abnormal. Homophilia is just one variant among many other sexual practices.'[42] This can be read both as an attempt to depathologize homosexuality and to render it as unthreatening, as unspectacular, as 'normal' as possible.

Not coincidentally, these were also the terms on which the liberal media sought to advance the tolerance of homosexuality. *Der Spiegel* chose the occasions of both reforms to Paragraph 175 for two front-page specials on homosexuality, in May 1969 and in March 1973 (see Figures 2.1 and 2.2). In both issues *Der Spiegel* cited the contention of the sexologist Gunter Schmidt, that homosexuality was but 'one feature in people who are in all other respects boringly normal' [*stinknormal*].[43] For the 1969 story, *Der Spiegel* also used the line as a secondary caption for an image of two men tidying up the kitchen: the main caption read 'homosexuals in the household'.[44] The point was emphasized in an accompanying article, which presented the couple Eberhard K. and Joachim H. According to *Der Spiegel*, 'One knows the "gays" and "fags", the exhibitionists and rent boys', but this was a distorted picture. In fact, hundreds of thousands of homosexuals lived in bourgeois partnership, 'in faithful reproduction of heterosexual marriage'.[45]

This is precisely the image that the IHWO (and the producers of the 1970 *Monitor* broadcast) wanted to convey, with the camera showing Fischdick and Stoewahs delicately setting out crockery on their balcony table.[46] Their self-presentation chimed with one of the dominant liberal discourses on homosexuality prior to the advent of gay liberation, that homosexuals were a misunderstood, non-threatening minority, which needed defending against 'one of German citizens' most stubborn prejudices.'[47] In January 1972, homosexuals were again

---

[42] My transcription from the footage. *Monitor*, 9 July 1970. Produced by the WDR and broadcast on the ARD.

[43] 'Späte Milde', *Der Spiegel* 20 (1969), 55–76 (63); 'Bekennt, daß ihr anders seid', *Der Spiegel* 11 (1973) 46–62 (57).

[44] 'Späte Milde', 63.

[45] '"Wir tanzen so gern zusammen": Homosexuelle in einer westdeutschen Kleinstadt', *Der Spiegel* 20 (1969), 62.

[46] The influence of the *Spiegel* 1969 story is evidenced not least by the marked similarity between passages from the text and the narrator's script from the 1970 *Monitor* footage (at times, these are nearly identical).

[47] 'Späte Milde', 55.

Figure 2.1 'The law falls – will the ostracism remain?'
Source: © *Der Spiegel* 20/1969.

featured on national television, this time on ZDF, the second channel. Unsurprisingly, a cosy domestic setting was once more highlighted. The documentary *And What If Your Son Was This Way?* concluded with another (anonymous) gay couple, who lived in a flat together with one of the men's mother. Against

Figure 2.2 'Homosexuals – freed, but ostracized.'
Source: © *Der Spiegel* 11/1973.

a background of dainty crockery and coffee and cake being served in their front room, the narrator summed up: 'Homosexuality has always existed. It is neither perversion nor sickness but a variation of nature.'[48]

---

[48] *Und wenn Ihr Sohn so wäre. Über Homosexuelle berichtet Eva Müthel* (ZDF, 14 January 1972). ZDF *historisches Archiv* 06432/00340.

The two stories in *Der Spiegel* highlight the dramatic transformation in homosexual politics between 1969 and 1973. The first appeared in print before decriminalization had come into effect. The couple Eberhard K. and Joachim H. were prepared to be interviewed for the story, but admitted that they burned correspondence from fellow homosexuals in case the police should ever pay them a visit.[49] By the time of the second story, a reduction in the age of consent to 18 was around the corner, and gay liberation was in full swing. The 1973 story featured the sociological study *The Ordinary Homosexual*, giving its left-wing authors a rare opportunity, in the form of a short article, to directly address the reader. Martin Dannecker and Reimut Reiche aimed their call at homosexuals, demanding that they stop conforming to an idealized image of the heterosexual masculine man, repressing everything about themselves that did not fit into the 'normal façade'. By affirming their sexuality, in all its difference, the fronts would become clearer, fronts which had recently been hidden behind a 'veil of sanctimonious tolerance'.[50] Indeed, the cover story itself took its title from another statement by Dannecker and Reiche, 'Acknowledge that you are different.'[51] The 1969 story had lambasted popular ignorance and prejudice, describing this as a throwback to Nazi times. The 1973 story was just as damning about the discrimination of homosexuals, but also adopted a rather caustic tone on the gay activism that had since emerged: the reader learns that activists 'don't quite know what they actually want, but they want it resolutely'. Those associated with the film *Not the Homosexual* were described as tending towards 'boundless political gibberish' and the IHWO as Germany's largest 'homo squad'.[52]

Der Spiegel, for one, did not seem overly impressed by homosexuals taking matters into their own hands and making a claim for self-determination. As cited above, both 1969 and 1973 stories included Gunter Schmidt's line on homosexuals being 'boringly normal'. In 1969, this appeared in the context of illustrating the scientific consensus that 'without doubt' homosexuality was neither vice, perversion of sickness. Yet in 1973, Schmidt's contention was cited as an example of the *lack* of scientific consensus: apparently the most recent research had still not resolved the question of whether homosexuality was congenital or acquired, whether just one feature among many others or in fact a sickness.[53] The liberal media's ambivalence about homosexuality is also an example of their ambivalence over the need for social reform and political activism more generally. The same political and generational conflicts that took place in wider society in the

---

[49] 'Wir tanzen so gern zusammen', 62.
[50] Dannecker and Reiche, 'Nur als Kranke toleriert', *Der Spiegel* 11 (1973), 50.
[51] 'Bekennt, daß ihr anders seid', *Der Spiegel* 11 (1973), 46–62.
[52] 'Bekennt, daß ihr anders seid', 47, 49 and 60.
[53] 'Späte Milde', 63; 'Bekennt, daß ihr anders seid', 49. The only name cited in this respect was Charles Socarides, whose psychoanalytic work had already been published in the 1960s. On Socarides, see Dagmar Herzog, *Cold War Freud: Psychoanalysis in an Age of Catastrophes* (Cambridge, 2017), 73–80.

aftermath of '1968', and the subsequent waves of protest associated with that year, were also to be found within editorial boards, including television broadcasters and *Der Spiegel*.[54] The liberal media were prepared to represent and take up activist concerns, but only up to a point. As Christina von Hodenberg has argued—focusing on broadcasters—television 'functioned as a catalyst, accelerator' but also as a 'sanitizer of the Sixties cultural revolution'.[55]

Nevertheless, broadcasters in this period also at times pushed homosexuals further than some of them preferred to go. Claus-Ferdinand Siegfried's documentary *Paragraph 175: Questions to Homosexuals and to Ourselves*, filmed in 1971 and broadcast on the WDR's third channel in early 1972, was prescient about the direction of travel. Fischdick and Stoewahs reprised their earlier role as living-room interviewees, citing their earlier experience as evidence that homosexuals should take the risk of acknowledging their homosexuality in public. But the documentary's narrator made sure to add that not all homosexuals live like Fischdick and Stoewahs, merely that the public prefers them that way, because they more closely resemble the marital norm.[56] The documentary went on to criticize wider society for forcing homosexuals into a ghetto. Being ostracized creates neuroses, and in reality homosexuals were not as nice and virtuous as heterosexuals might like them to be.[57]

In didactic fashion, the documentary proposed five ways forward. The first two, to come out and to inform society, were exemplified (in the documentary) by Fischdick, Stoewahs, and the IHWO. Another was to accept the sexual nature of humans, which was described as innately bisexual. The other two suggestions reveal the new leftist politics of Siegfried but also the latent stirrings of gay activism. The role of women must be improved because they, like male homosexuals, could not fully develop in West German society. Finally, it was less a case of *informing* than *changing* society. To make this case, the camera panned to footage of street theatre in the Netherlands by a group referred to as 'Dutch Student Homophiles', and of a gay liberation demonstration in the United States: the narrator expressed the possibility, and evidently, the hope, that such phenomena could soon take place in West Germany.

Choosing the same two national examples as Siegfried, in 1970 *him* columnist Wolfgang Selitsch had compared the domestic scene in homosexual politics unfavourably with that of the United States and the Netherlands. Calling on German homosexuals to catch up, he suggested that homophile students set up

---

[54] Christina von Hodenberg, *Konsens und Krise: Eine Geschichte der westdeutschen Medienöffentlichkeit 1945–1973* (Göttingen, 2006), 432.

[55] Hodenberg, *Televisions's Moment. Sitcom Audiences and the Sixties Cultural Revolution* (New York, 2015), 2. See also Michael Schwartz, 'Warum machen Sie sich für die Homos stark?' Homosexualität und Medienöffentlichkeit in der westdeutschen Reformzeit der 1960er und 1970er Jahre', *Jahrbuch Sexualitäten 2016*, ed. by Mari Borowski et al. (Göttingen, 2016), 51–93.

[56] *§175: Fragen an Homosexuelle und an uns selbst* (WDR, 1971). First broadcast 31 January 1972.

[57] Cited from the film. A copy is available at the SMB archive.

grassroots groups at their universities.[58] Though not in direct response to Selitsch's call, these duly followed, with the first groups being founded at the Universities of Bochum and Münster. The Homosexual Action Group (HAG) in Bochum was founded in December 1970 after a meeting was organized with the assistance of the university's counselling and advice centre.[59] The fact that the initiator of this meeting was a lesbian demonstrates that there did exist some co-operation between gays and lesbians in the 1970s, especially at the decade's start: Christiane Leidinger polemically concludes her article on the HAG with the line 'the first autonomous gay group in the Federal Republic was a woman!'[60] However, by summer 1971 only 7 out of 40 members were women, and there do not seem to have been any women at all involved beyond May 1972.[61]

The group's first initiatives were to secure a meeting room and official recognition by the university. Their example also served to inspire the founding of the HSM in Münster, in April 1971. The acronym HSM initially stood for Homophile Student Group Münster, but by January 1972 the group called itself the Student Action Group Homosexuality.[62] A HSM member criticized the use of 'homophile' in an article for the group's newsletter in 1973: 'Whoever calls himself homophile apologizes for homosexuality and begs for tolerance – without realizing that in so doing he implies that sexuality, especially same-sex sexuality, is something bad, that society is actually right in condemning homosexuals, just as privately he does so himself.' Rather, every homosexual should adopt the usage 'gay', thus announcing that 'he knows he is in the right. He holds the view that he can be as gay as he likes, and that this should bother no one. And only he who wants his rights, not mercy, has the chance of receiving them. Therefore we're gay—and not homophile!!!'[63]

Both Bochum and Münster groups were committed to 'internal' and 'external' activities, not only providing sociability but also engaging in the public sphere. However, the description 'action group' remained at this stage more of an aspiration than a reality. In 1971, the Bochum group listed the actions it had conducted so far: helping to found the HSM in Münster, providing a place to meet, displaying posters in the university, and organizing a discussion with heterosexual students. There was no mention of more visible or militant actions, nor of action beyond the confines of the university. A member of the group admitted that those who understood themselves as activists were outnumbered

---

[58] Selitsch, 'Das war nicht unsere letzte Aktion', *him* 8 (1970), 21.
[59] Christiane Leidinger, 'Gründungsmythen zur Geschichtsbemächtigung? Die erste autonome Schwulengruppe der BRD war eine Frau', *Invertito—Jahrbuch für die Geschichte der Homosexualitäten* 13 (2011), 9–39 (20).
[60] Ibid., 39.   [61] Ibid., 23 and 29.   [62] Wolfert, *Gegen Einsamkeit*, 138.
[63] 'Die Preisfrage', *Wir: Info der HSM* 4 (1973), 23.

by those who wanted only the chance to meet other people.[64] The HSM, too, was rather circumspect in its earliest phases. Not least because Münster was a strongly Catholic city, one of the priorities of the HSM was to engage with the Church and to come to a theoretical understanding of homosexuality and Christianity.[65] According to its charter of founding principles, the group's goal was to reach an integration of homophiles into society not through provocation, but through information.[66] As it turned out, the HSM struggled even to achieve integration into the university, never succeeding in achieving official university recognition.[67] While the role of the Bochum and Münster groups in these early days of gay liberation should not be overlooked, it would take another event to catalyse a wave of other action groups, which would soon outnumber and outmanoeuvre homophile organizations such as the IHWO.

'It Is Not the Homosexual Who Is Perverse'

In the programme notes for *It Is Not the Homosexual Who Is Perverse, But the Society in Which He Lives*, Rosa von Praunheim praised the 'historical act' of the Stonewall riots in New York City in June 1969, and expressed the hope that it would act as an example, since the 'inhibition and cowardice amongst German gays still stinks to high heaven'.[68] Despite the fact that the film's director implicitly linked the two phenomena, the broadcast of *Not the Homosexual* was not West Germany's 'Stonewall moment', if we understand 'Stonewall' as a signifier for an event that changed everything and founded gay liberation.[69] Firstly, it was not the first time that homosexuality had been transmitted into living rooms around the country. Secondly, various forms of homosexual organizing already existed by the time of the film's broadcast in 1972 and 1973. Thirdly, as suggested in the introduction, the film's striking portrayal of affirmation and gay pride was accompanied by an emphasis on respectability and a tone informed by gay shame. Seen in this light, *Not the Homosexual* demonstrates not only departure but also continuity in homosexual politics.

It was not therefore a watershed moment, but the early history of West German gay liberation cannot be written without reference to the film, not only because of

---

[64] 'HAG – Homosexuelle Aktionsgruppe Bochum', *kaktus: Zeitschrift der Homophilen Studentengruppe Münster* 1 (1971), 12; Heribert Scheerer, 'Emanzipation der Homosexuellen', *kaktus* 1 (1971), 13–15.

[65] 'Aufbruch an deutschen Universitäten', *him* 9 (1971), 16–17 (17).

[66] *kaktus* 1 (July 1971), 6. The charter was serialized in *him*, in issues 4, 5 and 6 of 1972.

[67] Rosa Geschichten (ed.), *Eine Tunte bist du auf jeden Fall: 20 Jahre Schwulenbewegung in Münster* (Münster: KCM, 1992), 13.

[68] *Internationales Forum des jungen Filmes* 25 (1971). SMB archive, Sammlung Holy.

[69] For accounts which compare the film's broadcast to Stonewall—but do not equate them—see Michael Holy, 'Lange hieß es, Homosexualität sei gegen die Ordnung', 92, and Jim [James] Steakley, 'The Gay Movement in Germany Today', *Body Politic* 13 (1974), 14–15, 21 and 23 (14).

the array of action groups founded in its wake, but also because no other event in the decade was as influential in inciting discourse about homosexuality. Written with Martin Dannecker, and produced by the WDR, Rosa von Praunheim's *Not the Homosexual* was first shown during the Berlin film festival in July 1971, but would achieve greater importance and notoriety due to its planned broadcast on national television in January 1972.[70] In the event, the film was screened only in North Rhine-Westphalia, on the WDR's third channel, with a federal broadcast (except in conservative Bavaria) belatedly taking place on the first channel, the ARD, in January 1973. Both screenings were followed by a televised studio discussion, with the film-makers, WDR representatives, and various commentators taking part.

According to its openly gay director, *Not the Homosexual* is 'anti-gay and thoroughly confirms every prejudice held by heterosexuals. From the oft-cited woman in the Bavarian Forest to the ignorant liberal, a new wave of hate will rise against gays.'[71] *Not the Homosexual* offered a compilation of scathing broadsides at aspects of contemporary homosexual life, taking aim at the sentimentality, selfishness, and political apathy of gay men. The viewer follows the journey of Daniel, after he excitedly arrives in West Berlin and progresses from a failed attempt at a monogamous relationship to residing with a wealthy clique in thrall to luxury and cultural consumption. Abandoned by his older suitor, Daniel then discovers the world of gay bars, cruising at public toilets, and leathermen, falling into line with the vanity, cult of physicality, and absence of meaningful communication to be found in the gay scene. Thoroughly depressed and isolated, Daniel eventually chances upon a commune of naked gay men, who proclaim the film's central message: 'Out of the toilets and into the streets!' Instead of aping the heterosexual norm, gays were told to organize, come together, and come out.[72]

The WDR was surprised by the fact that viewer feedback received during and after the 1972 regional broadcast, in the form of 400 phone calls and over 100 letters, was rather positive, noting in a press release that with controversial productions it was generally those who are critical who register their opinion with the broadcaster.[73] Since the WDR was the largest member of the regionally organized ARD public broadcasting consortium, this screening on its third channel would have theoretically reached almost a third of the West German population, mostly in the state of North-Rhine Westphalia. However, the third channel

---

[70] *Nicht der Homosexuelle ist pervers, sondern die Situation, in der er lebt* (Bavaria Atelier, 1971). Rosa von Praunheim is the *non de plume* of Holger Mischwitzky, which the director uses to this day.

[71] Cited from the original 1971 programme distributed at the film festival. *Internationales Forum des jungen Filmes* 25 (1971). SMB archive, Sammlung Holy.

[72] The film's parole 'Out of the toilets and into the streets!' is a mistranslation of the American slogan 'Out of the closets and into the streets!', but is nevertheless rather fitting. There is no direct German equivalent to 'the closet'—the phrase used by gay activists with the closest meaning was *Raus aus euren Löchern!*, 'come out of your holes!'

[73] 'Die Homosexuellen-Filme im WDR', 23 March 1972. WDR *historisches Archiv*, folder D 2023.

was known for 'highbrow fare', and its audience was further limited by viewers having both channels one (ARD) and two (ZDF), broadcast nationally, at their disposal.[74]

The response after the national ARD broadcast in January 1973 more closely resembled Praunheim's prediction.[75] In a flood of protest letters, hundreds of viewers expressed their outrage at the film. Several compared the situation unfavourably with the Nazi period, bemoaning the recent reform to Paragraph 175 and recommending castration, work camps or other forms of punishment for homosexuals.[76] Many argued that the film was unsuitable for television since homosexuality was degenerate or 'abnormal', with the vocabulary 'swines' often used as an anti-gay slur. For one discontented viewer, the reform to Paragraph 175 in 1969 had been 'absolutely sufficient'. He argued that 'From this changed situation no homosexually-inclined person should derive the right to beat the drum for homosexuality in public. [...] It is not comprehensible why the public should be animated by and for the minority who live abnormally.' A 60-year old man was not alone in connecting the film to a litany of WDR productions also found wanting, and the contemporary political climate: 'Even after a two-day interval I still feel sick to my stomach when I remember the scenes – men kissing, men screeching. Ugh! How low decency and morality have sunken. [...] After porn, sex, pot, drugs and criminality, it's only logical that homosexuality must be paraded on our screens. Indeed, why not. In the social-liberal state everyone can ultimately do as they please.'[77] The broadcast had negative financial consequences for at least one homosexual: a woman informed the WDR that she had changed her will the very next day to disinherit a close relative who was one of 'these pitiable people', calculating that it was better to leave her money to cancer research than having it changing hands for sexual acts in public toilets.[78]

Another viewer counselled the WDR that when it came to deciding what was and what was not normal, what people thought about the matter was irrelevant: all that mattered was what is and what is not against nature.[79] Even if homosexuals did act in accordance with their sexual drives, the anonymous letter writer continued, theirs still cannot be classified as normal sexuality—after all, Jürgen Bartsch had acted in accordance with his when he murdered four children. This reference to the paedophile serial killer must be understood in the context of the

---

[74] Hodenberg, *Television's Moment*, 55.

[75] Viewing figures for this broadcast are not available, but by this point 95% of households owned a TV set and average daily exposure stood at about 2 hours. Commercial channels did not arrive on the scene until 1984, when the public monopoly on broadcasting was lifted. So in 1973 viewers could choose from only the two national channels, and their regional third channel (or two regional channels, depending on their location). Hodenberg, *Television's Moment*, 93.

[76] These letters can be viewed at the WDR's archives in Cologne (primarily in folders 08584, 08585 and 08586).

[77] 17 January 1973. Folder 08584; 2 February 1972. Folder 08586.

[78] 5 February 1972. Folder 08586.   [79] 16 January 1973. Folder 08585.

pernicious long-standing assumption that male homosexuals posed a threat to youth. Jürgen Bartsch had been tried twice, in 1967 and 1971. The first trial lasted only nine days and Bartsch was given five life sentences, despite only being 15 years old at the time of the first murder.[80] The second trial was much longer, with more expert witnesses called to testify. Bartsch's sentence was reduced to ten years with subsequent transfer to an asylum.

As Kerstin Brückweh has argued, the juridical reform evident between these two trials was only part of the story. Analysing 250 letters sent by members of the public to newspapers, magazines and to lawyers and judges involved in the case, Brückweh identifies a clear continuation of anti-democratic positions and retaliatory logic, with many letter-writers calling for Bartsch to be executed and others insinuating that lawyers and judges shared the same sexual fantasies as the accused. The rhetorical strategy of linking one's opinions to the Nazi past was widespread, as was interpreting Bartsch as but one manifestation of a wider social decay, and even a growing communist threat.[81] These same themes can also be seen in the hundreds of letters sent to the WDR following the broadcasts of *Not the Homosexual*, which leaves little doubt that homosexual law reform had failed to magically transform stubbornly homophobic public opinion.

In the event, the film had barely managed to make it through to test public opinion in the first place. The unusual decision taken by the ARD programming conference to postpone the film's planned nation-wide broadcast in 1972 was denounced as an act of censorship by the Association of German Film and Television Directors and in several newspaper and magazine articles.[82] While each state broadcaster within the federal ARD was supposed to be politically independent, in reality the broadcasters were accountable to each state government. Thus the debate over *Not the Homosexual* was in part the result of a political struggle between the two most influential state broadcasters: the WDR, representing strongly social democratic North-Rhine Westphalia, against the much more conservative Bavarian state broadcaster. In 1972, CDU representatives began a campaign to rebrand the WDR (*Westdeutscher Rundfunk*) as *Westdeutscher Rotfunk* (Red Radio), or even the 'house of Mao'. Günter Rohrbach, the producer of the film, head of the Department for TV Drama, and a SPD member, was one of the figures especially singled out for criticism.[83]

---

[80]   Kerstin Brückweh, 'Fantasies of Violence. German citizens expressing their concepts of violence and ideas about democracy in letters referring to the case of the serial killer Jürgen Bartsch (1966–1971)', *Crime, Histoire & Sociétés/Crime, History & Societies* 10:2 (2006). Not paginated.

[81]   Ibid.

[82]   'Protest gegen Absetzung des Homosexuellen-Filmes', *Aachener Nachrichten* (24 January 1972); Klaus Schwidrowski, 'Schweinkram, Sünde oder Schock?', *Stern* 7 (1972); 'Vormund und Mündel', *Frankfurter Rundschau* (14 January 1972).

[83]   Hodenberg, *Television's Moment*, 56–8. See further Frank Bösch, 'Campaigning against "Red Public Television": Conservative Mobilization and the Invention of Private Television in West Germany', in *Inventing the Silent Majority in Western Europe and the United States: Conservatism in*

On paper, the ARD's majority decision (6:4) on *Not the Homosexual* was based on the consideration that the film ran the risk of cementing or worsening prejudice against homosexuals.[84] Other concerns were also evidently at play. Even in 1973, when the film was belatedly given its federal broadcast on the ARD first channel, the Bavarian state broadcaster opted out, meaning that over ten million Bavarian residents could not watch the film.[85] Writing in the *Süddeutsche Zeitung*, Uwe Heye speculated that the explicit call for social change contained within the film had influenced the ARD's decision, while an unnamed WDR spokesperson was quoted in *Stern* arguing that the concern for worsening prejudice was but a fig-leaf for the opinion of television directors that the film was full of smut and sin. Günter Rohrbach put the decision down to a case of bad conscience, since television as a medium had long failed to meet the needs of West Germany's homosexuals.[86] Consider the views expressed in a contemporary television journal. According to one article, the decision to postpone the screening was correct, and concerns over increased prejudice were legitimate. Yet this article also revealed notions of a quite different nature: since sexuality was not purely constitutional in nature, but could be acquired, a film such as *Not the Homosexual* had nothing to seek on the TV screen. It was not the task of television to allow representations of homosexuality, since this would encourage the adoption of the practice, thus making a mockery of attempts to protect youth.[87] These considerations may have also influenced the decision to screen the film at a late hour. As Rosa von Praunheim would complain, the belated national broadcast did not begin until 2250 and thus the studio discussion did not get under way until after midnight.[88]

Homosexuals, too, were far from unanimously positive about the film. Indeed, the majority of self-defined homosexuals writing to the WDR regarding the broadcasts also expressed negative sentiments. In 1972, when the overall feedback was more positive than a year later, homosexuals tended to be more critical than heterosexuals (according to the WDR's rough division of sentiments regarding the film, and using the self-definition of letter-writers). Roughly two-thirds of

the 1960s and 1970s, ed. by Anna von der Goltz and Britta Waldschmidt-Nelson (Cambridge, 2017), 275–94.

[84] *Bayernfunk* press release 711–23 [1830], 12 January 1972. WDR archive, folder D2023.
[85] The decision to broadcast the film was taken at a subsequent ARD programming conference in April 1972. This time, only *Bayerischer Rundfunk* (Bavaria) and *Norddeutscher Rundfunk* (representing Hamburg, Mecklenburg-Vorpommern, Lower Saxony and Schleswig Holstein) voted against a national broadcast. Cited from Klaus von Bismarck [WDR director] to *Gesellschaft Katholischer Publizisten*, 16 March 1973. WDR archive, folder 14177.
[86] 'Der Homosexuelle und die Gesellschaft', *Süddeutsche Zeitung* (2 February 1972); Klaus Schwidrowski, 'Schweinkram, Sünde oder Schock?', *Stern* 7 (1972); Rohrbach, 'Ohne Maske und Tarnkappe', *Der Spiegel* 5 (1972), 100.
[87] 'Ständige Programmkonferenz bewirkt Absetzung einer ungeeigneten Sendung', *Aktueller Fernsehdienst* 3/4 (1972). WDR archive, folder D 2023.
[88] Cited from the studio discussion, 15 January 1973. A copy is available at the SMB archive.

heterosexuals were positive about the film, whilst this was the case for no more than half of homosexuals.[89] Some displayed attitudes not far removed from those espoused by avowedly heterosexual letter-writers. One 72-year-old homophile complained that the effeminate figures portrayed on screen had nothing to do with real homosexuals; rather, they represented the 'scum of humanity'.[90]

Another homosexual concluded his letter with the statement 'That homosexuality is deviant must surely be clear to all.'[91] After watching the film, 'I was for the first time ashamed of being homosexual', lamented a man who justified his decision to remain anonymous on the grounds that he was active in public life.[92] Clearly, these individuals did not identify with what was presented on screen. The homosexual who referenced his shame may not have been representative. Yet his remark that he felt ashamed for the first time is telling, for while this shame may have been nurtured by isolation and silence before 1969, it was in fact let loose not by exclusion but by representation. As Elspeth Probyn writes, exposure is key to shame, and thus the increased depiction of marginalized groups on television was very much a double-edged sword: 'While a lack of representation may have been painful, it may have been less shaming.'[93]

For some homosexuals, the film helped in the process of coming to terms with their sexuality. 22-year-old Wolfgang Jahn wrote to the WDR praising the film and for the first time acknowledging to another person his homosexual feelings.[94] Jahn described how the film had made it more likely that he would finally affirm his homosexuality more widely, but before doing so, he wanted to join a circle of gay men, inspired by the commune presented at the conclusion of *Not the Homosexual*. These letters provide evidence not just of specific reactions to the stylistic merits of the film, but of how individuals understood their sexuality and their place in a disapproving society. Jahn answered his own question as to whether the film might increase the fear and isolation of homosexuals by means of stating that he could not imagine feeling more scared or more lonely than he did at present. Another viewer expressed his alienation from mainstream society in the strongest possible way, positing that the only way forward was his dream of an area of land being put aside, along with the provision of housing and factories, so that homosexuals could turn their backs on the 'diehard pharisees' and thus solve the problem for both sides.[95]

This radically separatist view was not an unique occurrence, with *du&ich* publishing an article in 1970 that in all seriousness put forward the utopia of a 'homo state'. Given the amount of money in homophile circles, there should be more than enough to purchase an island somewhere, the anonymous writer

---

[89] 'Die Homosexuellen-Filme im WDR', 23 March 1972. WDR archive, folder D 2023.
[90] 16 January 1973. Folder 08585.   [91] 2 February 1972. Folder 08586.
[92] Dated January 1973. Folder 08585.   [93] Probyn, *Blush: Faces of Shame*, 86.
[94] I have used a pseudonym. 1 January 1972, folder 08586.
[95] Cited from 'Die Homosexuellen-Filme im WDR', 23 March 1972. WDR archive, folder D 2023.

suggested, drawing an analogy to Jews and the state of Israel.[96] Yet the letters to the WDR also reveal interest in and desire for gay activism. Alongside several others, Wolfgang Jahn asked whether there were any gay groups active in his local area. He wanted to help others come to terms with being gay, but added that this required the same recognition himself.[97] Subsequently, Jahn was indeed able to involve himself in gay activism, becoming an active member of the Homosexual Action Group Bonn (AHB) and appearing himself in a film produced in 1976, *Pink Triangle? But That's Ages Ago* (of which more in Chapter 5).[98] While in 1972 Jahn for the first time told someone—or rather, the WDR public relations department—that he was gay, six years later he would proclaim his sexuality to the millions who read the weekly *Stern*, in a famous front-page action alongside 681 other gay men.[99]

The IHWO, meanwhile, had attempted to ensure that *Not the Homosexual* would never be shown in the first place. The couple Claus Fischdick and Carl Stoewahs did not reject media portrayals of homosexuality per se, having appeared in both the *Monitor* news report in 1970 and Claus-Ferdinand Siegfried's *Paragraph 175*. Alarm bells started ringing, however, once they realized that Siegfried's documentary was intended to be broadcast as an adjunct to *Not the Homosexual*, offering a less (melo)dramatic representation of gay life. They called on the WDR to cancel the screening of Praunheim's film, which they argued would be better suited to private viewings amongst homosexuals. The IHWO was engaged in 'arduous legwork' to challenge prejudice 'bit by bit'. In contrast, a national broadcast of *Not the Homosexual* would have 'devastating consequences' for homosexuals and negate all their efforts thus far. Günter Rohrbach, who had produced the film, replied that it would not produce any prejudice amongst the population that did not already exist.[100] In an article for *Der Spiegel*, Rohrbach drew the comparison to a struggle for racial equality, asking if a film would contribute to the liberation of 'negroes' if they were all presented on screen in whiteface.[101] Not content with this response, Fischdick and Stoewahs demanded that their interview from *Paragraph 175* be cut, since they rejected the coupling of the two films. This was roundly rejected by the WDR's legal department.[102]

---

[96] 'Der Homo-Staat: Modell einer Utopie', *du&ich* 7–8 (1970), 11–12 (12). In her book on gay liberation in the San Francisco Bay area, Hobson discusses a project which she describes as 'gay nationalist', the campaign to set up an autonomous gay reserve in Alpine County. *Lavender and Red*, 34–9.

[97] 1 January 1972. WDR archive, folder 08586.

[98] *Rosa Winkel? Das ist doch schon lange vorbei*, dir. by Detlef Stoffel, Christiane Schmerl, and Peter Recht (Universität Bielefeld, 1976).

[99] '"Wir sind schwul" - 682 Männer bekennen', *Stern* 41 (1978). Here, p. 117.

[100] Fischdick and Stoewahs to Bismarck, 30 November 1971. WDR archive, folder 12285; Rohrbach to IHWO, 14 December 1971. Folder 06818.

[101] Rohrbach, 'Ohne Maske und Tarnkappe', 100.

[102] Fischdick and Stoewahs to Bismarck, 3 December 1971. Folder 12285; WDR *Justiziariat* to Fischdick and Stoewahs, 14 January 1972. Folder 12285.

The IHWO had some cause to be frustrated by the WDR's attitude. Fischdick and Stoewahs complained not only about Praunheim's film but also that their interview in *Paragraph 175* had been cut and decontextualized. The WDR assured them that although the segment including their interview had been shortened for programming reasons, this had not altered the meaning of their statements. In fact, all mention of the name of the IHWO had been removed.[103] The documentary, in its final form, made oblique references to 'emancipation groups' but failed to provide the name or details of a single homosexual organization. In defending *Not the Homosexual*, Rohrbach had glibly written 'Whoever wants real change cannot baulk at an interim intensification of the situation.' In reply, Stoewahs and Fischdick described this as an 'outrageous imposition', pointing out that Rohrbach himself was hardly likely to be affected by any prospective 'interim intensification'.[104] In the event, Fischdick and Stoewahs would stand down from the IHWO executive shortly after this heated exchange.[105]

Their successor, Erhard Richter, was similarly minded. After the national broadcast, Richter penned an editorial in the IHWO's newsletter, stating that the film was completely unsuitable to challenge negative perceptions of homosexuality.[106] Unlike Fischdick and Stoewahs, who declined an invitation to take part in the studio discussion following the 1972 broadcast, Richter did attend the discussion in January 1973. Besuited, ill at ease and furiously puffing on his cigar, he cut rather a disconsolate figure, and did not attempt to speak during the 90-minute debate.[107] He was joined in this decision by Dieter Michael Specht, the chief editor of *him*, who sat in the row in front of Richter wearing oversized sunglasses. In the IHWO newsletter, Richter criticized the behaviour of 'left-extremist students' during the discussion, and rationalized his silence by referring to the undesirability of internal divisions amongst homosexuals being broadcast to the viewing public. This explanation did not satisfy at least one IHWO member, who wrote in the following issue that Richter's stance was ridiculous, and had nothing at all to do with tactical considerations.[108]

Raimund Wolfert has argued that the controversy over *Not the Homosexual* shows the dividing line between the IHWO and the 'new, student-influenced gay movement' like no other issue.[109] Certainly, differences were particularly acute during the studio discussion in 1973. The 'experts' invited to the discussion, parliamentary representatives and sympathetic academics, were precisely the IHWO's favoured interlocutors. Richter and others had met with SPD and FDP

---

[103] Fischdick and Stoewahs to Bismarck, 23 December 1971. Folder 12285.
[104] Rohrbach to IHWO, 14 December 1971. Folder 06818; Fischdick and Stoewahs to Bismarck, 23 December 1971. Folder 06818.
[105] Wolfert, *Gegen Einsamkeit*, 132.   [106] *IHWO Rundbrief* 2 (1973). Not paginated.
[107] A copy of the televised discussion is available at the SMB archive.
[108] *IHWO Rundbrief* 2 (1973); Detlef Goldbaum to IHWO, *IHWO Rundbrief* 3 (1973).
[109] Wolfert, *Gegen Einsamkeit*, 128.

parliamentarians in advance of the 1972 federal election and in October organized a podium event with those standing for election in Hamburg.[110] But during the televised studio discussion, Richter watched on in silence as Martin Dannecker harangued SPD member of parliament Ostman von der Leye, one of the leading figures in sexual reform efforts, as an 'agent of the system'. For Dannecker, the liberalization of Paragraph 175 was a reform in the interests of capitalism, as the economic resources of homosexuals could now be better exploited. In light of this exchange, the moderator told the assembled homosexuals that they were wasting a chance to talk specifically about homosexuality. Of course, gay activists refused this instruction: for them, gay oppression was inseparable from other oppressions and the nature of the socio-economic system.[111]

Rather than cultivating contacts with 'experts', Dannecker and Praunheim took the opportunity as soon as the discussion began to leave the podium and cross over to the part of the audience where their fellow homosexuals were seated: subsequent comments from the remaining experts that were protracted or critical were met with whistles and interjections. For Randall Halle, 'Certainly heterosexuals continued to speak about homosexuality, but with *Not the Homosexual* a counter-public emerged that inserted its voice into the public sphere through a radical demand for self-determination.'[112] The 1973 studio discussion did mark something of a turning point. Refusing to be talked at, or talked about, this was the most explicit claim to speech and agency made by homosexuals in German history. Yet for the IHWO, it was something of a missed opportunity. One member of the audience commented towards the end of the discussion that surely legal and social reform and the presence of action groups were *both* needed and that these were not mutually exclusive. This was in many ways precisely the position adopted by IHWO figures, but which they failed to defend on this significant occasion.

Action Groups and the Gay Movement

The significance of *Not the Homosexual* lies not least in that the film functioned as a catalyst for the founding of a wave of gay action groups. Rosa von Praunheim and Martin Dannecker took their film on tour around the Federal Republic, initiating discussions after screenings, thus providing a vital impetus to gay activism.[113] Groups including the Homosexual Action West Berlin (HAW), the Würzburg Homosexual Action (WüHSt), the Homosexual Action Saarbrücken

---

[110] *IHWO Rundbrief* 1 (1973).
[111] All cited from the televised discussion, 15 January 1973. SMB archive.
[112] Halle, 'Rainer, Rosa, and Werner', 546.
[113] Praunheim, *50 Jahre pervers: Die sentimentalen Memoiren des Rosa von Praunheim* (Cologne: Kiepenheuer & Witsch, 1993), 140.

(HAS) and the Homosexual Interest Alliance Düsseldorf (HID) were formed immediately after screenings of the film, or organized screenings as their first public event.[114] A member of the Initiative Group Homosexuality Stuttgart (IHS) recorded the studio discussion broadcast after the film, so that it could be analysed in a group meeting.[115] Praunheim also took his film overseas, attending screenings of the film at the Museum of Modern Art in New York City in April 1972 and at the National Film Theatre in London later that year: a reviewer for the British *Gay News* opined that the film was 'made with all the expertise of a ten-year-old psychopath turned loose with a Super-8 camera and a roll of Kodachrome II'.[116] Activists from the Gay Liberation Front in South London were no more impressed than the IHWO, since they confiscated the director's copy of the film after a screening at London's Institute of Contemporary Arts in 1974: a group spokesperson accused the film of reinforcing prejudice and added that 'we are holding the copy to ransom until von Praunheim agrees not to show it to straights any more'.[117] Back in West Germany, Praunheim would also play a financial role in aiding activism, providing the use of the studio floor that became the first home of the HAW, set up in November 1971. Dannecker, a founding member of *Rotzschwul*, cemented his influence over the movement by his appearances in the gay and mainstream press, in connection with his sociological study published in 1974, *The Ordinary Homosexual*.[118]

Not unlike the wider left-alternative scene, the gay movement was soon saturated by a range of confusing acronyms. Initially, the first gay action group in Munich was simply called HAG (Homosexual Action Group),[119] just like the original group in Bochum, but also groups in Düsseldorf, Bonn, Marburg, and Göttingen.[120] In hindsight, one is almost grateful to the German coffee firm *Kaffee HAG* for flexing its caffeinated muscles and threatening to sue the Munich gay action group in 1973. This led to the organization adopting the acronym HAM (Homosexual Action Group Munich) instead.[121] By December 1973, there were at

---

[114] 'Unsere Alternative: Angriff oder weitermogeln,' *konkret* 5 (1973), 42–3; 'Die Aktiven profitieren', *Emanzipation* 1 (1975), 3–4 (3); *him* 7 (1972), 49; *du&ich* 7 (1976), 41.

[115] 'Protokoll zum IHS Treffen' (20 January 1973). SMB archive, folder deutsche überregionale Gruppen—IHS.

[116] Vito Russo, 'Gay liberation from Germany with reluctance', *Gay Activist* (April 1972), 9; Peter Holmes, 'In all probability it's the movie maker who is perverse', *Gay News* (November 1972), 5.

[117] 'GLF "borrows" German gay film', *Gay News* (December 1974), 3.

[118] Praunheim, *50 Jahre pervers*, 141; Dannecker and Reiche, *Der gewöhnliche Homosexuelle*.

[119] Gustl Angstmann, 'Dokumentarische Information der Schwulenbewegung in München 1971–1975, HAG, HAM und Teestube', 1. SMB archive, folder München–Schwulenbewegung–HAG/HAM.

[120] *him* 2 (1972), 2; HAG Bonn was one of the six signatories to an open letter to the *Bundesprüfstelle für jugendgefährdende Schiften*, 1 October 1972. SMB archive, IHWO box one; HAG Marburg to WDR, 16 January 1972. WDR, folder 08584; HAG, 'Repression gegen Homosexuelle', *Anti-Repressions-Info* 1 (1977), 11–12. SMB archive, folder Schwulenbewegung–überregional–NARGS 1.

[121] Florian Georg Mildenberger, *Die Münchner Schwulenbewegung 1969-1996: Eine Fallstudie über die zweite deutsche Schwulenbewegung* (Bochum, 1999), 31.

least 37 homosexual organizations in the Federal Republic. These included groups in Aachen, Bochum, Bielefeld, Bonn, Bremen, Cologne, Dortmund, Düsseldorf, Essen, Frankfurt, Giessen, Göttingen, Hamburg, Hanover, Heidelberg, Kassel, Kiel, Konstanz, Mainz, Marburg, Munich, Münster, Saarbrücken, Stuttgart, Tübingen, West Berlin, and Würzburg (see further, Figure 2.3).[122]

Attempts to create unity within the movement in the form of an umbrella organization were unsuccessful, other than the short-lived German Action Alliance Homosexuality (DAH), founded in Bochum in late 1972.[123] The

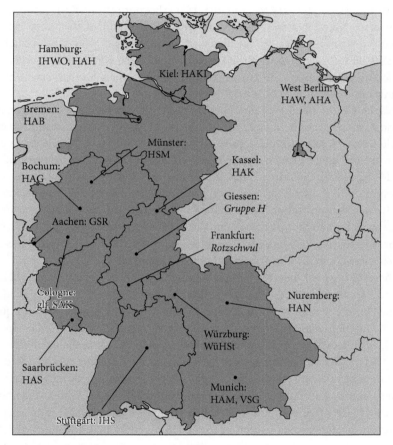

Figure 2.3 Map indicating the locations of various gay groups, ca. 1973.

Source: Adapted by the author, based on an image produced by wikimedia user TUBS, license CC BY-SA 3.0.[124]

[122] *him* 12 (1973), 7.   [123] Salmen and Eckert, *20 Jahre bundesdeutsche Schwulenbewegung*, 34.
[124] TUBS, 'Germany, Federal Republic of location map January 1957 – October 1990.svg' <https://commons.wikimedia.org/wiki/File:Germany,_Federal_Republic_of_location_map_January_1957_-_October_1990.svg> [date accessed 15 July 2018].

organization's platform, agreed in Heidelberg in February 1973, reiterated the programmatic independence of each member group, the spectrum of which was described as ranging from social-liberal to socialist. What separated the groups— namely, divergent 'long-term socio-political perspectives'—should be set aside, in favour of waging a common struggle against discrimination and for the realization of basic and human rights for homosexuals.[125] Due to this legalistic perspective, the presence of the IHWO, and also the leading role of the HSM and its leader Rainer Plein within the DAH, more than half of the action groups founded by 1973 did not join the umbrella organization, including the likes of *Rotzschwul*, the HAW, the HAH, the HAM, and the HAG Bochum.[126] A DAH meeting in Münster in May 1973 was derailed (in the leftist idiom of the time, 'refunctioned'—*umfunktioniert*) by members of these groups, who rejected Rainer Plein's attempt to engage with the Church, dubbed the convention a 'Catholics' Conference' and coined the phrase 'Not the homosexuals are perverse, but the organizations which they establish!'[127]

Despite all the criticism of the HSM, that group had been the first to organize a national demonstration. Indeed, West Germany's first ever demonstration by gays and lesbians, which took place in Münster on 29 April 1972. In a letter sent to other groups inviting them to the event—to mark the first anniversary of the HSM—organizers underlined that the action was 'not about homosexual self-presentation in the sense of "gay and proud" or "gay is beautiful"'. The occasion was to be a demonstration, not a demolition: participants travelling to Münster were warned not to act up or freak out, just because no-one knew them in the city. All prospective publicity material was to be sent to the HSM a week in advance; no leaflets were allowed to be distributed without approval.[128]

The HSM would not have been amused by the inventive slogan Martin Dannecker devised for the occasion 'Brüder und Schwester, warm oder nicht, Kapitalismus bekämpfen ist unsere Pflicht' ('brothers and sisters, whether queer or not, fighting capitalism is a duty we've got': see Figure 2.4).[129] *Der Spiegel* criticized this message in its front-page special in 1973, while the chief editor of *him*, Dieter Michael Specht, berated 'left-militant' elements for ruining the demonstration by rejecting relevant slogans in favour of revolutionary rallying cries.[130] Even so, some locals did not share the careful approach of the HSM: five members broke away later that year, to form the Gay Action Münster (SAM). In particular, the renegade faction took exception to the HSM's 'reformist, anti-gay politics of integration'.[131] Though no negative reactions were reported from passers-by at the

---

[125] 'DAH Rahmenpapiere', 4. SMB archive, folder IHS.   [126] *him* 12 (1973), 7.

[127] Wolfert, *Gegen Einsamkeit*, 186.

[128] 'Einladung an Alle', 13 April 1972. *Spinnboden Lesbenarchiv*, HAW Frauengruppe—Sammlung Monne Kühn 3 1972–1973.

[129] Also cited in Herzog, *Sex after Fascism*, 155, from whom I have adapted this translation.

[130] 'Bekennt, daß ihr anders seid', 49; *him* 7 (1972), 6.   [131] *him* 8 (1972), 47.

Figure 2.4 Martin Dannecker, pictured at West Germany's first demonstration by gays and lesbians, 29 April 1972.

Source: Photo: Udo Plein. By permission of Rosa Geschichten: Schwul-lesbisches Archiv Münster.

demonstration, the caution of the HSM is further evidence that gay liberation was never a 'free-for-all'. Just as for the earlier homophile movement, what was said, where, and in what manner remained fundamentally alive issues.

While those involved in homosexual politics were of diverse ages, action groups were overwhelmingly made up of students or recent graduates. Empirical data on activists is hard to come by, given that many groups kept few records and some did not have a membership structure. The Frankfurt-based *Rotzschwul* was unique among gay groups of the period in that it operated initially as a closed group. From its inception in November 1971 until January 1973 membership was therefore only in the region of 10–12, all but two of them students.[132] After the group was opened to new members the number involved rose to approximately 20–30, with an average age of 26, the oldest being only 31.[133] The Homosexual Action West Berlin (HAW) was larger, with approximately 120 members by 1975, most of them between the ages of 20 and 30.[134] Erwin Kirchner remembers the oldest member as being in his early forties, which was considered 'ancient' by the rest of the group.[135]

The Homosexual Action Nuremberg (HAN), founded in May 1974, had a core membership of about 12, aged between 18 and 26.[136] By the end of the decade, the Homosexual Action Hamburg (HAH) had an estimated 35 members, with another 100 described as 'sympathizers', 90 per cent of whom were aged between 16 and 29.[137] The Initiative Group Homosexuality Stuttgart (IHS) would estimate that there were 24,000 gays in Stuttgart (assuming that 4 per cent of the population was homosexual). Their own membership was put at around 200 'passive' members and 20 active participants.[138] The Homosexual Action Kiel (HAKI) was one of the smaller gay action groups, launching in 1974 with only about ten members, again mostly students. This limited reach was put down to what was described by one activist as their provincial location: 'being gay is something totally exotic here'.[139]

A large student population in Giessen, in the state of Hesse (approximately 13,000 from a total of 80,000), was the source of members for the city's gay group, the *Gruppe H*. Yet this group struggled with activist fluctuation, especially since the vast majority of graduates did not stay in Giessen after their degrees.[140] The

[132] Wackernagel, *Die Gruppe Rotzschwul*, 25–7.   [133] Ibid., 58.

[134] Hedenström (ed.), *Schwule sich emanzipieren lernen*, 65.

[135] Oral history interview (28 August 2012). I have used a pseudonym.

[136] Joachim Hohmann, 'Nürnberg', *du&ich* 8 (1975), 41–5 (44).

[137] Cited from a completed survey by a HAH representative, as part of a study on 'citizens' initiatives' by the University of Munich. SMB archive, folder München–Schwulenbewegung–HAG/HAM.

[138] *Emanzipation* 2 (1975), 2.

[139] *Schwuchtel* 1 (1975), 12. In June 1969, the population of Kiel stood at 277,000. The statistic for nearby Hamburg was 1.82 million. *Statistisches Jahrbuch für die Bundesrepublik Deutschland* (Wiesbaden, 1971), 32.

[140] Joachim Hohmann, 'Giessen', *him* 1 (1975), 22–4.

Society for Sexual Reform (GSR—Aachen) was founded in June 1972 after a screening of *Not the Homosexual* at the university. Membership thereafter fluctuated between 15 and 50. The group focused on engaging with local citizens, since media elites and opinion-makers tended not to be resident in Aachen: 'Here in the provinces we see our task rather as performing *direct* enlightenment of the Aachen population.'[141] As discussed in Chapter 1, the group was beset in this aim by the banning of its information stall in 1973.

Writing in 1985, Michael Holy argued that notions of 'public' and 'publicity' very much depend on the geographical location of each action group. In the provinces, it may be difficult to do any public actions at all, whereas for gay activists in the bigger cities a demonstration might not be considered public enough until there were 1000 participants.[142] In any case, it seems as if homosexuals were more likely to live in large cities than the average West German in this period. Of the 789 respondents surveyed in *The Ordinary Homosexual*, 70 per cent lived in cities with more than 500,000 residents: this was true of only 30 per cent of the general population.[143] This was a problem for groups such as the Homosexual Action Kassel (HAK). Kassel had a population of around 230,000 but a HAK spokesperson complained that there was a high turnover within his group, with members soon departing for either Munich or West Berlin, drawn by the much larger gay scenes there.[144]

Since so many of them were students, gay activists generally had a middle-class background. Despite the expansion to higher education in the 1960s, which saw the founding of several new universities (including in Bochum, where the country's first student gay group was formed), in 1973 only 6 per cent of the West German population possessed the *Abitur*, the educational qualification necessary to enrol at university.[145] In contrast, fully 36 per cent of those homosexuals surveyed by Dannecker and Reiche possessed the *Abitur*.[146] The social background of students in the late 1960s was not at all representative of the population at large. According to a sample of 500 students in July 1967, only 5 per cent of students' fathers were workers, as compared to 44.6 per cent for the wider population, whereas 31 per cent of students had fathers working in the civil service, as compared to just 7.7 per cent nationally. However, of those homosexuals surveyed by Dannecker and Reiche in employment, only 10 per cent were

---

[141] 'GSR Aachen', *him* 8 (1974), 44–5; Helmut Frings, 'Nicht die GSR ist pervers', *GSR Information* 2 (1974), 6–8 (8). Emphasis in the original.

[142] Holy, ' "Macht euer Schwulsein öffentlich!" Zum Verhältnis von "privat" und "öffentlich" in der zweiten deutschen Homosexuellenbewegung', in *Schwule Regungen*, ed. by Frieling, 37–46 (44).

[143] Dannecker and Reiche, *Der gewöhnliche Homosexuelle*, 323.

[144] Joachim Hohmann, 'Kassel: emanzipationsfaule Schwule?, *him* 9 (1974), 13–15 (15).

[145] *Jahrbuch der öffentlichen Meinung 1968–1973* (Allensbach, 1974), 4. This figure increased, but was still only 10% in 1982. *Allensbacher Jahrbuch der Demoskopie 1978–1983* (Munich, 1983), 5.

[146] Dannecker and Reiche, *Der gewöhnliche Homosexuelle*, 309.

identified as workers compared to 53 per cent of the wider population.[147] Thus, while the West German student population formed a social elite, gay students may have been somewhat more representative of West Germany's homosexual population.

Homosexual Generations

Given the lack of understanding and reciprocal denigrations between younger and older homosexuals, between those who tended to call themselves 'gay' and those who tended to call themselves 'homophile', it is tempting to read the emergence of gay liberation as a classic story of generational conflict.[148] For Franz, a 40-year old member of the HAW, homosexuals of his own age were not prospective sexual partners. Acknowledging the impact of Paragraph 175, he bemoaned that most gays of his age had resigned themselves to their lot. Either they fully joined in the 'terror of youth', fearful of being 'left on the shelf', or they attempted to construct a 'safe homo world' by conforming to the system.[149] Another HAW activist would write that in light of the political wrongdoings of their mothers and fathers his generation had been right to adopt the slogan 'trust no-one above thirty!', but admitted that they were nevertheless blinded by the fetish of youth. Now that he himself was on the cusp of turning 30, the gulf between himself and older gays was narrowing, while another chasm opened up behind him. Every day, every hour, every minute was being irrevocably lost. Optimism and zest for life were vanishing, leaving behind only the prospect of 'a wrinkled sack of what-could-have-been, dreariness, disappointment and ice cream.' Spurred on by this realization, he wished to reach out to older gays, in so doing challenging the fetish of youth in himself and helping an older generation to become involved in gay politics, to discover more meaning in their lives and to overcome their loneliness.[150]

The paucity of intergenerational contact within homosexual politics mirrored a similar phenomenon in the gay scene more widely. Regular articles on the problem of age appeared in the commercial gay press, often rather condescending and fearful about the process of ageing and the lot of older homosexuals. In 1975,

---

[147] *Jahrbuch der öffentlichen Meinung 1968–1973*, 455 (figures for the general population relate to the 1970 census); Dannecker and Reiche, *Der gewöhnliche Homosexuelle*, 310.

[148] After all, developments in modern German history have often been analysed through this lens. Referencing the frequent changes in constitutional order since German unification in 1871, and the experiences of dislocation following defeat in two world wars, Mark Roseman writes 'Few other national histories offer such obvious potential for dividing one cohort from another and rendering them unable to communicate across the gulf between their respective socialisations and experiences.' Roseman (ed), *Generations in Conflict: Youth Revolt and Generation Formation in Germany, 1770–1968* (Cambridge, 1995), 2.

[149] Franz, 'Schwul und Alter', *Schwuchtel* 2/3 (1976), 11.

[150] Claire, 'Erkundungsprojekt: Zur Lebenssituation und Lebenserfahrung alter Schwuler', *HAW Info* 21 (1976), 68.

du&ich featured a young gay couple, the 19-year-old Bert and Herbert, a year younger. Seeming to have no knowledge of the recent illegality of homosexuality whatsoever, Bert mocked older homosexuals who at the age of 50 would place a contact ad seeking a 'friend for life'. Rhetorically asking what they had been doing for the last 30 years, he supposed 'screwing around' in public toilets. The attention he and his partner received from older gay men disgusted him, their 'pushiness' and 'self-pity' made him sick—after all, they had been young once and had had the opportunity to make something out of their lives.[151] A previous piece in 1972 had offered a glimpse into the psychological difficulties caused by being socialized in an era when homosexuality remained illegal. Leopold, 47 years old, bemoaned the cruelty of younger homosexuals, particularly in respect to his baldness: were it not for the fact that he had to care for his ailing mother, he would have long since departed from this 'shitty life'.[152]

According to Georg, 63, young people simply did not understand the freedom they enjoyed, able to sleep with whomever they liked. In contrast, he had been restricted to 'fleeting pick-ups', and now had to make do with photos, which at least meant he could dream and not run the risk of being taunted as an 'old dirt-bag'.[153] Another compared his enforced lack of sexual contact due to Paragraph 175 to being plagued by an injured groin, but remarked that at least the latter would have qualified him for a disability pension.[154] While I do not want to call into question the suffering of these men, the inclusion of such accounts in the gay press, and in activist material such as the HAW newsletter, says just as much about the fear of ageing on the part of younger gay men as it does about the reality of life as an older homosexual. Septuagenarian Adolf would point out in his letter to *du&ich* that there was in fact such a thing as happy ageing, and criticized the magazine for painting such a bleak picture.[155]

One generational interpretation of homosexual politics might envisage gay liberation as a straightforward achievement of the '1968 generation', those born roughly between 1938 and 1948.[156] This generation either did not experience the Nazi period, or were only young children at the war's conclusion. They came of age not in the immediate post-war period of occupation and reconstruction, but in the 1960s, a time of greater affluence and consumption. Confronted by a reso-lutely conservative political culture, authoritarian modes of teaching and a restrictive sexual morality, this generation played a significant role in transform-ing society, even if the immediate goal of a political revolution in the late 1960s failed. The age and social background of the average gay action group member

---

[151] 'Die Glücklichen sind unter uns', *du&ich* 4 (1975), 2–6 (4).
[152] 'Die Angst vor dem Alter', *du&ich* 4 (1972), 10–11 (10).   [153] Ibid., 10.
[154] Ibid., 10.   [155] *du&ich* 6 (1972), 9.
[156] Both Heinz Bude and Dirk Moses use these dates. Bude, 'The German *Kriegskinder*: Origins and Impact of the Generation of 1968', in *Generations in Conflict*, ed. by Roseman, 290–305 (291). Moses, *German Intellectuals and the Nazi Past* (Cambridge, 2007), 9.

tallies with the interpretation that gay liberation was a product of the '1968 generation', even if gay liberation was in part also a *response* to 1968, rather than its direct consequence.

A more sophisticated generational story recognizes the contribution not just of the '68ers' but also the '45ers'. The '1945 generation' were born roughly between 1920 and 1930, meaning they were between 15 and 25 years old at the end of the Second World War. 1945 marked both the 'turning point of their lives and the beginning of their own and Germany's intellectual and emotional reorienta-tion'.[157] The 1945ers formed the first post-war generation of university students, and came to occupy influential positions in education, law, politics, and the media. It was members of the '1945 generation' who had successfully liberalized political culture to the extent that the protests and activism we associate with 1968 were even possible. The '45ers often sympathized with students' critiques of the ruling order, but cooperation broke down over the lengths to which some parts of this younger generation were prepared to go, particularly regarding the question of violence. It was in this context that prominent '45er and erstwhile ardent sup-porter of the student movement, Jürgen Habermas, warned Rudi Dutschke and other student leaders about the dangers of giving rise to 'leftist fascism'.[158]

Adapting this template to homosexual politics, we might plausibly posit 'gays' who organized in action groups as the '68ers and 'homophiles' who filled the ranks of more moderate associations such as the IHWO as the '45ers. The IHWO was fond of underscoring both the size and diversity of its membership, in that students made up only a minority of members. According to their own calcula-tions, in 1973 17 per cent of their members were between 35 and 50, with 25 per cent older than 50.[159] Carl Stoewahs, one half of the couple who appeared on national television in 1970 and 1972, was born in 1929 and his replacement as head of the IHWO, Erhard Richter, was born in 1927. Both can therefore be called '45ers. The agenda of the IHWO—reform not revolution, enlighten rather than provoke, engage with institutions instead of taking part in street demonstrations— also maps onto the rough dividing lines between the '1945' and '1968' generations.

Generation as a methodological apparatus should nevertheless be used with caution. Generations are not themselves 'motors of historical change', not 'object-ively existing quantifiable phenomena', but rather constructs.[160] By assuming the

---

[157] Moses, *German Intellectuals*, 9 and 50. Christina von Hodenberg also favours the '1945er' desig-nation. Helmut Schelsky coined the term 'sceptical generation' for this cohort, whereas several scholars use *Flakhelfergeneration* for those born between 1926 and 1928, referring to those teenagers who supported anti-aircraft batteries in the final stages of the war. Hodenberg, *Konsens und Krise*, 52 and 252.

[158] Timothy Scott Brown, *West Germany and the Global Sixties: The Antiauthoritarian Revolt, 1962–1978* (Cambridge, 2013), 103.

[159] *IHWO Report* 5 (1973), not paginated. One third were what the IHWO described as upper-class, one-third middle-class, 15% students and apprentices, and 11% workers. 93% were male, 7% female.

[160] Anna von der Goltz (ed), *Talkin' 'Bout My Generation': Conflicts of Generation Building and Europe's '1968'* (Göttingen, 2011), 15.

salience of generation, historians may end up themselves producing that which they intend to analyse.[161] In homosexual politics, like in all politics, age does not dictate political positions. While the IHWO had many older members, it had plenty of younger ones too: 33 per cent were aged between 25 and 35, with a quarter of members younger than 25.[162] Stoewahs' partner and fellow IHWO leader Claus Fischdick was born in 1939, so he could be classified as belonging to the '1968 generation' born between 1938 and 1948. Several prominent publicists were also young. Udo Erlenhardt, he who so roundly denounced the use of 'gay', was only 25 years old when he became chief editor of *him* in 1970. His successor, Dieter Michael Specht, was also a '68er, born in 1942. Grouping together in a single generation those who may be as much as ten years older or younger than each other runs the risk of obscuring important shifts within said generation. Elmar Kraushaar, active in the HAW since 1973, has written that by the time of the largest gay demonstration of the decade, at the conclusion of the *Homolulu* festival in Frankfurt in 1979, he no longer felt that he belonged to the generation of gay activists who organized the event, even though he was still only 29 himself.[163] Moreover, it is not the case that a majority of gay twenty-somethings involved themselves in the gay movement, with the membership of action groups never reaching particularly large numbers.

Since 1968 saw a mobilization of conservative students and other young people too, Anna von der Goltz has argued that we need to talk of generations of 1968 in the plural.[164] Although there is scant evidence of younger right-wing gays mobilizing, there is one notable exception. Jürgen Neumann, born in 1945, set up the German Homophile Organization (DHO) in West Berlin in 1971, and came into frequent conflict with the HAW. In 1972, Neumann warned DHO members in a newsletter to keep their distance from the HAW, a 'criminal left-radical pack of communists' whom he had reported to the police.[165] Like IHWO leaders Stoewahs and Fischdick, Neumann wrote to the WDR, opposing the broadcast of *Not the Homosexual*.[166] Neumann had been an avid member of the far-right NPD (National Party of Germany), describing this as a 'young, modern party' to readers of *him* in April 1971. Unfortunately for Neumann, the NPD did not take kindly to being featured in the gay press, and promptly suggested that he resign.[167]

---

[161] Ulrike Jureit and Michael Wildt (eds), *Generationen: zur Relevanz eines wissenschaftlichen Grundbegriffs* (Hamburg, 2005), 19.

[162] *IHWO Report* 5 (1973).

[163] Kraushaar, 'Höhenflug und Absturz – Von Homolulu am Main nach Bonn in die Beethoven-Halle', in *Rosa Radikale*, ed. by Pretzel and Weiß, 80–90 (81).

[164] Goltz, 'A polarised generation? Conservative Students and West Germany's "1968"', in *Talkin' 'Bout My Generation'*, 195–215. See also Goltz, 'A Vocal Minority: Student Activism of the Center-Right and West Germany's 1968', in *Inventing the Silent Majority*, 82–104.

[165] 'Berliner DHO-Mitteilungen!'. Copy in 'Vorbereitung: Besprechung IHWO-DHO-IHWO'. SMB archive, IHWO box one.

[166] Neumann to WDR, 4 January 1973. WDR, folder 08585.

[167] *him* 4 (1971), 4; 'Porzia hat das Wort', *him* 10 (1971), 36–7.

Neumann's politics were certainly not representative of others who used the term homophile, who tended to be liberal or centre-left in their political orientation. Other than Neumann, there were precious few homosexuals who openly favoured the political right in the 1970s. An exception was Johannes Werres, who was cited welcoming homosexual law reform at the top of this chapter. Werres presents a rare case, both in that he openly touted his support of the CDU in the gay press, and also because he represented continuity from the early post-war homophile movement, having written for *Der Kreis* and *Der Weg* since the 1950s. Though he was not a member of any homosexual organization in the 1970s, Werres set up a press agency, *Gay News*, which collected and syndicated relevant coverage on homosexuality from both the mainstream and gay press.[168] Looking back at the 1970s, Werres would bemoan the attitude of younger activists: 'They all acted more or less as if the world began with them. What had taken place earlier, what others had done or did parallel to them did not interest them.'[169]

Werres did not help his case by his frequent condemnation of leftist activists. Dannecker and Reiche, for example, were branded as 'agitators' in an article for the conservative broadsheet *Die Welt*.[170] He did, however, have a point about the distinct air of disdain with which younger gays frequently treated older homophiles. There are two main explanations for this conspicuous lack of identification: the first relates to questions of self-presentation. As Andreas Pretzel states, the retreat of homophiles to inconspicuous private circles, a response to the repressive socio-political climate they endured in the 1950s and 1960s, was met with a mixture of incomprehension and condescension by younger activists.[171] Homophiles tended to place a greater emphasis on conviviality than younger gay activists, not least because their freedom to socialize had been severely restricted before homosexual law reform. This made them easy targets for gay activists, who frequently mocked circles defined by the ostensibly apolitical, pompous, and gossipy nature of their participants as *Kaffeekränzchen* (roughly equivalent to 'tea parties').[172] Similarly, a columnist in *du&ich* expressed his concern in 1970 that the newly-founded IDH might go the same way as other homophile groups and become nothing more than a 'queens' tea party'.[173] Dress

---

[168] The title was rendered in English, and in 1975 changed to *Gay News Germany*, to avoid clashing with the British magazine *Gay News*. 'Sieben Jahre homosexuelle Emanzipationsbewegung in Deutschland', *Gay News Germany* 64 (1976), 14–19 (17). SMB archive, Personen/Journalist/Werres, Johannes.

[169] Werres, '"Alles zog sich ins Ghetto zurück": Leben in deutschen Großstädten nach 1945', in *Keine Zeit für gute Freunde: Homosexuelle in Deutschland 1933–1969*, ed. by Joachim Hohmann (Berlin: Foerster, 1982), 82–92 (90).

[170] The article was penned under a pseudonym. Hans Daniel, 'Homosexualität: Wie zuverlässig sind wissenschaftliche Aussagen von Agitatoren?', *Die Welt* (27 January 1973).

[171] Pretzel, 'Aufbruch und Resignation', 333.

[172] Not least by Martin Dannecker, as he rather apologetically admits. Dannecker, 'Der unstillbare Wunsch', 236.

[173] Dieter Müller-Geismar, 'Historischer Augenblick?', *du&ich* 3 (1970), 36.

was important too. Styles of attire had not just been transformed from the 1950s to the 1960s and into the 1970s, but had become increasingly politically coded, along with other personal preferences, such as hairstyle and taste in music.[174] In the action groups, jeans, unkempt or long hairstyle, and facial hair ruled the day. The decision to dress more formally, as those who used the denomination homophile tended to do so, may have been understood as indicative of a politically conservative outlook. According to a *him* columnist, activists rebuked him for attending a meeting wearing a shirt and tie, since this was seen as submitting to prevailing morality.[175]

The second reason some gays rejected older homophiles was because what little younger activists did know about their homophile predecessors and contemporaries struck them not only as closeted, acquiescent, and frankly boring, but also as politically suspect. Conformist behaviour was seen not just as misguided, but, informed by Frankfurt School readings, could also be taken as evidence of authoritarian or even fascistic personalities.[176] The reception of Herbert Marcuse and other Frankfurt School theorists was central to the way in which gay activists understood repression, tolerance, and liberation. For Marcuse, capitalism rarely needed to rely on terror and open repression of opposition, since its methods of indoctrination and manipulation had been so internalized by much of the population, who were left with no 'consciousness of servitude'. In this context, there emerged 'a pattern of one-dimensional thought and behaviour in which ideas, aspirations, and objections that, by their content, transcend the established universe of discourse and action are either repelled or reduced to terms of this universe'.[177]

Homophiles, in their rejection of 'gay', of provocation, in their supposed conformism, their upstanding behaviour, must have appeared as the archetypal one-dimensional men. In this light, they were part of the problem, not part of the solution. The irony here is that, later in the decade, a pronounced identification of gay activists with their predecessors did emerge. By the end of the 1970s, gay activists directly posited themselves as the 'subsequent generation' to the homosexuals who had perished in the concentration camps.[178] In contrast, activists saw no appeal in framing themselves as in any way the offspring of post-war homophiles. Identifying with those who had lost their lives in Nazi concentration

---

[174] See further Sven Reichardt, *Authentizität und Gemeinschaft: Linksalternatives Leben in den siebziger und frühen achtziger Jahren* (Berlin, 2014), 629–49.
[175] Georg Rethy, 'Gay Power – Nein!', *him* 5 (1972), 22–7 (22).
[176] Michael Holy, 'Der entliehene Rosa Winkel', in *Der Frankfurter Engel: Mahnmal Homosexuellenverfolgung*, ed. by Initiative Mahnmal Homosexuellenverfolgung (Frankfurt a.M.: Eichborn, 1997), 74–87 (76).
[177] Herbert Marcuse, *One-Dimensional Man. Studies in the Ideology of Advanced Industrial Society* (London and NY: Routledge, 2002 [1964]), 9 and 14.
[178] Leaflet distributed by the anti-fascist working group of the AHA at September 1979 rally organized by the Association of those Persecuted by the Nazi Regime (VVN). *AHA INFO Intern* (September 1979), 13–14.

camps, unblemished by any supposed conformism in the conservative moral climate of the early Federal Republic, proved altogether more straightforward.

Clearly, in the immediate aftermath of homosexual law reform, social conformity continued to exert a certain appeal. Only this can explain the emphasis on caution on the part of organizations such as the IHWO. Given that they were sexual outcasts in a hostile society, some homosexuals did everything in their power to stress their resemblance to the social majority, to convince others that they were fundamentally harmless, just responsible citizens like other men and women. Adopting confrontational forms of activism or leftist politics was simply not part of this programme. At the same time, there is also clear evidence of the desire to confront society. Self-defined homophiles agitated in the press, appeared on national television, and announced their homosexuality through a microphone in Hamburg, and all before gay action groups had even arrived on the scene. It would be quite wrong, therefore, to see in the transition from 'homophile' to 'gay' the eclipse of 'shame' by 'pride' Consider the *gay-journal* magazine, for whom Johannes Werres was a correspondent. Editors rejected what they referred to as a 'propagation and ideologisation of homosexuality'.[179] Yet this was seen as entirely compatible with the statement 'gay and proud'.[180]

Not the Homosexual had called on West German gays to be proud of their homosexuality. Yet in the film homosexuals were variously described as 'false half-gays', 'whores', 'urinal gays', 'infantile', and 'park fuckers'. Activities with which gay activists did not identify—or were ashamed of—could be relegated to the lives of the vain and inglorious homosexuals of the scene, whereas any hint of the conventional, the uptight, the desire to be accepted, could be maligned as 'homophile'. As we will see in the following chapter, members of the alternative left sought not just to change society but to change themselves. If leftist activists sought to abolish the 'bourgeois citizen' within, many gay activists clearly wanted rid of their 'homophile selves'. The politics of gay pride, of affirmation, did not erase the shame that endured in this period of transition, between 1969 and 1973. According to Eve Sedgwick, shame 'floods into being'.[181] On the occasions they were flooded by shame, gay activists found in homophiles an easy target, an instrument to gain relief from their shame. Deborah Gould asks 'How do you confront a society when you feel unrecognized and desire relief from that painful condition, when you want to be part of society but simultaneously reject it, in part because it has rejected you?'[182] For younger gay men, homophiles could help mop up all the shame that stubbornly persisted, whilst they proudly got on with the task of gay liberation.

[179] *gay-journal* 2 (1972), 2.   [180] Rendered in English. Ibid., 2.
[181] Sedgwick, *Touching Feeling*, 36.   [182] Gould, *Moving Politics*, 58.

3

Gay Liberation, '1968', and the Alternative Left

'We are gay'. So announced 682 men to the estimated 18 million readers of the *Stern* magazine in October 1978, in activists' most spectacular public action of the decade.[1] Ten years on, the front-page special owed much to the legacy of 1968, even if there was no *direct* line between gay liberation and the global wave of protest associated with that year. The perspectives and spaces opened up by 1968 profoundly influenced the course of homosexual politics in the ensuing decade. Consider the challenge posed by 1968 to authority and convention, its attack on sexual and moral conservatism, its broadening of political horizons to include matters of personal subjectivity, or its critique of the formal political party and the parliamentary arena as the best vehicle and space in which to advance collective interests. This influence is most apparent on the gay left, that is, those gay action groups such as the Homosexual Action West Berlin, *Rotzschwul* (in Frankfurt) and the Homosexual Action Hamburg, which linked homosexual oppression to the capitalist system, declaring their solidarity with other oppressed peoples (the Hamburg group recruited many of the 682 men who took part in the *Stern* action).[2]

'1968' has long since ceased representing a mere calendar year. Gerd-Rainer Horn uses 1968 to stand for a 'far larger moment in time', namely 1956 to 1976.[3] Martin Klimke and Joachim Scharloth suggest extending the 'generational periodization' associated with 1968 to a 'long 1960s' understood as dating roughly from 1956 to 1977.[4] This follows in the historiographical footsteps of Arthur

---

[1] 'Wir sind schwul' - 682 Männer bekennen', *Stern* 41 (1978). Based on a survey in early 1976 (sample size 4000–8000 people) the Allensbach Institute found that 29.9% read each issue of the magazine. This made *Stern* the most popular of any publication in the Federal Republic, with the exception of the tabloid *BILD*. *Allensbacher Jahrbuch der Demoskopie 1974–1976* (Allensbach, 1976), 268–9. According to the May 1970 census, the West German population was 60.65 million. *Statistisches Jahrbuch für die Bundesrepublik Deutschland* 1974 (Wiesbaden, 1974), 82.

[2] Wolfgang Zander, 'Von einem Schwulen, der auszog, das Fürchten zu verlernen', *Emanzipation* 2 (1979), 10–12.

[3] Horn, *The Spirit of '68: Rebellion in Western Europe and North America, 1956–1976* (Oxford, 2007), 2.

[4] Klimke and Scharloth, *1968 in Europe: A History of Protest and Activism, 1956–1977* (New York, 2008), 3.

The Ambivalence of Gay Liberation: Male Homosexual Politics in 1970s West Germany. Craig Griffiths, Oxford University Press (2021). © Craig Griffiths.
DOI: 10.1093/oso/9780198868965.003.0004

Marwick, whose 'long sixties' refers to the period 1958 to 1974.[5] Timothy Brown uses '1968' interchangeably with his phrase 'the global sixties', which he charts as extending from 1962 to 1978.[6] Belinda Davis prefers to talk of a 'long 1970s', in which '1968' represents the period from around 1965 to 1977, pulling together varied phenomena such as the student movement, youth culture, cultural and sexual revolutions, political democratization, and counter-cultural activism of all stripes into a single signifier.[7] Gay liberation can therefore be seen as part of this more expansive '1968', even if gay liberation had not yet emerged by that calendar year.

This chapter opens by focusing on the sexual politics of the West German student movement, which played the dominant role in the Extra-Parliamentary Opposition (APO) of the late 1960s. The APO, under the de facto leadership of the Socialist German Student League (SDS), reached its height between 1966 and 1968, before disintegrating in the period 1969-1970.[8] Although 1968 is often associated with 'free love' and the 'sexual revolution', not all tendencies in the APO were sympathetic to the mantra 'the personal is political': that questions of intimate life, the body, and personal autonomy were equally meaningful as wage disputes, imperialist interventions and the policing of protest; that individual personal experiences actually politically mattered; and that changing society was no good if along the way activists failed also to change themselves. In this section of the chapter, I also analyse the interconnections between women's liberation and gay liberation, for the gay movement can scarcely be imagined without the prior foundations provided by the women's movement. A case in point is the mass outing in *Stern*, which was inspired by the previous action conducted by feminists in 1971, when 374 women declared on the front cover of the same magazine that they had had an abortion.[9] In turn, both women's and gay movements were intimately connected with 1968. If the student movement, informed by new left theories and activist practices, gave rise to a 'dialectic of inspiration and anger' on the part of second-wave feminists, the same is equally true for gay liberationists.[10]

After exploring the sexual politics of 1968, I examine the relationship between gay liberation and the 1970s 'alternative left'. I use the term as a loose placeholder for those diverse movements, groups, and countercultural spaces to the left of the

---

[5] Marwick, *The Sixties: Cultural Revolution in Britain, France, Italy, and the United States, c. 1958-1974* (Oxford, 1998), 7.

[6] Brown, *West Germany and the Global Sixties*, 3.

[7] Davis, 'New Leftists and West Germany: Fascism, Violence and the Public Sphere, 1967-1974', in *Coping with the Nazi Past: West German Debates on Nazism and Generational Conflict, 1955-1975*, ed. by Philipp Gassert and Alan Steinweis (Oxford, 2006), 210-37 (210).

[8] The term APO drew attention to the virtual absence of parliamentary opposition, since between 1966 and 1969 the two main parties, the CDU/CSU and the SPD, were in coalition, commanding 90% of seats in the *Bundestag*. On the APO, see further Markovits and Gorski, *The German Left*, 1-104.

[9] 'Wir haben abgetrieben!', *Stern* 24 (1971).

[10] Geoff Eley, *Forging Democracy: The History of the Left in Europe, 1850-2000* (Oxford, 2002), 367.

governing Social Democrats: this 1970s 'alternative left' can be seen as the direct successor to the APO or the 'new left' of the 1960s. The alternative left provided the most readily available framework for gay activism; there were few political alternatives. The mainstream political parties were prepared to support homosexual law reform, but were not interested in calling into question gender roles or the exalted status of heterosexuality. Gay and lesbian caucuses in the SPD and the FDP did not arrive on the scene until the late 1970s.[11]

The alternative left provided not just ideological influences but also a *space* for gay action groups. I therefore explore not just the political connections but also the textual and spatial context of this alternative left. Gay leftists were often less preoccupied by the *Öffentlichkeit*, the wider public sphere, than by the left-alternative *Gegenöffentlichkeit*, the counterpublic, with its sprawling network of independently produced papers, posters, flyers, and zines, alongside its alternative spaces: bars, cafes, bookshops, grocery stores, and housing, film and theatre collectives. By examining the hitherto little unacknowledged gay participation in this counterpublic, I bridge the divide between narrower organizational histories of the new or radical left and the growing literature on the amorphous networks and spaces that the student movement and post-1968 protest groups gave rise to in the 1970s, generally historicized under the category 'milieu'.[12]

The 1970s alternative left was a melting pot of diverse and sometimes conflicting tendencies. It was a broader phenomenon than the 1960s new left, but I do not wish to set up a false divide between the two, in which the earlier movement appears as only sexist and homophobic in contrast to its supposedly more enlightened successor. Firstly, the 'alternative' in 'alternative left' does not necessarily mean inclusive, embracing of difference, or somehow quirky or cuddly. Notions of solidarity and anti-authoritarianism might spring to mind, but these were never sufficient to anchor gay liberation in the alternative left. This context explains why gay men's incipient status as a 'victim-group' of National Socialism proved so crucial, and is the focus of the following chapter. Secondly, we cannot afford to disregard the significance of 1968. For even as intellectual works popular in the student movement were silent on or antagonistic towards homosexuality, they also bequeathed to the gay left a foundational scepticism about the nature of liberalization in capitalist societies. Since no good could come from a rotten order, developments that might be seen as progressive steps in the right direction were denounced as anything but. This worldview allowed gay leftists to distance

[11] The Gay Socialists (*Schwusos*) were founded in 1979. 'Hallo, Gerda', *Der Spiegel* 34 (1979), 38–40. A homosexual caucus in the Young Democrats was officially recognized in November 1978. A group in the wider FDP was founded in 1980. See Jungdemokraten Arbeitskreis Homosexualität, 'Lieber ein warmer Bruder als ein kalter Krieger: Dokumentation' (1980). SMB archive.
[12] See Sven Reichardt and Detlef Siegfried (eds), *Das alternative Milieu: Antiburgerlicher Lebensstil und linke Politik in der Bundesrepublik Deutschland und Europa 1968–1983* (Gottingen, 2010); Sven Reichardt, *Authentizität und Gemeinschaft*; and Cordia Baumann, Sebastian Gehrig, Nicolas Büchse (eds), *Linksalternative Milieus und Neue Soziale Bewegungen in den 1970er Jahren* (Heidelberg, 2011).

themselves from more conservative homosexuals. In their supposed conformism, such men could be lambasted as insufficiently political, or in the idiom of the day, 'pseudo-political', *scheinpolitisch*. This dividing line in homosexual politics was directly provided by 1968.

The Sexual Politics of 1968

The appeal of free and unrestrained sexual activity to student activists was symbolically indicated by the parole scrawled onto a wall at Frankfurt University in 1967, 'Read Wilhelm Reich and act accordingly!'[13] Following Reich's teaching would not only lead to erotic pleasure, but was part of a political understanding that sexual repression was central to authoritarian personalities and fascist or protofascist societies. Wilhelm Reich's were among the most popular works reproduced by the bootlegging industry that surrounded the student movement, particularly his *The Sexual Revolution* and *The Function of the Orgasm*.[14] Offering an accessible blend of Marxism and psychoanalysis, Reich argued that sexual satisfaction lay at the core of all happiness, and that the communist movement in the 1920s and 1930s erred in ignoring the issue of sexual pleasure in their appeals to the working class.[15] According to Reich, sexual repression lay at the heart of all neurosis, and led to a lust for power and brutality.[16] His work thus offered the student movement added political legitimacy to that famous contemporary rallying cry, 'make love not war'.[17]

But what did the aforementioned scrawled slogan offer homosexuals? According to Reich, homosexuality was the result of an early inhibition of heterosexual love.[18] He supported the decriminalization of male homosexuality, and castigated its recriminalization in the Soviet Union under Stalin, but not least because he saw legal measures as an ineffectual way of abating the practice. Instead, homosexuality could be reduced only by 'establishing all necessary prerequisites for a natural love life among the masses'.[19] Moreover, in *The Function of the Orgasm*, Reich claimed that sexually satisfied heterosexuals had

---

[13] Reimut Reiche, 'Sexuelle Revolution – Erinnerung an einen Mythos', *Die Früchte der Revolte: Über die Veränderung der politischen Kultur durch die Studentenbewegung*, ed. by Lothar Baier et al. (Berlin, 1988), 45–71 (55–6).

[14] *The Sexual Revolution* was originally published as *Die Sexualität im Kulturkampf* in 1936, but an edition was released in 1966 used a Germanized version (*Die sexuelle Revolution*) of the English-language title. On the bootlegging industry, see Brown, *West Germany*, 127–30.

[15] Reich, *The Sexual Revolution: Toward a Self-Governing Character Structure*, trans. by Theodore P. Wolfe (New York, 1971 [1936]), xxviii.

[16] Reich, *Die Funktion des Orgasmus: Zur Psychopathologie und zur Soziologie des Geschlechtslebens* (Vienna, 1927), 14 and 168.

[17] Herzog, *Sex after Fascism*, 159. See further Häberlen, *The Emotional Politics of the Alternative Left*, 51–3.

[18] Reich, *The Sexual Revolution*, 209.   [19] Ibid., 209 and 210.

tended to oppose the First World War, whereas 'latent or manifest homosexuals' were among the most sadistic and the most brutal recruits.[20]

In his contribution to the Institute of Social Research's *Studies on Authority and Family*, originally published in 1936 but bootlegged in the late 1960s, Erich Fromm argued that sado-masochism tended to be accompanied by a relative weakness of heterosexual genitality. The 'average authoritarian man' was physiologically heterosexual, but mentally homosexual: he could marry and produce children but was cruel and hostile-minded towards women. Moreover, Fromm asserted that this latent homosexuality could be transformed into manifest homosexuality, citing as evidence the 'extreme authority structures' of recent times.[21] Although clearly alluding to the Nazis, he did not explicitly mention Ernst Röhm and the SA (*Sturmabteilung*, stormtroopers) as evidence of a supposed link between homosexuality and fascism. Prominent Soviet writer Maksim Gor'kii displayed no such restraint: 'Destroy the homosexuals – Fascism will disappear.'[22]

The contemporary philosopher Arno Plack argued in 1967 that the alleged homosexual complexion of the SA was no coincidence, but due to the fact that the 'inverts' had taken on leadership roles from the very start.[23] Plack's 1967 *Society and Evil* proved popular among student activists not only for its damning verdict of contemporary society, but also because Plack stressed the centrality of sexual repression to authoritarianism, evil, and the Holocaust. This argument reached its dubious conclusion with Plack's statement that what had happened in Auschwitz should not be considered 'typically German' but 'typical for a society which represses sexuality.'[24] Not the discrimination against and persecution of homosexuals were examples of sexual repression; instead, homosexuality itself was the problem, evidence of the repression of *heterosexuality*. Homosexuality and other 'abnormalities' such as incest were the result of hegemonic morality's taboo on free sexuality—that is, 'in its freedom affirmed heterosexuality', which for Plack was the only natural sexuality.[25] Challenging the repression of child sexuality, ending the taboo on pre- and extra-marital heterosexual activity, and tackling the jealousy of wives—jealousy which prevented their husbands from social contact with other women, thus forcing them to unduly socialize with men—were Plack's recommendations to reduce the unwanted occurrence of homosexuality.[26]

---

[20] Reich, *Die Funktion des Orgasmus*, 168.

[21] Fromm, 'Sozialpsychologischer Teil', in *Studien über Autorität und Familie*, ed. by Max Horkheimer (Paris, 1936), 77–135 (125 and p).

[22] Gor'kii's intervention was made in *Pravda* and *Izvestiia* on 23 May 1934. According to Dan Healey, the phrase had 'an unmistakably genocidal resonance'. Healey, *Homosexual Desire in Revolutionary Russia: The Regulation of Sexual and Gender Dissent* (Chicago, 2000), 189 and 332. The remark was also cited in Wilhelm Reich, *The Sexual Revolution*, 210.

[23] Arno Plack, *Die Gesellschaft und das Böse. Eine Kritik der herrschenden Moral* (Munich, 1970 [1967]), 236.

[24] Ibid., 309. Also cited in Herzog, *Sex after Fascism*, 138–9.   [25] Plack, 224, 226.

[26] Ibid., 228, 234, 235.

The presence of anti-homosexual passages in texts popular in the student movement and the alternative left does not mean that readers uncritically adopted these positions. The point is, however, that the powerful allure of a free and non-repressed sexuality never constituted a 'free for all', but was explicitly heteronormative in nature. Perhaps the most iconic example of this preoccupation with free (hetero)sexuality was the *Kommune I*, where monogamy and toilet doors were out of the question.[27] Yet communards would routinely denounce all political targets—police, university management, judges, mayors—as 'gays' or 'homos'.[28] It seems perhaps rather charitable to characterize this as an attempt to ironize, provoke, and reflect anti-homosexual positions of elite figures.[29]

There was little positive coverage of homosexuality in leftist publications in the late 1960s. *Konkret*, which enjoyed the highest circulation of any leftist magazine, did call for the repeal of Paragraph 175 in 1967, but gave scant coverage to developments in homosexual politics after that.[30] When homosexuality was mentioned, this was occasionally in crudely homophobic guises, as in narrative extracts which suggested that homosexuals were not real men or had simply not yet met the right woman.[31] Student movement and leftist discourse on sexuality was not only heteronormative but also patriarchal (or 'phallocentric', to use the contemporary idiom). This was the context which saw the genesis of second-wave feminism—facilitated by student and youth protest but also arising in opposition to the masculinist hue of this movement. *Konkret* blazoned images of topless or semi-nude women across its front cover almost every single issue, leading to regular letters from irritated female readers.[32] An article on 'lesbian love' in 1972 began by complaining that there was a lack of scientific writing on lesbianism, as opposed to titillating pieces for the voyeuristic pleasure of men.[33] Unsurprisingly, the article went on to offer exactly that, under the guise of an 'authentic self-portrayal by female homosexuals', replete with images of a naked inter-racial couple kissing and fondling each other.[34]

Editors regularly defended their representation of women by appealing to the need for greater sales, so as to avoid taking further advertising or raising the retail price of the magazine. In 1971, editors stated that *Konkret* should be sold to the widest possible audience, and that the number of those who were interested in sex

---

[27] Herzog, *Sex after Fascism*, 161.

[28] Stefan Micheler, 'Heteronormativität, Homophobie und Sexualdenunziation in der deutschen Studierendenbewegung', *Invertito: Jahrbuch für die Geschichte der Homosexualitäten* 1 (1999), 70–101 (81).

[29] Aribert Reimann, *Dieter Kunzelmann: Avantgardist, Protestler, Radikaler* (Göttingen, 2009), 305; see also his 'Zwischen Machismo und Coolness. Männlichkeit und Emotion in der westdeutschen Kulturrevolution' der 1960er- und 1970er Jahren', in *Die Präsenz der Gefühle: Männlichkeit und Emotion in der Moderne*, ed. by Manuel Borutta and Nina Verheyen (Bielefeld, 2010), 229–54 (242).

[30] Gerald Kienast, 'Schwul: §175 in Deutschland', *konkret* 1 (1967), 20–6.

[31] 'Gilly verführt einen Schwulen', *konkret* 7 (1970), 42–5.

[32] *konkret* 15 (1971), 2; *konkret* 23 (1971), 2.   [33] 'Lesbische Liebe', *konkret* 2 (1972), 40–3.

[34] Ibid., 40.

was higher than those interested in issues such as the dictatorship in Greece or labour disputes.[35] Yet in a cynical move, the article was followed by a call for greater reader involvement, subscribers being asked to choose their favourite between six photos and six short texts: all the photos were of topless women and all the texts offered various degrees of titillation, the last option being the aforementioned homophobic story.[36] Female leftists increasingly came to the view that the liberation of sexuality that their male comrades had in mind was 'the liberation of *their* sexuality, *their* desires, *their* pleasure'.[37]

Some argued that sexual liberalization¹ had made matters even worse for women: according to Annette Dröge, prudery or fear of pregnancy had at least allowed women to refuse sex, whereas after the introduction of the pill and 'sexual enlightenment' they were required to be permanently sexually available.[38] Similarly, while the massive expansion in the dissemination of erotica and pornography and its subsequent legalization may have been celebrated by some activists as breaking the taboo on nudity, for others it led only 'to the free sale of the female body'.[39] Accordingly, Christina von Hodenberg underscores the heterosexual and male domination of the 'sexual revolution': a verdict implicating not just wider society, but also the student movement, dominated as it was by heterosexual men. Critiquing the undue historiographical focus on a small number of elite male student protestors, Hodenberg argues that what we now see as the essential legacy of the sexual revolution, namely the sexual emancipation of women and homosexuals, had in fact little to do with 1968.[40]

The West German women's liberation movement is often dated to the 23rd SDS conference, in September and November 1968.[41] In her plenary speech on 13 September, Helke Sander criticized the marginalization of women and of issues such as child-rearing, the absence of women in leadership positions within the SDS, and the macho atmosphere which prevailed at SDS meetings.[42] After her speech drew no comments from male delegates and Hans-Jürgen Krahl moved onto the next item on the agenda, Sigrid Rüger arose from the audience and threw tomatoes directly, and accurately, at Krahl.[43] Equally (in)famously, at the

---

[35] 'Wieviel Sex in Konkret?', *konkret* 2 (1971), 36–41 (37).   [36] Ibid., 36–41.

[37] Michaela Wunderle, 'Lust und Liebe: Die feministische Sexualitätsdebatte', in *Die Große Unterschied: Die Neue Frauenbewegung und die siebziger Jahre*, ed. by Kristine von Soden (Berlin, 1988), 20–3 (21). Emphasis in the original.

[38] Dröge, *Sexualität und Herrschaft* (Münster, 1976), 8.

[39] Ibid., 29. See also Herzog, *Sex after Fascism*, 234–40 and Heineman, *Before Porn Was Legal*.

[40] Hodenberg, *Das andere Achtundsechzig: Gesellschaftsgeschichte einer Revolte* (Munich, 2018), 184. See also von Hodenberg's 'Writing Women's Agency into the History of the Federal Republic: "1968", Historians, and Gender', *Central European History* 52 (2019), 87–106.

[41] As Kristina Schulz notes, while the events during the conference were the catalyst for the founding of more women's groups, the *Aktionsrat zur Befreiung der Frauen* (Action Committee for the Liberation of Women) had already been founded earlier in 1968. Schulz, *Der lange Atem*, 72.

[42] *CheSchahShit: Die sechziger Jahre zwischen Cocktail und Molotov* (Hamburg, 1993), 273–82.

[43] Schulz, *Der lange Atem*, 82–4.

continuation of the same SDS conference in November later that year, activists from the recently formed Frankfurt Hag Council (*Frankfurter Weiberrat*) distributed leaflets depicting the penises of student leaders, among them Krahl, Dieter Kunzelmann, Bernd Rabehl, and Reimut Reiche, castrated and mounted on plinths: entitled 'Liberate the socialist pricks from their bourgeois dicks!'[44] Playing on the canard of hysteria and penis-envy in the most visually drastic way, the leaflet denounced the invisibility of women in the movement, the bombast of men, and the 'socialist screw-pressure' and 'socialist groping' that women had to endure. It is ironic indeed that the direct target of Rüger's tomatoes was Hans-Jürgen Krahl, a same-sex desiring man.[45] Whether unwilling or unable to claim a gay identity, Krahl was simultaneously a participant in and victim of the macho and heteronormative environment of the student movement and the radical leftist scene.[46]

Krahl died in a car crash in 1970, at the age of 27, so we do not know how his perspectives on women's liberation might have evolved. Gay men, of course, were not immune to charges of sexism, as can be seen by the sometimes strained relationship between gay and lesbian activists in the 1970s. Even in 1978 and 1979, when campaigning for an anti-discrimination bill saw a measure of cooperation between gay and lesbian activists, this came at the explicit behest of an external partner, a liberal civil rights organization. The Humanist Union set out to draft a wide-ranging anti-discrimination bill, seeking to emulate the British Sex Discrimination Act of 1975, but also to improve on this milestone, by including sexual minorities.[47] They approached the General Homosexual Action Alliance (AHA), which submitted a draft section on sexual orientation that failed to include any reference to lesbians. In response, a Humanist Union representative conceded that the discrimination of male and female homosexuals might be different, but posited that there would be enough similarities to justify a common law: 'Surely it could only aid the concern of homosexuals were they to have the greater (quantitatively!) power of women on their side? United strong together for a united law?'[48]

The Homosexual Action West Berlin (HAW) is an instructive case in examining the diverging paths of gay and lesbian activism. The HAW had a women's section for almost three years. Cristina Perincioli, co-founder of the group, remembers experiencing 'open-minded, fraternal encouragement and care' from

---

[44] Ibid., 88. Leaflet printed in *CheSchahShit*, 283. Translation 'Frankfurt Hag Council' taken from Hodenberg, 'Writing Women's Agency', 93.

[45] Reimann, 'Zwischen Machismo und Coolness', 243.

[46] On Krahl, see also Micheler, 'Heteronormativität,' 79.

[47] Humanistische Union, 'Ein Anti-Diskriminierungs-Gesetz für die Bundesrepublik'. SMB archive, AHA Sammlung, box Juristengruppe/Antifa Gruppe. On the Humanist Union, see Lora Wildenthal, *The Language of Human Rights in West Germany* (Philadelphia, 2013), 89–99.

[48] Bodo Erdmann to Mira Böhm, undated; Heide Hering to Bodo Erdmann, 14 August 1979. Both in SMB archive, AHA Sammlung, box Juristengruppe/Antifa Gruppe.

the men. In 1972, lesbian members explained their co-operation with the gay men by stating that 'our problems are the same'.[49] Nevertheless, it seems to have been women left cleaning the corridor in the factory floor that the HAW used as their meeting place.[50] Ilse Kokula, lesbian activist-turned-historian, and fellow founder of the HAW, argues that gay men uncritically adopted leftist rituals and bombast, exactly what women's movement activists came up against in the wider alternative left and in the student movement. Gay men, being men, still had their stake in the 'phallocracy'.[51]

In early 1975, HAW lesbian activists formally split from the rest of the group, renaming themselves the Lesbian Action Centre (LAZ).[52] This also indicates a significant shift in vocabulary. Until this point, 'lesbian' had not yet supplanted other designations for female homosexuality. Lesbians in the HAW often referred to themselves not only as 'homosexual women' but often as 'gay women' (schwule Frauen). In a 1972 poster, schwul was contrasted favourably with alternative terminologies: homophile ('the posh version'), homoerotic ('wistful'), lesbian ('Sappho has been dead for ages'), and homosexual ('even professors know something about this').[53] Schwul, a vocabulary that has since come to exclusively refer to male homosexuality in German (more so than 'gay' in English), was a less stable category in the 1970s. Jens Dobler has speculated that the 1970s saw the culmination of efforts by male homosexuals to claim schwul entirely for themselves, since there was no other vocabulary available that referred specifically to same-sex desiring men (unlike Lesbe or Lesbierin for women).[54]

In the course of the decade, lesbians tended to organize much more closely with and in the women's movement that with gay men. Some lesbian groups were sections of larger women's organizations from the very start. For other activists, the experience of homosociality and same-sex affection within the women's movement facilitated their coming-out as lesbian.[55] According to Monica Pater, there even existed a unity between the 'Women's/Lesbian movement'. She identifies a 'collective identity' between lesbians and other women's movement activists that came to the fore in the protests surrounding the trial of Judy Andersen and Marion Ihns in 1973–1974.[56] Both women stood accused of organizing the

---

[49] Perincioli, Berlin wird feministisch: das Beste, was von der 68er Bewegung blieb (Berlin, 2015), 64; 'Bericht der Frauengruppe', HAW Info 1 (1972), 12–13 (12).

[50] Ina Kuckuc [pseudonym], Der Kampf gegen Unterdrückung: Materialien aus der deutschen Lesbierinnenbewegung (Munich, 1977 [1975]), 71.

[51] Ibid., 14.

[52] Dennert et al., In Bewegung bleiben, 47. See further Henze, Schwule Emanzipation, 321–35.

[53] HAW Frauengruppe, 'Sind Sie...?' poster. Spinnboden archive, HAW Frauengruppe Sammlung G Necker 1972–1974.

[54] Dobler, 'Schwule Lesben', in Rosa Radikale, ed. by Pretzel and Weiß, 113–23 (120).

[55] Linhoff, Weiblich Homosexualität, 125.

[56] Pater, '"Gegen geile Männerpresse – für lesbische Liebe". Der Andersen/Ihns-Prozess als Ausgangspunkt für das Coming-out von Lesben', Invertito: Jahrbuch der Homosexualitäten 8 (2006), 143–68 (144).

murder of Ihns' husband, who had repeatedly beaten and raped his wife. To accompany the trial, the tabloid *BILD* commissioned a series of sensationalist articles on Ihns and Andersen, under the title 'The Crimes of Lesbian Women' and including such pearls of wisdom as 'She became lesbian because she hated her mother's men' and 'When women love [each other], a grave crime often follows.'[57] On demonstrations and during actions within the courtroom itself, lesbian activists focused on the issue of 'lesbian love being on trial', with their protests aided and facilitated not by gay men but by other women's movement activists who took up the issues of domestic violence and rape.[58]

In attempting to discover a relationship to their bodies that was not governed by men, many feminists experimented practically or theoretically with same-sex love. This was at times understood less as a sexual behaviour than as the logical conclusion of a feminist understanding, symbolized by the apocryphal line attributed to Ti-Grace Atkinson: 'feminism is the theory, lesbianism the practice'.[59] While this move enabled some lesbians to understand themselves as belonging to an avant-garde within the women's movement, it also led to distinctions being made between 'movement' and 'traditional' lesbians, i.e. between 'political' or 'theoretical' and 'real' or 'authentic' lesbians.[60] This was a phenomenon almost completely absent in the relationship between gay men and their heterosexual male counterparts on the alternative left.[61]

Pseudo-Liberalization

Even as gay liberation, following women's liberation, was in part a response to the discourse on sexuality in the student movement, gay leftists' take on sexual *liberalization* was unmistakably indebted to the intellectual ferment of 1968. Male homosexual behaviour was no longer subject to the Nazi version of Paragraph 175. It was now possible to come together and openly organize as gays or lesbians and homosexuality could now even be discussed on primetime television. Yet all of this was generally seen by the gay left as symptomatic of a deeply suspicious tolerance. This was why Martin Dannecker, as seen in the previous chapter, could denounce SPD parliamentarian Ostman von der Leye, a

---

[57] Ibid., 151–9.

[58] Annette Dröge, 'Jetzt reicht's! Lesbische Frauen werden öffentlich', in *Die Große Unterschied: Die Neue Frauenbewegung und die Siebziger Jahre*, ed. by Kristine von Soden (Berlin, 1988), 53–6 (54). See also Perincioli, *Berlin wird feministisch*, 206–14.

[59] Linhoff, *Weibliche Homosexualität*, 35; Terence Kissack, 'Freaking Fag Revolutionaries: New York's Gay Liberation Front, 1969–1971', *Radical History Review* 62 (1995), 104–35 (121).

[60] Dennert et al., *In Bewegung bleiben*, 50; Linhoff, *Weibliche Homosexualität*, 43.

[61] Rolf Schwendter would state in 1980 that there did exist 'movement gays', albeit not to the same extent as 'movement lesbians'. Schwendter, 'Nachwort, sieben Jahre später', in his *Theorie der Subkultur* (Frankfurt a.M., 1981 [1973]), 410.

key supporter of homosexual law reform, as an 'agent of the system'. It also explains activists' frequent usage of the prefix *Schein-*, meaning 'seeming', illusory, or 'pseudo-'. Homosexual law reform had been nothing more than a pseudo-reform, the Federal Republic was a pseudo-democracy, any space afforded to homosexuals was but pseudo-freedom, and any togetherness among homosexuals in the current socio-economic system did not go beyond mere pseudo-solidarity.[62] Meanwhile, any campaigning or activism that was too moderate, too insulated from wider social struggles, was pseudo-political, *scheinpolitisch*. The 'tolerance' offered by contemporary society was but *Scheintoleranz*, pseudo-tolerance, which offered no guarantees whatsoever: a point proven, according to one activist from Frankfurt, by the experience of the Weimar Republic.[63]

We can trace this intellectual legacy back to the 1960s new left, even if writers and activists in that decade rarely had homosexuality in mind. As early as 1963, Theodor Adorno identified the current trend towards sexual liberalization as illusory (*Schein*).[64] Discontent with the 'sexual revolution' was present from the earliest days of the new left, and only intensified as the public sphere became ever more saturated with nude, erotic, and pornographic images and as it became increasingly *de rigueur* to ignore conservative sexual norms or challenge the status of marriage and of the family.[65] In the words of anti-authoritarian child-rearing activists, 'even if screwing happens ten times as much as before, that would not amount to an actual liberation of sexuality'.[66] In his *One-Dimensional Man*, published in 1964, Herbert Marcuse argued that 'under the rule of a repressive whole, liberty can be made into a powerful instrument of domination'. Sexuality was being liberalized, but only in 'socially constructive forms'.[67]

His term for this process was 'repressive desublimation'—essentially the liberalization of that which was either unthreatening for the hegemonic order, or of that which would lead to greater submission to that order.[68] In his earlier *Eros and Civilisation*, Marcuse had set out his alternative for the future of sexuality. Rather than being de-sublimated in order to prop up the existing order, rather than being subordinated to the 'performance principle' and the need for 'non-gratifying labour', sexuality could instead be transformed into Eros, which would challenge the basis of the performance principle. Instead of

---

[62] 'OVG auf Schwulenhatz', *Rosa* 4 (1976), 32–6 (35); unnamed male homosexual, 1973 TV discussion following broadcast of *Not the Homosexual*; *Kampf der Schwulenunterdrückung!* (1977: Kommunisticher Bund), 1. SMB archive; HAW 'vorläufige Grundsatzerklärung' (November 1971). Printed as attachment to *HAW Info* 1 (1972).

[63] 'H', activist from *Rotzschwul*. As stated during an episode of the popular youth programme *Sparring*, 24 April 1976. *Sparring: Homosexualität—noch ein Tabu?*, ZDF. ZDF Archive, 06321/01373.

[64] Theodor Adorno, 'Sexualtabus und Recht heute', in *Sexualität und Verbrechen*, ed. by Bauer et al., 299–317 (300).

[65] See especially Herzog, *Sex after Fascism*, 141–83 and Heineman, *Before Porn Was Legal*, 101–28.

[66] 'Eine Bemerkung zur sogenannten Sexwelle', *Berliner Kinderläden: Antiautoritäre Erziehung und sozialistischer Kampf* (Berlin, 1970), 107–12 (108).

[67] Marcuse, *One-Dimensional Man*, 9 and 75.   [68] Ibid., 59–86.

being an instrument of work, the body would become an instrument of pleasure, which would in turn lead to the disintegration of institutions including the 'monogamic and patriarchal family'.[69]

Reimut Reiche, leader of the SDS in 1967–1968, was one of those unfortunate enough to have been symbolically castrated by women's movement activists in 1968. He was also the leading theorist amongst student movement activists of the relationship between sexuality and social change. His popular book *Sexuality and Class Struggle*, first published in 1968, owed an unmistakable intellectual debt to Marcuse, and is just one example of the ways in which the work of older Frankfurt School scholars was further disseminated within the new left.[70] Critiquing Wilhelm Reich, Reiche followed Adorno and Marcuse in stating that one must distinguish between an 'increased scope for sexual liberty' and 'real sexual freedom.'[71] In Wilhelm Reich's day, there had been a clearer link between the suppression of sexual impulses and economic conditions, for example due to housing shortages and the expense of contraception.[72] Exploitation was now a more advanced process, but the link continued. The reduction of sexuality to a commodity and an object of consumption were symptoms of a 'sexual manipulation', one way in which economic exploitation manifested itself. By incorporating the sexual into labour and into advertising, the current system allowed for controlled gratification and robbed the pleasure principle of any oppositional qualities, thus not only supporting the existing order, but leading to increased neurosis and aggression.[73] This informed Reiche's criticism of the communard Dieter Kunzelmann's infamous (and possibly apocryphal) statement, 'what do I care about the war in Vietnam when I'm having orgasm difficulties?' According to Reiche, the building of a movement against the war in Vietnam and tackling orgasm problems did in fact have a common prerequisite, namely the struggle against neurosis and repressive desublimation.[74]

Reiche's is only the most theoretically elaborate example of leftists' fundamental distrust of the 'sexual revolution' that they themselves were very much part of. Unlike those who ostensibly supported sexual freedom but were dubious about the merits of homosexuality, the likes of Reiche and Marcuse offered more direct appeal to gay activists. While Reiche quoted the aforementioned dubious passage from Erich Fromm at length, and wondered whether homosexuality would occur in a free (post-revolutionary) society, this was in the context of arguing that *both* homosexuality and heterosexuality were culturally acquired, whereas humans

---

[69] Marcuse, *Eros and Civilisation: A Philosophical Inquiry into Freud* (London, 1969 [1955]), 199–202.

[70] Krahl, for example, had been the PhD student of Theodor Adorno. See further Günter C Behrmann, 'Kulturrevolution: Zwei Monate im Sommer 1967', in *Die intellektuelle Gründung der Bundesrepublik: Eine Wirkungsgeschichte der Frankfurter Schule*, ed. by Clemens Albrecht et al. (Frankfurt a.M., 2000), 312–85.

[71] Reiche, *Sexualität und Klassenkampf*, 11.   [72] Ibid., 11.   [73] Ibid., 19 and 45.

[74] Ibid., 161.

were constitutionally bisexual in nature.[75] As we have seen, Reiche collaborated with gay activist Martin Dannecker on the sociological study *The Ordinary Homosexual*, published in 1974. Featured in *Der Spiegel* even before its publication, Reiche (himself heterosexual) would join Dannecker in urging gay men to come out and challenge their own conformism, thereby challenging society's 'veil of sanctimonious [*scheinheilig*] tolerance'.[76]

Marcuse, meanwhile, had heralded the transformative capacity of the 'substratum of the outcasts and the outsiders', having in mind the student and civil rights movements in the United States.[77] It did not take much imagination, of course, for gays to place themselves in this category. In a few cases, an adherence to the Frankfurt School and Marcuse was explicitly cited, as by the Red Gay Caucus (*Rote Schwule Fraktion*) in Oberhausen.[78] More generally, Marcuse and others offered a theoretical framework that leftists could use to justify their abandonment of the working class as the sole revolutionary subject. The HAW was at pains to point out in its statement of founding principles, in 1971, that the practice of homosexuality itself constituted a breach of the bourgeois restrictions on sexual behaviour and sexual norms.[79] Homosexual and paederast activist Peter Schult, meanwhile, argued that while homosexuality in itself was not revolutionary, the homosexual who learnt from his oppression and called the existence of the contemporary social order into question ceased to be merely a gay man, but would belong to the camp of the oppressed.[80] This kind of understanding offered gay men a potential cachet as righteous victims of an oppressive order, as will be seen in the next chapter. It also bequeathed gay leftists a somewhat avant-garde role within the wider homosexual population, making them responsible for lifting their fellow queers from the depths of their false consciousness.

Indeed, it is their deep suspicion of 'pseudo-liberalization', their axiomatic distrust of the very possibility of reform in liberal democracy, which most clearly marks gay leftists as members of the wider alternative left, and which signals their difference from other traditions of homosexual organizing. Occasionally, language in the vein of 'pseudo-tolerance' was to be found in the commercial gay press or amongst homophile activists.[81] In one of the last issues of the homophile journal *Der Weg*, Harry Stein welcomed what he (incorrectly) described as the complete repeal of Paragraph 175, but defined 'our new-found freedom' as only 'half a freedom' and raised the spectre of this even degenerating into 'pseudo-freedom'.[82] But not all gay men adopted this perspective. Having waited so long for decriminalization, homophile activists were generally unwilling to write off homosexual

---

[75] Ibid., 115–17.   [76] 'Nur als Kranke toleriert', *Der Spiegel* 11 (1973), 50.
[77] Marcuse, *One-Dimensional Man*, 260.   [78] *du&ich* 5 (1977), 29.
[79] HAW 'vorläufige Grundsatzerklärung'.
[80] Peter Schult, 'Für eine sexuelle Revolution! Wider die linken Spießer', *Autonomie* 5 (1977), 86–96 (92).
[81] *du&ich* 11 (1975), 6–7.   [82] Stein, 'Ein politisches Wort', *Der Weg* 221 (1969), 145.

law reform as being merely a fig-leaf, not least because some saw it in part as their own achievement. Being older than a younger generation of gay activists, they were more likely to have experienced the smaller and less diverse gay scene in the 1950s and 1960s, along with its higher levels of surveillance and discrimination, and could thus appreciate the changes that had come about, as opposed to seeing only the danger of the manipulation of sexual needs and repressive desublimation. From the 789 homosexuals surveyed in *The Ordinary Homosexual*, only 3 per cent of 18–20 year-olds had come into conflict with the law. For 21–25 year-olds this was 15 per cent, and for the 26–30 age group 12 per cent. But fully 39 per cent of those aged between 41 and 50 had experienced police harassment, or arrest, or prosecution, or imprisonment. For those older than 50, this was more than half, at 59 per cent.[83]

Here, questions of generation and of ideology are intertwined. To be sure, not every member of the gay left or every individual suspicious of liberalization was young. A case in point was that of the Frankfurt School scholars themselves. However, the age of activists was important, both in terms of whether they had the experiential vantage point of the 1950s and 1960s from which to judge the changed context of the 1970s, and whether they were part of a predominantly university-based leftist milieu where the reading and reception of the likes of Adorno and Marcuse, and of younger theorists such as Reiche, was commonplace. For this leftist scene, gay leftists included, every mark of liberalization, every sign of progress, was almost instinctively called into question or rejected altogether. Liberalization or reform within current West German society was met with a scepticism simply anathema to many older homophiles.

Johannes Werres, for one, was not impressed, writing in 1978 that leftist homosexuals 'see only oppression and exploitation, only bans on careers, only terror and unhappiness. [...] I don't know what these people live from, or what sort of world they live in; not in mine and yours in any case. We accept this society and want to live in it.'[84] He was not alone in this verdict. Carlo R., from Hamburg, wrote to *du&ich* editors in 1970 to praise what he perceived as the gay magazine's new-found more professional and less political style. Hectographed leaflets would get homosexuals nowhere, which could be seen by the fate of the extra-parliamentary opposition (APO), which was unable to engage with the wider populace. To be accepted by society, homosexuals needed a mass basis: 'After all, we want to leave the ghetto behind, we don't want to be the APO of sexuality.'[85]

---

[83] Dannecker and Reiche, *Der gewöhnliche Homosexuelle*, 368. The figure for 31–5 year-olds was 19% and for those aged between 36 and 40 17%. Older homosexuals were statistically underrepresented in the survey.
[84] 'Wir sind nicht mehr unter uns'!', *unter uns* 13 (1978), 8–10 (8).   [85] *du&ich* 10 (1970), 10.

The Alternative Left in the 1970s

The APO and the student movement had disintegrated by 1970, but that was by no means the end of the story regarding left-wing protest. In September 1969, following the federal election, Willy Brandt became Chancellor, the first time a social democrat had held the post since the Weimar Republic. With his promise to 'dare more democracy', Brandt won over some student activists; others entered the SPD and its youth wing in a tactical move, embracing student leader Rudi Dutschke's dictum to 'march through the institutions', in the process launching thousands of teaching, legal and other civil service careers.[86] Other activists, whether searching for reorientation following 1968, or fresh on the scene in the 1970s, threw themselves into building social movements, including the women's, gay, lesbian, peace, and anti-nuclear movements; some organized in so-called *Sponti* or 'spontaneous' groups such as the *Revolutionärer Kampf* (RK: Revolutionary Struggle); others turned to Marxist-Leninist or Maoist cadre parties known as the *K-Gruppen*, which focused on mobilizing workers; still others organized in larger umbrella organizations such as the *Sozialistisches Büro* (SB: Socialist Bureau), or in student organizations such as the *Sozialistischer Hochschulbund* (Socialist University League) or the MSB (Marxist Student League). Not a few eschewed formal political allegiances, forming grassroots countercultural tendencies such as *Gammler* or hippies and the *Haschrebellen* (Hash Rebels). A minority, meanwhile, turned to violent protest and terrorism.[87]

This broad spectrum, which I call the alternative left, was the successor to the 1960s new left. General characteristics of this new left include: a rejection of Cold War logic, and thus a rejection of *both* the capitalist system *and* Soviet communism; the marrying of Marx and Freud; a departure from viewing the working-class as the only revolutionary subject; a focus on personal subjectivity; a loose adherence to pursuing change in the here and now, including new forms of lifestyle and communication; and a visceral antipathy to the established Left, especially the SPD and the German Trade Unions' Federation.[88] The new left can also be characterized by its variety of action forms, which ranged from the more traditional—demonstrations, panel events, petitions—to more innovative forms of direct action, whether civil disobedience, sit-ins, 'happenings', or occupations.[89]

---

[86] In the case of media careers, Christina von Hodenberg has shown that this quest to 'transform and overcome the capitalist system from within' had limited success, either because revolutionaries morphed into reformers, or because all along they had had more of a 'pleasant walk' rather than an aggressive 'march' in mind. 'Mass Media and the Generation of Conflict', 395.

[87] Häberlen, *The Emotional Politics of the Alternative Left*, 7–14. See also the multitude of accounts in Roland Roth and Dieter Rucht (eds), *Die sozialen Bewegungen in Deutschland seit 1945: Ein Handbuch* (Frankfurt a.M., 2008). On political violence, see Alexander Sedlmaier, *Consumption and Violence: Radical Protest in Cold-War West Germany* (Ann Arbor, 2014) and Terhoeven, *Deutscher Herbst in Europa*.

[88] Ingrid Gilcher-Holtey (ed.), *1968: Vom Ereignis zum Gegenstand der Geschichtswissenschaft* (Göttingen, 1998), 15–17; Markovits and Gorski, *The German Left*, 1–104.

[89] Horn, *The Spirit of '68*, 152–5.

To be sure, not everything about the new left was 'new', nor was everything about the alternative left 'alternative'. For example, the *K-Gruppen* have generally been classified as 'dogmatic' in contrast to the 'undogmatic' and more 'anti-authoritarian' *Spontis*.[90] The fact that these cadre parties, bearing abbreviations such as the KPD-(AO), KPD/ML, KB, KBW, and GIM, returned to the proletariat as the only acceptable revolutionary subject and turned their backs on personal subjectivity can be taken as evidence of 'old' rather than 'new' left: it certainly does not sound very 'alternative'.[91] When Marxist-Leninist members of the Homosexual Action Bremen wrote to the Communist League of West Germany (KBW) in 1974, a spokesman replied that in the KBW's view homosexuality might not occur in a post-revolutionary society, and that homosexual action groups were reformist in nature and as such counter-revolutionary.[92] The German Communist Party (DKP), founded in 1969, sought to emulate the model of the Communist Party of Germany (KPD), which had been banned in 1956.[93] Accordingly, the DKP and its chapter in West Berlin, the SEW (Socialist Unity Party West Berlin), not only followed the line of the East German State but was directly funded by the GDR, a political allegiance uncharacteristic of the alternative left as a whole.[94]

Yet while older members of the illegal KPD took on most of the leadership roles in the newly constituted DKP, its ranks were filled by much younger activists influenced by the student movement and other parts of the alternative left.[95] Additionally, the explicit inclusion of the *K-Gruppen* in this alternative left is intended here as a corrective to the notion that the only 'true' spirit of post-1968 protest movements was utopian or anti-authoritarian. In fact, the compulsion to follow particular political lines and concomitant rampant sectarianism was common across much of the alternative left. It was not restricted to what Geoff Eley calls 'the absurdly proliferating mosaic of mainly Maoist groups', whose 'sectarian militancy' he describes as 'little more than a noisy side-show', in contrast to the larger and presumably less parochial 'alternative scene'.[96] Just because from a

---

[90] See for example Michael März, *Linker Protest nach dem Deutschen Herbst: Eine Geschichte des linken Spektrums im Schatten des 'Starken Staates', 1977–1979* (Bielefeld, 2012), 49–54.

[91] On the *K-Gruppen*, see Koenen, *Das rote Jahrzehnt* and Andreas Kühn, *Stalins Enkel, Maos Söhne: die Lebenswelt der K-Gruppen in der Bundesrepublik der 70er Jahre* (Frankfurt a.M., 2005). The KPD-AO (Communist Party of Germany—Buildup Organisation) was founded in 1970 and removed the 'AO' from its name in 1971. The KPD/ML (Communist Party of Germany: Marxist-Leninists) was founded in 1968, the KB (Communist League) in 1971, the KBW (Communist League of West Germany) in 1973 and the GIM (Group of International Marxists) in 1969.

[92] 'Dokumentation: Schriftwechsel zwischen Kommunistischer Bund Westdeutschland und Homosexuelle Aktion Bremen' (March 1974), 3 and 11. SMB archive.

[93] Confusingly, the KPD(-AO) was not the de facto successor party to the banned KPD; this was instead the DKP. Koenen, *Das rote Jahrzehnt*, 262.

[94] Ibid., 269.   [95] Ibid., 268.

[96] Klaus Hartung, 'Versuch, die Krise der antiautoritären Bewegung wieder zur Sprache zu bringen', *Kursbuch* 48 (1977), 14–44 (15); Eley, *Forging Democracy*, 458.

contemporary perspective it may be more difficult to identify with what Andreas Kühn has described as the 'totalitarian, inhumane ideology' of the *K-Gruppen* does not mean that these manifestations should be written out of history.[97] The gay activists from Bremen who wrote to the KBW in 1974 expressly defined themselves as Marxist-Leninists and a significant faction in the Homosexual Action West Berlin were members of the SEW. There was an active caucus of gay members in the Communist League (KB), who compiled various articles concerning homosexuality for the KB's newspaper, *Arbeiterkampf* (Workers' Struggle).[98] This caucus was one of four West German groups to represent the country when the International Gay Association (IGA) was formed in Coventry, in 1978.[99] We therefore need a broad understanding of 'alternative left', not least to underscore the ideological diversity of the gay left.[100]

Demarcations between this and that wing of the alternative left are fraught with difficulty. What may be gained in analytic clarity is counteracted by the impos- ition of essentially arbitrary distinctions between that which did in fact exhibit much in common. Massimo Perinelli, for example, distinguishes between 'Marxist-Leninists' and 'militants' (where do the militant Marxist-Leninists belong, one wonders?) and then confuses matters further by referring to distinct 'anti-authoritarian and the radically militant wings of the New Left'. Andrei Markovits and Philip Gorski, meanwhile, sum up the period 1969–1977 under the bracket of 'Marxist/revolutionary cadre politics and terrorism' and distinguish this both from an earlier phase of the new left and an overlapping period (dating from 1975) of 'New Social Movements'.[101] This runs the risk of giving rise to the impression that until 1977, or at any rate until 1975, most new leftists were either engaged in cadre politics or terrorism, which was far from the case, with mem- bership of *K-Gruppen* or terrorist organizations never reaching great heights. The KBW, the only communist organization other than the DKP to have a presence across West Germany, had a peak membership of approximately 2600. The DKP is somewhat of an exception, reaching a membership of 34,000 by 1972. Still, this

---

[97] Kühn, *Stalins Enkel*, 294. Andrew Tompkins also argues that the *K-Gruppen* have been subject to a dismissive attitude from historians (focusing, in his case, on the anti-nuclear movement). Tompkins, *Better Active than Radioactive! Anti-Nuclear Protest in 1970s France and West Germany* (Oxford, 2016), 22, 52–6.

[98] Hedenström (ed.), *Schwule sich emanzipieren lernen*, 66; *Arbeiterkampf: Kampf der Schwulenunterdrückung!* (n.d.) and AG Schwule im KB, *Schwule Rechte jetzt!* (1979). Both SMB archive.

[99] Now ILGA, the International Lesbian and Gay Association. The other West German groups to have joined by 1979 were the AHA, the AHB (Homosexual Action Group Bonn) and NARGS (National Working Group Repression against Gays). *Emanzipation* 4 (1979), 14–16.

[100] My understanding of 'alternative left' is informed by Michael März's conceptualization of the 'leftist spectrum', seeking to capture the diversity of all that was 'left' in 1970s West Germany. März, *Linker Protest nach dem Deutschen Herbst*, 49.

[101] Perinelli, 'Longing, Lust, Violence, Liberation: Discourses on Sexuality on the Radical Left in West Germany, 1969–1972', in *After the History of Sexuality*, ed. by Spector, Puff, and Herzog, 248–81 (272, 274); Markovits and Gorski, *The German Left*, 31.

was dwarfed by the membership of the parties represented in the *Bundestag*: in 1972, the FDP had 58,000 members, the CDU/CSU 530,000 and the SPD 954,000.[102]

The alternative left had no membership directory or list of demands. It was not an organization, nor even a network of organizations, but instead a variegated, amorphous political space. Accordingly, left-alternative *aims* were diverse, nebulous and at times mutually contradictory. Yet what the alternative left *opposed* was rather more straightforward. The alternative left can be considered a 'negative alliance', in which the rejection of shared opponents loosely held together individuals, groups and networks that could often agree on precious little else.[103] Boiled down to their essentials, these shared opponents were: the state, certainly including the centre-left federal government; the capitalist system; and the concept of progress, for genuine 'liberalization' was understood as impossible in the current social order.[104] Therefore, manifold ideological differences notwithstanding, 'alternative' captures the common search for 'concrete [...] and autonomous forms of existence', beyond the state and society which alternative leftists experienced as fundamentally alienating.[105]

Concepts of authenticity and autonomy were important here, but this was no individualists' paradise.[106] Central to the alternative left was the multi-directional nature of its participants' allegiances. Few activists contained themselves to one specific movement or issue, least of all gay leftists, who under the aegis of *Doppelmitgliedschaft*, double or twin-track membership, often organized in a socialist group alongside the particular gay group they were involved with.[107] As activists from Munich explained, 'it is only through the social emancipation of all groups that the social-sexual emancipation of homosexuals is possible'.[108] When the Homosexual Action Hamburg decided to campaign in the 1978 state elections—in a departure from the gay left's previous antipathy to the parliamentary sphere—they did not stand a candidate independently, but as part of the *Bunte Liste* ('multicoloured list', a precursor to the Greens), alongside environmental, feminist and migrant-rights groups. According to members, this 'unity of action' was necessary, because 'alongside the struggle against anti-gay prejudice'

---

[102]   Koenen, *Das rote Jahrzehnt*, 422 and 270; Oskar Niedermayer, 'Mitgliederentwicklung der Parteien bis 1989', <http://www.bpb.de/politik/grundfragen/parteien-in-deutschland/168030/mitgliederentwicklung-der-parteien-bis-1989> [accessed 8 December 2016].

[103]   I take 'negative alliance' from Markovits and Gorski, *The German Left*, 47.

[104]   Doering-Manteuffel and Raphael, *Nach dem Boom*, 51.

[105]   Reichardt and Siegfried, *Das alternative Milieu*, 22. See further Häberlen, *The Emotional Politics of the Alternative Left*.

[106]   Reichardt and Siegfried, *Das alternative Milieu*, 22.

[107]   'Doppelmitgliedschaft' (29 October 1972). Printed as appendix to Pareik, 'Kampf um eine Identität', 289–91.

[108]   From an article in a student magazine, December 1971. Cited in Gustl Angstmann, 'Dokumentarische Information der Schwulenbewegung in München 1971–1975, HAG, HAM und Teestube', 2. SMB archive, folder München–Schwulenbewegung–HAG/HAM.

gays had other interests, which 'arise first and foremost from our roles as worker, employee, pupil, student, tenant and so on'.[109] Almost no-one was committed to a model of absolute autonomy, but instead adopted various forms of what Nikos Papadogiannis has termed 'dual militancy'.[110] Oppression was understood as multi-directional and interrelated, as was liberation from that oppression—this, more than anything else, held the alternative left together.

The Gay Left, between Public and Counterpublic

'Mach dein Schwulsein öffentlich!', 'make your gayness public!' was a central tenet of the gay left. The perspective of Horst, from the Homosexual Action Munich, was symptomatic in this regard: 'Being gay, after all, does not mean being gay hidden somewhere or other in dark corners. Instead, it must be brought to the public, else it's just a half-measure.'[111] As Josie McLellan has shown with reference to East German homosexuals, *Öffentlichkeit* comes up again and again in their personal accounts. The term is usually translated as 'the public sphere', but can also mean 'in public', 'publicity', or 'the general public'. Michael Warner, meanwhile, suggests 'publicness' or 'openness'.[112] In West Germany, many gay groups had specific working groups that focused on *Öffentlichkeitsarbeit* ('public work' or 'public relations'). When the GSR group was banned from holding an information stall in Aachen, this was described as an *Öffentlichkeitsverbot*: in an English-language press release, this was translated as being 'barred from the public'.[113] The Homosexual Action Hamburg rationalized its participation in the 1978 state elections by arguing that the campaign would create new partners on the Left through dialogue in the communal list (*ein Stück Gegenöffentlichkeit*, an 'exemplar of counterpublic'), whilst also helping the gay movement enter the wider public sphere (*in die breite Öffentlichkeit gehen*).[114]

Gay leftists' preoccupation with *Öffentlichkeit* and *Gegenöffentlichkeit*, public and counterpublic, is a hallmark of their status within the alternative left, and an example of a direct influence hailing from '1968'. In 1967, the SDS passed a resolution calling for the creation of an 'enlightening counterpublic' (*aufklärende Gegenöffentlichkeit*), to break 'the dictatorship of the manipulators'.

---

[109] HAH, *Schwulen-info* 1 (April 1978). Not paginated. SMB archive, folder Hamburg: HAH—gay lib center—IHWO.

[110] He uses the term in reference to female communist party members who also agitated in feminist groups outside of the party. Papadogiannis, *Militant Around the Clock?: Left-wing Youth Politics, Leisure, and Sexuality in Post-dictatorship Greece, 1974–1981* (New York, 2015), 17.

[111] 'Eine Selbstdarstellung der HAM', *Schwuchtel* 2/3 (1976), 15–16 (15).

[112] McLellan, *Love in the Time of Communism: Intimacy and Sexuality in the GDR* (Cambridge, 2011), 119; Warner, *Publics and Counterpublics* (New York, 2002), 47.

[113] NARGS, 'A Case of Anti-Gay Discrimination was dealt with after all by the Russell Tribunal'. SMB archive, NARGS Box 1, Folder 1979/1.

[114] Untitled letter, March 1978. SMB archive, folder Hamburg–Schwulenbewegung–HAH.

This was seen as necessary to challenge the monopoly on information held by the capitalist mass media, especially Axel Springer and his BILD tabloid, described as a 'terroristic opinion machine'.[115] A year later, after the attempted assassination of Rudi Dutschke, the SDS executive launched its 'expropriate Springer!' campaign. Blaming the Springer press for launching a campaign of hate against the student movement and Dutschke in particular, the SDS argued that the democratic public sphere had been destroyed. The means of communication were in the service of manipulation. Every social class was thus systematically held in their 'false consciousness'.[116]

The left-alternative understanding of manipulation and false consciousness was most clearly indebted to Herbert Marcuse. For Marcuse, control and domination in capitalist societies takes place via 'the manipulation of needs by vested interests'. Since 'false needs' are fulfilled in these societies, there is no possibility of a 'consciousness of servitude' arising.[117] Individuals are easy targets for media indoctrination, since they are already 'preconditioned receptacles'. Their psychic processes are 'one-dimensional', preventing the formation of any critical opposition to the status quo. To strike at the 'material heart of domination', then, is to challenge advertising and media. The non-functioning of this complex 'might thus begin to achieve what the inherent contradictions of capitalism did not achieve – the disintegration of the system'.[118]

To be sure, concern about the state of the West German public sphere was not limited to student activists. An older generation of liberals and leftists, the '45ers', had long since articulated this disquiet, the most famous product of which was Jürgen Habermas' *The Structural Transformation of the Public Sphere*, published in 1962. But while Habermas and others set out to 'rescue' the liberal public sphere, the dominant understanding of new leftists was that the public sphere had been so compromised by manipulation that it could not be salvaged.[119] Instead, false consciousness could only be overcome through the construction of new publics: to this end, the mid-1960s onwards saw an extraordinary proliferation of independently-produced magazines, newsletters, leaflets, and posters as well as the constitution of publishing, artistic, film, and theatre collectives.

This trend intensified throughout the 1970s, a phenomenon most often historicized under the term 'alternative' or 'left-alternative milieu'. According to Sven

[115] 'SDS schreibt an BILD', undated. Printed in Astrid Czubayko, *Die Sprache von Studenten- und Alternativbewegung* (Aachen, 1997), appendix 24. On the anti-Springer campaign, see further Sedlmaier, *Consumption and Violence*, 168–204.

[116] 'Grundsatzerklärung des SDS zur Kampagne für die Enteignung des Springer-Konzerns' (14 April 1968). Printed in Czubayko, *Die Sprache*, appendix 26.

[117] Marcuse, *One-Dimensional Man*, 5 and 9.   [118] Ibid., 10, 14, 250.

[119] Christina von Hodenberg, 'Konkurrierende Konzepte von "Öffentlichkeit" in der Orientierungskrise der 60er Jahre', in *Demokratisierung und gesellschaftlicher Aufbruch: Die sechziger Jahre als Wendezeit der Bundesrepublik*, ed. by Matthias Frese et al. (Paderborn, 2003), 205–26 (205 and 222).

Reichardt and Detlef Siegfried, by 1980 as many as 80,000 activists were involved with some 11,500 alternative projects.[120] This infrastructure included pubs, cafés, bookshops, car repair workshops, second-hand shops, grocery stores, printers, publishing houses, and shared flats. At the time, especially during the 'German Autumn' in 1977, amidst concern over the extent of support for left-wing terrorism, this manifestation was sometimes called a 'second culture'. According to Peter Glotz, a SPD state senator in West Berlin, left-wing activists—unlike in 1968—had little hope that any change could be achieved in existing society. Instead, 'we have today two completely different communication systems, [...] two cultures'.[121]

According to contemporary leftist theorist Rolf Schwendter, 'progressive subculture' was the better term. Klaus Hartung, writing in the leftist journal *Kursbuch*, opted for 'leftist ghetto'.[122] Whatever term we use, this network was described and given shape in the pages of the leftist press. The Frankfurt-based fortnightly magazine *Pflasterstrand* was billed as an attempt to forge a public, to lift the isolation of activists, to embed alternative projects in a public structure.[123] The *Informationsdienst* (ID: Information Service) sought to disseminate information and news that would otherwise go unreported by the 'bourgeois media', and understood itself as a 'building block towards a socialist news service'. Rather than news from mainstream or party politics, ID collected and disseminated information from the grassroots—'in factories, citizens' initiatives, youth centres, leftist groups, pubs, on the street'.[124]

If the student movement had already been concerned with bringing injustice to light, with putting forward a different interpretation of what 'public' should mean, this was all the more important for the women's movement. This is semantically more evident in the German case, because the ubiquitous slogan translated above as 'the personal is political'—in keeping with its transnational use—actually reads '*Das Private ist politisch*', the *private* is political. For the women's movement, this slogan meant that issues such as inequalities in income, child-rearing and housework were by no means manifestations restricted to the private sphere, but injustices that were collectively experienced, and which required public discussion and a collective solution. To politicize these matters, and to offer a platform for women's voices, feminists established a network of bookshops, journals, publishers, theatre collectives, meeting places, women's centres, and rape crisis

---

[120] Reichardt and Siegfried, *Das alternative Milieu*, 11.
[121] Glotz, 'Jeder fünfte denkt etwa so wie Mescalero', *Der Spiegel* 41 (1977), 49–63 (57).
[122] Schwendter, *Theorie der Subkultur* (Frankfurt a.M., 1981 [1973]); Hartung, 'Über die langandauernde Jugend im linken Getto. Lebensalter und Politik – Aus der Sicht eines 38jährigen', *Kursbuch* 54 (1978), 174–88 (180).
[123] 'Wir wollen eine 14-Tägige Zeitung machen', *Pflasterstrand* 0 (1976), 2.
[124] *Informationsdienst zur Verbreitung unterbliebener Nachrichten* 1 (1973), 11.

centres: for Nancy Fraser a 'feminist subaltern counterpublic' and for Dagmar Herzog a 'female-centred public countersphere'.[125]

The gay left did the same, following in the footsteps both of the women's movement and the wider left-alternative scene. The movement's first national journals were founded in 1975, *Emanzipation* and *Schwuchtel*. In the same year, Peter Hedenström and Volker Bruns, two activists from the HAW, founded the *Rosa Winkel Verlag* (Pink Triangle Press).[126] In 1978, the gay bookshop *Prinz Eisenherz* opened in West Berlin. The movement's first theatre collective, *Brühwarm*, staged its inaugural play in 1976.[127] Several gay groups established telephone helplines, a forerunner of 'self-help' groups that proliferated after the onset of HIV/AIDS.[128] Groups in Dortmund, Frankfurt, Munich, and elsewhere opened their own centres or cafés in order to reach a wider public than solely gay activists: tellingly, these were often called 'communication centres'.[129] In 1977, activists from the HAW set up their gay centre, *Schwuz* (to replace the group, which was dissolved). Schwuz was defined as 'part of the gay subculture', but distinguished from gay bars in that it was not profit-oriented. According to activists, *Schwuz* was 'a place where gays can meet: to speak to each other, to work together, to experience tenderness, to organise actions, to find understanding and sex, to hear what others think, to not be alone'.[130]

Gay leftists, like other homosexuals, were members of the wider public sphere in West Germany, alongside everyone else living in the Federal Republic. They sought to gain enough publicity to be in with a chance of influencing public opinion, in order to challenge popular public (mis)conceptions about homosexuality, sometimes to seek to change policy. At the same time, as gay men, they were part of a 'gay public'. They would address other members of this gay public, not least because this was the most likely pool of 'recruits' for the movement. But they actually spent more of their time during the 1970s addressing another arena: the left-alternative public. These overlapping publics placed gay leftists in a particularly ambivalent position. Not all homosexuals saw the need to engage on the alternative left. The International Homophile World Organization (IHWO), for example, rejected a proposed poster design for a collaborative action against

---

[125] Fraser, 'Rethinking the Public Sphere: A Contribution to the Critique of Actually Existing Democracy', in *Habermas and the Public Sphere*, ed. by Craig Calhoun (Cambridge, MA, 1992), 109–42 (123); Herzog, *Sex after Fascism*, 226. See further Ilse Lenz, 'Das Private ist politisch!? Zum Verhältnis von Frauenbewegung und alternativem Milieu', in *Das alternative Milieu*, ed. by Reichardt and Siegfried, 375–404.

[126] 'Unternehmen Rosa Winkel', *him* 2 (1976), 18–19.

[127] *AHA Info Intern* (December 1978), 6; Ödipus Kollektiv (ed.), 'Brühwarm: ein schwuler Jahrmarkt' (1976). SMB archive.

[128] 'Homosexuelle helfen Homosexuellen', *Emanzipation* 6 (1976), 13–16.

[129] In 1977, gay cafes called *Anderes Ufer* opened in both Frankfurt and West Berlin. 'Anderes Ufer: Ein Kaffeehaus in Berlin', *him* 7 (1977) 18–19; 'An's andere Ufer gerettet', *Pflasterstrand* 15 (1977), 30–1.

[130] 'Schwulenzentrum Information und Termine'. APO archive, folder 1052. See further Chapter 5.

Paragraph 175 in 1973. With its background of a sickle and a clenched fist, the poster would lend homosexuals an 'APO image', thus cementing prejudice as opposed to challenging discrimination.[131] The IHWO did not want to be associated with extra-parliamentary opposition, with left-wing protest. Instead, the group focused on quiet lobbying of politicians, and on building a sense of community amongst homosexuals. Gay leftists were less prepared to restrict themselves to these spheres: the 'gay public' was diagnosed as suffering from a lack of political consciousness, whereas the parliamentary arena—at least until towards the end of the decade, with the arrival of the Greens—was more or less written off. Yet, the gay left could never rest on its laurels when it came to the left-alternative public either, given the scepticism expressed in some quarters over the political merits of sexual liberation. Perhaps this was why the proposed poster, rejected by the IHWO, was suitably discreet, with no reference to 'gay', to 'homosexual' or even to sexuality.[132]

Nevertheless, the gay left was never 'stuck' between publics, ground down in some existential dilemma. The ambivalence of their position was a productive one. Victoria Hesford argues that the public sphere should be considered 'a malleable discursive space in which groups do not simply articulate established positions but actually come into being through their dialogical interactions with others'.[133] Similarly, Nancy Fraser contends that public spheres are not just about deliberation but are also 'arenas for the formation and enactment of public identities'.[134] Oscillating from public to counterpublic involved not just a question of who to address, but *who gay activists were*. Implicated in all three of these spheres, negotiating these poles would shape not only the course of the gay left but its members' very identities as gay activists.

Consider the case of action forms. Bernhard Gotto has shown how women's liberationists, despite the sexism they endured, 'transferred their repertoire of action to a great extent from the 1968 protest movement'. This was not a question of copycat actions, but of inspiration, with street theatre, sit-ins and public art installations jostling with other forms of action that long predated 1968, such as open letters and mass demonstrations.[135] Gay activists followed in these footsteps. The basic units of the gay left, the various 'action groups' (*Aktionsgruppen*) dotted around the country, organized demonstrations, rallies, and public information stalls, often as part of, or to coincide with, wider feminist or leftist concerns: for example, on annual 1 May rallies. More imaginative actions include the

---

[131] *IHWO Report* 5 (1973), 12. The sickle was shaped so as to resemble § for paragraph.
[132] A copy of the poster can be found in Wolfert, *Gegen Einsamkeit*, 183.
[133] Hesford, *Feeling Women's Liberation* (Durham, NC, 2013), 260.
[134] Fraser, 'Rethinking the Public Sphere', 125. See also Warner, *Publics and Counterpublics*.
[135] Gotto, 'The best thing that remained of '68? Experiences of protest and expectations on change in the West German women's movement during the 1970s and 1980s', paper presented at *Social Movements after '68: Germany, Europe, and Beyond* conference at Rutgers University (9 November 2018). Publication forthcoming. My thanks to the author for permission to cite this draft paper.

'happening' orchestrated by activists in Bielefeld, who rented a city tram for a few hours, serenading passers-by, or the enormous papier-mâché phallus that the *Brühwarm* troupe cast off into the audience during their performances.[136] These types of actions, or spectacles, owed much to the influence of situationism, even if this movement was rarely explicitly cited in gay liberation.[137]

The interconnections between different parts of the alternative left were also transnational in scope. Activists in Bielefeld specifically described their stunt on the tram as a 'happening', a term which was popularized in West Germany by the student movement, but which emanated from the United States: the language of 'Go-ins', 'Sit-ins', 'Teach-ins', and 'Happenings', other than the capital letters, was not altered or translated into German.[138] French influences were particularly important. Alice Schwarzer, the central activist behind the 1971 action in *Stern*, when 374 women declared that they had had an abortion, suggested the idea to editors after her time working as a journalist in Paris, where she witnessed a similar action by 343 women in *Le Nouvel Observateur*.[139] Activists from France and Italy travelled to West Berlin in June 1973 to take part in a demonstration organized by the HAW: invites were also sent to the London Gay Liberation Front.[140] The French gay activist and theorist Guy Hocquenghem was particularly influential. His *Homosexual Desire* was published in German in 1974, while Pink Triangle Press made Hocquenghem's *L'Après-mai des faunes* one of its first publications.[141] Pink Triangle Press also published a collection of translated French gay-related texts in 1979, including works by Hocquenghem, Roland Barthes, Gilles Deleuze, and Félix Guattari (not incidentally, the preface to the volume was entitled 'Against Americanisation').[142] Even the name of the publishing house belies transnational links, for Pink Triangle Press was the name chosen

---

[136] Recorded and broadcast on the WDR's third channel, as part of the feature *Schauplatz Gerichtstrasse—Schwulengruppe Bielefeld* (30 January 1979). On the phallus, see Roland Lange, 'Brühwarm: der erfüllte Traum von der Selbstverwirklichung', *Emanzipation* 5 (1976), 12–14.

[137] On the legacy of the Situationist International in the alternative left more broadly, see Häberlen, *The Emotional Politics of the Alternative Left*, 65.

[138] Siegfried Jäger, 'Linke Wörter. Einige Bemerkungen zur Sprache der APO', *Muttersprache: Zeitschrift zur Pflege und Erforschung der deutschen Sprache* 3/4 (1970), 85–107 (91).

[139] Schulz, *Der lange Atem*, 145.

[140] It seems that the Italian and French activists were from the *fuori!* (United Front of Italian Revolutionary Homosexuals) and FHAR (Homosexual Revolutionary Action Front) groups respectively. *HAW Info* 12 (1973), 16–19. The HAW sent an English-language letter to British gay activists inviting 'Sisters, Friends and Comrades' to the event. Letter dated 25 April 1973. Hall-Carpenter Archives, Ephemera/222/14.2.

[141] Guy Hocquenghem, *Homosexual Desire*, trans. by Daniella Dangoor (Durham, NC, 1993 [1972]). The German edition of *L'Après-mai des faunes* was published in December 1975.

[142] Bernhard Dieckmann and Francois Pescatore, 'Gegen die Amerikanisierung: Ein Vorwort der Herausgaber,' in *Elemente einer homosexuellen Kritik: Französische Texte 1971–1977* (Berlin, 1979), 9–20. Michel Foucault was not included in this collection, but the *Schwuchtel* editorial collective drew upon his work when producing a special issue on the role of prisons and the plight of gay prisoners: *Schwuchtel* 7 (1977), 1.

not just in West Germany but also by Canadian gay liberationists.[143] *Schwuchtel*, meaning 'fag', may have been inspired by the American gay liberation newspaper *Fag Rag*, published in Boston.[144]

Many of the spaces where gay leftists cut their teeth were organized around international issues, especially committees against the war in Vietnam and the military putsch in Chile. The slogan 'freedom for Chile' adorned the front cover of the HAW's newsletter in late 1973 (see Figure 3.1). In the issue, activists reported on their participation in demonstrations organized by the wider Chilean solidarity campaign. The iconography displayed is also suggestive of collective belongings, with the logo in the top-left corner comprising biological symbols, indicating same-sex sexuality, surrounding the clenched fist of socialism. Even the subsequent debate in the HAW over whether to donate money to *Unidad Popular*, the alliance behind the deposed president Salvador Allende, or instead to the Maoist *Movimiento de Izquierda Revolucionaria*, displays a sectarianism indicative of the HAW's place in the wider alternative left.[145] The HAW's reporting on the plight of Chilean homosexuals, which cited the Argentinian Homosexual Liberation Front, seems to have been dependent on an article in the Canadian journal *Body Politic*. In turn, that piece relied on material from American magazines *The Gay Liberator*, *Gay Sunshine*, and *Fag Rag*.[146]

Borders between the gay public, left-alternative (counter)public, and the wider public sphere always remained porous. For example, we cannot possibly identify all of the 682 men who outed themselves in *Stern* as inhabiting a single political position or lifestyle. The same goes for the 374 German women who declared that they had had an abortion. Bands such as *Flying Lesbians* (rendered in English) or *Ton Steine Scherben*, both of which had significant lesbian and gay involvement, were influential in the left-alternative scene, but produced music whose reach cannot be limited to those circles.[147] The same applies to the spaces of gay activism. Until some had the capacity to rent their own factory floors, cafés or centres, gay groups often met in rooms provided by student unions—dominated by left-alternative parties in the 1970s. The student union in Aachen went further,

---

[143] As announced in *Body Politic* 22 (1976), 1. HCA/Journals/184. James Steakley, an American student active in the HAW while studying in East Berlin, may well have played a role in this transnational dissemination of the pink triangle, because he had earlier introduced Canadian readers to the West German gay movement. Steakley, 'The Gay Movement in Germany Today', *Body Politic* 13 (1974), 14–15, 21, and 23.

[144] Hobson, *Lavender and Red*, 75.

[145] Wolfgang Theis, 'Mach dein Schwulsein öffentlich – Bundesrepublik', in *Goodbye to Berlin? 100 Jahre Schwulenbewegung: Eine Ausstellung des Schwulen Museums und der Akademie der Künste* (Rosa Winkel: Berlin, 1997), 279–93 (285).

[146] HAW Info 17 (1975), 4; 'Chilean Fascists terrorize gays', *Body Politic* 14 (1974).

[147] Lenz, 'Das Private ist politisch!', 394. Rio Reiser, the lead singer of *Ton Steine Scherben*, was open about his homosexuality from 1976. Timothy Brown, 'Music as a Weapon? *Ton Steine Scherben* and the Politics of Rock in Cold War Berlin', *German Studies Review* 32:1 (2009), 1–22 (8).

Figure 3.1 'Freedom for Chile'. Front cover of *HAW Info* 12 (September/October 1973).

Source: By permission of the *Schwules Museum Berlin*.

covering the legal costs of the GSR in their effort to overturn the banning of their information stall.[148]

Other groups did not restrict themselves to these spaces. For example, the Bochum chapter of the Humanist Union functioned as one of the gay groups in the city.[149] Notwithstanding the role of the Humanist Union, which campaigned for greater secularization, spaces provided by the Protestant Church were also influential. Several gay groups held their regular meetings in rooms run by Protestant Christian Unions (*Studentengemeinden*). This was the case for the GSR in Aachen: the Christian Union there similarly supported groups campaigning on behalf of foreign workers, against homelessness, and within the peace movement.[150] In 1977, theologians, priests and church workers founded the umbrella organization Homosexuals and Church (HuK). This cannot be seen as entirely separate from the left-alternative scene: firstly, because 1968 was never an 'innately secular' moment, with religious bodies also influenced by protest, and secondly, because of the manner in which the organization was set up. The initiative sprang from the attempt by the AHA to hold a stall at the Protestant Church Congress in West Berlin. This was blocked by Church authorities but gay activists were harboured by the 'Christians for Socialism' working group instead.[151]

Gay leftists' ambivalent position between gay public, the left-alternative counterpublic, and the wider public sphere is reflected in terms of print culture, too. The gay left had limited influence over the commercial gay press, the major means by which images and representations of queer desire circulated in West Germany. While the two largest magazines, *du&ich* and *him,* did offer limited coverage to the gay movement, this was always on the terms of the magazines' editors. A sense of what was to come was provided in September 1971—by which point only a handful of groups had been founded in West Germany—when an article on the London Gay Liberation Front in *du&ich* was entitled 'militant homosexual APO stretches its tentacles to Europe'.[152] Astonishingly, the same magazine carried an interview with the Iranian Shah Reza Pahlavi in 1974, in which he assured readers that homosexuals were tolerated in Iran and that any student 'agitator' executed in his country had deserved it (this was the same Shah whose visit to West Berlin in

---

[148] AStA (*Technische Hochschule,* Aachen) to Maczkiewitz-Nigge, 5 December 1973. SMB archive, NARGS box one, folder 'Dokumentation Aachener Info-Tisch-Fall'.

[149] Leidinger, 'Gründungsmythen', 31.

[150] Lutz Olbrich, 'Die ESG und wir', *GSR Info* 2 (1974), 12–13.

[151] Peter Apor, Rebecca Clifford and Nigel Townson, 'Faith', in *Europe's 1968, Voices of Revolt,* ed. by Robert Gildea et al. (Oxford, 2013), 211–38 (211); 'Kurzinformation über die Arbeitsgruppe Homosexuelle und Kirche'. SMB archive, Sammlung HuK, folder HuK Regionalgruppe Berlin.

[152] 'Homo Power: GLF-Ableger in London? Militante Homosexuellen-APO streckt ihre Fühler nach Europa aus', *du&ich* 6 (1971), 9.

June 1967 had sparked off student demonstrations and was a key flashpoint in the West German student movement).[153]

While *him* was the magazine most supportive of the movement it nevertheless carried the occasional article mocking gay activists and their ideological excesses: for example under the title 'On trotskyist cock-suckers, Mao fags and anal revisionists'.[154] As we have seen, the *him* columnist Wolfgang Selitsch explicitly called for the founding of homophile student groups in August 1970.[155] Exactly a year later, Selitsch struck a more cautionary note. While welcoming the groups set up in Bochum and Münster, he warned against 'all too great emancipation strides', which in light of experience would only bring more social condemnation. Entitling his article 'Homo-Power in Deutschland?', he answered his own question with 'Gay Power in moderation – okay! – but please no Queens' revolt' (*Tuntenaufstand*).[156]

Given political differences between activists and publicists, and the relative dearth of coverage from the mainstream press, the left-alternative press offered a crucial alternative avenue, allowing gay action groups in Nuremberg, Frankfurt, Munich, Berlin, Heidelberg, and elsewhere to present themselves to readers of *ID*, *Pflasterstrand*, *Blatt*, *Info-BUG*, *Carlo Sponti*, and many others.[157] Articles in the leftist journals *Probleme des Klassenkampfs*, *Kursbuch* and *Das Argument* were central in launching the *Tuntenstreit*, the 'Queens' Dispute'. While this important debate over gender presentation was internal to the gay movement, it was facilitated by the left-alternative public (only later were the texts collated and reprinted, aimed this time at a more specifically gay audience).[158] Some of these journals, newspapers, and zines had small circulations and were local or regional, not national, in scope. Nevertheless, the left-alternative press was a growing part of the West German media landscape, with up to 390 different titles and a combined monthly circulation of 1.6 million by 1980.[159]

Inspired by the left-alternative press, in particular the success of feminist journals such as *Courage*, gay action groups launched their own periodicals in the mid-1970s. Many groups had from their earliest days disseminated internal, or local, news through hastily compiled 'information sheets' (*Infos*): these were generally distributed free of charge, and their readership rarely went beyond the confines of the group (for an example, see Figure 3.1). Later in the decade, groups

---

[153] *du&ich* 6 (1974), 12–13.
[154] 'Von trotzkistischen Bläsern, Mao-Schwuchteln und Anal-Revisionisten', *him* 8 (1972), 18–19.
[155] 'Das war nicht unsere letzte Aktion', *him* 8 (1970), 21.
[156] Selitsch, 'Homo-Power in Deutschland?', *him* 8 (1971), 30–1 (31) 'Gay Power' was rendered in English.
[157] 'Die Homosexuelle Aktionsgruppe Nürnberg', *ID* 83 (1975), 8; Von der Roten Zelle Schwul zum Schwulencafe', *Pflasterstrand* 14 (1978), 35–8; *Blatt* 145 (1979), 14–16 and 27–8; *INFO-BUG* 62 (1975), 6–7; 'Rosa Winkel: Historisches Zeichen der Schwulenunterdrückung', *Carlo Sponti* 14/15 (1975), 9.
[158] For citations, see section 'The *Tuntenstreit*' in Chapter 5.
[159] Reichardt and Siegfried, *Das alternative Milieu*, 12.

began cooperating to produce lengthier, better designed tracts, which were initially regional in scope. *Schwuchtel* was run mostly by activists from West Berlin, along with Heidelberg.[160] *Emanzipation* was initially the product of five gay groups in South Germany: in Munich, Stuttgart, Nuremberg, Tübingen and Würzburg. In 1976, the magazine removed the reference in its subtitle to South Germany, and other groups joined the editorial collection, including the AHA from West Berlin.[161] *Rosa*, meanwhile, was originally the newsletter of a single group, the Homosexual Action Hamburg, but grew to include groups from Bielefeld and Bremen.[162]

Just as activist-led cafes or communication centres never succeeded in displacing the commercial imperative of the wider gay scene, the activist press did not come close to replacing commercial gay magazines. There was no enterprise in the 1970s that successfully managed to bridge the divide between the activist and the commercial press; nothing along the lines of the French *Le Gay Pied*, which was said to have a circulation in the region of 35,000.[163] In 1979, *Emanzipation* attempted to make the leap from being sold only by the groups that formed its editorial collective to being made available through newspaper kiosks. This was unsuccessful, with that year's first issue costing 8000 DM to produce and distribute, but bringing in only 4000 DM of revenue. Of the copies sold, 200 came via regular subscribers, 1000 through the groups and 1000 were sold directly at kiosks.[164] This pales in comparison to the circulation of the commercial gay press. According to a *du&ich* editorial in 1976, the lowest number of monthly copies ever sold had been 9000.[165] *Emanzipation* editors warned that higher sales, more subscribers and greater advertising revenue were all needed to secure the future of the magazine. This failed to transpire, with the final issue of 1980 proving to be the last. *Rosa* also ceased publication in 1980 and *Schwuchtel* survived only until mid-1977.[166]

Engaging with the mainstream media, meanwhile, offered an opportunity to reach an audience of which the gay commercial press, the gay activist press, or the left-alternative press could only dream. When 682 men outed themselves in *Stern* in October 1978, this was the occasion when gay men reached their largest popular audience in the decade. Dagmar Herzog has argued that the *Stern* special

---

[160] *Schwuchtel: eine Zeitung der Schwulenbewegung* 1 (1975).

[161] *Emanzipation: Homosexuelle Aktionsgruppen informieren* 2 (1976).

[162] The magazine removed its reference to the HAH in 1977. *Rosa: Eine Zeitung der Schwulenbewegung* 8 (1977).

[163] 'Zeitungstreffen', *Homolulu: Schwule Tageszeitung* 4 (27 July 1979), 9. SMB archive, NARGS box two, folder NARGS 79.

[164] *Emanzipation* 1 (1979), 3.

[165] '6 Jahre du&ich: Ein Rückblick auf Gelungenes und Misslungenes', *du&ich* 10 (1976), 8–11 (9).

[166] *Emanzipation* 1 (1979), 3; *Emanzipation* 6 (1980). The largest and longest-lasting activist magazine of the 1980s was *Rosa Flieder*, founded in late 1978 and ceasing publication in 1989. Sebastian Haunss draws upon this source in his *Identität in Bewegung: Prozesse kollektiver Identität bei den Autonomen und in der Schwulenbewegung* (Wiesbaden, 2004).

marked the moment 'when the mainstream media (albeit still with considerable ambivalence) officially aligned itself with the demands of gay rights activists'.[167] It is important to underscore that ambivalence. The text introducing the alphabetical list of all 682 gay men read 'We've had enough of the game of hide and seek! We are homosexual and enjoy being so!'[168] This positive evocation of same-sex desire was in stark contrast to the general tone of the *Stern* article, which painted a depressingly familiar picture of discrimination, self-hate, suffering, and suicide.

Clearly, *Stern* found it easier to talk about the marginalized and oppressed rather than the happy and fulfilled homosexual, and despite the text cited above, gay desire barely featured. The gay left came across decidedly poorly, with journalist Niels Kummer opining that although many emancipation groups were founded, 'their impact often did not go beyond absurd agitprop or crazy provocations' (he did not see fit to mention the role of such emancipation groups in bringing the special issue to pass).[169] As Manfred Herzer would state in *Emanzipation*, *Stern* proudly claimed to be breaking the taboo on homosexuality, but in reality the activists who helped put the feature together had long since been open about their homosexuality, and indeed been involved in a movement for seven years on which *Stern* had barely reported.[170]

As indicated by the *Stern* special in 1978, as the decade wore on, there was a gradual increase in the reporting on the gay movement and on homosexuality more widely by the mainstream press. This can be seen through the media response to *Homolulu*, the international gay festival which took place in Frankfurt in July 1979, an event reported on—largely positively—by almost every significant German newspaper, including the conservative tabloid *BILD* and the conservative broadsheets *Die Welt* and *FAZ*. *Homolulu* organizers were rather taken aback by the dramatically increased volume of coverage: 'What a feeling it is to appear in all of these otherwise so anti-gay papers. So now we've made it: gayness is public, the press have registered us, sought us out and reported on us to the world.' However, this kind of press coverage was not typical for the decade, and when it finally arrived, activists reacted with an ambivalence symptomatic of gay liberation. The same activist who admitted his pleasure at the *Homolulu* coverage also worried about what it entailed: 'But it takes me aback, reading BILD or FAZ or the FR, watching television, with the report included alongside dispatches on the economy, from parliaments, from the whole well-functioning bourgeois world. [. . .] Have we been fitted in?'[171]

A feared institutionalization was less of an issue when it came to coverage in the left-alternative press. Nevertheless, while the alternative left provided the model

---

[167] Herzog, *Sex after Fascism*, 223.   [168] 'Ich bin schwul', *Stern* 41 (1978), 116.
[169] Ibid., 113.   [170] 'Schwule im Stern. Helden und Mäuschen', *Emanzipation* 3 (1978), 21–2.
[171] 'Pressespiegelungen', *Homolulu: Schwule Tageszeitung* 4 (27 July 1979), 3. 'FR' indicates the liberal *Frankfurter Rundschau* newspaper.

and ideological underpinning for the construction of alternative publics, gay activist initiatives often arose out of a dissatisfaction with left-wing attitudes. For example, the leftist theatre collective *Rote Rübe* ('red beet': i.e. beetroot) served as an important model for the gay collective *Brühwarm*, but the only openly gay member of *Rote Rübe* joined *Brühwarm* after the former apparently refused to stage a gay play (though he soon switched back, since *Rote Rübe* could offer him a paid position).[172] Paul Seidenberg, one of the 682 men who took part in the *Stern* action, specifically cited his membership of the DKP in the feature. This did not please party functionaries, who accused him of exhibitionism: under constant pressure, Seidenberg left the party in 1980.[173] Reflecting on the largely unsuccessful gay participation in the International Russell Tribunal, held in West Germany in 1978 and 1979 to investigate alleged civil rights abuses, one activist concluded that the action forms of 'hetero leftists' had left no space 'for our [own] articulation'.[174] The editors of *Schwuchtel*, meanwhile, expressed their frustration with the left, declaring 'whoever is made an outsider by this society remains an outsider amongst leftists too'. An article in the first issue expressed the journal's rationale: 'Us gays continue to occupy the lowest rung of the human value ladder in the Federal Republic. Therefore no-one will champion our cause if we fail to create a public ourselves.'[175]

~ ~ ~

1968 was deeply significant for gay liberation, despite the sexism and heteronormativity of the student movement. While the sexual politics of the 1960s new left and the student movement were hardly favourable for those seeking to organize around gender or sexuality, other parts of the intellectual framework provided by 1968 were formative. In particular, the gay left acquired from the student movement and the new left a deep and abiding scepticism of liberalization, of whether true freedom was possible in the current socio-economic order. This worldview allowed activists in gay action groups to demarcate themselves from other homosexuals whose consciousness was still in need of liberation. 1968 was important also because it gave rise to the 1970s alternative left, the necessary political environment for gay action groups. Notwithstanding its variegated ideological positions, this alternative left provided a crucial space, a forum, a counterpublic, for the gay left.

Instead of single-issue politics, the gay left demanded nothing less than a fundamental transformation of society. Activists were committed to a programme of multi-dimensional liberation, and in this sense might be seen as one of the forces picking up the utopian mantle of 1968 after the student movement

---

[172] *Brühwarm: ein schwuler Jahrmarkt*, 5. See also Bernhard Rosenkranz and Gottfried Lorenz, 'Brühwarm: Die erste Theatergruppe der Schwulenbewegung', in *Hamburg auf anderen Wegen. Die Geschichte des schwulen Lebens in der Hansestadt* (Hamburg, 2005), 184–90.

[173] 'Wir sind schwul', 108; Schwartz, 'Warum machen Sie sich für die Homos stark?', 69.

[174] 'Russel [sic], NARGS, Homolulu', *Rosa* 16 (1979), 22–5 (23).

[175] *Schwuchtel* 1 (1975), 1, 17.

disintegrated in the late 1960s. Yet it was above all gay leftists' deep-seated mistrust of the West German state and the very possibility of liberalization that marked them out as members of the alternative left. This was a double-edged sword. If gay leftists frequently maligned their more conservative counterparts as insufficiently political, this was to some extent because they were sensitized to this critique. Leftist scepticism about the political merits of liberalization led to a certain scepticism about the political value of gay liberation: a movement, at least in part, based on sexual preference and which could therefore easily be associated with the wider 'sexual revolution'.

Accordingly, gay activists were under constant scrutiny to prove their legitimacy, to prove that gay liberation was not just part of the commercialized 'sexual revolution' distracting progressive forces from the 'real' task of transforming the social order. I therefore show in the next chapter how reference to oppression, and especially oppression that could be framed as having a fascist legacy, proved to be gay activists' most reliable mechanism to appeal to their left-alternative interlocutors. Relying on a supposed spirit of antiauthoritarianism was never enough. Looking at conflicts over sexuality as a whole, including sex education, Dagmar Herzog has argued that by the time of the 1970s, unlike in 1968, leftists 'no longer required the use of references to Nazism as a kind of moral battering ram to advance sexual liberation'.[176] This verdict does not apply to all types of sexual liberation: for in homosexual emancipation the tendency to invoke the fascist past ran throughout the 1970s. It is to the memory of the Third Reich, and its impact on homosexual politics, that we now turn.

---

[176] Herzog, *Sex after Fascism*, 229.

4

The Pink Triangle

Persecution Past and Present

In 1975, Alfred Heinlein, from the Homosexual Action Nuremberg, argued in *Emanzipation* that 'us gays must learn to become more conscious of history, not to forget and repress our specific history but to embrace it and to learn from it'.[1] The 'specific history' referred to by Heinlein, prompted by the thirtieth anniversary of the downfall of the Third Reich in 1945, was the National Socialist persecution of homosexuals. On account of their real or supposed homosexuality, approximately 10,000 men were incarcerated in the Nazi concentration camps, where they were forced to wear the pink triangle on their uniforms. More than half of them died.[2] Bemoaning the fact that in all the commemorations marking the anniversary nobody had found time to mention the gay victims of the Nazis, Heinlein moved on to look at the contemporary situation:

Must we not especially in recent times ascertain that fascist tendencies and inclinations have once again been on the rise? [. . .] Certainly, the forms have changed, but oppression and discrimination continue. [. . .] The sanctimonious tolerance [*scheinheilige Toleranz*] allegedly practiced today could very quickly revert back to active persecution. It is therefore imperative to recognize and resist the onset of a new development to the Right.[3]

This chapter explains how West German gay liberationists reclaimed the pink triangle, a process that began in 1972 with the landmark publication of Heinz Heger's *The Men with the Pink Triangle*, a homosexual survivor's first-hand account of life in the camps.[4] The symbol was used on badges and on demonstrations, and in 1975 the gay movement named its first publishers after the insignia, the *Verlag Rosa Winkel* (Pink Triangle Press).[5] This was also the name chosen by Canadian activists in 1976 for their publishing house, indicating how

---

[1] 'Massenmord an Homos bis heute unaufgeklärt', *Emanzipation* 3 (1975), 1–3 (1).
[2] These estimates put forward by Rüdiger Lautmann in 1980 still represent the scholarly consensus. 'The Pink Triangle: The Persecution of Homosexual Males in Concentration Camps in Nazi Germany', *Journal of Homosexuality* 6 (1980), 141–60.
[3] Heinlein, 'Massenmord an Homos', 2.
[4] Heger, *Die Männer mit dem Rosa Winkel* (Hamburg, 1989 [1972]).
[5] 'Unternehmen Rosa Winkel', *him* 2 (1976), 18–19.

The Ambivalence of Gay Liberation: Male Homosexual Politics in 1970s West Germany. Craig Griffiths, Oxford University Press (2021). © Craig Griffiths.
DOI: 10.1093/oso/9780198868965.003.0005

from its German roots the symbol soon spread to other gay movements.[6] Indeed, before the rainbow flag emerged on the scene later in the 1980s, the pink triangle became arguably the most influential international gay symbol.[7]

In this sense, Heinlein's plea to his fellow gays to become 'more concious of history' was reflective of a wider transnational 'memory boom' in homosexual politics.[8] This memory boom went hand-in-hand with the growing salience of human rights language, and in particular the increased purchase of portrayals of suffering in the public sphere.[9] The 1970s saw not only the 'rediscovery' of the pink triangle, but also the rise of Amnesty International (awarded the Nobel Peace Prize in 1977), the human rights agreements that were part of the 1975 Helsinki Accords, and the 'human rights policy' of United States president Jimmy Carter.[10] Gay liberationists sought to capitalize on a climate in which the crimes of the Nazis—and their victims—were finally being better represented in political culture, symbolized by Chancellor Willy Brandt's dramatic gesture of contrition in Warsaw in December 1970, as he knelt in memory to the victims of the Warsaw ghetto uprising.[11] Armed with the pink triangle, gay activists demanded to be part of this picture.

At the same time, the pink triangle was used by gay activists not merely to commemorate a *history* of persecution, but to indicate that persecution had continued in the post-war Federal Republic and into the present. There was much about gay liberation that was playful and fun, but it was never free from seriousness, from the conviction of some gay men that they were living in a deeply authoritarian state which was on the verge of sliding back into fascism. This was an ambivalent legacy directly inherited from 1968, for while the student rebellions

---

[6] *Body Politic* 22 (1976), 1. The book that had facilitated this transnational transfer, Heinz Heger's memoir, was later translated: into English in 1980 and into French in 1981. On the French publication, see further Dan Callwood, 'Re-evaluating the French Gay Liberation Moment 1968–1983' (unpublished doctoral thesis, Queen Mary University of London, 2017), 93.

[7] Unlike the rainbow flag, the pink triangle referred more specifically to gay men. Given that the pink triangle was only used to designate male homosexuals in the concentration camps, the symbol did not carry the same significance for lesbian activists after it was 'rediscovered'. Discussions over whether the black triangle, used in the concentration camps to mark so-called 'asocial' prisoners, and whether this could be used as a lesbian symbol, seem not to have arisen until the 1980s. See further Erik Jensen, 'The Pink Triangle and Political Consciousness: Gays, Lesbians, and the Memory of Nazi Persecution', *Journal of the History of Sexuality* 11 (2002), 319–49 (333–8) and R. Amy Elman, 'Triangles and Tribulations: The Politics of Nazi Symbols', *Journal of Homosexuality* 30 (1996), 1–11.

[8] On 'memory booms' see Jay Winter, *War beyond Words: Languages of Remembrance from the Great War to the Present* (Cambridge, 2017), 204. Winter argues that a second memory boom took off in the early 1980s (the first had followed the First World War). In terms of homosexual politics, this second memory boom needs backdating slightly, to the mid-1970s.

[9] Jan Eckel, 'The Rebirth of Politics from the Spirit of Morality: Explaining the Human Rights Revolution of the 1970s', in *The Breakthrough: Human Rights in the 1970s*, ed. by Jan Eckel and Samuel Moyn (Philadelphia, 2014), 226–59 (247).

[10] See Eckel and Moyn (eds), *The Breakthrough*; Samuel Moyn, *The Last Utopia: Human Rights in History* (Cambridge, MA, 2010), and Wildenthal, *The Language of Human Rights*.

[11] Robert Moeller, *War Stories: The Search for a Usable Past in the Federal Republic of Germany* (Berkeley, 2003), 176–7.

are 'usually understood as outbreaks of youthful exuberance in the name of freedom and countercultural experimentation', they were, just as importantly, 'intended as defensive acts against a state perceived to be in thrall to German traditions that had led to 1933'.[12] Student protestors and their detractors alike were afflicted by what Dirk Moses has called the 'Weimar syndrome': the fear that the Federal Republic would meet the same fate as the Weimar Republic.[13] The totemic issue in this regard in 1968 had been the emergency laws, which would grant emergency powers to the federal government in the case of national crisis. From 1972, that baton passed to the *Extremistenbeschluß*, the 'Extremists' Resolution', dubbed the *Berufsverbot* ('ban on careers') by its opponents, which sought to prevent radicalized student activists from entering the civil service.[14]

According to the gay left, the 'ban on careers' claimed two gay victims in 1974, the church youth worker Klaus Kindel and the school teacher Reiner Koepp. Addressing the leftist 'Committee against the *Berufsverbot*', activists from the Homosexual Action West Berlin called on the audience to demonstrate solidarity with Koepp and Kindel and supported this call by reference to history: 'For it is really nothing new that communists and homosexuals in Germany are deprived of their citizenship.'[15] So unfolded a strategy in which activists juxtaposed the pink triangle with the red triangle, worn by political prisoners in the concentration camps. This move enabled the connection to be made between shared persecution in the past, in the Third Reich, and shared persecution in the present, chiefly in the form of the state's attempt to police left-wing activism.

Gay leftists were far from alone in making reference to the Nazi past. They were following in the footsteps of the deeply conservative historian of religion Hans-Joachim Schoeps, who dramatically claimed in 1962 'for homosexuals the Third Reich never ended'.[16] Schoeps had a point, because until homosexual law reform in 1969, the version of Paragraph 175 introduced by the Nazis in 1935 remained in force, totally unchanged. Gay activists in the 1970s found themselves on the other side of this legal reform, but they, unlike Schoeps, had access to a powerful symbol straight from the world of the concentration camps, the pink triangle. The gay left found in the history of Nazi persecution a useful framework both for understanding and for framing contemporary discrimination, claiming political capital from homosexuals' newly 'rediscovered' status as a 'victim group' of National Socialism. Yet this was never merely a strategic consideration. Memory of the Nazi

---

[12] Moses, *German Intellectuals*, 13.   [13] Ibid., 48.

[14] See further Braunthal, *Political Loyalty and Public Service in West Germany*.

[15] 'Radikale, Schwule, Kommunisten', *HAW Info* 20 (1975), 14–19 (15).

[16] Schoeps, 'Soll Homosexualität strafbar bleiben?', *Der Monat: Eine internationale Zeitschrift* 171 (1962), 19–27 (22). In an unsuccessful attempt to engage with the Nazi regime, Schoeps had founded the Nazi Jewish Vanguard in 1933, and in the post-war period he campaigned for the reestablishment of the monarchy and of the Prussian state. See further the collection of articles in *Nexus: Essays in German Jewish Studies* 2 (2014), 6–42.

persecution, combined with the experience of contemporary discrimination, produced a profound alienation on the part of gay leftists from the West German state. Indeed, in fearing that 1970s gay liberation would meet the same end as the 1920s homosexual emancipation movement, gay leftists came to display their own version of the 'Weimar syndrome'. Following an analysis of how the pink triangle was used by gay action groups, I therefore use the symbol as a window onto discourses of victimhood in gay liberation. Though the pink triangle had been reclaimed from its origins as a badge of shame in the concentration camps, it never became an unequivocal symbol of pride.

Although the pink triangle was used most widely in the various action groups that made up the gay left, the theme of Nazi persecution was never confined to that political trajectory. As early as 1972, the International Homophile World Organization (IHWO) wrote to Rainer Barzel, the Christian Democrat candidate for Chancellor in the forthcoming federal election, referring to a history of persecution to justify their demand for a rethinking of policy in the present: 'Have we already again gone so far, as in the Third Reich when Jews and homosexuals were persecuted, that a party aiming to come to government calls for preying on a minority?'[17] By the end of the decade, activists of all stripes, the commercial gay press, and the first openly gay parliamentary candidates coalesced around making the history of past persecution a central plank in their efforts to insert themselves into the West German mainstream.

Most influentially, this took the form of demanding compensation for surviving homosexual victims of the concentration camps. The politics of restitution—the German term *Wiedergutmachung* translates literally as 'making good again'—became a mechanism for gaining traction in the public sphere, putting adversaries on the back foot. By the time of a panel event organized by the gay and lesbian movements in advance of the 1980 federal election, even the Christian Democrat representative was promising to raise the question of compensation in parliament—a process that reached its next stage in 1985, when homosexual men were for the first time officially recognized as a victim-group of fascism by Federal President Richard von Weizsäcker.[18] The most radical exclusionary act committed against homosexuals in German history became, 40 years on, a key means of their inclusion. This chapter tells that story.

---

[17] Letter dated 8 August 1972. SMB archive, IHWO box one.

[18] The CDU representative was Friedrich Rahardt, from Hamburg. *Alle Schwestern werden Brüder*, ed. Dieter Bachnik and Rainer Schlädlich (Berlin, 1986), 222–41 (231). For the speech, see 'Gedenkveranstaltung im Plenarsaal des Deutschen Bundestages zum 40. Jahrestag des Endes des Zweiten Weltkrieges in Europa' <http://www.bundespraesident.de/SharedDocs/Reden/DE/Richard-von-Weizsaecker/Reden/1985/05/19850508_Rede.html> [date accessed 3 September 2018].

The 'Rediscovery' of the Nazi Persecution of Homosexuals

In the first account of the concentration camp system, published as early as 1946, Eugen Kogon described how homosexuals had been incarcerated in the camps, marked by a pink triangle badge.[19] In January 1946, at the Nuremberg war crimes trial, one of the American prosecutors stated that homosexuals had been a prisoner group at Dachau concentration camp.[20] Despite this knowledge, the historical profession showed a singular lack of interest. The first popular historical accounts were not written until the late 1960s, while the first academic study was not published until 1977, an article by Rüdiger Lautmann, Winfried Grikschat, and Egbert Schmidt.[21] Indeed, after the initial focus on Nazi crimes provided through the forum of the Nuremberg trial, Nazi persecution as a whole faded from view. This did not just affect homosexuals, but all groups persecuted by the Nazis, especially the Jews. As Nikolaus Wachsmann states, 'Within ten years of liberation, the camps had been sidelined – a result not of survivors unable to speak, but of a wider audience unwilling to listen.'[22]

It was only in the wake of the *Einsatzgruppen* trial in Ulm in 1958, the trial of Adolf Eichmann in Jerusalem in 1961, and then the Auschwitz trials in Frankfurt between 1963 and 1965, that the genocidal murder of the Jews achieved public prominence.[23] Until this point, Jewish victimhood was begrudgingly acknowledged, but diluted as only one part of a wider West German public memory in which the vast majority of Germans featured not as perpetrators but as victims, in the form of suffering from Allied bombing campaigns, being taken prisoner by the Red Army, or by being expelled from their homes in Eastern Europe in 1945.[24] As Robert Moeller has shown, Nazi persecution was never straightforwardly 'forgotten' in the Federal Republic, but rather selectively remembered. In the case of homosexuals, 'West Germans heard, discussed, and rejected their claims to victim status.'[25] This was symbolized by the decision of the Federal Constitutional Court, in 1957, that the continued application of the Nazi-era version of Paragraph 175 was legitimate: the judges argued that male homosexuality

---

[19] Kogon, *Der SS-Staat. Das System der deutschen Konzentrationslager* (Düsseldorf, 1946), 210–11.
[20] Footage available at 'Persecution of religious and other victim groups presented at Nuremberg trial', US Holocaust Memorial Museum <https://collections.ushmm.org/search/catalog/irn1002364> [accessed 10 April 2018].
[21] Lautmann, Grikschat and Schmidt, 'Der rosa Winkel in den nationalsozialistischen Konzentrationslagern', in *Seminar: Gesellschaft und Homosexualität*, ed. by Rüdiger Lautmann (Frankfurt a.M., 1977), 325–65. An abridged English-language version of this article appeared three years later, without acknowledging Grikschat and Schmidt. Lautmann, 'The Pink Triangle'.
[22] Wachsmann, *KL: A History of the Nazi Concentration Camps* (London, 2015), 12.
[23] Wilfried Mausbach, 'Wende um 360 Grad? Nationalsozialismus in der "zweiten Gründungsphase" der Bundesrepublik', in *Wo '1968' liegt: Reform und Revolte in der Geschichte der Bundesrepublik*, ed. by Christina von Hodenberg and Detlef Siegfried (Göttingen, 2006), 15–47 (26).
[24] Moeller, *War Stories*. See also Alan Confino, *Germany as a Culture of Remembrance: Promises and Limits of Writing History* (Chapel Hill, NC, 2006).
[25] Moeller, *War Stories*, 28.

contravened moral law and that the paragraph was not contaminated by specifically Nazi ideas.[26] In the prevailing 'memory regime' of the time, there was simply no space for homosexuals.[27]

More surprising than the lack of interest from historians and wider society is the fact that even in the various homophile journals of the 1950s and 1960s precious few references to Nazi persecution can be found. Such an intuitive figure of identification—the homosexual victim of National Socialism—was almost entirely absent from homosexual politics until the arrival of gay liberation.[28] A rare exception came in 1954, when L. D. Classen von Neudegg recounted his experiences in the concentration camps in a series of short articles in the homophile monthly *Humanitas*.[29] Neudegg's account, after over a decade's interlude, was to prove influential, as other homosexuals would subsequently rely on his testimony: in part, because he had suggestively used the description 'final solution of the homosexual problem' (*Endlösung des Homosexuellenproblems*).[30]

The contention that the Nazi persecution of homosexuals had culminated in a 'final solution' was taken up in the first two historical works pertaining to this topic, by Wolfgang Harthauser in 1967 and Harry Wilde in 1969.[31] Although both were short and impressionistic studies, their significance should not be understated. Harthauser's demand to 'shed light on one of the darkest chapters of recent German history' was amplified when repeated in a documentary aired on Radio Bremen in 1966, while Rüdiger Lautmann began his influential research in 1976 by reading Harthauser's article.[32] Meanwhile, Harry Wilde's baseless assertion that the persecution of homosexuals constituted 'a type of dress rehearsal for the final solution of the Jewish question' found a wider audience after being

---

[26] *Entscheidungen des Bundesverfassungsgerichts* (Tübingen, 1957), 389–443.

[27] Drawing on Omer Bartov, Samuel Moyn posits two memory regimes: the first represented the war as a 'site of near universal victimhood' and was replaced in the 1960s by a discourse which focused on the particularity of Jewish suffering. Moyn argues that the first regime 'implicitly or explicitly recognized that there had been "a mosaic of victims"', including homosexuals. In fact, at least in West Germany, it was only the latter memory regime that allowed the belated recognition that homosexuals had been victims of the Nazis. Moyn, 'Two Regimes of Memory', *American Historical Review*, 103:4 (1998), 1182–6. On 'memory regimes', see further Jay Winter, *War Beyond Words*, 122.

[28] Riechers, 'Freundschaft und Anständigkeit', 41.

[29] 'Die Dornenkrone: ein Tatsachenbericht aus der Strafkompanie Sachsenhausen', *Humanitas* 2 (1954), 58–60. See also 'Ein Blick zurück', 3 (1954), 85–6; 'Aus meinem Tagebuch 1939-1945: KZ Oranienburg', 5 (1954), 163–4; 'Versuchsobjekt Mensch', 7 (1954), 225; 'Ecce Homo – oder Tore zur Hölle', 12 (1954), 359–60.

[30] *Humanitas* 2 (1954), 58. An abridged version of Neudegg's testimony was later reprinted in *Emanzipation*: 'Die Dornenkrone: Ein Bericht aus dem KZ-Sachsenhausen', *Emanzipation* 2 (1977), 26–8. An article by James Steakley in *Body Politic* also drew on Neudegg's account: 'Homosexuals and the Third Reich', *Body Politic* 11 (1974), 1 and 20–1.

[31] Harthauser, 'Der Massenmord an Homosexuellen im Dritten Reich', in *Das große Tabu*, ed. by Schlegel, 7–37; Wilde, *Das Schicksal der Verfemten*.

[32] Harthauser, 'Der Massenmord', 8; *Der rosa Winkel* (Radio Bremen, 27 June 1966); Lautmann, 'Homosexuelle in den Konzentrationslagern: Zum Stand der Forschung', *Homosexuelle in Konzentrationslagern*, ed. by Olaf Mussmann (Berlin, 2000), 31–8 (31).

uncritically quoted by *Der Spiegel* in its front-page special on homosexual law reform in 1969.[33]

Homosexual law reform was also the topic that gave rise to Hans-Joachim Schoeps' famous formulation, 'For homosexuals the Third Reich never ended.' Writing in 1962, Schoeps did not specify that homosexuals had been incarcerated in the concentration camps. This information was only added in a nearly identical article a year later.[34] Perhaps he had since read an article published in 1963 by Heinrich Ackermann, who explicitly stated that homosexuals had been in the camps. This was in support of his contention that Paragraph 175 should be reformed, as part of a wider collection of essays calling for a fundamental reform of the sexual criminal code.[35] All these authors recognized the power of reference to the Nazi persecution of homosexuals. However, until the 1970s, this history was invoked only in isolated or schematic form. For example, neither Schoeps nor Ackermann mentioned the pink triangle itself. That would change in 1972, when powerful testimony led to what Michael Holy fittingly calls the 'rediscovery' of the pink triangle.[36]

Heinz Heger's *The Men with the Pink Triangle* was the first book-length memoir recounting the experiences of a homosexual survivor of the concentration camps. Strictly speaking, the book is not an autobiography, as the preface makes clear: 'The author did not himself suffer the treatment portrayed in this book; rather, he wishes only to reproduce what was said and shown to him by one of the very few surviving men with the pink triangle.'[37] Heinz Heger is in fact a dual pseudonym. In all likelihood, the author of the book was Hans Neumann, about whom little is known, whereas the concentration camp survivor was Josef Kohout.[38] This remains widely unrecognized, not least by some of the campaigners and city officials in Vienna responsible for renaming part of a city square—the *Zimmermanplatz,* an address where Josef Kohout used to live—to *Heinz-Heger-Park* in 2009.[39] Josef Kohout died in 1994, without ever having received acknowledgement of or compensation for his incarceration at Flossenbürg and Sachsenhausen concentration camps.[40]

[33] Wilde, *Das Schicksal,* 8; 'Späte Milde', *Der Spiegel* 20 (1969), 55–76 (57).

[34] Schoeps, 'Soll Homosexualität strafbar bleiben?', 22; Schoeps, 'Überlegungen zum Problem der Homosexualität', in *Der homosexuelle Nächste,* ed. by Hermanus Bianchi et al. (Hamburg, 1963), 74–114.

[35] Ackermann, 'Zur Frage der Strafwürdigkeit des homosexuellen Verhaltens des Mannes', in *Sexualität und Verbrechen,* ed. by Bauer et al., 149–60 (152).

[36] Holy, 'Der entliehene Rosa Winkel', 74.   [37] Heger, *Die Männer mit dem Rosa Winkel,* 7.

[38] Frank Gassner, 'Wer war Heinz Heger? Klärung eines Pseudonyms' (March 2011) <http://www.offener-buecherschrank.at/werwarheinzheger.pdf> [accessed 10 July 2016], 9.

[39] Ibid., 1.

[40] Kurt Krickler, 'Heinz Heger: Der Mann mit dem Rosa Winkel', *Lambda-Nachrichten* (2001), 42–4 <http://www.ausdemleben.at/heger.pdf> [accessed 24 February 2018].

The Men with the Pink Triangle was featured in *du&ich* in the same year as its publication and in *him* a year later, in 1973.[41] Until this point, the commercial gay press had followed the lead of the homophile publications of the 1950s and 1960s in barely mentioning the Nazi persecution of homosexuals. In the first issue of *du&ich* in October 1969, editors printed an open letter to the leader of the far-right National Democratic Party of Germany (NPD), Adolf von Thadden, responding to his alleged remarks that the recent reform of the criminal code should be reversed so it would be possible to 'once again have certain people locked up'. Alongside an image of forced labourers in a concentration camp, the letter stated that men with a homophile orientation had not only been locked up in Nazi Germany but murdered in their hundreds of thousands in the camps.[42] Thereafter, however, the publication seemed to be more interested in whether Adolf Hitler might have been queer.[43] Even when the matter at hand was indeed National Socialism and 'homo-hatred', as in a series of articles in *him* in 1972, the fact that homosexuals had been imprisoned in the concentration camps and forced to wear the pink triangle was not even mentioned; instead, the focus was on the murder of the SA leader Ernst Röhm.[44]

The Pink Triangle and the Gay Left

According to Dieter Schiefelbein, himself active in the gay movement in the 1970s, *The Men with the Pink Triangle* soon became 'political and moral set reading for gay movement activists.'[45] No other contemporary text was as widely read in gay liberation, and no other text spurred such a wave of activity, especially in the gay left. Gay action groups displayed the pink triangle on posters, leaflets and banners. The Homosexual Action Hamburg and the Paderborn Action Homosexuality adopted the symbol as their logo, while other groups incorporated the symbol into their name, such as the Pink Triangle Wuppertal (*Rosa Winkel Wuppertal*).[46] *Rotzschwul*, from Frankfurt, was the first action group to adopt the pink triangle in a public action, in March 1972. Activists distributed small pink triangles to

---

[41] 'Die Entarteten im KZ', *du&ich* 11 (1972), 10–12; Wilhelm Sorge, 'Unterdrückt, getreten, vernichtet', *him* 9 (1973), 22.
[42] Loose insert in *du&ich* (October 1969).
[43] 'Meine Liebesnacht mit Hitler: Protokoll einer Begegnung', *du&ich* 10 (1971), 40–1; 'War Hitler homosexuell?', *du&ich* 6 (1975), 12–13.
[44] Fedor Fackeltanz, 'Als Homohass die Welt in Flammen setzte', *him*; initially in June 1972 (30–3) and periodically thereafter. See further Holy, 'Der entliehene Rosa Winkel', 74.
[45] Schiefelbein, '"...so wie die Juden..." – Versuch, ein Mißverständnis zu verstehen', in *Der Frankfurter Engel: Mahnmal Homosexuellenverfolgung*, ed. by Initiative Mahnmal Homosexuellenverfolgung (Frankfurt a.M., 1997), 35–73 (35).
[46] Rosenkranz and Lorenz, *Hamburg auf anderen Wegen*, 150. On Paderborn, see 'Die Schwulen kommen!', *AHA Info* (June 1979), 17. On Wuppertal, see *Emanzipation* 2 (1978), 35–6.

passers-by during a demonstration.[47] The first attempt to theorize how the symbol created by the Nazis might be resignified for the purposes of gay liberation came from a sub-group of the Homosexual Action West Berlin (HAW), in October 1973. After providing a brief summary of *The Men with the Pink Triangle*, the HAW 'male feminists' proposed introducing the pink triangle as the group's logo, and argued that each activist should wear the triangle in badge form on their clothing.[48]

Their intervention came in the midst of a strategic debate within the wider group about the merits of drag and what might be called 'gender fuck': adopting elements of both masculine and feminine dress, style, and speech, and performing these in deliberately exaggerated ways (this debate will be examined in Chapter 5). The 'male feminists' envisaged that the pink triangle would serve a similar function to drag. By wearing the symbol, activists who did not want to adopt gender transgressive dress or behaviour could show their solidarity with those who did so. Both drag and pink triangle were intended to increase the visibility of homosexuality and to shatter the veneer of liberal tolerance in the Federal Republic. Moreover, the pink triangle was supposed to communicate that 'between gay oppression under National Socialism and our own oppression in the liberal Federal Republic and West Berlin there exists only a quantitative and not a qualitative difference'.[49]

Not all gay liberationists made the association between drag and the pink triangle, but the goal to communicate a link between gay oppression then and now was widely shared. A case in point is the documentary *Pink Triangle? But that's ages ago*, co-directed by the Bielefeld-based gay activist Detlef Stoffel, produced in 1976 and then shown around the country in a multitude of events normally arranged by local gay groups.[50] A poster advertising one screening summarized the film as concerning 'the straight line of gay oppression from fascism to today, and what gays are doing about it'.[51] Opening with a brief segment on the Nazi persecution of homosexuals, including uncontextualized stock footage of Auschwitz-Birkenau (where pink triangles, as a prisoner group, did not exist), the remainder of the film was dedicated to presenting several examples of contemporary discrimination.[52]

[47] Dominique Grisard, 'Zum Stellenwert der Farbe in der Schwulen- und Lesbenbewegung', in *Rosa Radikale*, ed. by Pretzel and Weiß, 177–98 (183).

[48] HAW Feministengruppe, 'Feministenpapier', 10. SMB archive. The authors also state that *Rotzschwul* was the first group to use the symbol (5).

[49] HAW Feministengruppe, 'Thesenpapier zur Strukturierung der Diskussion über das F[eministen]Papier', 1–2 (1). SMB archive.

[50] *Rosa Winkel? Das ist doch schon lange vorbei*, dir. by Detlef Stoffel, Christiane Schmerl and Peter Recht (Universität Bielefeld, 1976).

[51] 'Rosa Winkel?'. APO, folder 1052.

[52] Homosexuals were only classified as a prisoner group in the concentration camps, not in the extermination camps. See further Geoffrey Giles, 'The Denial of Homosexuality: Same-Sex Incidents in Himmler's SS and Police', *Journal of the History of Sexuality* 11 (2002), 256–90. Certainly there would

These examples included gay men being fired from their jobs due to their sexuality, medicalized forms of oppression, including experimental brain surgery aiming to change sexual behaviour, and the plight of the Society for Sexual Reform (GSR), the Aachen group that had been denied permission to hold an information stall by the city council. At the film's conclusion, the following text was displayed:

> The pink triangle has become an international symbol of the gay movement. A symbol of the history that others have tried to obliterate and which gays must discover. It is a reminder of where gay oppression can lead if gays do not actively struggle for their rights.[53]

This concluding message was addressed to (other) homosexuals, using the power of reference to Nazi persecution as a mobilizing device, exhorting them to engage in the gay movement, to 'struggle for their rights', not to settle for the limited liberalizations of Paragraph 175 in 1969 and 1973. In the same year, the gay magazine *Schwuchtel* used exactly the same text on its back cover, advertising the pink triangle, badges of which could be bought for one DM.[54] Indeed, an almost identical English-language version of this text was used to the same ends in *Body Politic*, a Canadian gay journal.[55]

Alfred Heinlein had urged gay activists to become conscious of their 'specific history'. In fact, gay activists at times actually needed to make this history somewhat less specific, in order to appeal to the alternative left. The gay left set about rediscovering, imagining, and creating a 'specific' or 'separatist' history, while ensuring that this history could lend itself to 'assimilationist' accounts too. At times, this was interpreted in its widest possible sense. Consider the case of the Homosexual Action Munich activists, who declared in 1975 'Today we wear the Pink Triangle again in order to show that we perceive this society as a new concentration camp', before swiftly adding: 'not only for gays, but for all, who want to be free'.[56] Usually, 'assimilationist' uses of the pink triangle were targeted at more particular audiences—the left-alternative circles in which gay action groups articulated themselves. Writing in the leftist magazine *Carlo Sponti*, an activist from Heidelberg explained that he wore the pink triangle to convey that the oppression of homosexual desire existed now just as it did then, but also as a symbol of the oppression of sexual desire in general, and to protest at the division

have been many thousands of homosexuals among the approximately one million Jews murdered at Auschwitz-Birkenau, but they were murdered because they were Jewish, not because they were homosexual.

[53] My transcript and translation from the film's conclusion. A copy is available at the SMB archive.
[54] *Schwuchtel* 4 (1976). Detlef Stoffel periodically contributed articles to the magazine, and presumably was responsible for this text too.
[55] *Body Politic* 22 (1976), 1.
[56] HAM, 'Wir tragen den Rosa Winkel', in *Der Rosa Winkel*, ed. by HAW (July 1975), 16.

of the personal and the political.[57] Explaining their understanding of the symbol, another sub-group of the HAW described the pink triangle as 'the historic symbol of sexual oppression here in Germany' and argued that it was a symbol of the struggle against reactionary gender norms.[58] These examples indicate the attempt by some in the gay left to work more closely with the lesbian and women's movements, hence labelling the pink triangle as a symbol not of gay oppression but of sexual oppression more generally. However, in an example of how 'assimilationist' and 'separatist' strategies were interwoven, activists moved on to specify that it was in fact gay men who had borne the brunt of the most virulent form of this ostensibly *general* sexual oppression.[59]

At times, the pink triangle was used as a rallying cry aimed particularly or exclusively at gay men—symbolizing difference, what set gays apart from wider society. Yet the pink triangle was not just used to stress difference, but also resemblance, emphasizing simultaneous and shared oppression, both in the contemporary Federal Republic and in the Third Reich. In other words, at times the *colour* of the pink triangle was predominant, its 'pinkness'—highlighting that prisoners were incarcerated on account of their sexuality. At other times the *shape* of the pink triangle was more germane, its 'triangularity'—in short, that the pink triangle was just another version of the red triangle, worn by political prisoners in the concentration camps. These tensions can be seen in debates over which symbol groups should officially endorse. The HAW 'male feminists' had suggested adopting the pink triangle as the HAW's insignia in part because they were dissatisfied with the current logo, a red clenched fist superimposed against a red heart. Their ultimately unsuccessful proposal would have involved changing the name of the HAW to the *Schwule Befreiungsfront*, a direct translation of Gay Liberation Front.[60] Symptomatic of the need to appeal to different audiences and display multiple allegiances, another group, the HAH, went on to adopt *both* the pink triangle *and* the clenched fist of socialist iconography in their official logo.[61]

For the gay left, the pink triangle functioned as a rhetoric of appeal, proof that activists were exhibiting the 'correct' political analysis—by focusing on issues of shared persecution of gay and heterosexual leftists. The prime instance of this kind was the *Extremistenbeschluß*, the 'Extremists' Resolution', more commonly

---

[57] Violet, 'Warum tragen wir den Rosa Winkel?', *Carlo Sponti* 16–17 (1975), 10.

[58] HAW *Sponti-Schwule*, 'Zum ROSA WINKEL', in *Der Rosa Winkel*, ed. by HAW (1975), 17–23 (17). The article was orginally published in the leftist weekly INFO BUG, in 1975.

[59] Ibid., 17.

[60] 'Feministenpapier', 6. Tracing the HAW's various logos is almost as complex as keeping track of its myriad sub-groups. See the banner depicted in Figure 5.1 for an example of the clenched fist against a heart. For a derivative, see Figure 3.1; at times, a clenched fist was depicted inside a circle. Protruding from the borders of the circle, two adjacent male and two adjacent female biological symbols were displayed (similar to ⚣ and ⚢).

[61] The clenched fist was first used by the KPD in 1924. See further Beate Schappach, 'Geballte Faust, Doppelaxt, rosa Winkel: Gruppenkonstituierende Symbole der Frauen-, Lesben- und Schwulenbewegung', in *Linksalternative Milieus*, ed. by Baumann, Gehrig and Büchse, 259–83.

referred to as the *Radikalenerlass* (radicals' decree) and invariably dubbed the *Berufsverbot* ('ban on careers') by its opponents. Introduced in 1972, the measure permitted the screening of current and prospective civil-service employees along the lines of current or past membership of 'radical' groups, which was usually taken to mean communist. Were sufficient evidence of a lack of support for the constitutional order to be found, individuals could have their applications rejected or contracts terminated. Since the civil service encompassed myriad posts, from teachers to train divers, the policy had a wide impact, leading to hundreds of thousands of screenings and several hundred rejections and dismissals.[62]

The 'ban on careers', according to gay activists, claimed two gay victims in West Berlin in 1974, the teacher Reiner Koepp and the Protestant Church youth worker Klaus Kindel. The authorities did not, in fact, draw on the *Extremistenbeschluß* in either case, though Koepp's 'role as a feminine homosexual' was explicitly cited in a court ruling justifying and upholding the decision of the school administration not to renew his contract in September 1974.[63] Addressing a convention calling for Koepp's reinstatement, HAW activists argued that there was now a 'ban on careers for gays' in the Federal Republic, from which any openly gay person was at risk.[64] Writing in *Emanzipation* in 1976, Ralf Dose and Friedhelm Krey referred to Kindel's case as a *Berufsverbot* and drew comparisons to similar treatment of political 'radicals', since Kindel had lost his job in May 1974 as a result of collecting signatures for the repeal of Paragraph 175: 'Kindel did no more (and no less) than exercise his democratic right to free expression of opinion and take part in the struggle of the gay minority against their special oppression. His court case is therefore part of the contemporary large-scale attempt to discipline active democrats, socialists and communists.'[65]

The *Berufsverbot* primarily targeted members of communist parties: accordingly, gay activism on this issue was largely channelled into seeking the support of communists. When the pink triangle was used in this regard, the emphasis was placed on shared oppression with communists, as opposed to the rarer example cited above, that the triangle represented 'general sexual oppression' and hence shared oppression not with (male) communists but with lesbian and women's movement activists. Dieter Runze explained that he wore the pink triangle in order to recall the division of various kinds of prisoner in the concentration camps and thus to raise consciousness about contemporary attempts to marginalize

---

[62] Braunthal, *Political Loyalty and Public Service in West Germany*, 47.

[63] 'Im Namen des Volkes', in *Schwule sich emanzipieren lernen*, ed. by Hedenström, 16–18 (18).

[64] Speech untitled and undated. Printed in *HAW Info* 16 (1974), 35–40 (40).

[65] Dose and Krey, 'Der Kindel-Prozeß in Berlin (West): Teilerfolg gegen Berufsverbot der Kirche', *Emanzipation* 3 (1976), 16–17 (16). Kindel legally challenged the church's decision to remove him from his post, and later in 1976 was given a post in a different area of the church's work. 'Klaus Kindel: Vergleich im Schwulenprozess', *Schwuchtel* 2/3 (1976), 8.

certain sections of the population.[66] In this context, part of the attraction of the pink triangle surely lay in its ability to undermine the myth, still current in some leftist circles, that there existed some form of connection between homosexuality and fascism.[67]

In 1976, Joachim Hohmann, a regular columnist in *him*, published his book *Homosexuality and Subculture*, which he dedicated to 'the men with the pink triangle': not only to the ostensible 80,000 who had perished in the concentration camps but also to those who wore the triangle in the 1970s.[68] One of his chapters pertained to the *Berufsverbot*, in which Hohmann compared the process of screening civil service personnel to the Inquisition. He argued that the 'modern inquisitors' did not discriminate when choosing whom or what to persecute: 'One had sold a copy of the *Rote Fahne* [Red Flag, a communist newspaper]. Another had read it. The third had marched against the war in Vietnam. The fourth is a member of the wrong party. The fifth kissed another man in public.'[69] The HAW's *Berufsverbot* group gave a more overtly ideological slant to this line of thought in a letter sent to other gay action groups in September 1975. Activists maintained that the cases of Kindel and Koepp were connected with the 'baiting' of 'so-called political radicals', as the *Berufsverbot* was aimed at all who called the structural fabric of society into question, whether economic *or* moral.[70] Thus, following Hohmann's example above, kissing a man on the street achieved a similar subversiveness to selling a communist newspaper. Activists added imagery of incarceration to illustrate their point: 'An invisible barbed wire fence of "radicality" (= "criminal") or "morality" (= "abnormal", "gay", "perverse", "work-shy") is being wrapped around these people.'[71]

This kind of understanding reached its height with the National Working Group Repression against Gays (NARGS), which adopted the pink triangle as part of its logo. Set up in 1977 following a call by the HAH, the umbrella group sought to ensure that cases of gay oppression would be investigated as part of the Third International Russell Tribunal on Human Rights.[72] Convened by the Bertrand Russell Peace Foundation, the Tribunal was split into two hearings: the first took place in Frankfurt in April 1978 and was dedicated to the *Berufsverbot*, while the second considered alleged censorship and rights abuses in the legal process, taking place in Cologne in January 1979.[73] Seeking to embed their cause

---

[66] Runze, 'Warum ist "Homosexualität" ein "soziales Problem"?', in *Seminar: Gesellschaft und Homosexualität*, ed. by Rüdiger Lautmann (Frankfurt a.M., 1977), 484–92 (490).

[67] Manfred Herzer, 'Das Dritte Geschlecht und das dritte Reich', *Siegessäule* 5 (May 1985), 31. See further Harry Oosterhuis, 'The "Jews" of the Antifascist Left', *Journal of Homosexuality*, 29:2–3 (1995), 227–57 and Laurie Marhoefer, *Sex and the Weimar Republic*, 146–73.

[68] Hohmann, *Homosexualität und Subkultur* (Offenbach, 1976), 4.   [69] Ibid., 176.

[70] Printed in *HAW Info* 20 (1975), 5–6 (5).   [71] Ibid., 5.

[72] *Rosa: Eine Zeitung der Schwulenbewegung* 8 (1977), 48.

[73] See further März, *Linker Protest*, 245–317. Organizers sought—in vain—to emulate the successes of the Foundation's first two Tribunals, which had been held in 1967 (on war crimes in Vietnam) and in 1974 (on political repression in Latin America).

in the Tribunal, NARGS produced a brochure called 'Gays against Oppression and Fascism', which was sold in the gay scene, in university canteens, at information stalls and through leftist bookshops.[74]

In a similar fashion to the film *Pink Triangle? But That's Ages Ago*, the brochure set out various examples of gay oppression, including the cases of Koepp and Kindel, police raids on the gay scene, denigration of homosexuals in the media, discrimination in the rental market, and the banning of the GSR's information stall in Aachen. In the brochure, NARGS attempted to connect these examples with the contemporary political situation facing 'all progressive forces'.[75] Seeking to underline this point, the group made sure to include a version of Martin Niemöller's famous poetic confession ('First they came for the communists, and I didn't speak out because I wasn't a communist [...]').[76] This move served to highlight the importance of various groups supporting each other, while also drawing attention to the fact that homosexuals were *not* among the groups of victims that Niemöller had mentioned in 1946. In the event, only one case put forward by NARGS was ultimately presented to the Tribunal's international jury members, that of the banning of the of GSR's information stall in Aachen.[77]

The pink triangle and the tactical approach of connecting this symbol to the red triangle is evidence not only of the suggestiveness of this parallel but also of the difficulty activists knew they had in gaining support from the alternative left. NARGS eventually succeeded in bringing an example of gay oppression before the Russell Tribunal in 1977 only because activists had stubbornly engaged in the Tribunal's 'supporters' movement' for the previous two years. At a congress in Göttingen convened by the myriad groups making up that supporters' movement, delegates passed a resolution calling on the Tribunal not to restrict its investigation of alleged human-rights abuses to censorship and the 'ban on careers' alone.[78] By excluding other oppressive measures, the will of the majority of those supporting the Tribunal would be ignored and this would trivialize the 'range and depth of political oppression' in the Federal Republic. The measures cited included the worsening of prison conditions, the security services' undermining of grass-roots campaigns, the criminalization of women protesting against the abortion law, and

---

[74] Untitled minutes of organizing meeting, January 1978. SMB archive: NARGS box 1, folder 1978. See further Craig Griffiths, 'Gay activism in Modell Deutschland', *European Review of History* 22 (2014), 60–76.

[75] NARGS, 'Schwule gegen Unterdrückung und Faschismus' (1977), 17. SMB archive.

[76] Ibid., 17. 'Als die Nazis die Kommunisten holten, habe ich geschwiegen; ich war ja kein Kommunist. / Als sie die Sozialdemokraten einsperrten, habe ich geschwiegen; ich war ja kein Sozialdemokrat. / Als sie die Katholiken holten, habe ich nicht protestiert; ich war ja kein Katholik. / Als sie mich holten, gab es keinen mehr, der protestieren konnte'.

[77] 'Verbot eines Informationsstandes der Homosexuellen Aktionsgruppe in Aachen', in *3. Internationales Russell-Tribunal: Zur Situation der Menschenrechte in der Bundesrepublik Deutschland* (Berlin: Rotbuch, 1979) [volume three], 53–4.

[78] 'Protokoll der 2. Arbeitskonferenz zur Vorbereitung eines Russell-Tribunals über die Repression in der BRD', 25–6.7.1977. APO archive, folder 1019. Not paginated.

the increasing pressure on trade unions to toe the line of the federal government. As part of this wider definition of political oppression, the gay left's voice was heard. Activists managed to have 'discrimination and agitation against gays *in the direct tradition of fascist methods*' added to the resolution.[79] Clearly, activists felt it important to underscore the perceived fascist heritage of contemporary discrimination, an association that the pink triangle perfectly symbolized. This was not least because activists had little confidence that their plight would otherwise be taken seriously. The wording of this part of the resolution, after all, suggests that it was not merely discrimination against gays that was seen as worthy of denunciation, but only discrimination that could somehow be linked to the Nazi past, discrimination therefore that leftists and human rights activists would have a moral duty to oppose.

Indeed, Elmar Kraushaar argues that the pink triangle was in fact the 'last means' of anchoring gay emancipation to the left.[80] Not all leftists found the juxtaposition of pink and red triangles convincing. When former concentration camp inmate Andreas K. attempted to seek the support of the Association for the Persecuted of the Nazi Regime (VVN), at their Hamburg office in the late 1940s, he was told that homosexuals were 'a bunch of dirty pigs'.[81] In East Germany, the VVN ruled that homosexuals could become members only if they could prove they had *resisted* National Socialism. Merely being persecuted was insufficient.[82] In April 1979, gay activists from the General Homosexual Action Alliance (AHA) sought to take part in an anti-fascist rally in Strasbourg, organized by the VVN. Having unfurled their banner, which read 'Gays in the concentration camps – never again!', they were unceremoniously removed from the march by two orderlies.[83] At a VVN congress in Dortmund later that year, the AHA was denied permission to distribute a leaflet. The leaflet, which was given out regardless, complained that homosexuals, too, were victims of National Socialism, but that they had never received respect or solidarity from the VVN, which essentially demarcated those persecuted by the Nazi regime into 'good' and 'bad' victims.[84]

The Yellow Star and the 'Weimar Syndrome'

In 1977, the Initiative Group Homosexuality Bielefeld (IHB) made the following assessment of the news that *Brühwarm* had been prevented from performing in a local youth centre: 'no wonder, in a state in which fascistoid thinking, speaking and acting are the order of the day. Whoever speaks today about "preventing"

---

[79] Ibid. Emphasis added.   [80] Kraushaar, 'Nebenwidersprüche', 158.
[81] Whisnant, *Male Homosexuality*, 47.   [82] McLellan, *Love in the Time of Communism*, 114.
[83] *Emanzipation* 4 (1979), 8–9.   [84] Leaflet reproduced in *AHA-Info* 9 (1979), 13–14.

might say tomorrow "gassing".'[85] Although the IHB made a conspicuously hyperbolic leap from censorship to the gas chambers, it was only later that year that the first serious piece of historical scholarship on the Nazi persecution of homosexuals was published.[86] This challenged widespread misconceptions such as prisoners wearing the pink triangle having been murdered in the gas chambers, victims reaching the tens or even hundreds of thousands, or that this had formed part of a 'final solution'. While many individuals and groups were honest enough to admit that the number of victims was simply unknown, inflated figures did sometimes appear: in May 1976, one HAW activist laid down a wreath at the site of the former Sachsenhausen concentration camp in memory of his '250,000 charred sisters', while according to the Homosexuality Working Group Braunschweig there had been 400,000 gay victims.[87] This tendency was by no means unique to gay groups, with the editors of the commercial gay magazine *unter uns* speaking of 250,000 victims in 1977.[88] The assumption that these kinds of figures were involved and that pink triangle prisoners had been sent not just to concentration camps, but also to the extermination camps, amounted to an appropriation of the model of the Holocaust. As Dieter Schiefelbein has shown, the Holocaust offered an obvious and easily accessible explanatory device to understand and imagine the course of Nazi homophobia, especially in the context of the paucity of historical research into the specific persecution faced by homosexuals.[89] The contemporary assumption, therefore, that gay men in the Third Reich had been sent to the gas chambers was understandable. The related argument, that gay liberationists in the 1970s might end up sharing their fate, is less intuitive and requires further explanation.

Knud Andresen contends that drawing parallels between contemporary political developments and the Holocaust is a hallmark of anti-Semitism after Auschwitz.[90] Wilfried Mausbach, meanwhile, has analysed what he refers to as the 1968 generation's 'flight from the national burden'.[91] The pattern was set in the late 1960s when West German peace activists compared the United States' actions in Vietnam to Nazi atrocities. In this interpretation, fascism had little to do with anti-Semitism, appearing instead as simply the worst manifestation of capitalism and militarism. After demonstrator Benno Ohnesorg was shot dead by police in June 1967, student activists displaced the position of Vietnamese peasants, beginning to imagine themselves as 'prospective victims of

---

[85] 'Über das gesunde Volksempfinden im Bielefelder Stadtrat', *Rosa* 10 (1977), 38.

[86] Lautmann, Grikschat and Schmidt, 'Der rosa Winkel'.

[87] 'Bettys Gedanken', *HAW Info* 22 (1976), 5; on Braunschweig, see newspaper clipping included in *HAW Info* 20 (1975), 22.

[88] *unter uns* 5/6 (1977), 3.   [89] Schiefelbein, 'So wie die Juden', 43–4.

[90] Andresen, 'Linker Antisemitismus – Wandlungen in der Alternativbewegung', in *Das Alternative Milieu*, ed. by Reichardt and Siegfried, 146–68 (162).

[91] Mausbach, 'Wende um 360 Grad?', 34.

extermination'.[92] After Ohnesorg's killing, the Socialist German Student League (SDS) produced a leaflet comparing media magnate Axel Springer, owner of the *BILD* tabloid, to Julius Streicher, editor of the rabidly anti-Semitic *Der Stürmer*. Streicher had incited the murder of Jews, for which he received the death penalty at the Nuremberg war crimes trial. According to the SDS, Springer incited the murder of students and was left free to continue doing so.[93] After the attempted assassination of student leader Rudi Dutschke in 1968, the SDS passed a resolution stating that the methods of anti-Semitism were now being used against 'new minorities': namely, themselves.[94] The potential victims of contemporary fascism came therefore to be seen not predominantly as the Jews, but as left-wing students.

Five years after Ohnesorg's killing, the publication of *The Men with the Pink Triangle* in 1972 allowed gay activists to follow in these footsteps, and to identify themselves as the most likely targets of a state potentially sliding backwards into fascism. The persecution of homosexuals, both in the concentration camps and in the 1970s Federal Republic, was juxtaposed not with the persecution of the Jews, but with that of communists and other left-wingers. The political expediency in drawing comparisons with the red triangle rather than with the yellow star, which Jews had been forced to wear in Nazi Germany, lay in the fact that this enabled the connection to be made between shared persecution in the past and shared persecution in the present, most significantly in the form of the *Berufsverbot*, the 'ban on careers'. This equation of two forms of Nazi persecution arguably came at the expense of downplaying a third and far more murderous persecution, that against the Jews. It also constituted a gay iteration of the 'flight from the national burden'. As Manfred Herzer would later reprimand other activists, only a small minority of homosexuals could be counted among the victims of National Socialism. A large majority, according to Herzer, had been 'willing subjects and beneficiaries' of the Nazi state, just like other German men and women.[95]

In his satirical novel *Lavendelschwert*, published in 1966, Felix Rexhausen documented a fictional homosexual insurgency, which temporarily succeeded in toppling the federal government in Bonn.[96] The novel was structured around a series of 'documents', all of which were fictitious, other than the draft of a bill published by the governing Christian Democrats in 1962.[97] As discussed in Chapter 1, that bill would have prolonged the criminalization of the 'depraved

[92] Wilfried Mausbach, 'America's Vietnam in Germany – Germany in America's Vietnam: On the Relocation of Spaces and the Appropriation of History', in *Changing the World*, ed. by Davis et al., 41–64 (47).

[93] Appendix 25 in Czubayko, *Die Sprache von Studenten- und Alternativbewegung*.

[94] 'Grundsatzerklärung des SDS zur Kampagne für die Enteignung des Springer-Konzerns'. Appendix 26 in Czubayko, *Die Sprache von Studenten- und Alternativbewegung*. See further Alexander Sedlmaier, *Consumption and Violence*, 168–204.

[95] Herzer, 'Das Dritte Geschlecht und dritte Reich', *Siegessäule* 5 (1985), 31.

[96] Rexhausen, *Lavendelschwert: Dokumente einer seltsamen Revolution* (Frankfurt a.M., 1966).

[97] Ibid., 50.

drive' of male homosexuality.[98] Seeking to underline the links between National Socialism and Christian Democracy in this area, one of Rexhausen's fictitious documents consisted of the minutes of a CDU meeting regarding a draft bill to enforce the registration of homosexuals. Homosexuals would have 'HS' stamped on their identity cards. Thus registered, landlords would not let to them, leading to whole areas populated by homosexuals alone. Moreover, the bill would have a secret clause. In times of emergency, homosexuals could be rounded up and incarcerated in camps. The allusions to the yellow star, to ghettoization, and to the deportation of the Jews could hardly have been any clearer.[99]

All these allusions were repeated in an article Rexhausen penned for *him* in 1972, in which he sought to urge the magazine's readers to reflect on the ramifications of voting Christian Democrat in the upcoming federal election. The magazine presented a double-page spread detailing the hypothetical minutes of a future Christian Democrat cabinet meeting. The hypothetical ministers discussed a hypothetical forced registration of homosexuals, before going on to speculate about a 'camp-like seizure'. This was all superimposed on a suggestive background image depicting SS guards conducting a roll call of concentration camp inmates.[100] Rexhausen, born in 1932 and a founding member of the West German chapter of Amnesty International, was perhaps afflicted by what Dirk Moses calls the 'Weimar syndrome'.[101] A lack of trust in West German institutions and fear that the Federal Republic might meet the same fate as the Weimar Republic was not limited to those on the left. Older liberals also shared this concern, especially in the 1960s. Karl Dietrich Bracher, for example, used an article in *Der Spiegel* in 1967 to ask whether Bonn would, after all, go the same way as Weimar.[102]

The 'Weimar syndrome' contextualizes the extraordinary regularity with which the Nazi past was invoked as a comparison to, or warning about, the West German present. Arguably, this tendency had lessened by the end of the 1960s, with the election of a social-liberal government in 1969 and with Willy Brandt, forced into exile during the Third Reich, becoming Chancellor, replacing Kurt Georg Kiesinger, who had been a member of the Nazi party. Yet in advance of the 1972 federal election, an article in the leftist magazine *konkret* warned that were the CDU to emerge victorious, steps would be taken to enable political concentration camps.[103] In the same year, victims of the *Berufsverbot* were described as 'the new Jews', with the process of screening civil service applicants compared to

---

[98] Full text of the bill included as an appendix to *Sexualität und Verbrechen*, ed. by Bauer et al., 405–12. Here, 411.
[99] Rexhausen, *Lavendelschwert*, 61–72.
[100] Felix Rexhausen, 'Ein HS in den Personalausweis!', *him* 11 (1972), 24–7.
[101] Wildenthal, *The Language of Human Rights*, 76.
[102] Moses, *German Intellectuals*, 48 and 160–85; 'Wird Bonn doch Weimar?', *Der Spiegel* 12 (1967), 60–8.
[103] Jürgen Roth, 'Störer in Stellung! Feuer frei!', *konkret* 21 (1972), 48–50 (49).

Nazi measures to aryanize the civil service in 1933.[104] In another allusion to the coming of the Third Reich, a caption on the front cover of the same magazine in April 1975 asked 'On the way to the police state – when will the *Bundestag* burn?'[105] Fears of Bonn meeting Weimar's fate endured in the 1970s, at least on the left, and at least in gay liberation. Felix Rexhausen may have been recycling material from 1966 in penning his dramatic warning to *him* readers in 1972, but the very fact that editors included this account says much about the continuing valency of the Nazi past. Because of homosexuals' marginalized position in society, and because of the 'rediscovery' of the pink triangle, such a potent symbol from the world of the concentration camps, the 'Weimar syndrome' would live on in 1970s homosexual politics.[106]

The 'Weimar syndrome' contextualizes what might otherwise be seen as some-what irresponsible exaggerations. With respect to the student movement in 1968, Christina von Hodenberg argues that references to fascism were essentially tac-tical: 'That a fall into a new fascism was imminent' may have been a 'politically effective' argument but was one that 'even the more radical activists did not fully believe'.[107] On the other hand, as Tim Brown has stridently reminded us, the postwar era was not a time 'in which fascism could be safely consigned to the past'. He cites the continued existence of two long-standing 'fascist or authoritarian conservative' regimes in Portugal and Spain and the establishment of fascist, 'authoritarian-nationalist' or military rule in Guatemala (1954), Paraguay (1954), Brazil (1964), Bolivia (1964), Argentina (1966), and Chile (1973).[108] Brown therefore cautions against understanding what I call here the 'Weimar syndrome' as 'some sort of German psychodrama in which young people proved incapable of distinguishing between liberal democracy and fascist dictatorship'.[109] Indeed, the Nazi frame of reference was open to a wider group of actors. Examples of using the Holocaust as a metaphor in the student movement, in the gay left and in the alternative left can usefully be juxtaposed by examples from other political traditions, for example the way the Christian Right attempted to rally support against the legalization of abortion. CSU representa-tive Maria Probst went so far as to state that 'Even to relax Paragraph 218

---

[104] Walter Leo, '"Die neuen Juden" oder das Kartell der Angstmacher', *konkret* 9 (1972), 44–5.
[105] *konkret* 4 (1975).
[106] I use 'Weimar syndrome' in a narrower sense than Dirk Moses, who refers not only to the fears of student protestors, but the fears of their detractors. Accusations of fascism were also directed at students themselves, as liberals who had previously supported calls for reform became concerned about threats to academic freedom and perceived links between the generations of 1933 and 1968. Moses, *German Intellectuals*, 192–6. These accusations tended not to be directed at gay activists in the 1970s; a rare exception came in 1973, when a viewer of *Not the Homosexual* wrote to the WDR after the film's screening and the subsequent studio discussion, describing Rosa von Praunheim, Martin Dannecker and the other homosexuals present as an ignorant 'horde of Nazis'. 22 January 1973, WDR archive, folder 08585.
[107] Hodenberg, *Das andere Achtundsechzig*, 75.   [108] Brown, *West Germany*, 99.
[109] Ibid., 101.

partially would mean the state was permitting murder. Here the course would be set whose final step must lead to a new Auschwitz.'[110] In 1973, Catholic doctor Siegfried Ernst described the prospective legalization of abortion as 'the largest Auschwitz in European history'.[111]

Just as making reference to the Nazi past was not a peculiarly left-wing trait, this tendency was by no means limited to West Germans. Writing in *Gay Sunshine* in 1970, Don Jackson alleged that homosexuals were being tortured in the Atascadero hospital in California, through the means of electric shock therapy and castration: his article was entitled 'Dachau in America'. Jackson issued the following warning: 'To my Gay sisters and brothers I say Reagan's paradise is restaging Dachau here. It can happen here. It is happening here. Wake up. Wake up before it's too late.'[112] Jackson did not mention the pink triangle, because the Nazi persecution of homosexuals had not yet been 'rediscovered'. Later in the decade, following in West German footsteps, gay liberationists in the United States also adopted the pink triangle as a gay symbol. In his analysis of the 'transnational quality of the gay and lesbian community's collective memory', Erik Jensen has shown that in the United States there was a more full-blown equation of the pink triangle with the yellow star.[113]

Just as in the Federal Republic, this history of persecution was used as rallying cry against contemporary discrimination. A case in point was the activist response to Anita Bryant's 'Save our Children' campaign, which in 1977 successfully overturned a civil-rights ordinance in Dade County, Florida: the law had briefly outlawed discrimination against gays and lesbians in education, housing and employment.[114] After the campaign spread from its Floridian roots to national exposure and an attempt to ban gay teachers from working in public schools in California, a review of one of Bryant's books in *Body Politic* was entitled 'Taking another crack at the final solution'.[115] Harvey Milk, the first openly gay elected official in California, also invoked the model of the Holocaust when addressing a gay-rights rally in San Francisco in 1978: 'We are not going to sit back in silence as 300,000 of our gay brothers and sisters did in Nazi Germany. We are not going to allow our rights to be taken away and then march with bowed heads into the gas chambers.'[116]

---

[110] Cited from Herzog, *Sex After Fascism*, 77.

[111] 'Abtreibung: Massenmord oder Privatsache?', *Der Spiegel* 21 (1973), 38–58 (46).

[112] Jackson, 'Dachau in America', *Gay Sunshine* (November 1970), 20. Hall-Carpenter Archives, LSE. HCA/Journals/198.

[113] Jensen, 'The Pink Triangle', 339.

[114] Gillian Frank, '"The Civil Rights of Parents": Race and Conservative Politics in Anita Bryant's Campaign Against Gay Rights in 1970s Florida', *Journal of the History of Sexuality* 22 (2013), 126–60.

[115] Cited from Jensen, 'The Pink Triangle', 329.

[116] James D Steakley, 'Selbstkritische Gedanken zur Mythologisierung der Homosexuellen verfolgung im Dritten Reich' in *Nationalsozialistischer Terror gegen Homosexuelle: verdrängt und ungesühnt*, ed. by Burkhard Jellonek and Rüdiger Lautmann (Paderborn, 2002), 55–70 (57).

In 1975, Ira Glasser, the executive director of the New York Civil Liberties Union, penned an editorial for the *New York Times* entitled 'The Yellow Star and The Pink Triangle'. Asserting that there had been almost 250,000 homosexual victims of National Socialism, Glasser compared the tolerance of contemporary discrimination against homosexuals to the tolerance of anti-Semitism before the Holocaust. According to Glasser, while discrimination in employment and housing on the basis of race, religion, or gender was illegal, the same kind of discrimination against homosexuals was still permitted: 'Just as the Jews of Europe had to hide or perish, so many homosexuals today must hide in New York City to avoid the penalties of "coming out" in the open: loss of job, harassment and abuse, even rejection by family and friends.'[117] To highlight this situation, Glasser commented that homosexuals were wearing pink triangles, and would continue to do so until the City Council passed an anti-discrimination ordinance. Among those opposing the ordinance were orthodox Jewish groups, and in August 1974 gay activists demonstrated against these groups, picketers wearing the pink triangle on armbands, in the effort to show that homosexuals had been fellow victims of Jews in the Third Reich.[118]

In West German gay liberation, focusing on the red triangle as opposed to the yellow star may have actually served to militate against some of the more egregious examples of the instrumentalization of the Holocaust that can be found in other national contexts. The most (in)famous example is perhaps *Bent*, a play first performed in London in 1979 but written by Martin Sherman, from the United States (Sherman is also gay and Jewish). The play was later adapted into a film, starring Clive Owen and Mick Jagger.[119] Presenting a tale of gay love against the backdrop of the concentration camps, pink triangle prisoners were depicted as occupying the lowest rung of the camp hierarchy. Indeed, one of the protagonists, Max, manages to swap his pink triangle for a yellow star, ostensibly because this would help him to escape the worst treatment.[120] James Steakley suggests that the German gay community has exhibited a 'more tactful and scholarly relationship to its history' than that in the United States.[121] Equally, that West German gay activists linked the pink triangle with the red triangle and not with the yellow star was probably related to the fact that Jews, unlike communists, were barely present in post-Holocaust Germany. In 1971, there were 6.1 million Jews in the United States, more than 2.5 million of whom lived in the State of New York. In the same year, the Jewish community in the Federal

[117] 'The Yellow Star and The Pink Triangle', *New York Times* (10 September 1975).

[118] Jensen, 'The Pink Triangle', 328.

[119] *Bent*, dir. by Sean Mathias (Channel Four Films, 1997). See further Jensen, 'The Pink Triangle', 340.

[120] Martin Sherman, *Bent* (New York: First Bard, 1980 [1979]), 39–41.

[121] Steakley, 'Selbstkritische Gedanken', 60.

Republic was estimated at only 30,000. Jews made up almost 3 per cent of the United States population. The figure for West Germany was 0.05 per cent.[122]

Christina von Hodenberg is surely correct to underscore that references to fascism were politically effective, and right to imply that those who made these references knew what they were doing.[123] In the case of homosexual politics, however, it is difficult—and unproductive—to demarcate political rhetoric and exaggerations from earnest and deep-seated concerns about the political situation in the Federal Republic. The Nazi past did not just offer a rhetorical opportunity to castigate the West German state but also provided the prism through which the contemporary Federal Republic was viewed, experienced, and understood. In 1976, activists from Würzburg Homosexual Action (WüHSt) organized a street action in the centre of the Bavarian city, in which they displayed a banner depicting pink triangles and the text 'Gays murdered in the concentration camps – and today?': this was filmed by the ZDF and broadcast on an episode of the youth television programme *Sparring*. Producers conducted a survey among passers-by, and the comments recorded included 'if my son were gay I'd have him castrated' and 'they should be gassed'.[124] The Nazi version of Paragraph 175 had departed the scene, but that did not prevent the endurance of these kinds of remarks. Such was their tone that a female passer-by berated a less sympathetic member of the public via the means of comparing his attitude to that adopted towards the Jews in the Third Reich.[125]

Certainly, 1970s West Germany was not on the verge of fascism. Equally, there is no doubting the reality of contemporary discrimination and the often hostile environment confronted by gay liberationists. Bonn was not Weimar, but focusing on homosexuality reveals pronounced limits of liberalization in the Federal Republic—despite homosexual law reform.[126] Reiner Koepp, the school teacher who lost his job in West Berlin in 1974, was told by the court upholding his dismissal that teachers had a special responsibility to observe the 'unwritten laws of honour, convention and decency'.[127] The gay group denied permission to hold an information stall in Aachen in 1973 took their struggle all the way to the Higher Administrative Court in North-Rhine Westphalia in 1976, but were told that the state retained the power to banish matters of the 'intimate sphere' from the public arena.[128] Suspicions that the police were registering homosexuals who had fallen

---

[122] Ira M. Sheskin and Arnold Dashefsky, 'United States Jewish Population, 2016', *The American Jewish Year Book* 116 (2016), 153–239; *Statistisches Jahrbuch für die Bundesrepublik Deutschland* 1974 (Wiesbaden, 1972), 96.

[123] Hodenberg, *Das andere Achtundsechzig*, 75.

[124] Ulrich Pramann, '… den würde ich kastrieren lassen', *Stern* 18 (1976), 209–10 (209).

[125] Cited from the footage: *Sparring: Homosexualität—noch ein Tabu* (ZDF, 24 April 1976). ZDF archive 06321/01373.

[126] See further the section 'Homosexual law reform and the limits of liberalization' in Chapter 1.

[127] Hedenström (ed.), *Schwule sich emanzipieren lernen*, 18.

[128] Verdict of the NRW *Oberverwaltungsgericht*, 15 March 1976. SMB archive, NARGS box one, folder 'Dokumentation Aachener Info-Tisch-Fall'.

foul of the law—a measure adopted by the authorities in the Third Reich—proved to be well-founded, at least in Hamburg, where the state police were forced to admit in 1980 that the practice had continued throughout the 1970s.[129]

Moreover, regardless of how historians interpret the limitations of legal reform, in gay liberation there was simply a lack of trust in the liberalization of the Federal Republic. This distrust was particularly evident in fears about the nature and permanence of the reforms to Paragraph 175 in 1969 and 1973. Even Rüdiger Lautmann, who robustly criticized exaggerations about the Nazi persecution, shared this conviction, appearing in *Pink Triangle? But That's Ages Ago* and stating that homosexual law reform may not prove definitive: 'However, in my opinion it would be illusory to assume that this spiral could not once again begin to turn with someday a sharpening of the paragraph [175] again coming into force.'[130] The pink triangle could be embraced in gay liberation partly because of activists' fundamental misgivings about just how liberal the liberal democracy they were living in really was, and was adopted not least due to the symbol's capacity to illustrate this conviction.

Victimhood and Pride

According to activist-turned-historian Michael Holy, the gay movement's adoption of the pink triangle in the mid-1970s formed part of a move away from 'gay pride' and towards a 'victim identity'. For Holy, after the reduction of the age of consent to 18, in 1973, the gay movement had no convincing answer to the question 'What more do you want then? We're free, after all!' and thus fell into a 'fundamental crisis of legitimacy' vis-à-vis homosexuals not engaged in the movement.[131] Activists' answer to this crisis was to double-down on complaints about contemporary discrimination, interpreting legal reform only as further evidence of the 'pseudo-liberality' of the Federal Republic. In this light, the pink triangle was appealing to activists because it visualized the idea that oppression, legal reform notwithstanding, had continued. Looking back at the 1970s, Holy's diagnosis is that reclaiming the symbol can be seen as an effort to reclaim the lost status of being persecuted. Moreover, adopting the 'replacement stigma' of the pink triangle led to an *Überidentifikation*, an extreme identification, with the homosexual victims of National Socialism.[132]

---

[129] Rosenkranz and Lorenz, *Hamburg auf anderen Wegen*, 164.
[130] Cited from the script accompanying the film. Peter Recht, Christiane Schmerl, and Detlef Stoffel, *Rosa Winkel? Das ist doch schon lange vorbei....: Materialien zum gleichlautenden Film* (Bielefeld, 1976), 15. On his critique of exaggerations, see Lautmann, Grikschat, and Schmidt, 'Der rosa Winkel', 327.
[131] Holy, 'Der entliehene Rosa Winkel', 81.   [132] Ibid., 75.

Gay liberationists were certainly not the first to claim the status of victimhood in support of a political argument. Hans-Joachim Schoeps and Heinrich Ackermann had done the same in support of their demands for homosexual law reform in the 1960s. Similarly, in 1969 *Der Spiegel* cited the history of the Nazi persecution of homosexuals in support of its contention that homosexual law reform had not gone far enough.[133] Ulrich Herbert has argued that 'anti-liberal bastions' in the political culture of the Federal Republic would have lasted longer were it not for their association with the Nazi past. This past offered reformers, from the 1960s onwards, a 'possibility of delegitimization', a vehicle through which to discredit their opponents.[134] The inverse of this process was also powerful: gay activists recognized a chance to legitimize themselves through their status as would-be descendants of a group persecuted by the Nazis. In a sense, gay liberation benefited from the zeitgeist of the period. Jan Eckel argues that the 1970s saw 'an increasing receptiveness to and public presence of depictions of suffering', which became 'decisive features of human rights advocacy'. For example, Amnesty International attempted to raise international awareness of the torture of political dissidents in Chile by pitching their coverage to deliberately appeal to 'sentiments of pity and moral outrage'.[135] The increasing salience of suffering in the present tense was accompanied by a renewed emphasis on past injustices. In this climate, many groups referred 'to their own history of suffering to justify claims for political participation and nondiscrimination'.[136] This was by no means limited to homosexuals, far less only to German homosexuals. Indeed, Wendy Brown has theorized that invoking histories of hurt and pain can be seen as a structural feature of identity politics more generally, in which 'politicized identity', in the process of seeking to gain political recognition, becomes 'attached to its own exclusion'.[137]

To the extent that a gay 'victim identity' did emerge, this must be situated in the context of the alternative left, because this was the formative political environment for the gay action groups that were responsible for first reclaiming the pink triangle. Sven Reichardt argues that 'alternative-left' identity was built upon a perception of pervasive state repression: through police, judges, prisons, and psychiatry but also through the forces of consumerism, environmental degradation, and patriarchal society.[138] This explains activists' enthusiasm for the Russell Tribunal on Human Rights coming to West Germany in 1978 and 1979. Here was an opportunity to document their victimhood to an international audience.

---

[133] 'Späte Milde', *Der Spiegel* 20 (1969), 55–76 (57).   [134] Herbert, *Wandlungsprozesse*, 48.
[135] Eckel, 'The Rebirth of Politics', 247 and 248.   [136] Ibid., 248.
[137] Wendy Brown, 'Wounded Attachments', *Political Theory* 21:3 (1993), 390–410 (406). See further Jensen, 'The Pink Triangle', 326.
[138] Reichardt, 'Inszenierung und Authentizität. Zirkulation visueller Vorstellungen über den Typus des linksalternativen Körpers', in *Bürgersinn mit Weltgefühl*, ed. by Knoch, 225–50 (230). See also Reichardt, *Authentizität*.

Possibly the most visually dramatic example of this victimhood, in this case self-inflicted, was provided by the Red Army Faction's (RAF) hunger strike campaign, led by imprisoned left-wing terrorists. This campaign allowed the 'fantasies of RAF victimhood to intrude starkly into the public realm', especially with the graphic images of Holger Meins' corpse that circulated after his death in 1974. During protests and demonstrations, photos from his autopsy were carried side by side with images of emaciated concentration camp prisoners, constructing a link between persecution then and now that resonated far beyond the limited number of those who directly supported terrorist organizations.[139]

In an article for the leftist journal *Kursbuch* in 1977, Klaus Hartung wrote that leftists had come to imagine themselves purely as the 'innocent victims of state persecution', since emphasizing this persecution was one means through which to rationalize their own political failure.[140] If gay leftists came to think of themselves as victims, their political and not just their sexual orientation was significant in this process. Focusing on contemporary oppression, for example the 'ban on careers', and linking this to the Nazi past, was a powerful tendency across the alternative left, a paradigm gay activists could hardly be expected to have escaped from. In this view, focusing on victimization seems less a tactical move than an almost instinctive emotional and ideological response to a contemporary society that was experienced as oppressive not just by gay leftists but by many left-wingers, regardless of sexuality.

Michael Holy is correct in arguing that a powerful identification with the homosexuals who had endured National Socialism developed in gay liberation. If political utility is part of the equation, this was never disconnected from attachments on a more empathetic level. Consider the testimony of Jakob Schepmann, who clearly distanced himself from exaggerations about Nazi persecution but spoke of the emotional connection he made between his own experience in the Federal Republic and a much more virulent form of oppression in the Third Reich:

> In a situation in which you are forced to get by on your own, you experience yourself, or I experienced myself, as oppressed. As misunderstood, unseen, on your own, [...] and in a situation like of this the identification with people who were oppressed is of course twice as large. Because of this identification, [...] you read about oppression, even when it is not the same oppression, experience your own oppression and say okay, we have something in common, even when the level is completely different.[141]

---

[139] Leith Passmore, 'The Art of Hunger: Self-Starvation in the Red Army Faction', *German History* 27 (2009), 32–59 (53). See also Terhoeven, *Deutscher Herbst*, 268.

[140] Hartung, 'Versuch, die Krise der antiautoritären Bewegung wieder zur Sprache zu bringen', *Kursbuch* 48 (1977), 14–44 (18).

[141] Oral history interview, 7 July 2012. Schepmann was active in the gay movement in Oldenburg and later involved with NARGS. Pseudonym used.

Other activists went further, such as Almut, who stated that after reading *The Men with the Pink Triangle* 'I could completely identify with the gays in the concentration camps, I could feel their pain in my very being.'[142] In our oral history interview, Ehrhard Forster, who still wears the pink triangle today, likened the symbol to the crucifix, thus placing an act of suffering and sacrifice at the centre of his gay identity.[143] Activists' empathic gestures were sometimes transnational in scope. The back cover of NARGS' brochure 'Gays against Oppression and Fascism' featured a poem in memory of Lola Punales, a Chilean homosexual murdered by Pinochet's forces after the military putsch in 1973. According to the poet, who was an activist in the HAW, Punales no longer represented just one name, but symbolized the verbal abuse suffered on a daily basis from 'hetero cops' and 'comrades' alike; no longer just a name, but a reminder of the time forty years ago, when the SS murdered gays; no longer just a name, but a symbol of freedom and unity among the 'queens of the world'. The poem concluded 'Lola Punales is all of us!'[144]

If gay liberationists were preoccupied with suffering, they were always at the same time busy developing strategies to overcome a sense of victimization. Though the above poem managed to link together the experience of West German gays with a Chilean murdered by the military junta, and with the homosexuals murdered by the Nazis, the author also added that Punales was a symbol of 'our hate': yes, hatred of uniforms and brutality, which could easily be projected onto the institutions of the Federal Republic, but also hatred of 'self-oppression' and 'self-pity'.[145] Indeed, the pink triangle was a vehicle through which activists attempted to challenge the social consequences of ostracization. Recall that in 1973, the 'male feminists' clearly identified the pink triangle as an emancipatory symbol, as a method of increasing the visibility of homosexuality, serving a similar function to drag. Other activists from the HAW expanded on this in a Berlin leftist weekly:

> The pink triangle, just like the word gay, should brand us and expose us – look, they're the swines! But we find that the aspects of ourselves that are to be 'exposed' by this symbol and these words are in no way shameful. We therefore affirm that of which we are accused, namely not being 'real men'! In this sense the pink triangle is a symbol of a new consciousness.[146]

---

[142] Almut, in *Der Rosa Winkel*, ed. by HAW (1975), 27.

[143] Oral history interview, 31 October 2013. Pseudonym used.

[144] Written by Mechthild Sperrmüll. NARGS, 'Schwule gegen Unterdrückung', 32. 'Sperrmüll' was the *non de plume* of HAW member Volker Bruns. Elmar Kraushaar (ed), *Schwule Lyrik, Schwule Prosa: Eine Anthologie* (Berlin, 1977), 191.

[145] NARGS, 'Schwule gegen Unterdrückung', 32.

[146] HAW *Sponti-Schwule*, 'Zum ROSA WINKEL', in *Der Rosa Winkel*, ed. by HAW (1975), 17–23 (23). Originally published in *INFO BUG*, in 1975.

Writing in *Schwuchtel* in 1976, Georg Linde argued that the pink triangle functioned as a prosthetic, serving only to distract attention from the need to overcome personal problems. According to Linde, gays needed to learn to do without their 'pink triangle ID' and instead develop a more honest relationship to themselves.[147] His argument seems to have impressed the magazine's editors, because in the subsequent issue they advanced a very similar position, positing that the symbol could suppress individual conflicts.[148] However, other activists clearly experienced the pink triangle as something of a liberating force:

> It is only through the pink triangle that I have become aware of my voids and have only just begun to fill them. The virtually permanent examination of my being gay has also shown me that it is not just my environment, that of the 'normal people', that is caught up in prejudiced mindsets passed down from the past, but often myself as well. [...] The pink triangle discussions are for me always a test of to what extent I am being problematised.[149]

Statements such as these do not support the contention that 'gay pride' had been supplanted by a focus on victimhood. Indeed, it seems unproductive to posit a dichotomy between pride and victimhood, just as between pride and shame: rather, it is the oscillations between these poles that structured the course of gay liberation and lent a powerful ambivalence to the pink triangle symbol. For example, consider the first show performed by the gay theatre collective *Brühwarm*, in 1976. 'A Gay Fete' featured representations of several examples of contemporary oppression, including attempts to change sexual orientation via stereotactic brain surgery or psychotherapy.[150] In one scene, an elderly fascist reminisced about his wartime service, boasting about how many homosexuals had been forced to wear the pink triangle in the concentration camps. His companion was a former constitutional court judge, who read out the 1957 verdict upholding the Nazi-era version of Paragraph 175. Yet, interrupting these narratives of persecution and victimhood, two men wearing t-shirts emblazoned with the pink triangle then burst onto the stage, overpower the fascist and the judge, and gaze forthrightly—proudly—at the audience.[151]

Related themes can be observed in how activists from Hildesheim used the pink triangle. To advertise their weekly meeting in a local bar, activists designed a poster that displayed an enormous pink triangle, followed by the caption 'gays are everywhere' (see Figure 4.1.). Within the triangle, scores of locations were listed,

---

[147] Linde, 'Komm süsser Schmerz', *Schwuchtel: Eine Zeitung der Schwulenbewegung*, 5 (1976), 16.

[148] *Schwuchtel* 6 (1977), 1 and 3 (3).

[149] Hans, 'Was ist das - Rosa Winkel?', in *Schwule sich emanzipieren lernen*, ed. by Hedenström, 28–36 (34).

[150] *Brühwarm: ein schwuler Jahrmarkt*, first performed in 1976. A programme is available at the SMB archive.

[151] The scene was filmed and reproduced as part of the aforementioned film *Rosa Winkel? Das ist doch schon lange vorbei*. SMB archive.

Figure 4.1 'Gays Are Everywhere', produced by activists in Hildesheim, ca. 1979.
Source: By permission of the *Schwules Museum Berlin*.

including in the café, on the street, at work, in parliament, in the family, at the grocers and on television.[152] In this instance, with no additional reference what-soever to oppression or fascism, the focus was on exposure, on emerging into the open, on strength in numbers. Here, the pink triangle had progressed from its origins as a stigmatizing badge of shame in the concentration camps to a method of highlighting queer presence and participation in every walk of life.

Equally, this does not mean that adopting the pink triangle inevitably paved the way for a transformed consciousness, because wearing the pink triangle did not always lead to exposure. Adding the caption *schwul* or *Schwule* ('gay' or 'gays'), as in the poster from Hildesheim, was crucial to activists' quest for greater visibility. When *Rotzschwul* first used the pink triangle in 1972, the badges produced by activists included this caption below the symbol, so that its intended meaning would not be lost, such as being misconstrued as a piece of fashionable jewel-lery.[153] The HAW 'male feminists' also suggested that the triangle should be worn with the addendum of 'gay'.[154] According to those activists, while the criteria for a successful gay symbol included calling to mind a history of oppression, the most important criterion remained that the symbol must show that he who wears it is gay.[155] When the HAW undertook their first public action involving the pink triangle two years later, six activists held individual cardboard triangles, each depicting a letter, collectively spelling out *schwul*. The result was an impressive performance of queer visibility, directly in front of the entrance to the *Kürfürstendamm* underground station, on Berlin's famous *Ku'Damm* boulevard (see Figure 4.2). However, the small pink triangles distributed by the activists during this action did not include the caption *schwul*.[156] Nor was it included on the various badges and buttons sold in shops or via magazines.[157] Since the 'rediscovery' of the pink triangle was so recent, it is unlikely that the pink triangle, taken by itself, would have successfully communicated the homosexuality of the person wearing it. While this may have frustrated the ambitions that some had in mind for the triangle—that it would essentially function as a substitute for drag, that it would increase the visibility of homosexuals—the fact that it was *not* an obviously gay symbol may have precisely represented part of its appeal to other gay people. For some homosexuals, the pink triangle served not as a loud symbol of pride, but largely as a 'discreet signifier'.[158]

According to activists from Heidelberg, the gay movement successfully 'refunc-tioned' the pink triangle, just as it had done with the word 'gay'—claiming a word

---

[152] 'Schwule sind überall!'. SMB archive, Sammlung Holy, box 24. Undated, but probably autumn 1979.
[153] Grisard, 'Zum Stellenwert der Farbe', 183.   [154] 'Feministenpapier', 9.   [155] Ibid., 9.
[156] Compare the front and back covers of HAW, 'Der Rosa Winkel' (1975). SMB archive.
[157] Rosenkranz and Lorenz, *Hamburg auf anderen Wegen*, 154.
[158] Elman, 'Triangles and Tribulations', 7.

Figure 4.2 Pink triangle action by HAW activists, 1975.

Source: Photo: Ludwig Hilgering. By permission of the *Schwules Museum Berlin.*

of abuse and transforming this into a positive terminology.[159] Giving this a further twist—quite literally—the activist collective ACT UP, in the United States, felt the need to invert the pink triangle when they adopted the symbol in their anti-AIDS activism in the 1980s.[160] In this light, the 1970s resignification of the pink triangle from its origins in the concentration camps had not been entirely successful, since according to ACT UP the triangle needed to be cast in its more familiar upwards-pointing presentation in order to be suitably transformed into a symbol of gay pride. Yet in 1995, when German activists were finally granted permission to install a plaque memorializing the homosexual victims of Dachau at the site of the former concentration camp, they chose as the date to unveil the plaque not 29 April, the anniversary of the camp's liberation, but 18 June, to coincide with the gay pride parade in Munich.[161] Pride and victimhood remained inextricably linked.

---

[159] 'Warum tragen wir den Rosa Winkel?', *Carlo Sponti* 16–17 (1975), 10.

[160] ACT UP was the acronym for the 'AIDS Coalition to Unleash Power'. Jensen, 'The Pink Triangle', 331.

[161] Cited from Steakley, 'Selbstkritische Gedanken', 61.

Generation and Memory

Heinz Heger's *The Men with the Pink Triangle* was a rare example in gay liberation of a vehicle through which the experiences of an older homosexual were communicated to a younger queer audience. Heinz Heger himself wrote to *du&ich* in 1975, complaining about the derogatory attitudes espoused in an recent article by a young gay couple towards older homosexuals.[162] A year earlier, an anonymous reader did likewise, this time to *him*, advising younger gays to read *The Men with the Pink Triangle* rather than mock him and other older homosexuals.[163] We have seen how older homosexuals, especially those who called themselves 'homophile', were generally treated with disdain by younger activists, especially in the gay left. Due to their style of attire, their supposed conformism, their politically suspect arrangement with the post-war social order, their focus on conviviality instead of political action, younger activists tended to make the implicit assumption that older homosexuals were simply a lost cause.

There is a painful irony in the fact that among these older generations of homosexuals there were many men who had experienced persecution first-hand under the Nazis, in the concentration camps or otherwise. So while in the course of the 1970s there certainly were instances of intensive identification with those homosexuals thought to have perished in the concentration camps, this was accompanied by an equally powerful *dis*identification with those older homosexuals who made their lives in the Federal Republic of the 1950s and 1960s, even if these objects of identification and disidentification happened to be the very same people.[164] This theme was highlighted in an episode of the youth television programme *Sparring* in April 1976. The topic for this episode was 'Homosexuality: still a taboo?' Producers from the ZDF broadcaster invited activists from both *Rotzschwul* and WüHSt to present themselves to the studio audience and the watching public, estimated at six million.[165] As part of the show, a skit was performed, in which a young gay man, Florian—identified by his badge with the English-language phrase 'Gay is beautiful'—is approached at a fast food stand by an older man, Herbert, who calls himself homophile.[166]

Herbert tells Florian that he is lonely, and unwelcome in the gay scene. He had been incarcerated in Bergen-Belsen concentration camp and his partner was

---

[162] *du&ich* 7 (1975), 6. It is unclear whether Hans Neumann or Josef Kohout used the pseudonym Heinz Heger in this instance.

[163] *him* 3 (1974), 4.

[164] On identifications and disidentifications, see further Helmut Puff, 'After the History of (male) Homosexuality', 24.

[165] On the viewing figures, see Ulrich Pramann, '...den würde ich kastrieren lassen', *Stern* 18 (1976), 209–10 (209). Martin Dannecker was also invited, but as an 'expert' rather than an activist. It was not mentioned that the co-author of *The Ordinary Homosexual* had himself co-founded the *Rotzschwul* group.

[166] *Sparring: Homosexualität—noch ein Tabu* (ZDF, 24 April 1976). ZDF archive 06321/01373.

murdered in the gas chambers at Dachau. Taken aback, Florian asks how many were imprisoned. Herbert replies 67,000, of whom 56,000 died.[167] Rather conceitedly, Florian enquires whether he shows a certain likeness to Herbert's murdered partner. Herbert answers in the negative, and adds that he would not have approached Florian had he understood the meaning of his badge. Asked by the presenter to reflect on the scene, a *Rotzschwul* activist argued that Herbert was wrong to hide his homosexuality: only by being open about their sexuality could gays develop a new consciousness. Experiences from the Weimar Republic had shown that relying on 'pseudo-tolerance' was not enough. A representative from WüHSt added that the scene depicted a generational conflict he had witnessed at first hand and that was widespread in the gay scene.[168]

Herbert was not the only one 'hiding' his homosexuality, if his objection to Florian's badge can be taken as evidence of such a concealment. 'Gay is beautiful', after all, was much more discreet in a German-speaking country than its direct translation, '*schwul[sein] ist schön*'. It would not only have been Herbert who did not understand its meaning, but probably the majority of the West German public.[169] Moreover, the WüHSt activists who appeared on the show wore comically oversized eye masks to disguise their appearance, citing the danger to their future careers. Viewers learned nothing about what older homosexuals might have thought about the skit, and whether they might have identified more with Herbert than with the younger Florian. *Sparring* was a television programme aimed specifically at a young audience, but it is not clear who producers would have invited even if they had wanted to include reactions from older participants. The IHWO, with its more mixed and less student-dominated membership, had had representatives appear in several television documentaries earlier in the decade, including on the ZDF, but the group was defunct by 1974. Even in the IHWO, relatively few members were old enough to have directly experienced the Third Reich. According to a survey conducted in 1973, only 17 per cent of its members were older than 35 (born in 1938 or earlier).[170] I have found no archival trace in the IHWO's circulars or newsletters of homosexuals referring to their own experience in the Third Reich: even after homosexual law reform in 1969, it was clearly exceedingly difficult for homosexual survivors of the concentration camps to talk about their experiences, much less to make their plight public. Herbert seems to have been a rare, fictionalized, example.

Precious few of the activists who wore the pink triangle in the 1970s attempted to reach across the generational divide in homosexual politics and come into

---

[167] No further details were given about these rather specific figures. It is unclear who was responsible for researching the sketch.

[168] *Sparring: Homosexualität*. Cited from the footage.

[169] As discussed in the introduction, the meaning of 'gay' was not grasped by at least one homosexual publicist in 1970. 'Liebe auf den Straßen', *du&ich* 11 (1970).

[170] *IHWO Report* 5 (1973).

contact with those who had actually worn the pink triangle in the concentration camps. A rare exception was Egmont Fassbinder, from the HAW, who placed an advert in *Emanzipation* in 1975. Superimposed against the background of a triangle and entitled 'Old gays urgently sought', the text of the advert read:

It is clear to us that we cannot overcome the problems of age and of loneliness on your behalf. We can only suggest that you help yourselves collectively (with us). *But we need your experiences.* We know from books what happened to gays under fascism. We know from books that many thousands of gays had to wear the pink triangle in the concentration camps and that only few of them emerged from the camps alive. But we do not know enough. We read that thousands were mutilated, tortured and murdered. We read it, but we barely comprehend it. We want to learn more about it from you.[171]

The advert, of which derivatives were also placed in *him* and *du&ich*, was met with little response.[172] In a letter later that year to Richard Plant, an academic in the United States who had left Nazi Germany in 1933, Fassbinder wrote that he had identified only two individuals.[173] Nevertheless, Fassbinder's efforts raise the question of what the experiences of older homosexuals were 'needed' for. Why, after all, did younger gay men 'need' the experiences of older homosexuals?

Perhaps activists required these experiences in order to bolster their credentials as the legitimate successors to this generation of homosexuals, to begin establishing a connection between the early 1930s and the 1970s—a connection symbolized by the pink triangle. A connection to the more recent past, to the early post-war Federal Republic, did not meet their purposes: for gay liberationists did not see anything worth identifying with in the homophile movement of the 1950s and 1960s. In any case, even this connection would have been hard to come by. As we saw in Chapter 2, not one homophile organization or publication from the late 1950s or early 1960s continued into the 1970s. Activists such as Fassbinder, by 1975, had not yet established a palpable attachment to the homosexual emancipation movement of the 1920s and early 1930s. This only happened towards the end of the decade, later symbolized by the founding of the Magnus Hirschfeld Society in 1982, named after the sexologist and leading figure in the Weimar-era

---

[171] 'Alte Schwule dringend gesucht', *Emanzipation* 3 (1975), 10. Emphasis in the original.
[172] *him* 10 (1975), 49; *du&ich* 8 (1976), 36. The IHWO also placed an advert in *him*, in 1972, urging homosexual victims of the concentration camps to contact them; they promised to raise the issue of lost pension contributions. 'Wiedergutmachung für Homosexuelle', *him* (August 1972), 47.
[173] Egmont Fassbinder to Richard Plant, 18 August 1975. New York Public Library, Manuscripts and Archives, Richard Plant collection, box one, folder ten. Plant was in the process of researching the history of Nazi persecution, which led to his book *The Pink Triangle: The Nazi War against Homosexuals* (New York, 1986).

movement.[174] Given that Hirschfeld's Institute of Sexual Science was ransacked by the Nazis and its books destroyed, there was no obvious avenue for the transmission of activist memory from the early 1930s to the 1970s.[175]

There were simply very few individuals still active in homosexual politics whose lived experience could have provided the basis for connections to previous iterations of homosexual emancipation. Johannes Werres was a rare exception. In 1945, aged 22, he was released from a prisoner of war camp.[176] In 1968, he wrote to the Federal Post Office, requesting that a special stamp be released to honour Magnus Hirschfeld on the centenary of his birth, but he was told that the sexologist was insufficiently well-known amongst the West German public.[177] Subsequently, Werres introduced readers of *him* to Hirschfeld. Up until that point, Hirschfeld had rarely featured either in the commercial gay press, or in the newsletters and journals produced by gay groups.[178] It seems that it took the 'rediscovery' of the pink triangle to in turn spark the 'rediscovery' of the homosexual emancipation movement crushed by the Nazis. Moreover, the first detailed historical account of Hirschfeld's legacy was provided not by a West German, but by an American activist, James Steakley, who published his *The Homosexual Emancipation Movement in Germany* in 1975.[179]

The concept of postmemory is instructive in thinking about the connection between 1970s gay liberationists and the experiences of older homosexuals. According to Marianne Hirsch, postmemory refers not to the memory of those who actually experienced events first-hand, but 'the relationship that the "generation after" bears to the personal, collective, and cultural trauma of those who came before'. Hirsch writes that 'postmemory's connection to the past is thus actually mediated not by recall but by imaginative investment, projection, and creation'.[180] Similarly, Michael Rothberg has drawn attention to the significance of 'negotiation, cross-referencing, and borrowing' in the production of memory about the Holocaust.[181] This kind of process was at play during the 'rediscovery'

---

[174] The *Magnus-Hirschfeld-Gesellschaft*, not to be confused with the *Bundestiftung Magnus Hirschfeld*, the federal foundation set up in 2011. On the Society, see further <https://magnus-hirschfeld.de/> [accessed 3 September 2018].

[175] See further Marhoefer, *Sex and the Weimar Republic*, 174–5.

[176] Werres, 'Als Aktivist erster Stunde: Meine Begegnung mit homosexuellen Gruppen und Zeitschriften nach 1945', *Capri: Zeitschrift für schwule Geschichte* 1 (1990), 33–51 (33).

[177] Werres, 'Bundespost Berlin hält Magnus Hirschfeld für "wenig bekannt"', *Der Weg* 228 (197), 59–60.

[178] *him* (May 1975), 41–7. An exception to this relative lack of interest was activist-turned-historian Manfred Herzer, who wrote to *him* commenting on Werres' article: *him* (December 1975), 5.

[179] Steakley was a PhD student based in East Berlin, but who was active in the HAW in the West. *The Homosexual Emancipation Movement in Germany* (New York, 1975).

[180] Hirsch, *The Generation of Postmemory: Writing and Visual Culture After the Holocaust* (New York, 2012), 5.

[181] Rothberg, *Multidirectional Memory: Remembering the Holocaust in the Age of Decolonization* (Stanford, 2009), 3.

of the Nazi persecution of homosexuals. Not being able to rely on their own experiences, having little or no contact with those who could do so, and having access to precious few written testimonies, gay activists in the 1970s were forced to imagine and create this history, as well as project their present onto this historic backdrop. While the danger of trivializing the experiences of those who lost their lives in the concentration camps looms large, Hirsch convincingly argues that postmemory can serve as a platform for 'repair and redress' in activism.[182] Despite their lack of contact with older homosexuals, gay activists consistently called for official recognition and compensation for the homosexual survivors of Nazi persecution. For example, when they proposed introducing the pink triangle symbol in 1973, the HAW 'male feminists' argued that wearing the insignia needed to be accompanied by 'practical solidarity' for the 'gay victims of fascism', in the shape of calling for compensation for their suffering.[183] This demand reached a wider audience in May 1978, when it was featured in the manifesto of Wolfgang Krömer, from the HAH, who became the first openly gay candidate in German history to stand for public office.[184]

In 1979, the AHA organized a podium event featuring those standing in the upcoming state elections in West Berlin, including representatives from all the major parties.[185] Demands to repeal Paragraph 175, for the passage of an anti-discrimination law, and for holistic sex education in schools, were all met with an equivocal response. However, all the representatives pledged to ensure that surviving homosexual victims of the Third Reich would be treated equally to any other victim group. Commenting on this result, a member of the AHA remarked 'we have the possibility for a campaign that can undoubtedly find worldwide resonance and that can very swiftly bring the gay problem in its historic and contemporary relevance before parliament'.[186] Indeed, the question of homosexual victims was raised in the parliamentary arena already later that year, when SPD member of the *Bundestag* Hajo Hoffmann asked the government if surviving homosexuals could apply for compensation under the auspices of the Federal Restitution Law (*Bundesentschädigungsgesetz*). He was told the answer was no, because that law was limited to those persecuted on the grounds of 'race, belief or worldview'.[187]

---

[182] Hirsch, *The Generation of Postmemory*, 16.
[183] HAW Feministengruppe, 'Thesenpapier', 2.
[184] HAH. 'Ab jetzt gibt's unser Programm: ein Schwuler kandiert sich zur Bürgerschaftswahl', 4. SMB archive, folder Hamburg–Schwulenbewegung–HAH.
[185] Gerhard Beier-Herzog, 'Zur Wahlveranstaltung der AHA. Nur ein Anlauf oder schon ein Sprung?', *AHA Info Intern* (March 1979), 3–5.
[186] Ibid., 5.
[187] 'Plenarprotokoll 8/179', *Deutscher Bundestag—8. Wahlperiode* (17 October 1979), 14128. <http://dipbt.bundestag.de/doc/btp/08/08179.pdf> [accessed 8 December 2018]. Hoffmann had been approached by a homosexual group from Saarbrücken, the 'Communication Circle Homosexuality'. Rudi Finkler, 'Für die Homosexuellen in der B.R.D. ist der Nationalsozialismus nocht nicht zu Ende', *du&ich* 9 (1979), 12–15 (12).

This stance did not change until as late as 2002, because successive governments claimed that homosexual victims could have instead applied to a different compensation scheme, the Law on the General Consequences of the War (*Allgemeines Kriegsfolgengesetz*).[188] For example, in June 1983, in response to a query from the Greens, the federal government stated that homosexuals were eligible under this law, but that the deadline for claims had passed at the end of 1959. This position overlooked—perhaps intentionally—that male homosexuality had remained criminal until 1969, under the very same version of the law introduced by the Nazis. Those who applied for compensation could have faced further prosecution.[189] Nevertheless, Katharina Ebner is right to argue that with the reference to past victimhood, in the Third Reich, a powerful new 'horizon of argumentation' regarding homosexuality entered the parliamentary arena. No longer could discussions around homosexual law reform revolve only around questions of morality and religion.[190] This applies not just to the *Bundestag* but to the wider public sphere. Consider the aforementioned play *Bent,* which received its German première in Mannheim in 1980. A reviewer for *Die Zeit* pithily identified the appeal of the play's narrative: 'Homosexuality on stage is still considered a sacrilege in Mannheim. Portraying the victims of National Socialism as victims is not a sacrilege.'[191] Reference to past persecution had become a potent weapon in the gay liberation toolbox.

Marianne Hirsch usefully distinguishes between familial and affiliative forms of postmemory.[192] The insight that postmemory need not be restricted to familial settings is particularly illuminating for memory amongst gays and lesbians, who are rarely connected by biological lineage but more likely to be affiliated by their shared sexuality. By the end of the 1970s, gay activists combined their demand for *Wiedergutmachung*—restitution for surviving homosexual victims—with the argument that they themselves were the legitimate descendants of the homosexuals persecuted by the Nazis. In July 1980, gays and lesbians held a podium event in Bonn, in advance of the federal election that year, a rare example both of organizing on the national level, and of cooperation between gays and lesbians: all the major political parties sent representatives. The first demand made was for restitution for the homosexual victims of National Socialism.[193] This demand went further than compensation for survivors. Organizers argued that many

---

[188] In 2002, following an amendment to a law originally promulgated in 1998, all verdicts passed down against Paragraph 175 in the Third Reich were quashed, meaning those men affected were now eligible to apply for compensation. 'Gesetz zur Aufhebung nationalsozialistischer Unrechtsurteile in der Strafrechtspflege' < https://www.gesetze-im-internet.de/ns-aufhg/index.html> [accessed 8 December 2018].

[189] Cited from Ebner, *Religion im Parlament*, 255. For more on the limitations of 1950s compensation schemes, see Moeller, *War Stories*, 28–31.

[190] Ebner, *Religion im Parlament*, 206.

[191] Helmut Schödel, 'Lotte in Mannheim: kunstlos', *Die Zeit* (18 April 1980).

[192] Hirsch, *Postmemory*, 36.

[193] 'Homosexuelle zur Bundestagswahl: Parteien auf dem Prüfstand', 4–6. SMB archive, folder Bonn–Beethovenhalle.

homosexual victims had been left in the lurch by their families and that they themselves should be considered as these victims' rightful successors. Therefore, *Wiedergutmachung* should also include 'collective restitution', in the shape of a fund put at the disposal of the gay movement.[194]

From this fund, activists in the Federal Republic and other European countries previously occupied by the Nazis would be able to finance their campaigning activities, for example by opening Centres similar to those which had existed until 1933.[195] This claim was described as analogous to previous acts of collective restitution; although this was not explicitly stated, organizers could only have had in mind the compensation package agreed between the Federal Republic and Israel in 1953.[196] For good measure, the title page of the pamphlet distributed at the event was illustrated by a pink triangle. The back cover displayed the front page of *Das Freundschaftsblatt* (subtitle: 'Central Organ of the German Homoerotic Movement'), from November 1932. The piece was entitled 'Should we vote?', and cited the positions of the KPD, SPD and NSDAP on Paragraph 175. Thus, the affiliation between the gay movement of the early 1980s and the homosexual emancipation movement of the 1920s and 1930s, soon to be crushed by the Nazis, was further underlined.[197]

The call for 'collective restitution' was not heeded, although even the CDU representative at the podium event promised to raise the issue of compensation for surviving victims in parliament.[198] Gay liberationists, unlike their homophile predecessors, benefited from a climate in which the injustices committed by the Nazi regime were finally being more widely acknowledged. This was symbolized at the start of the decade by Willy Brandt's act of contrition in Warsaw in December 1970, as he knelt in memory to the victims of the Warsaw ghetto uprising. At the end of the decade, in 1979, the American series *Holocaust* was broadcast on West German television, where it was watched by an estimated 63 per cent of the population.[199] Gay liberationists sought to capitalize on the resulting intensification of public interest in the Holocaust and in the victims of the Nazis, even as they complained that, once again, homosexuals were being left out of the picture. The anti-fascist caucus of the AHA was founded by group members angered by the exclusion of the persecution of homosexuals from the *Holocaust* series.[200] In a poster from 1980, they sought to explain why non-gays should show solidarity

---

[194] 'Homosexuelle zur Bundestagswahl', 6. A variant of the 'collective restitution' demand was successful in 2011, when the Magnus Hirschfeld Foundation was founded following a grant from the federal government. < https://mh-stiftung.de/ueber-die-stiftung/> [accessed 8 December 2018].

[195] 'Homosexuelle zur Bundestagswahl', 6. Organizers presumably had in mind Hirschfeld's Institute of Sexual Science in Berlin.

[196] Ibid., 6. See further Moeller, *War Stories*, 26–8.

[197] 'Homosexuelle zur Bundestagswahl', back page.   [198] *Alle Schwestern werden Brüder*, 231.

[199] *Allensbacher Jahrbuch der Demoskopie 1979–1983*, ed. by Elisabeth Noelle-Neumann and Edgar Piel (Munich: KG Saur, 1983), 552.

[200] Untitled flyer. SMB archive, AHA-Sammlung: Box Juristengruppe/Antifa-Gruppe.

with the gay movement: 'gay oppression concerns everyone, because sexual oppression has always been a means to control people. Gay liberation is a fundamental part of coming to terms with the past, of coming to terms with fascism.'[201]

That gay liberation was a necessary part of 'coming to terms with the past', of *Vergangenheitsbewältigung*, was an extremely powerful claim, which had a resonance far beyond the gay left. The front page of the tenth anniversary issue of *du&ich* in September 1979 posed the question '10 years of freedom?' The ambivalence implicit in that question was reflected a few pages further into the issue, by means of an article on the lack of compensation for homosexual victims of the Third Reich. The piece was entitled 'for homosexuals in the Federal Republic National Socialism never ended', thus echoing Hans-Joachim Schoeps' phrase, first published 17 years earlier. Back in 1949, Kurt Hiller, a key figure in the homosexual emancipation movement of the 1920s, wrote in the homophile journal *Der Kreis* that the theme of Nazi persecution, if successfully publicized, could become a springboard of a new homosexual movement.[202] If memory is the product of collective negotiation and exchange, gay liberation therefore succeeded in making its voice heard where the homophile movement—in the inauspicious social context of the 1950s—had failed.[203] This represented an ambivalent success, for achieving greater recognition and acceptance—a mission about which many gay activists in any case had decidedly mixed feelings—came about first and foremost not because of an increased state and public approval of difference and diversity, but from a positionality of victimhood.

---

[201] 'Vom KZ in's Gefängnis'. SMB archive, AHA box 2, folder AHA–Schwulenbewegung–Berlin.
[202] Cited from Andreas Pretzel, 'Aufbruch und Resignation', 289.
[203] On memory, see especially Confino, *Germany as a Culture of Remembrance*, 18.

5

Thinking and Feeling Homosexuality

In Chapter 3, we briefly met the gay theatre troupe *Brühwarm*, who would cast off into the audience an enormous papier-mâché phallus during performances of their inaugural play.[1] Not everyone was impressed. Roland Lange, an activist from Stuttgart, took to the pages of the gay liberation journal *Emanzipation* to argue that what he called *Brühwarm*'s 'cock fetishism' [*Schwanzfetischismus*] was anything but emancipatory. Emancipation, according to Lange, meant 'tackling prejudice though appropriate information'. *Brühwarm* were guilty of having offered up one of the crassest anti-gay clichés: that homosexuality was reducible to sex.[2] Corny Littmann, one of the troupe's members, returned fire. According to the activist and actor (and, in 1980, a parliamentary candidate for the Greens), Lange's path to emancipation was a blind alley. Gay liberation, for Littmann, was not about tackling prejudice. 'My problem with prejudices is that many in fact do hit home: I am an arse-fucker, sometimes a queen [*Tunte*], running through the neighbourhood on the prowl, fucking with many different men. The problem for me is not the prejudice but that I don't stand by my filth, I don't want to be the gay swine that I really am. I'd rather parade the clean, leftist homosexual and as such I'm tolerated/accepted. I try to tackle this problem by, for example, saying to others, in their face: yes of course I'm an arse-fucker.'[3]

It is tempting to see in this altercation a classic example of a radical, proud, sex-positive gay liberationist discourse coming up against a more moderate, restrained, objective style—a style perhaps inherited from the homophile movement, a terminology chosen to downplay the *sexual* in homosexual. In fact, throughout the 1970s, there was a tremendous diversity of opinion in gay liberation about the meaning of emancipation, about the best ways in which to engage with public audiences, and about the place of sex. We cannot use this diversity of opinion to analytically distinguish different versions of homosexual politics, to differentiate one wing of the gay movement from another, or to contrast 'radical' with 'integrationist' activists and groups (like Littmann from the Homosexual Action Hamburg and Lange from the Initiative Group Homosexuality Stuttgart).

---

[1] The name *Brühwarm* played on '*warme Brüder*', 'warm brothers', an anti-gay slur. Initially, the troupe was called the Oedipus Collective. *Brühwarm* came from the title of their first play, and was adopted soon afterwards. Ödipus Kollektiv (ed.), 'Brühwarm: ein schwuler Jahrmarkt' (1976). SMB archive. See also 'Wir heissen jetzt Brühwarm!, *Schwuchtel* 5 (1976), 21–2.

[2] 'Brühwarm: der erfüllte Traum von der Selbstverwirklichung', *Emanzipation* 5 (1976), 12–14.

[3] *Emanzipation* 6 (1976), 40.

The Ambivalence of Gay Liberation: Male Homosexual Politics in 1970s West Germany. Craig Griffiths, Oxford University Press (2021). © Craig Griffiths.
DOI: 10.1093/oso/9780198868965.003.0006

Instead, a deep-seated ambivalence over these issues ran through the very heart of groups and individuals themselves. Littmann, for example, was clearly caught between going on the offensive, loudly foregrounding homosexual desire, and instead fitting in: not necessarily fitting into mainstream society, but into the alternative left, which would best accept him—or at least tolerate him—in his guise as a 'clean, leftist homosexual'. Similarly, Littmann was prepared to claim an identity as a *Tunte* (a 'queen' or 'fairy'), but only, by his own admission, some of the time.

No other question so vexed West German homosexuals as that of gay male effeminacy. Letter after letter in the commercial gay press denounced effeminate self-presentation, which was seen as outmoded and responsible for solidifying homophobic prejudices. Only in the mid- to late 1970s, under the influence of sexologists such as Volkmar Sigusch, were clear analytic separations made between intersexuality, transvestism, transsexuality, and homosexuality.[4] One might think that gay liberationists would have revelled in the instability of these cultures and categories, expressing their commitment to multi-dimensional liberation, rather than the emancipation only of masculine gay men. Indeed, some activists—whether they called themselves *Tunten* or 'male feminists'—embraced effeminacy for political reasons, adopting elements of both masculine and feminine dress, style and speech (and names), and performing these in deliberately exaggerated ways. Yet this gender transgression was rejected by other gay activists, who accused *Tunten* of mistaking individual needs for collective liberation, and for endangering the efforts of the gay movement in seeking left-wing support. Debates over drag show that the politics of respectability proved to be remarkably tenacious, even as the vocabulary 'homophile' increasingly gave way to 'gay' over the course of the 1970s.

Following gender transgression, I then discuss the equivocal position of sex and desire in homosexual politics, focusing on how the political valorization of mutuality and reciprocity led to controversies over erotic sensibilities that did not seem to live up to these ideals, including sado-masochism. Glib assumptions about the hedonism of the 1970s have led in some quarters to a 'hypersexual caricature' of gay men's sexual urges—which Jim Downs, in his account of gay liberation in the United States, rightly criticizes.[5] Some have even sought to explain the HIV/AIDS crisis in the 1980s through the supposed sexual abandon of the 1970s. Notoriously, Rosa von Praunheim penned an article for *Der Spiegel* in 1984, in which he placed much of the blame for the worsening HIV/AIDS crisis at the door of promiscuous homosexuals. 'Every infection we cause can mean manslaughter', argued Praunheim, bemoaning that the freedom won by those who

---

[4] Sigusch, 'Aufklärung', *du&ich* 11 (1976), 9. See also Volkmar Sigusch (ed.), *Sexualität und Medizin* (Cologne, 1979).

[5] Downs, *Stand by Me: The Forgotten History of Gay Liberation* (New York, 2016), 6.

went on the streets in the 1970s was lived out by most gays 'in discos, orgy bars and commercial sex'.[6] We can call into question this type of narrative without suggesting that sex was somehow unimportant. One cannot entirely disagree with Downs' comments that 'the 1970s was more than a night at a bathhouse' or that 'Sex was only part of what had mattered to gay men as they began to make gay liberation meaningful in their lives.'[7] Yet this striking disavowal of sex is reminiscent of how much gay and lesbian scholarship has unintentionally marginalized the sexual in favour of less disreputable matters.[8] In John Howard's memorable phrase, 'Concerned with identity, culture, and politics, it sometimes politely overlooks the arguably defining feature of the enterprise, homo*sex*.'[9]

Given that gay and lesbian history began life as an activist project, we can trace historians' occasional uneasiness about 'homosex' directly back to gay liberation itself: for it was precisely over matters of sex and desire that activists' ambivalence was most keenly felt. To elucidate this ambivalence, I return to a theme introduced in Chapter 1: how activists responded to the gay scene, those places where same-sex desiring men met each other for the purposes of leisure, sociability, and sex. A shared antipathy to the gay scene resembled an important point of connection between gay action groups and organizations that still used the term 'homophile', including the International Homophile World Organization (IHWO). There was no clear transition here from the homophile movement of the 1950s and 1960s to gay liberation in the 1970s. Focusing on sex, the continuities in homosexual politics seem as least as striking.

In the final third of the chapter, having laid these foundations regarding debates over drag and sex, I focus on the emotional politics of gay liberation. After identifying the gay scene as a major culprit for psychological distress in homosexual life, activists set about imagining alternatives. For one activist in West Berlin, cottaging sites such as public toilets needed to be transformed into 'palaces of communication'.[10] I show how activists sought to move beyond diagnosing problems to actually tackling them, focusing on the rise of consciousness-raising and self-help groups and the first telephone crisis helplines. Yet these efforts were fraught with difficulty, not least because they carried with them the perceived danger of changing the homosexual so that he could better integrate into what was a deformed society, rather than tackling the structural issue, namely the deformed society itself. Gay liberation offered a route out of isolation and unhappiness for some same-sex desiring men, but not for all. Just as emotions such as hope and

---

[6] Praunheim, 'Gibt es Sex nach dem Tode? Thesen zum Thema AIDS', *Der Spiegel* 48 (1984), 228.
[7] Downs, *Stand by Me*, 6 and 4.
[8] Martin Duberman has accused Downs of writing a 'sanitized history of the 1970s'. Duberman, *Has the Gay Movement Failed?* (Oakland, CA, 2018), 54.
[9] Howard, *Men Like That: A Southern Queer History* (Chicago, 1999), 15. Emphasis in the original.
[10] 'Doris Night' [pseudonym], 'An meine Schwestern der Klappe', in *Schwule Lyrik, Schwule Prosa: Eine Anthologie*, ed. by Elmar Kraushaar (Berlin, 1977), 125–6.

pride existed before homosexual law reform in 1969, fear and shame endured thereafter. Heather Love has written that gay liberation seemed to possess a 'magical power' to 'transmute shame into pride, secrecy into visibility, social exclusion into outsider glamour'.[11] In keeping with her call to challenge the 'affirmative bias' in queer history, this chapter concludes by revealing the emotional continuities in homosexual politics that gay liberation was powerless to prevent.

The *Tuntenstreit*

In June 1973, the Homosexual Action West Berlin (HAW) organized a six-day gathering attended by activists from across the Federal Republic and internationally. This was the gay movement's second *Pfingsttreffen* ('Whitsun gathering'), an occasion when activists from different regions would come together over the long weekend marked by a public holiday in Germany, a tradition taken from the workers' movement.[12] Organized under the slogan 'The oppression of homosexuality is only a particular case of the general oppression of sexuality', the week included a public information stand, workshops, film viewings, street theatre, and fêtes, before culminating in a demonstration in central Berlin, which attracted around 700 participants (see Figure 5.1).[13] During this demonstration, some of the visiting French and Italian activists, in drag, refused to stay in the main body of the march and danced around in the surrounding streets, chanted slogans and interacted with passers-by.[14] Reporting in brief on the demonstration under the title 'March of the Eye Shadow', the tabloid *BILD* remarked 'Some of the participants had full beards and wore long dresses, eye shadow and blue nail varnish.'[15]

As the informal minutes of heated discussions that took place after the demonstration reveal, some West German activists reacted with anger.[16] Comments included that the appearance and behaviour of the *Tunten* was unpolitical, that as they did not wear drag in the workplace their behaviour on the demonstration was as exotic as the Easter Bunny or Father Christmas, and that the demonstration had been made into a carnival for the voyeurism of passers-by. *Tunten*, along with their supporters, responded by criticizing the conformism of other demonstrators,

---

[11] Love, *Feeling Backwards*, 28.

[12] The first such gathering had taken place the year previously, in both Münster and West Berlin. West Berlin was also the location for the *Pfingsttreffen* in 1974 and 1975, before Munich hosted the event in 1976 and Hamburg in 1977. On Munich, see *Rosa* 6 (1976), 34–7; on Hamburg see Erwin Gruhn, 'Pfingsten in Hamburg', *Emanzipation* 4 (1977), 31–2.

[13] HAW, 'Pfingstaktion '73: Die Unterdrückung der Homosexualität ist nur ein Spezialfall der allgemeinen Sexualunterdrückung' (1973). SMB archive.

[14] See *HAW Info* 12 (1973), 16–19. Personal accounts include Andreas, 'Meine persönliche HAW-Geschichte' in *Schwule sich emanzipieren lernen*, ed. by Hedenström, 38–45 and Hans Hermann, 'Ausgießung des heiteren Geistes', *him* 9 (1973), 6–7.

[15] 'Marsch der Lidschatten', BILD (12 June 1973).   [16] *HAW Info* 12 (1973), 16–19.

Figure 5.1 Demonstration organized by the HAW, 10 June 1973.
Source: Photo: Rüdiger Trautsch. Uploaded to wikimedia by James Steakley, license CC BY-SA 3.0.[17]

with one (French) activist decrying this 'typically German militaristic behaviour'.[18] These were the opening salvos in what became known as the *Tuntenstreit* ('queens' dispute'), a strategic debate within the gay left concerning the political value of drag and gender transgression. The conflict was particularly acrimonious in the HAW, but activists who attended the demonstration in West Berlin returned to their local groups and engaged in similar discussions there.[19] All participants in the debate sought profound changes to existing society, but sharply disagreed over what exactly these changes should constitute, in what manner they should be reached and whose support should be sought along the way. Some prioritized the socialist revolution, arguing that the gay left should not only collaborate with the workers' movement but subordinate itself to the cause of economic liberation. Others rejected this reading of liberation, emphasizing instead a politics of personal emancipation as a stepping-stone to working with

[17] <https://commons.wikimedia.org/wiki/File:HAW-Demo.jpg> [date accessed 15 July 2018].
[18] *HAW Info* 12 (1973), 16–19 (17). While this is not explicitly stated in the minutes, it seems that the French and the Italian activists were from the *FHAR* (Homosexual Revolutionary Action Front) and *fuori!* (United Front of Italian Revolutionary Homosexuals) groups respectively.
[19] On Hamburg, see Rosenkranz and Lorenz, *Hamburg auf anderen Wegen*, 151–6.

other forces, especially the women's movement, in a wider struggle against injustice.

Tunten can be loosely translated as 'queens' or 'fairies'. Writing about the 1950s and 1960s, Clayton Whisnant suggests the translation of 'fairy', insofar as *Tunten* 'were gay men who acted in effeminate ways without necessarily dressing completely like women'. According to Whisnant, this effeminacy was the most readily available means through which they could articulate their desire for other men.[20] Carsten Balzer, whose anthropological fieldwork was carried out in the 1990s and 2000s, locates *Tunten* as part of a 'transgender subculture' and contends that *Tunten* 'see their gender performativity as an expression of their inner femaleness as well as a criticism of a certain mainstream model of femininity'.[21] In the context of the 1970s, the term 'gender fuck' is more suitable than 'transsexual' or 'transgender', because there is no clear evidence that *Tunten* in this debate perceived their gender identity as at odds with the sex assigned to them at birth.[22] As Susana Peña has argued, we risk 'anachronistically imposing a contemporary category' by labelling 'outward manifestations' from previous historical contexts as transgender, given that these manifestations were not understood in this way at the time.[23]

Investigating the differences between *Tunten* and drag queens, Balzer writes that *Tunten* reject straightforward female impersonation, in favour of adopting elements of effeminate dress, style, speech, and mannerism and acting them out in theatrical, 'grotesque' or 'trashy' ways.[24] This performative critique of gender norms was a signal feature of the *Tuntenstreit*. West German *Tunten* in this debate therefore roughly map onto the proponents of 'political drag' or 'radical drag' in Britain, of 'faggotry' in the United States, or can be compared to the so-called *gazolines* in the Homosexual Revolutionary Action Front in France.[25] It is not possible, however, to make hard and fast distinctions between different identity categories. The *Tuntenstreit* saw complex interactions of sexual, gender and political identity. Some who called themselves *Tunten* adopted this category

[20]   Whisnant, *Male Homosexuality*, 142 and 126.
[21]   Balzer, 'The Beauty and the Beast: Reflections about Socio-Historical and Subcultural Context of Drag Queens and "Tunten" in Berlin', *Journal of Homosexuality* 46 (2004), 55–71 (60).
[22]   The first West German magazine explicitly addressing a transsexual audience did not appear until 1981. *EZKU: Vierteljahreszeitschrift von Transsexuellen für alle Terraner* (January 1981). APO archive, folder 1052.
[23]   Peña, 'Gender and Sexuality in Latina/o Miami: Documenting Latina Transsexual Activists', *Gender and History* 22 (2010), 755–72 (756).
[24]   Balzer, 'The Beauty and the Beast', 60.
[25]   On Britain, see Weeks, *Coming Out*, 202–3 and Robinson, *Gay Men and the Left*, 86–8. On the US, see Hobson, *Lavender and Red*, 3–75; Kissack, 'Freaking Fag Revolutionaries', 124; and Betty Luther Hillman, '"The most profoundly revolutionary act a homosexual can engage in": Drag and the Politics of Gender Presentation in the San Francisco Gay Liberation Movement, 1964–1972', *Journal of the History of Sexuality* 20 (2011), 153–81. On France, see Jackson, *Living in Arcadia*, 188–9 and Callwood, 'Reevaluating the French Gay Liberation Moment', 77–80; the name *gazolines* came from the gas canisters used to make hot drinks at meetings.

only briefly, or used it only at certain times. Other activists occasionally called into question whether this made them *Tunten* at all, for instance demarcating between 'real' and 'student' *Tunten*.[26] Confusing this further, gay activists routinely adopted female aliases, including those who were in fact antagonistic to *Tunten*.

Carsten Balzer argues that in the 1970s the label of *Tunte* was re-signified, previously having been used mainly as a slur term by those 'outside of the community'.[27] However, fundamental to the politicization of *Tunten* within the gay left was a growing consciousness not just of the discriminatory attitudes held by heterosexuals, but also by other gay men. This had been clearly articulated as early as November 1971, in the HAW's founding document: 'Whoever, in either his appearance or behaviour, does not conform to the ideal of the normal man, is considered a *Tunte*, and everyone can easily find someone else who seems more feminine than himself and who he can make into the object of his aggression, instead of demonstrating solidarity with him against social discrimination'.[28] The theoretical interpretation of this hatred of *Tunten* was provided by Martin Dannecker and Reimut Reiche, in their sociological study *The Ordinary Homosexual*. According to the authors, West Germany's gay men were suffering from a 'collective neurosis', evidenced primarily by their views towards *Tunten*.[29] In response to the leading question 'when homosexuals are discussed in public, it is often especially effeminate types who are mentioned: would you please briefly describe what you think about so-called *Tunten*?', 76 per cent of respondents expressed a negative opinion, ranging from aggression and disgust to complaints that *Tunten* made relations between gays and straights more difficult. The authors argued that this was an example of homosexuals projecting their guilt onto *Tunten*, blaming their effeminacy for the homophobia that they, the 'normal' homosexuals, had to face.[30]

If the commercial gay press is anything to go by, a rejection of gender transgression on the part of West German homosexuals was indeed widespread. Writing to *du&ich* to express his disappointment at *And what if your Son was this way?* (broadcast on the ZDF in January 1972), one reader described the homosexuals depicted in the documentary as 'intolerably feminine and diva-esque'.[31] Even long hair was too much for another subscriber, who asked *du&ich* editors why almost none of their models wore their hair short: 'But there are also the gays who reject everything feminine [...] Show some proper guys!'[32] One reader criticized the magazine for including a (rare) article on transvestites: 'These are the people who impair our reputation amongst the public;

[26] *HAW Info* 12 (1973), 17.   [27] Balzer, 'The Beauty and the Beast', 60.
[28] HAW, 'vorläufige Grundsatzerklärung' (November 1971).
[29] Dannecker and Reiche, *Der gewöhnliche Homosexuelle*, 345–76.   [30] Ibid., 351 and 356.
[31] *du&ich* 7 (1972), 10. *Und wenn Ihr Sohn so wäre. Über Homosexuelle berichtet Eva Müthel* (ZDF, 14 January 1972).
[32] *du&ich* 12 (1970), 8.

after all, wide sections of the population still think gays run around in women's clothing. Disgusting, simply disgusting.'[33] In its 1980 edition, the *Spartacus International Gay Guide* took issue with the contemporary state of 'gay entertainment', dominated by 'silly effeminate men dressed in women's clothes miming to records, usually rather badly'. Since 'transvestitism [sic] has so little to with the male homosexual world [...] it does seem to get rather too much limelight and public exposure'.[34] An article in *him* in December 1972 went further. *Tunten* failed to challenge gender roles and uncritically adopted prevailing stereotypes. Consequently, they were the 'most frustrated' and 'the psychologically weakest' homosexuals and numbered among the most 'deplorable creatures' of all.[35]

Gay activists were by no means immune to the rejection of gender transgression that prevailed in the gay scene at large. Seeking to challenge these discriminatory attitudes, *Tunten* within the HAW soon coalesced into a single 'feminist' caucus, cementing this process with their *Feministenpapier*, a programmatic document setting out what was termed 'male feminism' and the feminists' understanding of emancipation.[36] It is not clear if all members of the HAW's 'male feminist' group wore drag, or how often, when and where they did so. Andreas, for example, credits the French demonstrators with awakening many West German *Tunten* out of their 'Sleeping Beauty-esque self-oppression'. He subsequently wore drag for the first time during the discussion after the demonstration and in public at the HAW's information stand on the *Ku'Damm* in central Berlin. For Andreas, this was a revelatory experiment: 'I realised that I have many more possibilities to love, to live, to express myself than these guys, these blokes in their suits, who were really trembling in front of me. Oh, it was great!'[37]

In their *Feministenpapier*, the male feminists argued that the HAW and the gay movement at large must concentrate on working with the women's movement in challenging gender oppression, since this oppression pre-dated the advent of capitalism: 'The first class oppression is the oppression of women through men!'[38] Within this context, drag was seen as one means through which gay men could demonstrate their commitment to undermining the gender norms seen as responsible for this oppression. This argument was developed, whilst also reaching a wider audience, in an article entitled 'The Homosexuality in us', originally published in 1974 in the leftist journal *Kursbuch*.[39] The five authors, all of whom identified as HAW feminists, argued that fixed gender norms were the

---

[33] *du&ich* 10 (1974), 7.   [34] *Spartacus International Gay Guide* (Amsterdam, 1980), 9.
[35] Düsseldorfer Arbeitskreis Homosexualität und Gesellschaft, 'Wie hältst du's mit den Tunten?', *him* 12 (1972), 13 and 18–19 (18).
[36] HAW Feministengruppe, 'Feministenpapier.'
[37] Andreas, 'Meine persönliche HAW-Geschichte', 40.   [38] 'Feministenpapier', 20.
[39] Helmut Ahrens et al., 'Die Homosexualität in uns', in *Tuntenstreit: Theoriediskussion der Homosexuellen Aktion Westberlin* (Berlin, 1975), 5–34. Originally published in *Kursbuch* 37 (1974), 84–112. The five authors were Helmut Ahrens, Volker Bruns, Peter Hedenström, Gerhard Hoffman, and Reinhard von der Marwitz.

root cause of the oppression of homosexuality and that feminists, in drag, could call these norms into question:

> The specific approach of male feminism, to appear wearing make-up, 'feminine' or with the pink triangle, is *one* means and at the same time a necessity for gay men of rupturing the imposed division between private and public, a division that has become second nature.[40]

Debates over drag were charged by competing notions of the private and the political (or the personal and the political, as this contestation is better known). The male feminists did not insist that every activist wore drag. As we saw in the previous chapter, it was in this context that the pink triangle was theorized as a means of increasing the visibility of homosexuality, to be worn by those who preferred gender normative dress. Indeed, the male feminists had specific ideas about what type of drag was appropriate. The authors of 'The Homosexuality in us' criticized those *Tunten* whose gender transgression was seen as insufficiently 'political', whether because confined to the private arena, or merely serving the purposes of providing levity and entertainment at so-called 'drag balls'. Such occasions only made the *Tunte* appear 'as an imitator of "ladies"'.[41] Similarly, the article's authors denounced the 'hysterical imitation of the *Grande dame*' and the 'transsexuality' of stars like David Bowie, whose glam rock style was seen only as a commercial attempt to maximize profit.[42]

Despite the male feminists' attempt to demarcate their model of transgressing gender boundaries from earlier or parallel examples, it was precisely to this history of gender presentation that their critics would refer, with the HAW teachers' group asking whether the supposedly progressive behaviour of the feminists was not in fact a 'form of entrapment in a model that comes from the past'.[43] As intimated here, all sides in the *Tuntenstreit* made routine reference to homophile politics in order to support their case. Some asserted that as drag belonged in the private arena and was 'unpolitical' it was nothing more than an old-fashioned homophile relic, thereby landing at a rhetorical tool to fundamentally deny any radical political meaning to drag.[44] The feminists replied that in rejecting drag—or rather, their specific politicized form of drag—other gay liberationists were merely reproducing homophile conformism and the homophile refusal to politicize the personal.

The leading homophile journal of the 1950s and 1960s, *Der Kreis*, constantly exhorted its subscribers, and especially those who attended its club nights in

---

[40]   Ahrens et al., 'Die Homosexualität in uns', 29. Emphasis in the original.
[41]   Ibid., 26 and 27.   [42]   Ibid., 28.
[43]   Edith und ihre Lehrerinnen, 'Falsche Unmittelbarkeit? Gedanken zur "Feministenfrage" von der Pädogogengruppe', *HAW Info* 13 (1974), 25–30 (28).
[44]   For example, see *HAW Info* 12 (1973), 17–19.

Zürich, to behave themselves 'respectably', so as to avoid inviting further discrimination against homosexuals. A key part of this respectability was gender normative dress and appearance. Responding to a reader's letter in 1955, the journal's editor Karl Meier wrote that the *Tante* ('Auntie', an etymological variant of *Tunte*) should be offered support by *Der Kreis*, but only when 'he keeps himself within the necessary limits'.[45] For example, the presence of *Tunten* could be tolerated, but only on occasions such as at masquerade or drag balls.[46] With this history in mind, the authors of 'The Homosexuality in us' drew on Dannecker and Reiche's thesis of hatred against *Tunten*, but characterized the homosexuals caught up in this process as homophiles (even if homophile journals such as *Der Kreis* had long since departed the scene). They specifically defined homophile as meaning 'conformist gay' and proceeded to apply the term to those HAW members who refused to problematize their masculinity.[47]

Published a few months after the *Feministenpapier,* an article written by the HAW's teachers' group discussed the particularities of engaging with school pupils, youth clubs, colleagues and parents.[48] The authors stressed their 'fundamental sympathy' with the feminists, but wrote that it was impossible for them to adopt a feminist stance—understood as wearing make-up and drag—in their *Öffentlichkeitsarbeit,* their public work or outreach. They called on the feminists to restrict themselves to 'sensibly limited fields of activity, in which, with the agreement of the whole HAW, they can act in a mediated way'.[49] As 'total feminism' could not be 'classified' or 'digested' by the general public, this approach should only be considered when previous efforts had been made to open up 'possibilities for understanding'.[50] The notion that effeminate homosexuals should keep their gender transgression hidden away from the public sphere is of long currency, dating back at least to the so-called 'masculinist' wing of the homosexual rights movement in Imperial Germany and the Weimar Republic.[51] Concerns over potentially damaging interactions with the general public undoubtedly remained, and in this sense an antagonistic stance vis-à-vis *Tunten* on the part of some gay activists in the 1970s is an example of continuation from earlier traditions of homosexual politics. Generally, however, activists had more specific audiences in mind. The HAW teachers' group mentioned a public specific to their work: children, parents, and teachers. Yet, significantly, they also stated that

---

[45] Cited from Kennedy, *The Ideal Gay Man*, 172. See also Riechers, 'Freundschaft und Anständigkeit.'

[46] Whisnant, *Male Homosexuality*, 114 and 139.

[47] Ahrens et al., 'Die Homosexualität in uns', 25.

[48] Edith und ihre Lehrerinnen, 'Falsche Unmittelbarkeit?' This was the first of several incarnations of the teachers' group; a subsequent version achieved official trade union recognition in 1978. Detlef Mücke, 'Schwule und Schule: 11 Jahre Initiativen von schwulen Lehrergruppen', in *Schwule Regungen, Schwule Bewegungen: Ein Lesebuch,* ed. by Willi Frieling (Berlin, 1985), 151–70.

[49] 'Falsche Unmittelbarkeit?', 25.   [50] Ibid., 26.

[51] See further Beachy, *Gay Berlin*, especially 85–119.

demonstrations and meetings with leftist groups were inappropriate occasions for drag.[52]

Indeed, those who rejected drag in the course of the *Tuntenstreit* were primarily motivated by their desire to gain support from the working class and the left-alternative (counter)public. In the discussions after the demonstration in June 1973, one activist had argued that the working class should be the only addressee of the gay movement. Coming into contact with this constituency was so difficult, according to the activist, because 'we always comprehend emancipation as a private act of liberation'.[53] He admitted that reciprocal solidarity was not yet in evidence but maintained that 'we just have to struggle on with stubborn persistence, not through shocking actions which ultimately remain private and harmless'.[54] This 'stubborn persistence' belonged to the strategy of simultaneously organizing both in and outside of the gay movement. According to the 'plenary of socialist working groups in the HAW', while the wider group should advocate 'necessary reforms', the HAW could not itself lead a socialist struggle, as gayness was not a 'class feature'.[55]

This position was developed in an article published in the *Problems of Class Struggle* journal in 1974, written in response to the aforementioned 'The Homosexuality in us'. The article's pseudonymous authors criticized various past and contemporary examples of homophobia in leftist organizations, but classified the oppression of homosexuality as a so-called *Sonderunterdrückung*, a 'special' or 'additional' oppression. They urged homosexuals to recognize their majority position as exploited workers and aim for a gradual integration of the homosexual movement into the workers' movement.[56] Other activists were warned against a potential 'relapse to an unpolitical self-understanding [with] the adoption of fashionable bourgeois ideologies', rather than a 'consistently socialist orientation'.[57] Another activist in the HAW, meanwhile, denounced the 'exotic bunch of *Tunten*' as a 'new spawning of upper-class bluster', serving only as a distraction from 'actual' (socio-economic) problems.[58] Manfred Herzer, co-author of the article in *Problems of Class Struggle*, left the HAW in 1974, to join the General Homosexual Action Alliance (AHA): a group that had started life as the West Berlin chapter of the IHWO.[59] Herzer explained his decision in an open

---

[52] 'Falsche Unmittelbarkeit?', 28.   [53] *HAW Info* 12 (1973), 18.   [54] Ibid., 19.

[55] PSA, 'Doppelmitgliedschaft' (29 October 1972). Printed as appendix to Pareik, 'Kampf um eine Identität', 289–91.

[56] Thorsten Graf and Mimi Steglitz, 'Homosexuellenunterdrückung in der bürgerlichen Gesellschaft', in *Tuntenstreit*, 35–68. Originally published in *Probleme des Klassenkampfs: Zeitschrift für politische Ökonomie und sozialistische Politik*, 16 (1974), 17–50 (42 and 66).

[57] Ibid., 65.

[58] Helmer, 'Briefe an meine freunde, die Feministen!', *HAW Info* 13 (1974), 22–3.

[59] Around 20 further members would leave the HAW in the aftermath of the *Tuntenstreit*. See further the introductory editorial note in HAW, *Tuntenstreit* [unpaginated section]. Manfred Herzer used the pseudonym Mimi Steglitz in the piece for *Problems of Class Struggle*.

letter sarcastically entitled 'long live feminism!', in which the male feminists were castigated as a 'clique of bohemians and petite bourgeoisie [*Spießer*] gone wild'.[60]

In a subsequent co-authored article in the marxist journal *Das Argument*, Herzer—this time without a pseudonym—expanded his critique of the 'unpolitical' nature of drag by connecting this 'faux-radical' protest pose to a faulty understanding of emancipation.[61] Class, not gender, was presented as the central category of analysis. Herzer and his co-author argued that the 'polarity between gender roles' could probably be abolished within capitalism, without calling into question the forces that sustained the capitalist system: 'It would however be absurd to mistake these processes for emancipation, which can only be understood as liberation from exploitation and class rule.'[62] In this light, the male feminists were to blame not only for confusing private affairs with collective emancipation, but for hindering this collective emancipation by alienating the only force capable of bringing it about, the working class.

It is unclear whether activists actually experienced negative reactions from the working class when wearing drag. Perhaps these fears were inherited from the late 1960s. According to Reimut Reiche, the generally negative reception of the student movement within the general population may have been down to perceptions of student protesters being scruffy, licentious and having long hair, characteristics that were supposedly alien to the working class.[63] Herzer, along with several other erstwhile members of the HAW, were also activists in the Socialist Unity Party of West Berlin (SEW), which was funded by the East German state. This may have made them especially eager to avoid any impression that homosexuals were given to bourgeois tendencies, since according to one discourse in the GDR sexual acts between men were not only unmanly but also un-proletarian.[64] The titular character of Rainer Werner Fassbinder's 1975 film *Fox and his Friends*, played as a gay working-class man by Fassbinder himself, adopts a decidedly gender-normative presentation, whereas some of the dishonest homosexual clique with whom he comes into contact are presented as effeminate and dandified. According to a gay activist writing in *Schwuchtel*, the film thus made it more likely for the population to associate *Tunten* with 'bourgeois decadence'.[65]

The male feminists, those responsible for all this bourgeois decadence, did not oppose forms of leftist solidarity—one example cited was taking part in a demonstration against the war in Vietnam—but argued that the gay movement must

---

[60] 'Es lebe der Feminismus!', *HAW Info* 16 (1974), 32

[61] Thorsten Graf [pseudonym] and Manfred Herzer, 'Zur neueren Diskussion über die Homosexualität', *Das Argument: Zeitschrift für Philosophie und Sozialwissenschaften* 93 (1975), 859–87 (871).

[62] Ibid., 871 and 865.   [63] Reiche, *Sexualität*, 17

[64] Jennifer Evans, 'Decriminalization, Seduction, and "Unnatural Desire" in East Germany', 558.

[65] Walter Weber, 'Faustrecht der Freiheit: oder, stellt Fassbinder die Klassenfrage', *Schwuchtel* 1 (1975), 15

renew its support for personal emancipation.[66] Rather than being hidden in large groups of people, the first emancipatory step for each activist should be an affirmation of their own homosexuality.[67] The male feminists stressed that in gay liberation's rush to prove itself to the left, to demonstrate that it had the 'right' politics—such as taking part in *de rigueur* demonstrations, joining annual 1 May rallies, or collecting donations for imprisoned leftists—their specific position as gay men was being lost. They contended that while the gay movement *should* articulate an anti-capitalist stance, its task was also to focus on the oppression faced by homosexuals—and women—whether that occurred in wider society or within leftist circles. Therefore, a struggle on two fronts was deemed necessary, both against capitalism but also against the social situation of oppressed groups. An approach that did not combine both struggles was doomed to failure.[68]

The male feminists did not subscribe to a model of absolute autonomy, but sought to make common cause with the women's movement rather than with more traditional socialist organizations. The terms *Sonderunterdrückung* ('special oppression') and *Nebenwiderspruch* ('secondary contradiction'), both used in the course of the *Tuntenstreit* to stress the primacy of class struggle, had been employed previously by some student movement leaders to downplay the gender oppression thematized by the women's movement.[69] In criticizing what they perceived as the unquestioned masculinity of other gay activists, the male feminists were consciously treading in the footsteps of women's movement activists who had critiqued the masculinity and misogyny on the part of male student movement leaders. Their engagement therefore relativizes Benno Gammerl's assessment that activists in the West German gay movement only rarely reflected on the category of masculinity.[70]

However, there is little evidence that the male feminists enjoyed much success in seeking support from other (female) feminists. Male feminist drag did not lead to a successful re-orientation of the gay movement towards second-wave feminism. Lesbians within the HAW, for example, do not seem to have offered any support to the male feminist group, instead criticizing what they understood as the orientation of male feminists towards a traditional image of women.[71] One lesbian activist who attended the 1973 gathering came away with the impression that *Tunten* saw themselves as women and as victims of the oppression of women. This saddened her, as she took it as evidence that these gay men no longer had 'any

---

[66] 'Feministenpapier', 13.   [67] Ibid., 13.   [68] Ibid., 19.

[69] Dennert et al., *In Bewegung bleiben*, 38.

[70] Gammerl, 'Ist frei sein normal? Männliche Homosexualitäten seit den 1960er Jahren zwischen Emanzipation und Normalisierung', in *Sexuelle Revolution? Zur Geschichte der Sexualität im deutschsprachigen Raum seit den 1960er Jahren*, ed. by Peter-Paul Bänziger et al. (Bielefeld, 2015), 223–43 (224).

[71] Ahrens et al., 'Die Homosexualität in uns', 29. The male feminists, of course, rejected this analysis and argued that only unpoliticized *Tunten* were guilty of this.

identity whatsoever'.[72] Others were not convinced that gay men had anything to offer feminism, since they were not women. This was the perspective adopted by the author of an article in *Emanzipation* in 1977, who added that the male feminists should confess their 'unpolitical enjoyment of grotesque-theatrical performances'.[73] In response, another activist took to defending the role of fun within political activism, whatever form this might take.[74]

Sex

Benno Gammerl has argued that the 1970s saw a transition towards greater equality in homosexual relationships, with sexual partners increasingly being of a similar age and physique. The appeal of paederastic relationships had not only been intergenerational but also hierarchical: what the younger partner could learn from the older, more mature, more intelligent partner. Instead, there was a newfound focus on egalitarianism, and on *Zärtlichkeit* (tenderness, affectionateness).[75] Even those homosexuals who foregrounded their masculinity in contact ads generally sought equally masculine partners.[76] In the American context, David Halperin has argued that mutuality and reciprocity were the new erotic watchwords of gay liberation: 'Hence, successful sexual relationships involved equal partners of the same age, the same wealth, and the same social standing, each of them doing everything with and to the other with perfect reciprocity.'[77] This contributed to the rise of the so-called 'macho' or 'clone' style, with its ideal of the hyper-masculine muscled body, a culture that did not exist in such a visible way in West Germany.[78] Nevertheless, reciprocity was an important transnational trend. This seems to have been the model implicitly favoured by Martin Dannecker and Reimut Reiche. According to their sociological study *The Ordinary Homosexual*, those homosexuals who practised *both* active and passive anal sex were most likely to have 'relatively stable levels of homosexual

---

[72] Cited in Linhoff, *Weibliche Homosexualität*, 129.

[73] Golda von Ostheim, 'Machen Kleider Leute? Gedanken zum Schwulenfeminismus', *Emanzipation* 5 (1977), 24–5. For similar responses in the United States, see Hillman, 'The most profoundly revolutionary act', 173.

[74] *Emanzipation* 1 (1978), 5.

[75] Gammerl, 'Früher war mehr Lametta? Schwule Perspektiven auf die siebziger Jahre', paper presented at *Sonntagsclub*, Berlin (4 November 2013).

[76] Benno Gammerl, 'Frau Muskel-Ty Herr Hexe und Fräulein Butch? Geschlechtlichkeiten und Homosexualitäten in der zweiten Hälfte des 20. Jahrhunderts,' in *Zeitgeschichte als Geschlechtsgeschichte: Neue Perspektiven auf die Bundesrepublik,* ed. by Julia Paulus et al. (Frankfurt a.M., 2012), 225–45 (239).

[77] Halperin, *How to Be Gay*, 52.

[78] Rehberg, 'Männer wie Du und Ich', 474. On the United States, see further Hobson, *Lavender and Red*, 75 and Downs, *Stand by me*, 169–89.

self-esteem', combining pro-sex perspectives but with an emphasis on tenderness and harmony in relationships.[79]

Zärtlichkeit has more often been associated with the women's movement and lesbian activists in particular than with the gay movement. In September 1974, *Der Spiegel* entitled its front cover story on lesbianism 'Women loving women: the new tenderness'.[80] Within the prevailing alternative left 'emotional regime', men were presented as being especially emotionally deprived, incapable of being tender or affectionate.[81] Writing in a special sexuality issue of *konkret* in 1979, one activist criticized 'propaganda' from other lesbians, including an undue focus on faithfulness, stable relationships, and emotional connections. Anything that did not fit into this schema, such as aggression, sadomasochism, and penetration, was rejected and denounced as aping male sexuality.[82] Indeed, Siegfried Schäfer provided an example of this in the very same publication. According to Schäfer, in lesbian relationships the emotional connection was key, a phenomenon inverted in gay male sexuality: 'Many homosexual men immediately have sex with each other; friendship or tenderness is rarely a prerequisite, at best sometimes the consequence. [...] With lesbian women it rarely comes to the compulsive overemphasis and overvaluation of sexuality, as can be found with so many homosexual men.'[83]

Schäfer's account tells us less about the reality of male homosexual relationships than about the strategic gains evidently felt to be won by defining lesbian sexuality against what was seen as its polar opposite, disassociating lesbianism from the opprobrium attached to male homosexuality in the process. Nevertheless, gay activists were also far from comfortable with aspects of gay male sexuality, particularly those elements that were not readily reconciled with an egalitarian model of intimacy. This discomfort was informed, especially in the case of gay action groups, by changing left-alternative ideas about sexual expression. We have seen how the appeal of a free and unrestrained sexuality was central to the student movement, even if the sexual politics of that movement were often sexist and heteronormative. The leftist discourse on sex continued to ebb and flow. According to Massimo Perinelli, an increasing 'militancy and militarization of left-wing discourse' in the early 1970s saw the issue of sex 'crowded out' in the West German new left.[84] In his analysis of the magazine *Agit 883*, which ran from

---

[79] Dannecker and Reiche, *Der gewöhnliche Homosexuelle*, 215.

[80] 'Frauen lieben Frauen: Die neue Zärtlichkeit', *Der Spiegel* 36 (1974), 1.

[81] Häberlen and Smith, 'Struggling for Feelings', 622. See also Häberlen, *The Emotional Politics of the Alternative Left*, 177.

[82] Alexander von Streit, ' ... als ob Lesbischsein sich nur im Bett abspielt', *Sexualität konkret* (1979), 74–6. On the marginalization of butch-fem lesbian sexual culture, which involved the shunning of polarized sexual roles and penetrative sex, see Nan Alamilla Boyd, 'Talking about Sex: Cheryl Gonzales and Rikki Streicher tell their Stories', *Bodies of Evidence*, ed. by Boyd and Ramírez, 95–112.

[83] Schäfer, 'Lesbierinnen: Was sind das für Frauen?', *Sexualität konkret* (1979), 71–3.

[84] Perinelli, 'Discourses on Sexuality', 269.

1969 to 1972, Perinelli identifies a growing exclusion of that which did not fit into a 'fuck the system' attitude, such as tenderness and sexuality, a process reaching its apogee with the Red Army Faction and their 'contempt for the sexual'.[85]

The gay left was not the RAF, but activists never fully escaped the idea that sexual matters might be a distraction from the 'real' business of revolutionary politics. This was already implicit in a parole from Rosa von Praunheim's *It is not the Homosexual who is perverse, but the Society in which he lives*: 'being gay does not fill one's evenings' (*Schwulsein ist nicht abendfüllend*).[86] In the film, this was part of a message that gays should 'engage politically' and show solidarity with other oppressed groups. According to Manfred Herzer, writing in 1977, the gay movement had not lived up to this demand, especially in light of its failure to build links with the workers' movement.[87] In part, this message was influenced by the desire to avoid 'single-issue politics'. Yet it also reflected the idea, on some level, that there was perhaps something *wrong* with spending one's evenings having gay sex.[88]

As the women's movement increasingly made its presence felt, what emerged was less a 'contempt for the sexual' than a critique of the types of sex men and women were seen as capable of having in capitalist society. Roland Lange's usage of 'cock-fetishism' speaks to the dissemination of this critique, which especially challenged the primacy of penetrative sex. Joachim Häberlen has shown how the trumpeting of 'tenderness' was in part a reaction against the perceived restriction of sexuality to the genitals, and to the goal of reaching orgasm, alone: instead, according to this line of thought, the entire body should be sexualized.[89] In this vein, Häberlen cites a drawing from the HAW's newsletter in 1973, which depicted all parts of the body (male and female) as erogenous zones, not just the genitals.[90] Suggesting that the ears, nose, back, arms, and legs were equally erogenous sites as the penis, scrotum, anus or prostate can certainly be seen as contributing to an expansion of sexual possibilities and an exploration of new forms of eroticism. Yet the unease regarding penetrative sex among gay activists did not have as its only source the leftist critique of genital sexuality. It was also

---

[85]   Ibid., 274.

[86]   Cited from the footage. *Abendfüllend* can also mean 'feature-length', when applied for example to a film or television programme.

[87]   Herzer, 'Homosexuellenemanzipation und Arbeiterbewegung – am Beispiel der Gewerkschaften', in *Seminar: Gesellschaft und Homosexualität*, ed. by Lautmann, 480–4 (484).

[88]   Activist-turned-historian Hans-Georg Stümke describes this parole as 'phobic'. Stümke, 'Demokratie ist abendfüllend. Die alte Coming-out-Bewegung ist tot. Wir brauchen eine politische Schwulenbewegung', in *Was heißt hier schwul?: Politik und Identitäten im Wandel* (Hamburg, 1997), ed. by Detlef Grumbach, 45–56 (51).

[89]   He calls this a 'decategorized' sexuality. Häberlen, 'Feeling Like a Child: Dreams and Practices of Sexuality in the West German Alternative Left during the Long 1970s', *Journal of the History of Sexuality*, 25:2 (2016), 219–45 (225 and 234). This 'radically different, more wholesome, and unrestricted form of sexuality' was modelled on the perceived sexuality of children (239).

[90]   Ibid., 231.

influenced by a factor that had little to do with the specifics of left-alternative discourse: namely, the particular opprobrium attached to anal sex between men, something that affected all same-sex desiring men in West Germany.

In 1977, Alexander Ziegler, the chief editor of *du&ich*, argued that 'arse-fuckers' were one of the 'outgrowths' thoroughly unrepresentative of the homosexual community at large (those who wore make-up were another).[91] We have seen how *Der Spiegel* picked up on this theme in their front-page special on homosexual law reform in 1973, expressing extreme scepticism about the claim that those who enjoyed anal sex were but 'a minority in the minority.'[92] It would be mistaken to see gay liberationists as immune to this pressure. The most disreputable of homosexual sex acts constituted a stigma that even gay leftists struggled to confront. As part of their appearance in a 1976 episode of *Sparring*, activists from *Rotzschwul* filmed an action in central Frankfurt. When told by one passer-by that homosexuality was 'a joke' because it consisted mostly of 'abnormal' anal sex, a member of the group sought not to refute this evaluation of anal sex, but instead challenged the man's characterization of homosexuality as consisting primarily of that behaviour.[93] Just as with the HAW drawing, what in one context might be seen as calling into question the dominant role of the phallus might in another be seen as seeking to circumnavigate the stigmatizing activity of anal sex. To be sure, not identifying with a certain sexual activity does not equate to gay shame, but it does not much resemble stereotypical representations of gay pride, either.

Indeed, there may have been other emotions at play. The editors of *Medicine for Gay Men*, a manual on gay sexual health and practice first published in 1978, stated that their motivation was to provide information on sexually transmitted infections, but more importantly to help dispel the fear of their own bodies and its illnesses that was held by many gay men. According to the editorial collective, which included three members of the HAW, 'gay sex—that means sex between men—is often experienced in a listless and uptight fashion. The taboo of our sexuality, especially that of the arse, limits our capacity to sensually appreciate our bodies.'[94] Certainly, gay liberation was one of the forces increasing connectivity and communication between same-sex desiring men. But until grassroots sexual health manuals emerged towards the end of the decade—and then proliferated after the HIV/AIDS crisis emerged—personal accounts of sexual practice were rarely incorporated into published material. An exception was provided by the *Brühwarm* collective. Though the programme distributed at the troupe's first play did not capture the flying papier-mâché phallus, it did feature a piece by one of the

[91] *du&ich* 6 (1977), 11.   [92] 'Bekennt, daß ihr anders seid', *Der Spiegel* 11 (1973), 46–62 (52).

[93] *Sparring: Homosexualität—noch ein Tabu* (ZDF, 24 April 1976). ZDF archive 06321/01373.

[94] Autorengruppe schwule Medizinstudenten, *Sumpf Fieber: Medizin für schwule Männer* (Berlin, 1978), unpaginated foreword.

actors, on his first experience of 'arse-fucking'. Manfred recounted his fear, and his previous reticence about anal sex, but his account foregrounded pleasure, too: 'I enjoy being screwed.'[95]

Mutuality and reciprocity may have been the sexual forms increasingly valorized over the course of the 1970s, but they did not totally eclipse those erotic acts and sexual subjectivities brought into disrepute. That included intergenerational desire but also sexual behaviour and modes of self-presentation that suggested bipolarity, the adoption of asymmetrical sexual roles. This was another issue influencing the debate on gender transgression. Effeminacy was not compatible with the model of masculinity adopted by many gay activists not least because it was interpreted as signposting a passive sexual preference, that is, indicating a desire only to be fucked and not to return the favour. The 'political drag' or 'gender fuck' of the male feminists was not registered by all observers, not least the author of an article in Der Spiegel, who in 1978 commented that 'female-passive [sic] oriented homosexuals' used jewellery and make-up so as to more easily find their sought-after same-sex partner.[96] According to the frankly dubious scientific pedigree of 'Dr. W', writing in du&ich in 1971, 'very feminine' homosexuals would always hold themselves deficient for not being born women and for not possessing female genitals. The preferred sexual activity of such homosexuals was passive anal sex, since in this instance their anus could serve as a 'replacement vagina'.[97]

Equally, activists were confronted by the growing visibility of a sado-masochistic scene, pointing to the popularity of what represented (at least on the surface) the least reciprocal and mutual of sexual practices. In West Berlin, a particular flashpoint was the opening of Knolle in late 1975, a bar often frequented by leathermen and furnished with one of the first dark rooms in the country. A HAW activist described the bar as 'one of the most extreme expressions of male-fascistoid sexuality'. In its darkened cellar only silhouettes could be made out, in order to cover up any potential tenderness between men, and thus protect patrons from having to question their masculinity. Indeed, the author associated Knolle with other ostensibly retrograde developments that he thought emanated from the United States: a growing militarism and Nazi cult in the gay scene, along with leather, 'certain forms of male pornography' and, curiously, sex aids such as cock rings or poppers.[98]

In reply, another activist criticized this perspective, arguing that the darkness of what was referred to as the 'screw room' was more about preserving anonymity than masculinity, and that any frustration caused by anonymous sex was less than that caused by rejection. It was not the patrons of Knolle who needed to change,

---

[95] Manfred, 'Übers Arschficken', in 'Brühwarm: ein schwuler Jahrmarkt', ed. by Ödipus Kollektiv, 12. SMB archive.
[96] 'Irrtum der Natur', Der Spiegel 49 (1978), 31–3 (31).
[97] 'Wie Homophile leben', du&ich 3 (1971), 32–7 (32).
[98] 'Männer lasst das Knollen sein kommt herauf und reiht euch ein!, HAW Info 20 (1975), 60–2 (60).

but activists themselves: 'we [need to] learn to fulfil our own desires and to recognize that the rejection of queens and of trade [*Tunten und Kerle*] is a rejection of part of ourselves'.[99] Frank Ripploh, who would later go on to direct the cult film *Taxi zum Klo* ('Taxi to the Toilet'), posited that the reason so many activists reacted aggressively to the 'leather monsters' was due to their sense of inferiority.[100] According to Ripploh, 'perspective gays' (*Durchblickschwule*) such as himself tended to demonstrate their critique of consumerism through their 'scrap heap look'. This, along with their fondness for leftist clichés, cost them the 'most beautiful fucks'.[101]

The debate within gay liberation over sado-masochism was influenced by the context of the National Socialist past, particularly because the 'rediscovery' of the Nazi persecution of homosexuals was so recent. The individual who denounced *Knolle* admitted to having masturbated to thoughts of being tortured by a member of the SS, interpreting this as the unwanted product of his oppressed situation.[102] Two other HAW activists defended sado-masochism, writing that the desire to whip or be whipped had nothing to do with reactionary politics whatsoever, and that claims to the contrary were shameless and represented a trivialization of fascism.[103] The editorial collective of *Schwuchtel* seconded the view that no particular political trajectory should be read into sado-masochism, but rejected the notion that fascism could not be explained from a consideration of the sexual.[104] In this, the editors were recapitulating a (mis)understanding held by many new left figures, that the Third Reich was not only characterized by sexual repression, but could also be explained by it.[105] As we saw in Chapter 3, this discourse at times had homophobic overtones. According to Erich Fromm, whose texts were widely disseminated in the student movement, sado-masochistic impulses were linked to the popularity of the Nazis and particularly of Hitler, adored because of his strength and supremacy. Moreover, according to the Frankfurt School author, sado-masochism was particularly to be found among the 'petit bourgeois authoritarian type' and amongst homosexuals.[106]

The contemporary link between sado-masochism and authoritarianism may have been further underlined by Pier Paolo Pasolini's unrelentingly graphic film *Salò, or the 120 Days of Sodom*, which depicted the sexual depravity of Italian

---

[99] Claire [pseudonym], 'Zur SM-Diskussion: Thesen zur Funny', *HAW Info* 22 (1976), 18–19.

[100] Peggy von Schnottgenberg [pseudonym], 'Hilfe, ich liebe große Schwänze, Sperma, Schweiß und Leder', *Schwuchtel* 4 (1976), 2–3 (2).

[101] Ibid., 2.

[102] 'Männer lasst das Knollen sein kommt herauf und reiht euch ein!, *HAW Info* 20 (1975), 60–2 (62).

[103] Wilfried and Michael, 'Einige Gedanken zum Knolle-Artikel im HAW-Info 20', *HAW Info* 22 (1976), 21–2.

[104] *Schwuchtel* 5 (1976), 1.   [105] See especially Herzog, *Sex After Fascism*.

[106] Fromm, 'Sozialpsychologischer Teil', 125–36.

fascist libertines.[107] Although confused and ill-defined, the associations between sado-masochism and fascism informed the discomfort of some gay activists with sado-masochistic desire amongst homosexuals. Some may have internalized these associations; for others, it was more a case of seeking not to provoke latent prejudice. This affected even those individuals who identified with elements of the sado-masochistic scene. Hans Eppendorfer, the chief-editor of *him* from 1976, became known to a wider audience under the name 'The Leather Man', through a series of interviews with the novelist Hubert Fichte. According to Eppendorfer, at a leather gathering in Hamburg in 1970 there had been a room furnished with a gas oven and a trench, and he agreed with Fichte that this had 'something of the concentration camp about it'. He saw some leathermen as potential concentration camp guards, since behind their leather there existed a pronounced 'craving for recognition'. Indeed, the wider leather scene was described in its current form as 'simply purely fascist'.[108]

In July 1977, members of the AHA were invited to *Knolle* for 'leather coffee' by the West Berlin branch of the Motor Sport Club (MSC).[109] A spokesperson reassured AHA activists that the MSC encompassed the entire political spectrum, from extreme left to extreme right (this clarification may not have been that reassuring!) and that their members favoured the whole gamut of sexual activity, not just sado-masochism.[110] The only thing their members had in common was their style of attire, a mechanism of publicly avowing their sexuality.[111] Through this display of homosexual desire, MSC members argued that they possessed greater self-consciousness than the typical gay activist.[112] Encounters with such individuals may have influenced the author of a position paper submitted before an AHA meeting, which posed the question of whether being political was becoming a surrogate for being gay. The paper proposed that 'being involved in gay politics is [seen as] a morally superior substitute for the free acting out of sexual needs of all kinds, of which [activists] find themselves incapable'.[113]

---

[107] Released shortly after the director's death in 1975. The film and the manner of Pasolini's death (apparently, murdered by a male prostitute) were often discussed as interwoven issues. See for example Peter Jacob, 'Schönheit aus Elend', *du&ich* 3 (1976), 13–14.

[108] Hans Eppendorfer, *Der Ledermann spricht mit Hubert Fichte* (Frankfurt a.M., 1977), 203–4 and 207.

[109] Elsewhere, the acronym MSC was given as 'motorcycle club' and 'motorsport and contacts'. In any case, the MSC was less an organization for motor-sport enthusiasts than a loose umbrella group for leathermen, the majority of whom seem to have identified as homosexual. See further 'Bei Uns sitzt das Leder noch Stramm', *Die Zeit* (2 September 1977).

[110] Michael Faisst, untitled report on AHA-MSC meeting (17 July 1977). SMB archive, box AHA two.

[111] Clayton Whisnant states that one appeal of leather to homosexuals was that it 'contained a sexual message, yet offered a rebuke to effeminacy'. Whisnant, *Male Homosexuality*, 150.

[112] Faisst, untitled report on AHA-MSC meeting.

[113] Undated document, 'Leitfaden für ein Gespräch über das "Politische" und das "Unpolitische" in uns'. SMB archive, box AHA two.

The hypothesis put forward for the subsequent discussion was that 'political work keeps the "gay swine" in each of us in check'. While this was a perceptive insight, the activist or activists who wrote this position paper were clearly unsure over its ramifications, adding 'That is—thank God—correct? Or—unfortunately—correct? Or false?' This is precisely the kind of ambivalence expressed by Corny Littmann, who was caught between expressing the 'gay swine' within, or presenting as a 'clean leftist homosexual'. This ambivalence also speaks to the gap between 'what we want' and 'what we want to want', to use the words of Dominic Ording, from his analysis of English-language gay liberation manifestos. Political and sexual desires did not always go hand in hand, and gay activists struggled to come to terms with this fact: 'In short, they wanted to be conscientious and to get laid at the same time.'[114]

Appearances notwithstanding, gay groups were not just fora of political discussion, but also served sexual functions. Whether movement events were experienced as successful and enjoyable could depend not just on their perceived political efficacy, but whether activists 'got lucky' and discovered new sexual partners.[115] Based on interviews with seventeen *Rotzschwul* members in 1974, Barbara Wackernagel calculated that on average each individual had had at least three sexual partners from the Frankfurt-based group. Only one of her interviewees had not experienced any sexual contact within the group.[116] In light of these findings, Wackernagel expressed her surprise that not one single activist mentioned anticipated sexual contact amongst their expectations for the group, suggesting that this might be explained by sexuality being 'rationalized away' in favour of 'higher' motives.[117] Looking back at the 1970s, a former member of the HAW recounted in our oral history interview how his homosexuality was often lived out on a cerebral rather than a physical level, describing himself as a *Theorieschwuler*, translating as 'theory gay'—or even, to draw out the implied meaning, a 'theoretical gay'.[118] The director of *Not the Homosexual*, Rosa von Praunheim, was an irregular participant in HAW meetings and was fond of criticizing gay activists for their 'theorizing around'.[119] In the group's newsletter, he asked 'I'd like to know who has fun sitting in the inhibited, clinical HAW circle and acting as if he were not gay.'[120]

---

[114] Ording, 'Intimate Fellows: Utopia and Chaos in the early post-Stonewall gay liberation manifestos,' in *Anarchism and Utopianism*, ed. by Laurence Davis and Ruth Kinna (Manchester, 2009), 187–206 (188).

[115] Elmar Drost, 'Mit dem Schwanz gedacht', in *Schwule Regungen, Schwule Bewegungen: Ein Lesebuch*, ed. by Willi Frieling (Berlin, 1985), 9–24 (22).

[116] To be precise, an average of 3.25. Wackernagel, 'Die Gruppe Rotzschwul', 133–4.

[117] Ibid., 132.   [118] Erwin Kirchner (pseudonym). Oral history interview (28 August 2012).

[119] 'Protokoll des HAW Plenums' (30 July 1972), 1. *Spinnboden Lesbenarchiv:* HAW Frauengruppe, Sammlung Monne Kühn 2/3 1972–1973.

[120] *HAW Info* 5 (1972), 7.

Of course, there was, and is, more than one way to be gay. Indeed, one of the signal contributions of gay liberation was to add to the many different ways that same-sex desiring men might feel, think about, or express their homosexuality. But gay liberation was never a simple matter of 'anything goes'. Instead, activists constructed a certain hierarchy out of the manifold ways of being gay, even if the contours of this hierarchy were never definitive. A final example to elucidate this point: how activists responded to the phenomenon of cruising for sex in public, and particularly at public toilets. Along with anal sex, make-up, and prostitution, this was one of those 'outgrowths' lambasted by Alexander Ziegler in *du&ich*. It was also one of the chief culprits identified by 1950s homophile activists as responsible for the public's poor opinion of homosexuals.[121] Where do the 1970s activists fit in, those who in the conventional narrative supposedly challenged normalizing impulses and celebrated queer sexual difference? As we saw in the introduction, Rosa von Praunheim's *Not the Homosexual* told West German gays to be proud of their homosexuality, but not *all* forms of homosexuality. This is evidenced by language such as 'park fuckers' and 'urinal gays' (*Pissbudenschwule*), and even by the film's mistranslation of the English-language parole 'out of the closets', which was rendered in German as 'out of the *toilets* and into the streets!' Cottaging was seen as simply incompatible with the dictates of emancipation.

Occasionally, gay activists directly reached out to the denizens of cruising grounds, for example in 1976 when the Gay Action Cologne (SAK) organized a gathering in the trees near a city lake. Some 50 people came, about half of them 'dragged out of the bushes' from the surrounding area.[122] According to one SAK activist, providing sexual opportunities was an important way of making the gay movement seem interesting to prospective members.[123] Of the 789 homosexuals whose responses informed *The Ordinary Homosexual*, 45 per cent had met a sexual partner over the previous 12 months in a park, and 41 per cent in a public toilet (slightly fewer then had sexual relations in those locales: 40 per cent and 29 per cent respectively).[124] Among *Rotzschwul* members, 11 of the 17 activists interviewed by Wackernagel admitted to frequenting these sexual sites.[125] In 1973, the group organized an action at a particularly popular public toilet in Frankfurt, seeking to draw attention to police oppression and to challenge the prejudice against those who cruised for sex.[126]

Those who organized in the HAW's working group on public toilets (or *Klappen*, to use the contemporary idiom) seemed less interested in engaging with this location. Erwin Kirchner, in our oral history interview, recalled how

---

[121] *du&ich* 6 (1977), 11; Riechers, 'Freundschaft und Anständigkeit', 21.
[122] 'Fete am Kölner Schwulentreff', *Schwuchtel* 5 (1976), 18.   [123] Ibid., 18.
[124] Dannecker and Reiche, *Der gewöhnliche Homosexuelle*, 103–7. The period in question was between mid-1970 to mid-1971.
[125] Wackernagel, *Die Gruppe Rotzschwul*, 81.   [126] Ibid., 80.

activists even discussed blowing up particularly notorious public toilets in West Berlin.[127] In a piece for the HAW's newsletter in 1976, group members defined themselves against those who frequented either the *Knolle* bar or public toilets. The way that *Knolle* patrons behaved towards each other's bodies had nothing in common 'with what *we* understand by emancipation'.[128] According to the rather chaotic article, group members would liberate themselves from the chains of monogamy and from the toilet cubicle walls that divided them, by coming together, by dancing, and by exploring their bodies. The 'cottaging sisters' (*Klappenschwester*), meanwhile, were also to be liberated, from attacks by the police, but also from their own 'deathly muteness'.[129] (Indeed, fears about the police surveillance of public toilets were later proven well-founded, at least in Hamburg, when Corny Littmann—of *Brühwarm* fame—took a hammer to the mirrors above the sinks to reveal a chamber hidden behind.)[130]

According to a poem written by a member of the working group, gays needed to learn to articulate their desires, to liberate their fantasies, so as to 'smash the rules of the game' that restricted their pleasure, separated different bodies, and kept their sexuality in shackles. Yet the creative fantasy of liberated sexual relations went hand-in-hand with a somewhat censorious attitude: for those cottaging locations were described as sites of degradation.[131] Although gay activists were keen to stress that they did not consider themselves any better than those who cruised for sex in the scene—in contrast to how this theme had featured in homophile publications—one cannot help but identify a powerful disapproval of those whose sexual consciousness had not yet met the demands of liberation. Notwithstanding the protestations of *Rotzschwul* members, it was not only the 'bar gays' (*Kneipenschwulen*) who had a problem with the 'cottaging gays' (*Klappenschwulen*), but activist gays too: even if that problem might have fallen rather closer to home, perhaps part of themselves and their own desires.[132] Though their expressions of distaste were couched in different forms, Jennifer Evans is right in arguing that the homophile movement of the 1950s and 1960s

---

[127] Oral history interview (28 August 2012). Pseudonym used.
[128] AG Klappe, 'was wir wollen', *HAW Info* 23 (1976), 3. Emphasis in the original.
[129] Ibid., 3.
[130] 'Dicker Hammer', *Der Spiegel* 29 (1980), 80–2. A police spokesperson admitted that officials had used these hidden rooms to inspect goings-on in eight public toilets in Hamburg. They had been installed in the late 1960s, but the surveillance continued even after homosexuality was partially decriminalized in 1969 and 1973. Littmann's action came in the midst of an ultimately unsuccessful election campaign. He was the lead candidate in Hamburg for the Greens. Rosenkranz and Lorenz note that Helmut Schmidt—Federal Chancellor until 1982—was the Senator for the Interior in Hamburg at the time when the surveillance windows were installed. *Hamburg auf anderen Wegen*, 78.
[131] Written by 'Doris Night' [pseudonym], an activist in the HAW, originally from Bielefeld. 'An meine Schwestern der Klappe', in *Schwule Lyrik*, ed. by Kraushaar, 125–6.
[132] Wackernagel, *Die Gruppe Rotzschwul*, 83.

and the gay movement of the 1970s were to ultimately find 'affinity in their shared denigration of the gutter'.[133]

The Emotional Politics of Gay Liberation

Writing in *him* in 1973, gay publicist Jens Soerensen asked what ten years of the 'sex wave' had amounted to. He acknowledged that people now had more sexual information at their disposal, and that there was a somewhat greater tolerance of sexual minorities.[134] Yet he bemoaned that sex was turning into a 'competitive sport' (*Leistungssport*) and that the advent of sex shops had artificially created new sexual demands, leading to a lack of confidence and sexual dysfunctions such as impotency.[135] Similarly, an article in *du&ich* in 1973 did not deny that liberalization had taken place, but stressed that one must differentiate between libertinage and freedom. Constant change of sexual partners militated against 'real friendship', and liberalization brought the danger that 'emancipated sexual behaviour' would be exploited and manipulated by commerce.[136] While activists in gay action groups seldom used vocabulary such as 'real friendship', they shared the perspective that sexual excess did not amount to freedom. As Elizabeth Heineman has argued in relation to responses to the broader sex wave, 'sexual revolutionaries and conservatives' had at least one thing in common: a shared 'suspicion of consumption and pleasure'.[137] In homosexual politics, this can best be seen through a mutual antipathy to the gay scene, which represented a crucial point of connection between gay action groups, the gay press, and organizations that still used the term 'homophile', including the International Homophile World Organization.[138]

The IHWO explicitly wished to make the gay scene (or 'subculture') surplus to requirements.[139] Such was the taint of the gay scene that the organization refused to publish pieces in its members' magazine that expressed anything positive about the 'gay underground'. It seems that IHWO members needed this reminder, given the admonishment with which it was coupled: 'we've received these sort of submissions – *shame!*'[140] The IHWO opened its 'club-centre' in July 1971, in an area of Hamburg deliberately located away from the main part of that shameful gay scene. Here, IHWO members (and others, for the payment of a small fee) could experience a different atmosphere to that which could be found in the

---

[133] Evans, 'The 1950s as Radical In-Between', 14.
[134] Soerensen, 'Sex Bilanz', *him* 4 (1973), 12–13 (12).   [135] Ibid., 13.
[136] Ludwig, 'Unter uns gesagt', *du&ich* 2 (1973), 60.
[137] Heineman, *Before Porn Was Legal*, 126.
[138] See also Benno Gammerl, 'Ist frei sein normal?', 236.
[139] *IHWO Rundbrief* 3 (1973). Not paginated. SMB archive, IHWO box one.
[140] Ibid. Emphasis in the original. Exactly the same wording was used for submissions which 'bordered on or even crossed into pornography'.

commercial gay scene.[141] However, the executive were forced to admit two years later that the centre had failed to offer anything substantially different to the ambience to be found in regular gay bars, just at cheaper prices (and those cheaper prices ensured that the venture soon proved financially unsustainable).[142]

For the *glf-Köln* (GLF Cologne), before he could engage in the public sphere, the homosexual had to overcome personal weaknesses, not the least of which was fear and a lack of trust.[143] The group therefore sought to provide opportunities for homosexuals to overcome their loneliness by organizing discussion evenings, theatre visits, film nights, trips, and parties. Here, they could meet like-minded people without being confronted by 'the four Gods of homosexuals': sex, youth, beauty, and fashion. In time, they could improve their self-confidence and tackle their guilt complexes, taking advantage of the GLF, which sought to offer an alternative to 'anonymous sex'.[144] Following in the footsteps of the IHWO—not that this was recognized at the time—the group opened its own 'club-centre' in Autumn 1974, fulfilling a long-time desire to offer a reliable meeting space but also an alternative to gay bars in Cologne.[145] Similarly, the Initiative Group Homosexuality Stuttgart (IHS) arranged activities such as hiking trips and coffee mornings to 'improve interpersonal relationships' in the group. According to an editorial in the group's newsletter, the IHS provided a 'healthy climate for human encounters', an alternative to the 'semi-darkness of parks, toilets, and bars', a welcome contrast to an 'atmosphere dominated by formalities and by pent-up sexual desire'.[146] The IHS opened its first 'club-centre' in 1973, which seems first and foremost to have been a venue for group meetings. Until then, these meetings had taken place in a Protestant Church building.[147] In 1976, the group attempted to provide a more visible alternative to the scene, announcing plans to open a public *Teestube* ('tearoom'), where there would be no compulsion to consume, no regulation of behaviour, and no 'gay insider atmosphere'.[148]

One IHS member was far from impressed by talk of coffee mornings, warning that the group was descending into a 'bourgeois institution'. If gays wanted to 'break out of their ghetto', he continued, they must become politically active: 'that means practical work internally as well as externally', in order to avoid 'complacent stagnation'.[149] Back in Cologne, members soon clashed over the correct role for their centre, as the goals of gay activism and sociability did not dovetail as

---

[141] Wolfert, 'Gegen Einsamkeit', 106 and 107.   [142] *IHWO Report* 8 (1973), 2.
[143] 'Was ist eigentlich GLF?', *GLF Info* 3 (1972), 1.   [144] Ibid., 1.
[145] Gerhard Grühn, 'Troubles in Paradise. 30 Jahre Schwulen- und Lesbenzentren in Köln', *Invertito* 7 (2005), 37–64 (40).
[146] 'Stuttgarter Homos verstärken ihre Aktivität', *IHS Info* 4 (1973), 1.
[147] 'ihs im eigenen Clubzentrum', *IHST Info* 1 (1974), 1. From the seventh issue of 1973, the IHS collaborated with the Initiative Group Homosexuality in Tübingen to produce a joint newsletter, hence the changed title. The collaboration did not last long, since by the fifth issue of 1974 the title had reverted to *IHS info*.
[148] *Emanzipation* 5 (1976), 31.
[149] Gerhard Wiegand, 'Initativgruppe ohne Initiative?', *IHST info* 2 (1974), 2.

nicely as had been expected: a conflict which Gerhard Grühn describes as featuring 'politically engaged activists' versus 'conservative leisure-club supporters'.[150] In reality, these dividing lines cannot so easily be drawn. While activists in gay action groups tended to be suspicious about any overdue emphasis on sociability, they also recognized the need for forms of socializing amongst their members. The Homosexual Action Nuremberg, for example, organized what was described as '*gemeinsame Freizeitgestaltung*', the common arrangement of recreational activities, in order to improve relationships and communication within the group.[151]

The Homosexual Action Hamburg shared this focus on communication. According to the HAH, the gay scene was 'inhumane'.[152] Gay bars offered only a climate of competitiveness and portal to a dream-world and the consumer society; instead, homosexuals needed to create new 'forms of communication', to bring them out of their isolation.[153] Deploying the same vocabulary, Frankfurt gay activists opened their 'communication centre' in 1974, but subsequently bemoaned that it had failed in its purpose: 'as soon as it reached 10.30, sisters hurriedly decamped to the scene.'[154] Using furniture from this centre, activists instead set up a gay café, the *Anderes Ufer*. With its floor-to-ceiling windows, the café possessed a visibility that was defined against the reputedly clandestine nature of the gay scene. The project was described as a 'permanent gay action.'[155]

As we saw in the introduction, a faction broke away from the GLF Cologne in 1976, becoming the Gay Action Cologne (SAK). Disharmony in the North-Rhine Westphalian city was played out in the pages of the national gay press, when the SAK advertised itself to *du&ich* readers as an attempt to rectify Cologne's poor reputation in gay activism.[156] Yet even groups that did explicitly place an emphasis on public actions could not escape internal discord over the correct approach to gay activism. A SAK activist noted in 1976 that group members were at very different stages in their 'development.' Some were still in the 'coming-out phase' whereas others had long since left this stage behind and wanted less time spent on mutual support and more on public actions.[157] These were not just abstract strategic differences, but demonstrate the significance of diverse personal needs, the different things that individuals wanted and needed from gay liberation.

---

[150] Grühn, 'Troubles in Paradise', 42.   [151] *Emanzipation* 3 (1975), 3.

[152] HAH, 'Zur Situation der Homosexuellen', May 1972. SMB archive, IHWO Box One.

[153] Ibid.

[154] 'Von der "Roten Zelle Schwul" zum Schwulencafe', *Pflasterstrand* 14 (1977), 35–8 (37).

[155] 'An's andere Ufer gerettet', *Pflasterstrand* 15 (1977), 30–1. *Anderes Ufer*, 'other bank', derives from the phrase 'vom anderen Ufer sein' ('to be from the other side'). Another café of the same name opened in West Berlin the same year: 'Anderes Ufer: Ein Kaffeehaus in Berlin', *him* 7 (1977) 18–19. These cafés were then the model for *Tuc Tuc*, which was opened by HAH activists in 1979. *him* (October 1979), 41.

[156] *du&ich* 5 (1976), 45. The GLF retorted a month later that they had been around much longer than the SAK, and had many more members, approximately 100 in contrast to just 15 of the renegade group: *du&ich* 6 (1976), 42–3.

[157] 'Schwule Gruppen in Köln', *Schwuchtel* 4 (1976), 17–18 (18).

According to HAW member Jürgen B., gay activists had to learn from the mistakes of the student movement. The gay movement needed to be more than just an interest group; instead, the task for activists was to change aspects of their behaviour. For Jürgen, this had been rejected as petit-bourgeois by many leftist student groups, and the communes had failed to integrate 'emotional interests' into activism.[158] In fact, 'emotional interests' had not featured very prominently in the founding document of the HAW, written in November 1971. The group used this opportunity to nail its ideological colours firmly to the mast. The discrimination of homosexuals was defined as inseparable from the 'conditions of the emergence and development of capitalism', and the oppression of homosexuality was described as 'just one case of the general oppression of sexuality, which serves the security of political and economic power'. Thus, so the understanding went, an emancipation of homosexuals could only take place under socialism.[159]

Many, however, were unwilling to postpone the task of emancipation until the establishment of socialism. Contemporary leftist thinkers such as Dieter Duhm proved influential in arguing that individual, not just collective, liberation mattered too. In his book on 'interpersonal fear' in capitalism, Duhm contended that dogmatic understandings of Marxist categories and an 'interpersonal climate of intolerable coldness and arrogance' was costing the left much-needed support. Capitalism, Duhm agreed, needed to be abolished in order to lift alienation, yet he insisted that emancipation was not just the result of this process, but rather the process itself.[160] The group was therefore a vital intermediary post where emancipation must be lived out if there was to be any hope of realizing this change in wider society. In their groups, activists needed to develop alternatives to the 'bourgeois system of competitiveness, animosity and isolation'.[161]

Similarly, psychoanalyst Horst-Eberhard Richter focused on the foundational role of the group in his bestseller from 1972. In his view, groups were an opportunity to 'give new meaning' to individuals' 'deformed and emptied relations'.[162] As Joachim Häberlen and Jake Smith have argued, in describing the fear, isolation and coldness that were perceived as endemic to capitalism, leftist activists did not so much analyse existing emotional conditions as produce an 'emotional regime', which told activists how they *should* feel in West German society. Capitalism was seen as engendering damaged personalities in three main ways: through an

---

[158] Minutes of HAW plenary, 4 June 1972. Spinnboden Lesbenarchiv, HAW Frauengruppe: Sammlung Monne Kühn 2/3 1972–1973.

[159] HAW 'vorläufige Grundsatzerklärung' (November 1971).

[160] Dieter Duhm, *Warenstruktur und zerstörte Zwischenmenschlichkeit: Dritter Versuch der gesellschaftlichen Begründung zwischenmenschlicher Angst in der kapitalistischen Warengesellschaft* (Lampertheim, 1975 [1973]), 20–1 and 161.

[161] Ibid., 161 and 175.

[162] Richter, *Die Gruppe: Hoffnung auf einen neuen Weg, sich selbst und andere zu befreien. Psychoanalyse in Kooperation mit Gruppeninitiativen* (Hamburg, 1972), 33. Cited from Häberlen, *The Emotional Politics of the Alternative Left*, 173.

'allegedly omnipresent sense of fear', through 'feelings of loneliness and the inability to engage in meaningful social relations', and by creating 'an overly rational' world that left no space for the expression of feelings.[163]

Whether this was an accurate description of capitalism is less important than the framework this understanding offered the gay left. In their diagnosis of the gay scene's ills, activists in gay action groups did not particularly differ from other political trajectories in gay liberation. However, they parted company when it came to identifying the root cause of this state of affairs. Groups such as the IHWO tended to see any unwanted manifestations of the gay scene as the product of the ostracization caused by decades of illegality. The gay left looked elsewhere, finding in anti-capitalism a useful explanatory structure for the emotional conditions they encountered in the gay scene—and in their own lives. According to *Rotzschwul*, any sense of freedom, escape or happiness in the gay scene was but an illusory solution to the desperation and unhappiness that prevailed among homosexuals.[164] Cruising grounds in parks, toilets and saunas were characterized by fear and the absence of affection or tenderness.[165] To be sure, these were not 'objective' assessments. Rather, these kind of emotions 'made sense' under an anti-capitalist logic, whereas feelings such as pleasure, satisfaction, even hope, gave rise to a certain ambivalence: for these emotions were not supposed to be compatible with a fundamentally rotten system. A happy homosexual was one who had yet to open his eyes.

Häberlen conceptualizes the alternative left as a 'space for experimenting with feelings in multiple ways'.[166] The chief unit through which this emotional experimentation, and exploration, took place was the consciousness-raising group (*Selbsterfahrungsgruppe*). Rainer Marbach, from the Initiative Group Homosexuality Göttingen, remembers taking part in such a group, partly inspired by the work of Horst-Eberhard Richter (even though other activists took Richter to task for his scant reference to homosexuality).[167] Looking further afield, a working group of the HAW acknowledged the work of Richter but found the model provided by the women's movement and the gay movement in the United States more significant.[168] In a position paper, these activists recommended the formation of groups consisting of not less than six and not more than ten participants, and that everyone should be allowed to speak without being

---

[163] Häberlen and Smith, 'Struggling for Feelings', 617 and 620.
[164] Rotzschwul, 'Die homosexuelle Subkultur', 6. SMB archive, folder Frankfurt.   [165] Ibid., 12.
[166] Häberlen, *The Emotional Politics of the Alternative Left*, 24.
[167] Marbach, 'Erinnerungen an die 1950er und 1960er Jahre und den Aufbruch der Schwulenbewegung: Autobiographische Anmerkungen', in *Ohnmacht und Aufbegehren*, ed. by Pretzel and Weiß, 27–36 (33). On the criticism, see 'Interview mit Horst-Eberhard Richter', *Emanzipation* 5 (September/October 1979), 5.
[168] HAW Freitagsgruppe, 'Selbsterfahrungsgruppen: Das amerikanische Model'. Printed as appendix to Pareik, 'Kampf um eine Identität', 262–6. As this paper referenced, 'consciousness-raising' was difficult to render in German. By *Selbsterfahrungsgruppen*, activists meant consciousness-raising groups, even though 'self-experience groups' would be a more direct translation.

interrupted. This format was best suited to overcoming the problem of trust, the difficulty of talking about intimate matters, and the presence of competitiveness and rivalry, which prevaricated against the discussion of weaknesses. By discussing personal issues—including childhood memories, problems in the workplace, with parents, in relationships, sexual fantasies—isolation could be overcome, and the first step taken towards a 'gay solidarity'.[169] The paper acknowledged that 'navel-gazing' should not be an end in itself, but that 'navel-gazing as a precursor to concrete political work is for the broken gays [*kaputte Schwule*] of our society a downright necessity'.[170]

Focusing on the role of consciousness-raising groups across the alternative left, Häberlen analyses how 'politics became 'a kind of self-therapeutization that required constantly working on the self.'[171] Because of its almost permanent nature, this was a demanding dictate. HAW activist Andreas recalls laying on a large mattress with other members of his consciousness-raising group, 'touching, stroking, feeling each other, with much fear, inhibited'.[172] What may have been for some activists a chance to overcome fear and inhibition, may for others simply have poured fuel on the fire of those emotional states. The same goes for 'political drag': Andreas giddily described his excitement when he first wore a skirt in public, but added that he later found himself furiously scratching off his nail varnish while riding the underground, because he could not cope with the uninterrupted stress caused by such experiments.[173] Expressing one's feelings was considered a route to liberation, but this liberation was twinned with the pressure to reveal one's most intimate details. Writing in *Autonomie* in 1976, Matthias Belz and Klaus Trebes took aim at what they perceived as the leftist taboo on masturbation. For the authors, this taboo was indicative of the fact that leftists had not yet discovered how to live in a spontaneous and liberated way. The cop and the priest had been internalized, the man on the street demanding law and order was also running around inside their communes or shared living arrangements. The dogma that the oppressors were always the others, never themselves, had blinded leftists to the way that 'self-repression' legitimized and supported state oppression. Continuing, the authors urged the readers of *Autonomie* to consider whether they fantasized during masturbation, whether they had violent dreams, whether they imagined being raped. To be in denial about fantasies and to be unable to talk politically about dreams led to widespread fear, and ultimately the 'daily reproduction' of 'our secret fascism'.[174]

---

[169] Ibid., 262 and 265.   [170] Ibid., 265.
[171] Häberlen, *The Emotional Politics of the Alternative Left*, 170.
[172] Andreas, 'Meine persönliche HAW-Geschichte', 38.   [173] Ibid., 41 and 43.
[174] 'Selbstbefriedigung', *Autonomie* 3 (April 1976), 77–9 (79). As the reference to rape foreshadowed, discussion on sexuality between alternative leftists led to increasingly aggressive and toxic disputes between men and women in the second half of the 1970s. See further Herzog, *Sex after Fascism*, 234–40.

These pressures were arguably intensified in shared living arrangements, known as *Wohngemeinschaften* (WGs). These can be translated simply as 'flatshares', but the more literal 'residential communities' captures the political investment made in these attempts to bring aspects of the group, and consciousness-raising group, into daily life. We have seen how *Rotzschwul* activists launched the city's first 'gay commune' in 1974, part of a wider struggle waged by various leftist groups and local residents over housing conditions in the city.[175] This experiment was short-lived, but activists continued to set up gay WGs throughout the decade, partly due to a simultaneous critique of the 'heterosexual nuclear family' and the 'bourgeois gay home', and partly for less ideological purposes—to save money on rent.[176] The five actors and two technicians in *Brühwarm*, for example, not only performed and travelled but also lived together in a collective.[177] Some activists rotated between living in WGs set up by gay action groups and living in more general leftist collectives, together with heterosexual activists.[178]

According to the narrator of a documentary produced by the WDR in 1979, on the Initiative Group Homosexuality Bielefeld, the group's *Wohngemeinschaft* fulfilled activists' need for tenderness and provided a sanctuary from 'daily humiliations'.[179] Looking back at this footage several decades later, one of the activists featured, Detlef Stoffel, remembered how the image of bliss and harmony depicted on screen was far from accurate: the 'extreme arguments', understandably, were not showcased to the watching public.[180] Erwin, from the IHS in Stuttgart, described how his group's WG offered activists a chance to overcome their loneliness and to practice shared living: 'We're learning again how to bear criticism from others, to exercise tolerance in daily life, to become less hard-headed.'[181] Yet Andreas recalled how members of his WG—all from the HAW—constantly talked about the need to communicate, but failed to actually practice that communication in their flat.[182]

Whether motivated by their reluctance to take part in this communication, or by a political preference in favour of organizing actions outside the confines of the group, not all activists were on board with the business of consciousness-raising. One member of the HAW, Wilfried, argued that consciousness-raising groups

---

[175] 'Wir sind geräumt!' Printed as appendix to Wackernagel, *Die Gruppe Rotzschwul*.

[176] On the first two factors, see Stephen Vider, ' "The Ultimate Extension of Gay Community": Communal Living and Gay Liberation in the 1970s', *Gender and History* 27 (2015), 865–81 (869).

[177] Rosenkranz and Lorenz, *Hamburg auf anderen Wegen*, 187.   [178] *Schwuchtel* 2/3 (1976), 5.

[179] Broadcast on the WDR's Third Channel on 30 January 1979. *Schauplatz Gerichtstrasse—Schwulengruppe Bielefeld* (WDR, 1979). SMB archive.

[180] *Detlef: 60 Jahre schwul*, dir. by Jan Rothstein and Stefan Westerwelle (Pro-Fun Media, 2012). Cited from the footage.

[181] Erwin, 'Die Wohngruppe', *IHS Info* 2 (1973), 9.

[182] Andreas, 'Meine persönliche HAW-Geschichte', 43.

were merely promoting 'narcissistic introspection'.[183] According to an activist from the Initiative Group Homosexuality Tübingen, gay consciousness-raising groups not only had the problem of overcoming a lack of trust—common to all such groups—but the additional issue of each member being a potential sexual partner of every other participant.[184] Dieter Michael Specht, the former chief editor of *him*, wrote in 1976 that such groups should only be facilitated under the guidance of a trained practitioner, to avoid potentially making psychological problems even worse.[185]

Access to those trained practitioners became somewhat easier in the 1970s, because psychoanalytic psychotherapy was belatedly added to the catalogue of treatments provided by health insurance companies.[186] An expert commission on the population's mental health reported to the *Bundestag* in 1975, arguing that the level of awareness about psychological difficulties in the Federal Republic had fallen at least a decade behind the level in many other countries. The report's authors wondered whether the reluctance to address this problem might be interpreted as a reaction against the inhumane treatment of the mentally ill in the Third Reich. The report noted that since homosexual law reform, the number of homosexuals ordered by the courts to undertake psychotherapeutic treatment had significantly decreased. Equally, the report observed an *increased* need for treatment and guidance from homosexuals, with respect to 'partner conflicts' and 'general crises'.[187]

Gradually, the psychoanalytic and psychotherapeutic professions sought to tackle these problems, instead of perceiving the difficulty to be the sexual orientation of homosexuality itself. In an influential article in 1974, Fritz Morgenthaler, a Swiss psychoanalyst, argued that the goal of therapy should not be to 'cure' a patient's homosexuality. Analysts who encouraged their patients to develop a 'normal' heterosexual object choice (the scare quotes were Morgenthaler's own) were but unconsciously acting out a social role afforded them by wider society.[188] In a subsequent article from 1979 that was featured in the gay press, Morgenthaler went further, and became, according to Dagmar Herzog, 'the first European analyst, of any nationality, to declare that homosexuality was not in and of itself pathological'.[189] For Morgenthaler, the greatest burdens to which homosexuals

---

[183] Wilfried L, 'Warum es den Schwulen so schwer fällt, solidarisch zu sein', *HAW Info* 6 (1972), 9–12 (9).
[184] Hanno, 'Schwule Gruppendynamik: Am Beispiel der Initiativgruppe Homosexualität Tübingen', *Emanzipation* 1 (1976), 2–5 (2).
[185] 'Nicht erst, wenn die Seele brennt', *Emanzipation* 6 (1977), 5–9 (6).
[186] Häberlen, *The Emotional Politics of the Alternative Left*, 172.
[187] 'Bericht über die Lage der Psychiatrie in der Bundesrepublik Deutschland', *Deutscher Bundestag* 7. *Wahlperiode* (November 1975) <http://dipbt.bundestag.de/doc/btd/07/042/0704200.pdf> [accessed 13 November 2018], 4 and 8.
[188] Morgenthaler, 'Die Stellung der Perversionen in Metapsychologie und Technik', *Psyche* 28 (1974), 1077–98 (1095). See further Herzog, *Cold War Freud*, 199–204.
[189] Herzog, *Cold War Freud*, 205.

were exposed came not from within, but from the society in which they live—thus echoing the title of Rosa von Praunheim's film from 1971, *Not the homosexual is perverse, but the society in which he lives.*[190] It was precisely this socially critical possibility of psychoanalysis that the editorial collective of *Emanzipation* sought to tap into, in a special issue published in late 1979. The collective defined psychoanalysis as partly 'a technique of treatment for the tackling of same-sex love, developed by heteros', but set this against its transformative potential in representing 'a critical theory of sexual oppression and liberation'. Indeed, according to the editors, any activist interested in 'the theory and strategy of gay liberation' could not afford to avoid engaging with psychoanalysis.[191]

On a less theoretical and more practical level, several gay groups began providing therapeutic services to the wider homosexual community, moving beyond the consciousness-raising groups aimed only at members. This was a decisive grassroots contribution to the so-called 'psycho-boom' that swept the Federal Republic in the 1970s.[192] In 1976, the counselling and advice [*Rat und Tat*] working group of the AHA began collaborating with the *Telefonseelsorge* in West Berlin—a counselling helpline funded and run by the Churches. Two AHA members were trained by the *Seelsorge* and began taking calls at their offices.[193] The GLF Cologne offered not only a telephone and letter service but drop-in counselling sessions three times a week at their centre.[194] The Association for Sexual Equal Rights (VSG—Munich) set up its *Rat und Tat* group as early as 1974, and engaged with the Churches and other partners such as youth workers and the city's mental health teams.[195]

Focusing on therapeutic work in the alternative left, Maik Tändler argues that this development should not be understood as an internal retreat, caused by political disappointment. Instead, exploring one's self—and helping others to do the same—was charged with 'great political-emancipatory expectations'.[196] Even so, that such therapeutic work was at times controversial within gay liberation is evidenced by the defensiveness of those groups that placed a focus on this activity. For example, the VSG—originally the Munich chapter of the IHWO—stressed

---

[190] Morgenthaler, 'Homosexualität: Das "Krankhafte" vom Homosexuellen trennen', *Berliner Schwulenzeitung* (June/July 1980), not paginated. Originally published as 'Innere und äussere Autonomie', *Neue Zürcher Zeitung* 153 (6 July 1979).

[191] 'Psychoanalyse und Homosexualität', *Emanzipation* 5 (September/October 1979), 3. The special issue included an interview with Horst-Eberhard Richter, who joined Morgenthaler in stating that homosexuality per se was not a clinical problem, but that homosexuals often presented with psychological difficulties because of social oppression and discrimination. The interview was conducted by Ralf Dose and Manfred Herzer. 'Interview mit Horst-Eberhard Richter', 5.

[192] Maik Tändler, '"Psychoboom". Therapeutisierungsprozesse in Westdeutschland in den späten 1960er- und 1970er Jahren', in *Das beratene Selbst: Zur Genealogie der Therapeutisierung in den langen' Siebzigern*, ed. by Sabine Maasen et al. (Bielefeld, 2011), 57–93.

[193] 'Homosexuelle helfen Homosexuellen', *Emanzipation* 6 (1976), 13–16 (13).   [194] Ibid., 15.

[195] 'Arbeitsgruppe Rat und Tat'. SMB archive, VSG Sammlung folder one.

[196] Tändler, 'Psychoboom', 58.

that members did not call into question the necessity of social change. While acknowledging that they could be accused of tackling the symptoms rather than the causes of unhappiness, VSG activists still believed that their work offered a 'small contribution to the emancipation of homosexuals'.[197] Similarly, the IHS in Stuttgart argued that offering therapy and advice was no 'conformist alternative to the struggle for emancipation', but rather a constituent part of that struggle.[198]

Contrasting definitions of how political the personal was taken to be were not the only concern at play. For some activists, engaging with institutions of church or state was a slippery slope, threatening the autonomy of gay liberation. Nevertheless, groups that avoided working with local telephone hotlines often had other versions of outreach and therapeutic services. Several groups set up *Rosa Hilfe* ('Pink Aid') initiatives, at least partly inspired by the *Rote Hilfe* ('Red Aid'), which supported imprisoned leftist protestors. The *Rote Hilfe* in West Berlin, for example, directly approached the HAW in 1972, asking them to mentor gay prisoners.[199] In the course of the decade, 'pink aid' evolved into a shorthand for self-help, often without any reference to the specific needs of gay prisoners. The *Rosa Hilfe* caucus within the Homosexual Action Hamburg was formed by 12 members of the wider group, who came together in the understanding that 'nothing will be given to us gays in this society unless we help ourselves'. They insisted that there was no clear division between themselves and those who rang their telephone helpline each Monday evening: for any advice or support they gave came directly from their own 'painful experiences' in the workplace, in their families, in public, during flat hunts, or at the doctors.[200] Due to the sheer number of such projects that sprang up in the second half of the decade, activists began attempting to coordinate these activities. For example, a meeting in West Berlin in April 1979 was attended by 'pink aid' groups from Hannover, Dortmund, Hamburg, Bremen, and Oberhausen. In addition to the *Rat und Tat* groups mentioned above from the VSG in Munich and the AHA, a gay doctors' caucus also took part. There was another such workshop at the *Homolulu* festival in Frankfurt later that year: here, *Rat und Tat* was translated into English as 'Aid and Action'—underlining what by then was the dominant view in gay liberation, that self-help and political action were by no means mutually exclusive.[201]

~   ~

[197] 'Arbeitsgruppe Rat und Tat', *Emanzipation* 2 (1976), 25–6 (26).
[198] Roland Dreyer, 'Beratung in Stuttgart: Ergebnisse einer Umfrage', *Emanzipation* 6 (1976), 10–12 (10).
[199] Minutes of HAW plenary, 12 November 1972. *Spinnboden Lesbenarchiv*, HAW Frauengruppe: Sammlung Monne Kühn 2/3 1972–1973.
[200] HAH, 'Rosa Hilfe', undated. Leaflet in SMB archive, folder Hamburg—Schwulenbewegung—HAH.
[201] 'Rosa Hilfe Treffen in Westberlin', *Emanzipation* 3 (1979), 34; Bilingual poster advertising *Homolulu*. SMB archive, NARGS box two.

Eva Rieger, a lesbian member of the women's section of the HAW—before this section left the group in 1975, to form the Lesbian Action Centre—fondly remembers the role that the HAW played in her life in the early 1970s. In an interview with Cristina Perincioli, Rieger recounts how she perceived the lesbian scene as a 'wicked and immoral place', before finding orientation in the HAW:

> This is what the HAW brought about: I no longer had to think that my sexuality was deviant, instead, this way of life could be fully recognised. The psychological was for me the most important thing in the HAW: you're not ill, not perverse, you don't belong on the rubbish heap of society, instead you can live out your love for other women.[202]

Coming together to discuss their sexuality was indeed a liberating experience for many same-sex desiring women and men. Interviewed by Jim Downs, activist-turned-historian Jonathan Ned Katz credits a reading group organized by the Gay Socialist Action Project in New York City with helping him understand, quite suddenly, that he and other homosexuals were not sick, but oppressed. This was a transformative experience, so much so that Katz 'would get dizzy and have to lie down'.[203]

Not everyone experienced gay liberation as a joyous release, a breaking of chains. Towards the end of our oral history interview, the former *Rotzschwul* activist Gerhard declared 'You cannot say that this gay movement made people happier.'[204] Gerhard clearly included himself in this conclusion, as he went on to express that the 1970s had in fact been a personally 'catastrophic decade' in which he endured long spells of loneliness and isolation. Feelings such as these were certainly discussed and acknowledged in the 1970s, but as Gerhard testifies, rarely tackled collectively, consciousness-raising groups notwithstanding. In December 1977 a former member of the HAH, Rainer Rüstig, committed suicide. He had left the HAH to join the Action Analysis Organization (AAO), a radical therapeutic sect in Vienna, run under the auspices of Otto Mühl. Members lived together in a collective and shared their property, labour and their sexuality.[205] According to the HAH, Rüstig had been subjected to daily 'exorcisms' on account of his homosexuality, which was interpreted as deformed and due to his hatred of women and his mother in particular.[206] In response, the AAO claimed that Rüstig had in fact left their organization several months before his suicide and

[202] Cited in Perincioli, *Berlin wird feministisch*, 67.   [203] Cited in Downs, *Stand by me*, 95.
[204] Oral history interview (30 January 2013). Pseudonym used.
[205] On the AAO, see Reichardt, *Authentizität*, 686–98.
[206] 'Wir trauen um Rainer', undated leaflet. Printed in *Schwulen-Info* 1 (1978), not paginated. SMB archive, folder Hamburg, HAH–gay lib center–IHWO. See also 'Selbstmord bei der AAO', *ID* 215 (1978), 15.

that he had been fully aware of their stance on homosexuality. Apparently, Rüstig had gradually succumbed to 'the great fear of every homosexual: fear of ageing and of loneliness', until he came to see his situation as hopeless.[207] While the HAH clearly held the 'charlatans' of the AAO partly responsible for Rüstig's suicide, the group also acknowledged that he would never have gone to the AAO had he found the measure of security and support he originally sought in the HAH.[208] Also in 1977, Rainer Plein, the co-founder of the HSM in Münster and dubbed by some as the 'mother of the movement', made the decision to end his life.[209] Clearly, difficult feelings did not just disappear once individuals joined the gay movement. Coming together and coming out may have been emotionally transformative for some homosexuals, but not for all.

Feelings such as loneliness, isolation, despair, and shame are rarely offered up for public consumption in the context of modern queer history. Of course, their enunciation can be painful. Yet these feelings are also muted because they clash with the standard narrative of gay liberation, which sees the shame and isolation of the post-war period overcome by collective action and the politics of visibility. Focusing on oral history, Nan Alamilla Boyd has characterized lesbian and gay history-making as a 'political project aimed at social uplift'.[210] In this light, feelings that are perceived as irreconcilable with social uplift, that are not affirmative, can be downplayed or elided in the interview process, both by the narrator and the interviewer. Other historical methodologies are also far from immune to this problem. For one, these types of feelings were less likely to be recorded in the first place. Second, they can easily escape our attention. Thirdly, they can be too much to bear. Historical research can at times be an upsetting and depressing affair. Indeed, while I was struck by Gerhard's statement—'You cannot say that this gay movement made people happier'—I was left deeply unsure over how best to respond to his sadness. Similarly, regular articles in the gay press on mental distress and teenage suicide do not make easy reading.[211]

Perhaps, researching and writing about emotions such as pride and hope is a psychologically easier task. The structural conditions in West Germany that might help facilitate these emotions changed in 1969: not primarily because of the Stonewall riots in New York City in June of that year, but because of homosexual law reform, in the shape of the liberalization to Paragraph 175. Let us not underestimate the psychic consequences of illegality. August Brackenbusch, a pensioner interviewed by researchers at the University of Bonn in 1968, did not

---

[207] 'Die AAO zum Tod von Rainer Rüstig', *ID* 218 (1978), 29.   [208] 'Wir trauen um Rainer'.
[209] Dieter Michael Specht, 'Zum Tode Rainer Pleins', *Emanzipation* 1 (1977), 16.
[210] Boyd, 'Talking about Sex', 110.
[211] 'Wenn Sie anderen helfen, so weiß ich, warum ich gestorben bin', *du&ich* 8 (1972), 18–19; 'Die Selbstmörder sind unter uns', *du&ich* 2 (1973), 10–13.

use the word homosexual to describe himself, but recounted how ashamed he felt when neighbours called him a '175er'. 'I've carried this cross my whole life', he told his interviewers, before continuing: 'I despise my body. I'll be glad when it's all over. If I hadn't had religion, I'd have long since ended things.'[212] Yet homosexual law reform was no magic wand—and neither was gay liberation. Emotions such as shame and fear did not, and have not, departed the scene. Emotional continuities, devalued in part because they clash with the idea that everything changed in 1969, can also be neglected because the scholarly recognition of these continuities can induce affective responses that recapitulate the very feelings in question. In tracing texts for a 'tradition of queer backwardness,' Heather Love also considers the 'backward feelings'—such as shame, depression, and regret—that they can 'inspire in contemporary critics'. As she writes, 'the history of queer damage retains its capacity to do harm in the present.'[213]

---

[212] Brackenbusch is the pseudonym taken from the original psychological study (on ageing and the life-course). Cited from Hodenberg, *Das ansere Achtundsechzig*, 154.
[213] Love, *Feeling Backward*, 8 and 9.

Conclusion

Where did gay liberation stand at the end of the 1970s? *Homolulu* offers us a good vantage point. The week-long festival, which took place in Frankfurt in July 1979, was billed as an 'autonomous island with gays for gays'.[1] Even though *Homolulu* was partly inspired by the success of the leftist congress Tunix, held the previous year in West Berlin, the festival also speaks to activists' disappointment with the relative lack of support gay liberation had won from the heterosexual left.[2] The most recent setback had been the Third International Russell Tribunal on Human Rights, which despite the best efforts of the National Working Group Repression against Gays (NARGS), had only considered—in brief—a single example of gay oppression when it convened for its second session earlier that year. According to one activist, working with heterosexuals in the future should not be ruled out, but *Homolulu* would be a chance to do politics 'the other way round' (*andersrum*), from the bottom up, 'in which *we* decide what we need, how *we* will discuss it, and which interaction *we* want to develop with each other'.[3]

Given that NARGS was one of the groups behind the festival, it is unsurprising that a focus on oppression continued during *Homolulu*. In an issue of the festival's daily newspaper, police raids in the gay scene, bans on careers, censorship and self-oppression were summarily given the shorthand 'everyday gay life'. Workshops were held on the Nazi persecution of homosexuals, on medical repression and on international cases of discrimination.[4] Ticking all the boxes, including a nod to the anti-nuclear movement, one participant told *Der Spiegel* that *Homolulu* was a 'radical gay encounter against this compulsory heterosexual capitalist atomic state'. Yet the festival also promised a 'blossoming of gay culture', an opportunity for self-discovery and intimacy.[5] The English-language invitation promised 'Here it will be fun to be gay. Free of the constraints forced on us by hetero-terror, we plan to stage theatre pieces, sing, love each other, work, dance,

---

[1] Trilingual (untitled) flyer. SMB archive, NARGS box two.
[2] Tunix-Schwester in Schwuz, 'Reise nach Tunix!'. SMB archive, box Rosa Winkel Verlag. On *Tunix* more generally, see März, *Linker Protest*, 203–44 and Sabine von Dirke, *All Power to the Imagination! The West German Counterculture from the Student Movement to the Greens* (Lincoln, NE, 1997), 111–21.
[3] 'Russel [sic], NARGS, Homolulu', *Rosa* 16 (1979), 22–5 (25). Emphases in the original.
[4] *Homolulu info* 3 (1979). Not paginated; Poster 'Homolulu. Die Geburt eines Vulkans, oder der Versuch, eine Utopie, konkret zu machen'. SMB archive, NARGS box two.
[5] 'Heiße Lava', *Der Spiegel* 29 (1979), 58; *Homolulu info* 3 (1979).

The Ambivalence of Gay Liberation: Male Homosexual Politics in 1970s West Germany. Craig Griffiths,
Oxford University Press (2021). © Craig Griffiths.
DOI: 10.1093/oso/9780198868965.003.0007

celebrate and discuss with each other.' To this end, workshops were held on art, yoga, shared living arrangements, the gay scene, gay alcoholics and on self-help.[6]

At the closing rally of the demonstration that concluded *Homolulu*, activists pronounced a long list of demands. Several claims, such as calling for the repeal of Paragraph 175 and for compensation to be paid to homosexual survivors of concentration camps, were long-standing. Others, however, included calling for equality of treatment for unmarried couples, funding for gay counselling centres, representation on the broadcasting council, and the passing of an anti-discrimination law.[7] During *Homolulu*, NARGS organizers refused to give an interview to a reporter from the conservative tabloid *BILD*, but a resolution to ban all 'radical right-wing' media from the festival failed to pass. Calling for representation on the broadcasting council proved controversial, with at least one activist at *Homolulu* arguing that the gay movement should struggle against the heterosexual norm inherent in society, rather than for thirty minutes pro-gramming time for gays.[8] Nevertheless, this policy, alongside the proposed anti-discrimination law, was also included in a similar catalogue of demands presented to the party representatives who attended a podium event in Bonn in July 1980, ahead of the federal election later that year.[9]

The demands read out at *Homolulu*, and the podium event in Bonn, reveal a gradual and partial turn towards the language of civil and human rights, and towards electoral politics. This could be understood as representing the eclipse of a 'radical' discourse of liberation by an 'assimilationist' discourse of rights: defend-ing homosexuals' place in existing society, rather than seeking to fundamentally transform that society. In fact, while we can chart the relative prevalence of different activist approaches and assumptions, and thus identify general trends, there was no caesura or turning point in 1979 or 1980. Some activists had conceptualized gay liberation all along through the prism of rights, or had sought party political influence from the very start, while others maintained their anti-parliamentary stance far beyond 1979. Most were caught somewhere in the middle, subject to conflicting feelings about their place in society. This ambiva-lence was not just about society, but about themselves. Just as throughout the decade, West German same-sex desiring men in 1979 had very different ideas about the meaning of homosexuality and how it should be lived. Take Johannes Werres. Reacting to *Homolulu*, Werres was appalled by the behaviour of demon-strators, in various stages of undress, bearing out-there placards and many in drag. According to Werres, not all homosexuals, and especially bisexuals and married

[6] Trilingual (untitled) flyer; *Homolulu: Schwule Tageszeitung* 0 (23 July 1979), 2.
[7] *Homolulu: Schwule Tageszeitung* 5/6 (28–9 July 1979), 3.
[8] *Homolulu: Schwule Tageszeitung* 3 (25 July 1979), 1; Corny, 'Wir waren im BILD: Homolulu – bekannt aus Presse, Funk und Fernsehen', *Rosa* 18 (1979), 5–6 (6).
[9] 'Homosexuelle zur Bundestagswahl: Parteien auf dem Prüfstand', 23. SMB archive, folder Bonn–Beethovenhalle.

men, could afford to take part in an event of that nature, not to mention a gay bank director or businessman. He even expressed his understanding if parents, teachers and the police wanted to keep their children away from such carryings-on.[10]

We could easily write off Werres as an obsolete lost cause. This is precisely what many younger gay activists did. To be sure, Werres' deeply conservative world-view, influenced by Hans Blüher's work from the 1910s on the patriotic *Männerbund* ('male association'), was not characteristic of 1970s gay liberation.[11] Yet the exuberance and 'anything goes' spirit of *Homolulu* was not fully representative of the decade, either. Werres did not take kindly to drag, but then neither did some of the activists in the Homosexual Action West Berlin whom we met in the previous chapter. While the gay left remained singularly uninterested in the perspective of gay bank directors in 1979, achieving positions of influence and respect was not an ambition limited to those in the financial sector. For all that some activists proudly paraded their difference from the heterosexual norm, the affirmation of difference never wholly sup-planted normalizing impulses. As Mary Bernstein has observed, identity-based movements 'often shift their emphasis between celebrating and suppressing difference from the majority'.[12] In the case of the gay left, activists felt less pressure than Werres to fit into mainstream society, but they were at times deeply preoccupied with demonstrating their resemblance to other alternative leftists. Ambivalence, the prism through which I have made sense of the tensions and complexities in gay liberation, was not so easily escaped.

Parliamentary Politics

According to activists from the Homosexual Action Munich, the West German gay movement had reached a state of stagnation by 1979. In their analysis, this was repeating what had already happened in the United States, a situation only overcome on the other side of the Atlantic by the impact of Anita Bryant's homophobic 'Save our Children' campaign.[13] Covering the success of this cam-paign in overturning a gay rights ordinance in Dade County, Florida, in June 1977, a correspondent for *Der Spiegel* quoted an American gay activist describing Anita Bryant as 'the best thing that could have happened to us'.[14] This might seem counterintuitive, given that years of hard work by Floridian gay and lesbian activists had been torn asunder. Yet the new-found threat personified by Anita

---

[10] Letter from Johannes Werres and Heinz Liehr [his partner], *Emanzipation* 6 (1979), 3.
[11] Werres, 'Als Aktivist erster Stunde', 38. On Blüher, see Beachy, *Gay Berlin*, 140–59 and Bruns, 'Der homosexuelle Staatsfreund'.
[12] Bernstein, 'The Strategic Uses of Identity', 234.   [13] *Blatt* 145 (1979), 14–16 (14).
[14] 'Feuer der Hölle', *Der Spiegel* 25 (1977), 188–91 (191).

Bryant—previously better known for her singing career and orange juice commercials—offered a measure of unity between disparate elements in American gay liberation. The 'Save our Children' campaign also made heterosexual leftists (and liberals) finally sit up and take notice. These constituencies began to take gay liberation claims more seriously.[15]

Back in West Germany, in 1978, an activist in NARGS complained about the unsatisfactory participation of homosexuals in the umbrella group. His diagnosis: 'We need a German Anita!'[16] No such galvanizing figurehead of oppression existed in the Federal Republic. The individual who came closest to filling this role was Franz-Josef Strauß, head of the Bavarian Christian Social Union (CSU) and the joint CDU/CSU candidate for Chancellor in the October 1980 federal election. Strauß was certainly no fan of homosexuality, declaring back in 1971 '*Ich will lieber ein kalter Krieger sein, als ein warmer Bruder*', loosely translating as 'I'd rather be a cold war hawk than a flaming faggot'.[17] Although not the individual directly responsible for taking the decision, Strauß was head of the ruling CSU when the Bavarian broadcaster (the *Bayerischer Rundfunk*, part of the federal ARD consortium) refused to screen Rosa von Praunheim's *It Is Not the Homosexual Who Is Perverse, But the Society in Which He Lives* in January 1973. The ARD television signal was simply turned off.[18]

The Bavarian broadcaster repeated the move in November 1977, when Bavarian residents were unable to watch *The Consequence*, a dramatized gay love story, loosely based on an autobiographical novel by Alexander Ziegler, chief editor of *du&ich*.[19] Such was the aversion to Strauß that activists and publicists temporarily set aside their differences to set up the action 'Pink Front against Strauß' in 1979. Led by the Homosexual Action Hamburg (HAH) and by the magazine *him* (with its editorial offices based in Hamburg), the campaign took its name from a similar, but unspecified, initiative in the Netherlands.[20] Launching the campaign, organizers called on West German homosexuals to wake up to the threat posed by Strauß, and finally recognize their electoral strength, which was estimated at between two and three million (larger, the organizers noted, than the combined membership of the Christian Democrats, Social Democrats (SPD) and Free Democrats (FDP), and larger than the population of the federal states Hamburg and Bremen put together).[21]

[15] Hobson, *Lavender and Red*, 87.

[16] Untitled minutes of organizing meeting, January 1978. SMB archive, NARGS box one, folder 1978.

[17] 'Worte des Jahres', *Die Zeit* (1 January 1971).

[18] Each state broadcaster in the federal ARD was nominally politically independent, but in reality accountable to each state government. The CSU held an absolute majority in the Bavarian state parliament throughout the 1970s.

[19] *Die Konsequenz*, dir. by Wolfgang Petersen (WDR, 1977). See further Wolfgang Petersen and Ulrich Greiwe (eds), *Briefe und Dokumente zum Film 'Die Konsequenz'* (Frankfurt a.M., 1980), especially 144–54.

[20] 'Rosa Front gegen Strauß', *him* 11/12 (1979), 24–7 (25).   [21] Ibid., 24.

Gay liberation did not emerge as a central theme in the 1980 election campaign, notwithstanding the title of one of the CSU's election pamphlets: 'For homosexuals, communists and violent criminals – the true face of the FDP.'[22] Attacking the FDP may not have been the wisest decision, since the Christian Democrats ultimately needed to detach the FDP from their coalition partner, the SPD, in order to take power in Bonn. When this eventually happened in October 1982, ending 13 years of the social–liberal coalition, SPD Chancellor Helmut Schmidt was replaced not by Strauß, but by the more moderate Helmut Kohl.[23] Although Strauß was no Anita Bryant, the reaction to his candidacy is more broadly reflective of an electoral turn in homosexual politics, as the parliamentary arena moved closer to activists' centre of attention. For example, one of the groups that signed up to 'Pink Front against Strauß' was the homosexual caucus within the FDP's youth organization, which had been set up in late 1978.[24] A homosexual sub-group in the wider FDP followed in 1980, hot on the heels of its counterpart in the SPD (the Gay Socialists, or *Schwusos*), a group set up in 1979.[25]

Until the late 1970s, engaging with the parliamentary system had been a priority only for associations like the International Homophile World Organization (IHWO), not for gay action groups. The IHWO, which sought to inform the 'opinion-forming classes' rather than the 'man on the street', organized a podium event with prominent regional representatives of the three main parties in Hamburg in October 1972, in advance of the federal election later that year.[26] Following in the IHWO's footsteps, there was more activity surrounding the federal election in 1976. The GLF Cologne organized a discussion event for group members which featured parliamentary candidates for the CDU, SPD, and FDP.[27] The Initiative Group Homosexuality Stuttgart did likewise. Representatives from two communist parties were also invited, but could not attend, while the regional CDU in Baden-Württemberg declined to take part. An organizer noted with satisfaction that the politicians who did attend seemed prepared to recognize gay 'emancipation groups' as interlocutors in the sense of an *Interessenvertretung* (a special interest, or lobby group). According to the organizer, the event was a significant step forward from earlier in the decade, and evidence that gay groups were starting to become more socially acceptable (*salonfähig*). However, more needed to be done to make groups better organized

---

[22] Cited from Schwartz, 'Warum machen Sie für die Homos stark?', 86.

[23] The change of power took place not via an election, but through a 'constructive vote of no-confidence'. Axel Schildt argues that Strauß' polarizing candidacy cost the Christian Democrats victory at the 1980 election. Schildt, 'Die Kräfte der Gegenreform', 477.

[24] Jungdemokraten Arbeitskreis Homosexualität, 'Lieber ein warmer Bruder als ein kalter Krieger: Dokumentation' (1980), 13. SMB archive.

[25] 'Hallo, Gerda', *Der Spiegel* 34 (1979), 38–40.

[26] *du&ich* 6 (1973), 42; 'Weg mit §175', *IHWO Report* 6 (1973), 7. On the podium event, see *IHWO-Rundbrief* (November/December 1972), not paginated. SMB archive, IHWO box one.

[27] *Emanzipation* 6 1976), 32–3.

and united, so that a national lobby would be able to exert some political influence.[28]

The national lobby group that this activist had in mind may have been modelled on the German Action Alliance Homosexuality (DAH), founded in Bochum in late 1972, but which was boycotted by many groups and soon collapsed. A more durable equivalent was not founded until 1986, with the Federal Federation Homosexuality (BVH: *Bundesverband Homosexualität*), but an important stepping stone towards organizing on the national level was the podium event organized in Bonn in July 1980, three months before the federal election.[29] The CSU turned down an invitation, arguing that 'there are certain things in human life' that belong 'in the most intimate personal sphere,' making them unsuitable topics for election campaigns.[30] The CDU, after initially declining an invitation, did participate, sending Friedrich Rahardt, a member of Hamburg's state parliament. He was joined on the podium by the General Secretary of the FDP, Günther Verheugen, alongside Herbert Brückner, a member of the SPD state government in Bremen, and two representatives from the Greens: Barbara Retzlaff and none other than Corny Littmann, a member of the HAH and the Greens' lead candidate in Hamburg for the federal election.[31] Back in 1978, the HAH had sponsored another activist, Wolfgang Krömer, to stand for election to the state parliament, as part of the *Bunte Liste* ('multicoloured list', a precursor to the Greens).[32] It was partly this rise of the 'alternative' political party, in the shape of the Greens, that allowed some action groups to overcome their previous rejection of the ballot box as a valid means of gay liberation.[33]

Michel Foucault turned down an invitation to chair the event, citing his inadequate German-language ability, but a prominent chair was found in Reinhard Münchenhagen, who had moderated the studio discussion following the 1973 broadcast of *Not the Homosexual*.[34] A prestigious location was secured (the *Beethovenhalle*), and political representatives seemed to be courting the gay vote. However, trouble began almost immediately once the evening got underway. Neither Münchenhagen nor Günther Verheugen were impressed by the sudden arrival of a representative from the German Communist Party (DKP). The party had been invited but had not confirmed its attendance. Only minutes of the

---

[28] *Emanzipation* 6 (1976), 34.

[29] On the BVH, see Salmen and Eckert, *20 Jahre bundesdeutsche Schwulenbewegung*, 71.

[30] Florian Harlander to AHA, 4 November 1979. Materialien Bonner Beethoven-Veranstaltung, Detlef Mücke private collection.

[31] Dieter Bachnik and Rainer Schädlich (eds), *Alle Schwestern werden Brüder* (Berlin: Trifolium, 1986), 222.

[32] HAH, 'Ab jetzt gibt's unser Programm: ein Schwuler kandidiert sich zur Bürgerschaftswahl.' SMB archive, folder Hamburg–Schwulenbewegung–HAH.

[33] See further Stephen Milder, *Greening Democracy: The Anti-Nuclear Movement and Political Environmentalism in West Germany and Beyond, 1968–1983* (Cambridge, 2017).

[34] *Rundbrief* 2 (15 February 1980), not paginated. Materialien Bonner Beethoven-Veranstaltung, Detlef Mücke private collection.

subsequent discussion could take place, as members of the audience interrupted proceedings amid boos, heckling and whistling.[35] As the microphone was turned off, one unnamed participant summed up the proceedings as a 'destructive gay dictatorship'. Peter Föhrding, from the GLF Cologne, shouted that the derailing of the event was tearing asunder a decade of hard work.[36] In a subsequent English-language press release, the Gay Action Cologne (SAK) described the podium event as a 'catastrophe unique in the German and international gay movement'.[37]

This was a rather exaggerated verdict, for there do not seem to have been any catastrophic consequences. The disruption of the event, however, certainly reveals some of the underlying conflicts running through gay liberation. The reaction of the two Cologne groups—groups that, as we have seen, were usually mutually antagonistic—underlines the importance some activists increasingly placed on presenting the gay movement as a serious, respectable political force. This aim, evidently, was not shared by all. A leaflet written by activists from the Initiative Group Homosexuality Bielefeld (IHB) deplored the strategy behind the podium event. Electoral politics, according to the IHB, was leading gay liberation down a blind alley, and calls to unite against the threat posed by Franz-Josef Strauß were spreading the same illusions as Magnus Hirschfeld had done in the 1930s. Continuing, activists argued that public institutions would simply never accept free expressions of homosexuality. An anti-discrimination law, for example, would only protect the interests of those capable of inclusion within a 'gayness defined by the state'. If the gay movement really wanted to challenge the division between the private and the public, according to the IHB, it needed a new discourse—not one to be found in parliaments, but one which could accommodate 'our desire for masturbation, incest, the seduction of minors, promiscuity, arse-fucking, perversion' and 'craziness'.[38]

Homosexuals, as this dispute exemplifies, had always disagreed about what emancipation might mean. For some, emancipation meant the full integration of homosexuals into existing society. Back at the start of the decade, the editorial team of *du&ich* wrote that they had set themselves the task of furthering the emancipation and the integration of 'the homophile minority'. Indeed, they sought 'total emancipation'.[39] Martin Dannecker, when interviewed by the same publication, expressed a diametrically opposed position. Integration into existing society would only mean exchanging one lack of freedom for another, more subtle form of oppression. Therefore, homosexuals needed to seek emancipation, which

---

[35] See the transcript of the audio recording, in *Alle Schwestern werden Brüder*, ed. by Dieter Bachnik and Rainer Schädlich (Berlin, 1986), 222–41.

[36] Ibid., 233 and 234.

[37] 'Conference with German Politicians' (12 July 1980). SMB archive, box Rosa Winkel Verlag.

[38] IHB, 'Schwule auf dem Prüfstand'. Materialien Bonner Beethoven-Veranstaltung, Detlef Mücke private collection.

[39] *du&ich* 7/8 (1970), 1.

Dannecker saw as the opposite of integration.[40] This could not be accomplished armed with language such as 'homophile', which amounted to a 'purification of the homo', conforming to a system for which sexuality was impure.[41] By the end of the decade, the vocabulary 'homophile' has virtually disappeared. Yet, as the possibility of public recognition and integration into society became more tangible, the ambivalence engendered by this prospect became all the more pronounced.

The matter of integration begs the question of who and what was to be integrated. In its acerbic leaflet, the IHB had raised the spectre of 'the seduction of minors'. In the run-up to the podium evening in Bonn, the most controversial topic had been to what extent, if at all, the event should represent paedosexuals as well as gays and lesbians. A compromise was temporarily reached whereby the gay, lesbian, and paedophile movements were to have two representatives each on the podium (alongside the invited politicians).[42] Drafting an anti-discrimination bill, to be presented to the participating politicians on the podium, had seen a rare measure of cooperation between gays and lesbians. But this newfound collaboration became frayed over the question of whether the bill should demand only the repeal of Paragraph 175, or the repeal of the entire sexual criminal code. Repealing Paragraph 175 would have equalized the age of consent between male homosexual and heterosexual relations at 16. Repealing Paragraphs 174 and 176, meanwhile, would have removed the age of consent altogether, thus legalizing all intergenerational relationships.

The lesbian group *L'74* would only countenance a reform to those two paragraphs, so that intergenerational relationships would not be subject to prosecution providing that they were voluntary, non-violent, and consensual.[43] This move was rejected by paedophile activists, who demanded the complete repeal of these laws. The Lesbian Action Centre (LAZ) still supported the podium event, subject to the provision of gender parity on the podium. The group did not oppose the inclusion of paedophiles, since they were 'those of us most criminalized and those who sit in jail because of their sexual orientation'.[44] *L'74*, though, did withdraw their backing for the event. According to the group, Paragraph 176 pertained in 80 per cent of cases only to heterosexual paedophile relationships, which almost always involved an adult male forcing his sexuality onto a female child. In their eyes, lesbian paedophilia did not exist, and they were not convinced by the 'idealized presentation of gay paedophile relationships'. The podium event could not be supported

---

[40] Dannecker, 'Integration oder Emanzipation?', *du&ich* 2 (1971), 36–7 and 43 (36).

[41] Ibid., 37.

[42] Gerhard Beier-Herzog, 'Anmerkungen zur Veranstaltung in der Beethovenhalle', *AHA Info* (July/August 1980), 19–25 (20).

[43] 'Entwurf der L74 für ein ADG' (undated). SMB archive, AHA Sammlung, box Juristengruppe/Antifa-Gruppe.

[44] 'Stellungnahme von Frauen aus dem LAZ' (February 1980). Printed in *Alle Schwestern werden Brüder*, ed. by Bachnik and Schädlich, 84–5.

if it provided a platform for paedophiles, who were using the occasion as a Trojan horse.[45]

Following a trend in the alternative left, there was wide support within gay liberation for the liberation of childhood sexuality, and this often coincided with a measure of tacit or explicit support for the rights of self-defined paederasts or paedophiles.[46] One subscriber wrote to *du&ich* in 1973, urging the publication to cease depicting paedosexuality as something natural, because otherwise 'normal homosexuals' like himself would be considered in the same way as paederasts: 'You preach tolerance and understanding, and what emerges is that you're bringing us all into disrepute.'[47] But in 1978, an article in *Emanzipation* stated that the non-paedophile should learn to accept the paedophile. The author of another article asserted that paedophilia was a crime without victims, and urged paedophiles to organize and defend themselves against discrimination, for which they should receive unconditional support from the gay movement.[48]

For Johannes Werres, homosexual relationships between younger and older men served not only erotic but also social purposes, and in 1970 he argued that the repression of such relationships was one cause for the student revolts, growing challenges to authority, misunderstanding of sexual freedom, and increased youth criminality.[49] At the other end of the scale politically, a few gay action groups had their own paederast or paedophile subsections. One of them, the *Päderastengruppe* in the HAH, explained why gay activists should support their initiative: 'Have we in the gay movement arduously resisted the hetero concept of normality only now to subjugate ourselves under that of the gay scene?'[50] All along, gay activists were keenly aware of the power of the prejudice that homosexuals preyed on boys, and sought to refute this characterization. Franz G. wrote to *du&ich* in 1975, arguing that 'normal' homosexuals should publicly distance themselves from those who were attracted to boys: 'when the paedophiles are finally out of the picture...better times for us homosexuals will beckon.'[51] The closer to respectability and to positions of influence that gay activists came, the greater the pressure to define what was and what was not considered part of gay liberation, since the taint of paedophilia threatened this potential respectability. Ultimately, this led to the renunciation of support for the repeal of age of consent

---

[45] Isis, 'Abgesang auf Beethoven', *Unsere kleine Zeitung*, 4 (1980). Reprinted in *Alle Schwestern werden Brüder*, 116–18.

[46] For a fuller discussion, see Griffiths, 'Sex, Shame and West German Gay Liberation', 451–9. See also Häberlen, 'Feeling Like a Child'.

[47] *du&ich* 3 (1973), 49.   [48] *Emanzipation* 1 (1978), 4 and 29.

[49] Under the pseudonym Norbert Weißenhagen. 'Kann man für die Homosexualität "werben"?', *Der Weg*, 226 (1969–70), 279–81 (281). Werres later stated that his form of 'boy love' was partly based on the ideas of Hans Blüher. Werres, 'Als Aktivist erster Stunde', 38.

[50] 'Päderasten?' (undated). SMB archive, folder Hamburg–Schwulenbewegung–HAH.

[51] *du&ich* 3 (1975), 11.

laws and the total exclusion of paedosexuals from the international gay movement in the 1990s.[52]

Human Rights

A growing emphasis on rights—which included the rights of children—was one factor influencing changing definitions of sexual liberation, and the process of deciding what did and did not belong in what became known as 'gay rights'.[53] To be sure, this was not a totally new development. The post-war homophile movement had already deployed a 'discourse of citizenship', drawing upon human rights language.[54] One of the earliest post-war homophile groups was called the Society for Human Rights (*Gesellschaft für Menschenrechte*), which was established in Hamburg in 1948 and directly cited the Universal Declaration of Human Rights in its founding document.[55] In 1973, the short-lived DAH umbrella group stated that its mission was to fight the social discrimination faced by homosexuals, and to support the realization of the human rights promised by the UN Charter, a document which came into legal force in the Federal Republic later that year, when both German states finally joined the United Nations.[56]

In the gay left, the need to formulate discrete, concrete responses to oppression had previously been somewhat ameliorated by an all-embracing anti-capitalism, but a turn to an activism more approximating a civil-rights model was well under way by the end of the 1970s. The clearest example of this tendency came with the notion of campaigning for an anti-discrimination bill, first proposed by the General Homosexual Action Alliance (AHA) in 1977. The centrepiece of this proposed package of legislative changes was an amendment to the Basic Law to make discrimination on the basis of sexual orientation or family status unconstitutional.[57] The AHA's rights-based stance was clear from its support for the Russell Tribunal, which was explicitly predicated on the understanding that the task for gay activists consisted of having existing constitutional rights fulfilled and extended, rather than challenging the socio-economic basis on which those rights were constructed.[58] NARGS, by contrast, was more suspicious about relying on the liberal defence of rights, at least according to a 1979 press release, published

---

[52] David Paternotte, 'The International (Lesbian and) Gay Association and the Question of Pedophilia: Tracking the Demise of Gay Liberation Ideals,' *Sexualities* 17 (2014), 121–38.

[53] On the case of France, see Julian Bourg, *From Revolution to Ethics: May 1968 and Contemporary French Thought* (Montreal, 2007), especially 204–25.

[54] Jackson, *Living in Arcadia*, 113.   [55] Riechers, 'Freundschaft und Anständigkeit', 22.

[56] DAH, 'Rahmenpapiere' 12 March 1973. SMB archive, folder IHS. On the Charter, see Michael März, *Linker Protest*, 265.

[57] AHA, 'Entwurf eines Antidiskriminerungsgesetzes der AG Juristen'. SMB archive, AHA Sammlung.

[58] 'Aufruf und Unterstützung', *him* 8 (1977), 6.

after the Russell Tribunal had closed its second hearing: human rights were described as reliant on the prevailing morality and therefore 'by their very nature repress gays'. Nevertheless, according to the invitational flyer for *Homolulu*, written by a NARGS representative, one of the aims of the festival was 'developing a strategy for getting us into the human rights discussion'.[59]

This vocabulary became more widely used not for reasons idiosyncratic to gay liberation, but because of the contemporary international boom in human rights language. Samuel Moyn has identified 1977 as the 'breakthrough year' in this regard. The year began with United States President Jimmy Carter using his inaugural address to express his wholesale commitment to human rights around the globe, and ended with Amnesty International winning the Nobel Peace Prize.[60] The West German chapter of Amnesty was founded back in 1961, but by the late 1970s it was the largest section in the international organization, which by this time had some 300,000 members.[61] According to Lora Wildenthal, human rights 'absorbed energies formerly directed at projects on the left', while Moyn conceptualizes human rights as 'the last utopia', one that became more widespread because 'other visions imploded.'[62]

Certainly, the realization on the part of some activists that existing society was not on the verge of fundamental transformation was an important factor in the turn to human rights language. Jeremy Varon argues that activists from across the progressive spectrum moved away from the 'grand project,' however that was variously defined, to instead pursuing 'the more modest goal of changing at least parts of the world in small but meaningful ways'.[63] However, this was not necessarily a matter of either/or. For gay liberation, human rights vocabulary was not just a pragmatic replacement for crushed political hopes, but a language that jostled with and even complemented other allegiances. Consider *Homolulu* and the series of rights-based demands made at the festival, which failed to drown out more utopian messages: 'Just as the Deutsch Mark [sic], Dollar, Franc and Lira are superfluous, borders, states, the army, governments and other instruments of power and repression are equally unnecessary for our life together'.[64]

The language of rights is closely connected to the question of minority, because some gay liberationists rejected the view that homosexuals represented a stable

[59] NARGS, 'A Case of Anti-Gay Discrimination was dealt with after all by the Russell Tribunal'. SMB archive, NARGS box one, folder 1979/1; Poster 'Homolulu. Die Geburt eines Vulkans, oder der Versuch, eine Utopie, konkret zu machen'. SMB archive, NARGS box two.

[60] On 20 January and 10 December respectively. Moyn, *The Last Utopia*, 155. See also Eckel and Moyn (eds), *The Breakthrough: Human Rights in the 1970s*.

[61] Wildenthal, *The Language of Human Rights*, 76 and 88. On the international membership figure, see Moyn, *The Last Utopia*, 146.

[62] Wildenthal, *The Language of Human Rights*, 16; Moyn, *The Last Utopia*, 4.

[63] Varon, *Bringing the War Home: The Weather Underground, The Red Army Faction, and Revolutionary Violence in the 60s and 70s* (Berkeley, 2004), 309.

[64] Poster 'Homolulu. Die Geburt eines Vulkans, oder der Versuch, eine Utopie, konkret zu machen'. SMB archive, NARGS box two.

group—akin for example to a racial minority—which could be identified as a specific minority and hence afforded protection from discrimination. As we have seen, the 'Pink Front against Strauß' spoke confidently of there existing between two and three million homosexuals in West Germany, a statistic one frequently encounters in the gay press.[65] At times, the mainstream media was also fond of citing this number: two million according to *Der Spiegel* and *Stern*, three million according to the *Süddeutsche Zeitung* and the *Frankfurter Allgemeine Zeitung*.[66] These statistics derive from the 4 per cent of American men posited to be exclusively homosexual by the Kinsey Report, extrapolated onto the West German population. As Rolf Gindorf and Rüdiger Lautmann noted in 1974, the figure of 4 per cent led many to the misconception that therefore 96 per cent of the population must be heterosexual, rather than focusing on Kinsey's finding that exclusive heterosexuals made up less than half of all men.[67] In a rare exception to the minority model to be found in the gay press, a *du&ich* columnist warned in 1971 against circumscribing a 'homophile minority' from a heterosexual majority, since homo- and heterosexuality were two extreme poles, with the sexuality of most laying in the broad spectrum in between.[68]

Some gay activists joined this publicist in rejecting the notion of any particularity or difference in homosexuality, in their understanding of desire as more fluid that identity categories can allow. *Sexuality is more*, an alternative sex education book produced by gay, feminist and education reform activists in 1976, challenged the idea that homo- and heterosexuality represented particular forms of sexuality. Rather, both belonged to the one human sexuality, both 'are to be found in a latent or manifest way in every human being.'[69] One of the suggested lesson plans sought to raise awareness of the discrimination facing gays and lesbians, but so as to make pupils aware that this discrimination also impacted them; that a part of their self was also being stigmatized and rejected.[70] This kind of understanding opened up space to consider homo- and heterosexuality as equally problematic categories, both concealing a universal bisexual potential.

Yet escaping the homo/hetero binary in the here and now was an altogether murkier affair. The bisexuality postulated by some gay liberationists was a hypothetical bisexuality, 'less an identity or a practice in the present tense than it was a

---

[65] 'Wir sind stärker als die FDP', *du&ich* 3 (1970), 1; 'In Medias Res', *du&ich* 9 (1971), 2; *du&ich* 5 (1980), 4.
[66] 'Gesteuerte Lust', *Der Spiegel* 10 (1969), 152; 'Ich bin schwul', *Stern* 41 (1978), 104–18 (104); 'Toleranzgrenze', *Die FAZ* (30 July 1979); 'Ungewöhnliches Festival gegen Vorurteile', *Süddeutsche Zeitung* (30 July 1979)
[67] Gindorf and Lautmann, 'Homosexualität und Normalität: Vom Irrtum unserer Kategorien', *Vorgänge: Zeitschrift für Gesellschaftspolitik* 10 (1974), 108–16 (114). On Kinsey, see further Steven Angelides, *A History of Bisexuality* (Chicago, 2001), 107–14.
[68] 'Zur Lager der Verbände', *du&ich* 2 (1971), 54–5 (55).
[69] Dorothea Assig et al. (eds), *Sexualität ist mehr. Eine Unterrichtsreihe zum Thema Sexualität* (Wuppertal, 1976), 24.
[70] Ibid., 62.

future aspiration or utopian ideal'.[71] For all his disdain for most utopian ideals, Werres was one of the very few voices in 1970s homosexual politics who consistently acknowledged those same-sex desiring constituencies who were not 'gay'— as in his caustic response to *Homolulu*, when he mentioned married men and bisexuals.[72] The increasing invoking of rights towards the end of the decade hardened the gay movement's focus on those who claimed a gay male identity. For those rights were still very much 'gay rights', not yet the more pluralistic 'LGBT rights' (that initialism, denoting lesbian, gay, bisexual, and transgender, was not popularized until the 1990s).

In 1978, the HAH described its electoral participation in Hamburg as a first step in the direction of gays themselves representing their demands for 'equal rights and human rights'. According to the group, taking part in the election was the 'logical consequence' of gays' social situation, which required an activist response: 'being gay means defending oneself!'[73] The HAH's campaign illustrates how three trends gradually came together at the end of the decade: a focus on 'self-help', the language of rights, and a greater engagement with the parliamentary system. So many groups had set up counselling or 'pink aid' (*Rosa Hilfe*) initiatives by the end of the decade that in December 1980 the umbrella group Homosexual Self-Help was founded, which sought to 'support homosexual people and groups in social, economic and legal regards'.[74] The association provided legal costs to those who came into conflict with the law on account of their homosexuality, and distributed funds to proposed projects. It was open to both gay and lesbian groups.[75]

In 1981, applications included those made by the Pink Triangle Press, for the publication of a reader on homosexuality; by a lesbian group for an advert in a mainstream magazine; by the gay magazine *Rosa Flieder*; by film-makers for a planned documentary on a gay teacher; and by Berlin activists for the training of two telephone counsellors.[76] Since the limited funds at the association's disposal were spent on legal defence, none of these projects could be funded in the first instance. In conjunction with this focus on self-help, some gay activists therefore began to seek funding for their activities. The first documented case of public funding for the gay movement came in late 1979, when the Kreuzberg District Assembly voted to provide 5000 DM towards the new AHA centre in West Berlin.[77] These moves in the direction of self-help and state-funding were then

---

[71] Angelides, *A History of Bisexuality*, 119 and 123.
[72] Other examples include Werres, 'Schweigende Mehrheit', *Sexualmedizin* 5 (1974), 268; Werres 'Kinderfreunde – Kinderfeinde?', *du&ich* 11 (1975), 22–4.
[73] HAH, 'Ab jetzt gibt's unser Programm', 8; 2.
[74] *Homosexelle Selbsthilfe* terms of reference (18 November 1980). SMB archive, AHA Sammlung: unnamed box, folder 'Eingangspost bis Ende '85'.
[75] Untitled press release (1981). Folder 'Eingangspost bis Ende '85'.   [76] Ibid.
[77] The proposal was made by the FDP, and passed with the votes of the SPD and the Alternative List (a precursor to the Greens). Jungdemokraten Arbeitskreis Homosexualität, 'Lieber ein warmer Bruder.'

accelerated by the arrival of the HIV/AIDS crisis in 1983, which necessitated on the one hand grassroots care and support groups, and on the other increased healthcare funding and state-funded medical research. Creating a significantly different and more urgent context, HIV/AIDS would open up a dialogue between gay activists and state officials that had only just begun by the end of the 1970s.[78]

The Persistence of Ambivalence

The partial decriminalization of homosexuality in 1969 offered West German homosexuals a precarious foothold in society. A decade on, that foothold had become somewhat more secure. Alexander Ziegler, chief editor of du&ich from 1972 to the last issue of 1979, took the opportunity of his final editorial to argue that the 1970s could justly be described as the 'decade of the emancipation of homosexuals'. Rather than being consigned to the margins, the homosexual was now, according to Ziegler, accepted by wide sections of the population.[79] Conversely, Michael Föster, writing in him—the main commercial rival to du&ich—argued at the close of the decade that homosexuals had won 'barely one iota of public recognition.'[80] If Ziegler was guilty of a somewhat rose-tinted interpretation, Föster underestimated the contribution of gay liberation. With respect to the ultimately unsuccessful backlash against gay men in 1980s Britain, Matt Cook has written 'In ways that were hard to resist or counter, they had become a much more tangible part of the social and cultural fabric.'[81] This verdict undoubtedly applies to the Federal Republic too, for even as the HIV/AIDS crisis opened up new opportunities for the demonization of homosexuals, the most reactionary interventions were not able to win public support.

For example, the proposal put forward by CSU politician Peter Gauweiler in 1986, that those infected with HIV should be forcibly quarantined, was rejected by the Christian Democrat-led federal government. In response, Rita Süssmuth, CDU minister for Youth, Family, Women, and Health, initiated a publicly funded sexual health campaign and allowed Der Spiegel to use an image of her covered in a giant condom for a front cover in February 1987.[82] Certainly, homophobia endured, not least from the Christian Democrats, but this was still quite a transformation from 1970, when Süssmuth's SPD counterpart in the same

---

[78] On self-help and dialogue between homosexuals and state officials in Hamburg, see Henning Tümmers, '"Heaven can Wait": Reaktionen auf die Aids- Bedrohung in Hamburg', Zeitgeschichte in Hamburg (2011), 13–30.

[79] Ziegler, 'Das letzte Wort', du&ich 12 (1979), 52.

[80] Föster, 'Zehn Jahre danach—Das Ende der schwulen Angst', him 11/12 (1979), 46–7 (47).

[81] Cook, 'AIDS, Mass Observation, and the Fate of the Permissive Turn', 246.

[82] Dagmar Herzog, Sexuality in Europe: A Twentieth-Century History (Cambridge, 2011), 180. For the front cover, see Der Spiegel 7 (1987).

ministry, Käte Ströbel, had attempted to place *him* on the index of 'youth-endangering materials', due to its supposedly 'sexual-ethical misorientation'.[83]

This book has sought to integrate the history of the 1970s into a longer history of homosexual emancipation. German-language sexology was central to the emergence of a homosexual identity in the nineteenth century, and it was in German that the term 'homosexual' was first used.[84] Wilhelmine Germany was home to the first homosexual rights movement anywhere in the world, which we can date to the founding of Magnus Hirschfeld's Scientific-Humanitarian Committee in 1897. As the movement grew in size and confidence in the Weimar Republic, even in the absence of legal reform, it was in Berlin that *Die Freundschaft* was published, the world's first homosexual paper to be placed on public sale.[85] Fifty years before Stonewall, Magnus Hirschfeld opened his pioneering Institute of Sexual Science, in Berlin in 1919.[86]

With the Nazi destruction of this movement the centrality of the German case to the story of homosexual emancipation seemed to come to an end. Work on homosexual emancipation in the second half of the twentieth century often ends up classifying gay and lesbian life as either 'pre' or 'post' Stonewall, turning the Stonewall riots of June 1969 in Christopher Street, New York City, into somewhat of a mythical turning point. This tendency not only fails to give due weight to previous iterations of homosexual emancipation, but also privileges the American context over others. What Elizabeth Kennedy has called the 'meta-narrative' of Stonewall was not invented by historians, but speaks to the success of American activists in commemorating the Stonewall riots.[87] This commemoration took shape as early as 28 June 1970, when activists marked the first anniversary of the riots with the first Christopher Street Liberation Day, part of a wider 'gay pride week'. Those who took part at that first Liberation Day rally were told 'We are all participants in the most important Gay event in history'—meaning not Stonewall, but its first annual celebration.[88]

Activists' commemorative success story became increasing global in the 1970s. On 30 June 1979, activists in Bremen, Stuttgart, Cologne, and West Berlin celebrated what was variously described as 'gay carnival', 'gay freedom day', 'Christopher Street Day' or 'ten years Stonewall day'.[89] They were celebrating Stonewall, but the riots in Christopher Street had not been the most important event back in 1969, certainly not for West German homosexuals. Instead, this was the liberalization of Paragraph 175, which came into effect on 1 September 1969.

---

[83] *him* 6 (1970), 14–18.   [84] See further Beachy, *Gay Berlin*.   [85] Ibid., 164.
[86] See especially Marhoefer, *Sex and the Weimar Republic*.
[87] Kennedy, 'Telling Tales', 73. On the commemoration, see Armstrong and Crage, 'Movements and Memory: The Making of the Stonewall Myth.'
[88] Christopher Street Liberation Day Umbrella Committee, 'Welcome' (undated, but 1970). Craig Rodwell Papers, box four, folder CSLDUC 1970. New York Public Library.
[89] Michael Rosenkranz, 'Schwuler Karneval in Bremen', *him* 10 (1979), 18–19; 'Zehn Jahre Stonewall Day', *Emanzipation* 5 (1979), 28–31.

An article in *him* in 1979, deploring the lack of attention paid to this latter anniversary, was entitled 'Ten years on: The end of gay fear'.[90] Tellingly, despite the article making no reference whatsoever to Stonewall, to Christopher Street Day, or to the United States, the double-page photo chosen to illustrate the piece depicted a massive rally in New York's Central Park (there was no caption, but the photo was probably taken during the closing rally of one of the Christopher Street Liberation days which had taken place annually since 1970). The American context seems to have been considered sexier, more vibrant, and—perhaps—less fearful. Indeed, the article was far from positive about the contemporary situation in the Federal Republic: 'The majority of homosexuals in this country remain conformist, and therefore invisible'.[91]

Paragraph 175 was finally repealed altogether in 1994 (partly due to the fact that since German unification in 1990, the law had only applied to the West of the country, not to the newly created federal states that previously made up the GDR). A few years later, Eike Stedefeldt angrily accused his fellow gay activists of having moved significantly to the right since the heyday of gay liberation. The gay movement no longer found itself on the 'left-alternative margins of society', but operated 'full of pride in its centre'.[92] To be sure, Stedefeldt's account of corruption and right-wing tendencies in the gay movement is both somewhat exaggerated and highly partisan, but there is no doubting the transformation that has taken place regarding the place of gays and lesbians within German society. Since 2001, same-sex couples have been able to enter into civil partnerships, and in 2009 an openly gay politician, Guido Westerwelle (FDP), became vice-chancellor and foreign minister. Two of my interviewees have recently been awarded the Order of Merit (*Bundesverdienstkreuz*), Germany's highest civil decoration, in recognition of their work in the gay and lesbian movements.[93] Then, in June 2017, the German parliament legislated both to introduce equal marriage and to annul the convictions of those same-sex desiring men prosecuted against Paragraph 175. Although, as of January 2019, only 129 men have came forward to claim the meagre compensation for the legal injustice they suffered, this was the final step in undoing the notorious legal statute, and came 50 years after the infamous Federal Constitutional Court decision upholding its legitimacy.[94]

1970s activists have witnessed this social transformation with a variety of shock, pride, and disappointment. For one of my interviewees, the relative integration of gays and lesbians into mainstream society demonstrates the incredible flexibility

---

[90] Michael Föster, 'Zehn Jahre danach—Das Ende der schwulen Angst', *him* 11/12 (1979), 46–7.
[91] Ibid., 47.
[92] Stedefeldt, *Schwule Macht. Oder, Die Emanzipation von der Emanzipation* (Berlin, 1998), 204.
[93] Names omitted. Interviews took place 7 July 2012 and 25 August 2014.
[94] 'Bisher kaum Anträge auf Entschädigung für Homosexuelle', *Der Tagesspiegel* (12 January 2019). The compensation package amounts to €3000 per individual, plus €1500 for each year spent in prison. Approximately 64,000 men were sentenced for infringing Paragraph 175.

possessed by the capitalist system, a flexibility vastly underestimated back in the 1970s.[95] For many gay liberationists, emancipation under the current socio-economic system was unimaginable. Nevertheless, for some of those same activists, emancipation has clearly taken place. This has led to decidedly mixed feelings about what was won by gay liberation, and how it has been remembered. In an article published in 2001, Egmont Fassbinder, a former activist in the Homosexual Action West Berlin, writes 'we kicked off within a brief period virtually unbelievable social changes.' However, there is no triumphalism in his account, because he relativizes the contribution of gay liberation on the same page of that article: 'we advanced our emancipation by a few steps'. According to Fassbinder, 'we struggled for our liberation bit by bit. That wasn't always easy, but we fought also for those who came after us and for whom many things have fallen into their laps.' He then asks: 'will they know to appreciate this, to maintain and develop what has already been achieved?'[96]

Claus-Ferdinand Siegfried, in the book which accompanied his documentary from 1972, *Paragraph 175: Questions to Homosexuals and to Ourselves*, declared that West German homosexuals found themselves in a 'historic situation', having only about a five-year window in which to fight for their sexual self-determination, before they would be integrated into society and accepting of their lot.[97] In this sense, gay liberation can be seen as a brief window of opportunity, a utopian interlude between the homophile movement of the 1950s and 1960s and the accommodationist gay and lesbian politics of the 1980s and 1990s.[98] The reverse of this interpretation frames gay liberation as a time of cavalier excess, before gays and lesbians got on with the real business of seeking and achieving equality. Both of these accounts end up trampling over the historical integrity of 1970s homosexual politics, because they fail to recognize that gay liberation was not some pristine (or horrifying) radical wilderness, but a profoundly ambivalent, messy affair.

Laurie Marhoefer argues that a basic dilemma, 'the choice between a more radical movement and a narrower one based on respectability, privacy, assimilation, and citizenship claims', was not only present in the Weimar-era movement, but 'ought to be recognized as characteristic of queer politics' more broadly across the twentieth century.[99] Directing our gaze towards ambivalence suggests that we cannot hope to neatly divide homosexual emancipation into warring camps of those who sought radical change and those who wanted merely liberal inclusion. In the 1970s, at least, this ideological contestation ran through the very heart of

[95] Oral history interview (21 November 2013).
[96] Fassbinder, 'Mein schönes "schwules" Schöneberg', in *Berlin-Schöneberg. Blicke ins Quartier. 1949–2000*, ed. by Petra Zwaka und Johanna Muschelknautz (Berlin, 2001), 153–60 (160).
[97] Siegfried, *Gesellschaft und Homosexualität: Beginn einer Auseinandersetzung* (Berlin, 1972), 103.
[98] For a recent example, see Duberman, *Has the gay movement failed?*
[99] Marhoefer, *Sex and the Weimar Republic*, 213.

groups, publications, and individuals themselves. Crucially, ways of thinking and talking were intimately connected with ways of feeling about homosexuality. Gay liberation has until now been historicized and remembered only through the prism of pride; that the annual rallies and festivals to commemorate the Stonewall riots and celebrate queer culture have become simply known as 'pride' is only the most visible manifestation of this fact. By challenging oppressive attitudes and institutions, through learning to accept the fact of homosexuality, by proudly proclaiming its normality and goodness—so the narrative goes—young gays and lesbians strode out of the closet and rescued homosexuals from their shame and from their fear. But shame was never fully conquered by pride, and the politics of confrontation was never the only game in town. Gay liberation did not only revolve around pride, hope, visibility, and radicalism, but also shame, fear, respectability, and confusion. Ambivalence about the very meaning of gay desire and sexuality, about whether the 'resemblance' or 'difference' of homosexuality should be stressed, whether society could find a home for its same-sex desiring population, and what that home should look like, ran through the decade: indeed, this was a structural feature of gay liberation.

References

Primary material

Archival collections
Archive, *APO und soziale Bewegungen, Universitätsarchiv der FU Berlin* (APO)
Archive, *Centrum Schwule Geschichte*, Cologne
Archive, *Schwules Museum Berlin* (SMB)
Hall-Carpenter Archives, London School of Economics (HCA)
Historisches Archiv des Westdeutschen Rundfunks (WDR)
LGBT Community Center National History Archive, New York City
New York Public Library, Manuscripts and Archives division
Spinnboden Lesbenarchiv, Berlin

Personal papers
Detlef Mücke, Berlin

Journals, magazines and newspapers consulted
AHA Info
Autonomie
Blatt
Body Politic
Carlo Sponti
Come Out: A Liberation Forum of the Gay Community
Der Kreis
Der Spiegel
Der Weg
Die Zeit
du&ich
Emanzipation
Frankfurter Allgemeine Zeitung (FAZ)
gay-journal
glf-journal
GSR Info
HAH Info
HAW Info
him
Humanitas
IHS Info
IHWO Report
IHWO Rundbriefe
Informationsdient (ID)
kaktus: Zeitschrift der Homophilen Studentengruppe Münster

konkret
Kursbuch
Pflasterstrand
Rosa
Schwuchtel
Stern
unter uns
VSG Info

Audiovisual sources

§175: Fragen an Homosexuelle und an uns selbst, dir. by Claus-Ferdinand Siegfried (WDR, 1971). SMB archive
Bent, dir. by Sean Mathias (Channel Four Films, 1997)
Detlef: 60 Jahre schwul, dir. by Jan Rothstein and Stefan Westerwelle (Pro-Fun Media, 2012)
Die Konsequenz, dir. by Wolfgang Petersen (WDR, 1977). SMB archive
Faustrecht der Freiheit [Fox and his Friends], dir. by Rainer Werner Fassbinder (1975)
Monitor news programme (ARD, 9 July 1970). SMB archive
Nicht der Homosexuelle ist pervers, sondern die Situation, in der er lebt, dir. by Rosa von Praunheim (Bavaria Atelier, 1971)
'Persecution of religious and other victim groups presented at Nuremberg trial', US Holocaust Memorial Museum <https://collections.ushmm.org/search/catalog/irn1002364> [accessed 10 April 2018]
Rosa Winkel? Das ist doch schon lange vorbei, dir. by Detlef Stoffel, Christiane Schmerl, and Peter Recht (Universität Bielefeld, 1976). SMB archive
Schauplatz Gerichtstrasse—Schwulengruppe Bielefeld (WDR, 1979). SMB archive
Sparring: Homosexualität—noch ein Tabu? (ZDF, 1976). ZDF *historisches Archiv*, 06321/01373
Und wenn Ihr Sohn so wäre. Über Homosexuelle berichtet Eva Müthel (ZDF, 1972). ZDF *historisches Archiv* 06432/00340

Statistics, opinion polls, parliamentary and legal documentation

Allensbacher Jahrbuch der Demoskopie 1974–1976 (Allensbach, 1976)
Allensbacher Jahrbuch der Demoskopie 1976–1977 (Allensbach, 1977)
Allensbacher Jahrbuch der Demoskopie 1979–1983 (Munich, 1983)
'Bericht über die Lage der Psychiatrie in der Bundesrepublik Deutschland', *Deutscher Bundestag 7. Wahlperiode* (November 1975) <http://dipbt.bundestag.de/doc/btd/07/042/0704200.pdf> [accessed 13 November 2018]
Bundesgesetzblatt [1973: 98] (Bonn, 1973), 1725–35
Entscheidungen des Bundesverfassungsgerichts (Tübingen, 1957)
'Gesetz zur Aufhebung nationalsozialistischer Unrechtsurteile in der Strafrechtspflege' <https://www.gesetze-im-internet.de/ns-aufhg/index.html> [accessed 8 December 2018]
Jahrbuch der öffentlichen Meinung 1958–64 (Allensbach, 1965)
Jahrbuch der öffentlichen Meinung 1968–1973 (Allensbach, 1974)

'Plenarprotokoll 5/230', *Deutscher Bundestag—5. Wahlperiode* (7 May 1969). <http://dipbt. bundestag.de/doc/btp/05/05230.pdf> [accessed 8 December 2018]

'Plenarprotokoll 8/179', *Deutscher Bundestag—8. Wahlperiode* (17 October 1979). <http:// dipbt.bundestag.de/doc/btp/08/08179.pdf> [accessed 8 December 2018]

'Schriftlicher Bericht des Sonderausschusses für die Strafrechtsreform', *Deutscher Bundestag—6. Wahlperiode* (14 June 1972), p. 30. <http://dipbt.bundestag.de/doc/btd/ 06/035/0603521.pdf> [accessed 25 June 2018]

Statistisches Jahrbuch für die Bundesrepublik Deutschland (Wiesbaden [published annually])

Strafgesetzbuch (Munich, 1970)

Strafgesetzbuch der DDR (Berlin, 1981)

Von Weizsäcker, Richard, 'Gedenkveranstaltung im Plenarsaal des Deutschen Bundestages zum 40. Jahrestag des Endes des Zweiten Weltkrieges in Europa' <http://www. bundespraesident.de/SharedDocs/Reden/DE/Richard-von-Weizsaecker/Reden/1985/05/ 19850508_Rede.html> [date accessed 3 September 2018]

Published primary sources

Ahrens, Helmut, Volker Bruns, Peter von Hedenström, Gerhard Hoffman, and Reinhard v. d. Marwitz, 'Die Homosexualität in uns', in *Tuntenstreit: Theoriediskussion der Homosexuellen Aktion Westberlin* (Berlin, 1975), 5–34

Altman, Dennis, *Homosexual: Oppression and Liberation* (London, 1974 [1971])

Andreas, 'Meine persönliche HAW-Geschichte', in *Schwule sich emanzipieren lernen: Materialien zur Ausstellung*, ed. by Peter Hedenström (Berlin, 1976), 38–45

Assig, Dorothea, Michael Baurmann, Ralf Dose, Horst Kirchmeier, and Eckehard Kunz (eds), *Sexualität ist mehr. Eine Unterrichtsreihe zum Thema Sexualität* (Wuppertal, 1976)

Autorengruppe schwule Medizinstudenten, *Sumpf Fieber: Medizin für schwule Männer* (Berlin, 1978)

Bachnik, Dieter and Rainer Schädlich (eds), *Alle Schwestern werden Brüder* (Berlin, 1986)

Bauer, Fritz et al. (eds), *Sexualität und Verbrechen: Beiträge zur Strafrechtsreform* (Frankfurt a.M., 1963)

Berliner Kinderläden: Antiautoritäre Erziehung und sozialistischer Kampf (Berlin, 1970)

Berlin-Report (1973 and 1975–1978). SMB archive

Dannecker, Martin and Reimut Reiche, *Der gewöhnliche Homosexuelle: eine soziologische Untersuchung über männliche Homosexuelle in der Bundesrepublik* (Frankfurt a.M., 1974)

Dieckmann, Bernhard and Francois Pescatore (eds), *Elemente einer homosexuellen Kritik: Französische Texte 1971–1977* (Berlin, 1979)

Die schwulen Medizinmänner, *Sumpf Fieber: Medizin für schwule Männer* (Berlin, 1982)

Dröge, Annette, *Sexualität und Herrschaft* (Münster, 1976)

Drost, Elmar, 'Mit dem Schwanz gedacht', in *Schwule Regungen, Schwule Bewegungen: Ein Lesebuch*, ed. by Willi Frieling (Berlin, 1985), 9–24

Duhm, Dieter, *Warenstruktur und zerstörte Zwischenmenschlichkeit: Dritter Versuch der gesellschaftlichen Begründung zwischenmenschlicher Angst in der kapitalistischen Warengesellschaft* (Lampertheim, 1975 [1973])

Eppendorfer, Hans, *Der Ledermann spricht mit Hubert Fichte* (Frankfurt a.M., 1977)

Fromm, Erich, 'Sozialpsychologischer Teil', in *Studien über Autorität und Familie*, ed. by Max Horkheimer (Paris, 1936), 77–135

Gindorf, Ralf and Rüdiger Lautmann, 'Homosexualität und Normalität: Vom Irrtum unserer Kategorien', *Vorgänge: Zeitschrift für Gesellschaftspolitik* 10 (1974), 108–16

Graf, Thorsten and Manfred Herzer, 'Zur neueren Diskussion über die Homosexualität', *Das Argument: Zeitschrift für Philosophie und Sozialwissenschaften*, 93 (1975), 859–74

Graf, Thorsten and Mimi Steglitz, 'Homosexuellenunterdrückung in der bürgerlichen Gesellschaft', in *Tuntenstreit: Theoriediskussion der Homosexuellen Aktion Westberlin* (Berlin, 1975), 35–68

Hedenström, Peter (ed.), *Schwule sich emanzipieren lernen: Materialien zur Ausstellung*, (Berlin, 1976)

Heger, Heinz, *Die Männer mit dem Rosa Winkel* (Hamburg, 1989 [1972])

Herzer, Manfred, 'Homosexuellenemanzipation und Arbeiterbewegung – am Beispiel der Gewerkschaften', in *Seminar: Gesellschaft und Homosexualität*, ed. by Rüdiger Lautmann (Frankfurt a.M., 1977), 480–4

Herzer, Manfred, 'Ein Brief von Kertbeny in Hannover an Ulrichs in Würzburg', *Capri: Zeitschrift für schwule Geschichte 1* (1987), 26–35

Hoffmann, Gerhard, Reinhard v. d. Marwitz, and Dieter Runze, 'Wie können Tunten Sozialisten sein? Zur Kritik der Homosexuellenunterdrückung in der bürgerlichen Gesellschaft durch Graf/Steglitz', in *Tuntenstreit: Theoriediskussion der Homosexuellen Aktion Westberlin* (Berlin, 1975), 69–106

Hohmann, Joachim, *Homosexualität und Subkultur* (Aschenbach, 1976)

Hohmann, Joachim (ed.), *Keine Zeit für gute Freunde: Homosexuelle in Deutschland 1933–1969* (Berlin, 1982)

Internationales Russell-Tribunal: Zur Situation der Menschenrechte in der Bundesrepublik Deutschland [volume three] (Berlin, 1979)

Italiaander, Rolf (ed.), *Weder Krankheit noch Verbrechen: Plädoyer für eine Minderheit* (Hamburg, 1969)

Kameny, Franklin E., 'Gay is Good', in *The Same Sex: An Appraisal of Homosexuality*, ed. by Ralph W. Weltge (Philadelphia, PA, 1969), 129–45

Kraushaar, Elmar (ed.), *Schwule Lyrik, Schwule Prosa: Eine Anthologie* (Berlin, 1977)

Lemke, Jürgen Lemke (ed.), *Gay Voices from East Germany* (Bloomington, IN, 1991)

Linhoff, Ursula, *Weibliche Homosexualität: Zwischen Anpassung und Emanzipation* (Cologne, 1976)

Marbach, Rainer, 'Erinnerungen an die 1950er und 1960er Jahre und den Aufbruch der Schwulenbewegung: Autobiographische Anmerkungen', in *Ohnmacht und Aufbegehren: Homosexuelle Männer in der frühen Bundesrepublik*, ed. by Andreas Pretzel and Volker Weiß (Hamburg, 2010), 27–36

Marcuse, Herbert, *Eros and Civilisation: A Philosophical Inquiry into Freud* (London, 1969 [1955])

Marcuse, Herbert, *One-Dimensional Man. Studies in the Ideology of Advanced Industrial Society* (London, 2002 [1964])

'Persona Humana: Declaration on Certain Questions Concerning Sexual Ethics'. <http://www.vatican.va/roman_curia/congregations/cfaith/documents/rc_con_cfaith_doc_1975 1229_persona-humana_en.html> [accessed 25 June 2018]

Petersen, Wolfgang and Ulrich Greiwe (eds), *Briefe und Dokumente zum Film 'Die Konsequenz'* (Frankfurt a.M., 1980)

Plack, Arno, *Die Gesellschaft und das Böse. Eine Kritik der herrschenden Moral* (Munich, 1970 [1967])

Praunheim, Rosavon, *50 Jahre Pervers: Die sentimentalen Memoiren des Rosa von Praunheim* (Cologne, 1993)

Reich, Wilhelm, *Die Funktion des Orgasmus: Zur Psychopathologie und zur Soziologie des Geschlechtslebens* (Vienna, 1927)

Reich, Wilhelm, *The Sexual Revolution: Toward a Self-governing Character Structure*, trans. by Theodore P. Wolfe (New York, 1971 [1936])

Rexhausen, Felix, *Lavendelschwert: Dokumente einer seltsamen Revolution* (Frankfurt a.M., 1966)

Richter, Horst-Eberhard, *Die Gruppe: Hoffnung auf einen neuen Weg, sich selbst und andere zu befreien. Psychoanalyse in Kooperation mit Gruppeninitiativen* (Hamburg, 1972)

Runze, Dieter, 'Warum ist "Homosexualität" ein "soziales Problem"?', in *Seminar: Gesellschaft und Homosexualität*, ed. by Rüdiger Lautmann (Frankfurt a.M., 1977), 484–92

Schlegel, Willhart (ed.), *Das große Tabu: Zeugnisse und Dokumente zum Problem der Homosexualität* (Munich, 1967)

Schoeps, Hans-Joachim, 'Soll Homosexualität strafbar bleiben?', *Der Monat: Eine internationale Zeitschrift* 171 (1962), 19–27

Schoeps, Hans-Joachim, 'Überlegungen zum Problem der Homosexualität', in *Der homosexuelle Nächste*, ed. by Hermanus Bianchi et al. (Hamburg, 1963), 74–114

Schwendter, Rolf, *Theorie der Subkultur* (Frankfurt a.M., 1981 [1973])

Sexualkunde-Atlas: Biologische Informationen zur Sexualität des Menschen (Opladen, 1969)

Sherman, Martin, *Bent* (New York, 1980 [1979])

Siegfried, Claus-Ferdinand, *Gesellschaft und Homosexualität: Beginn einer Auseinandersetzung* (Berlin, 1972)

Sigusch, Volkmar (ed.), *Sexualität und Medizin* (Cologne, 1979)

Spartacus International Gay Guide (Brighton, 1970)

Spartacus International Gay Guide (Brighton, 1972)

Spartacus International Gay Guide (Amsterdam, annually 1973–1980)

Tuntenstreit: Theoriediskussion der Homosexuellen Aktion Westberlin (Berlin, 1975)

Wackernagel, Barbara, *Die Gruppe Rotzschwul: Eine Analyse homosexueller Subkultur* (Unpublished *Diplomarbeit*: Saarbrücken, 1975)

Werres, Johannes, '"Alles zog sich ins Ghetto zurück": Leben in deutschen Großstädten nach 1945', in *Keine Zeit für gute Freunde: Homosexuelle in Deutschland 1933–1969*, ed. by Joachim Hohmann (Berlin, 1982), 82–92

Werres, Johannes, 'Als Aktivist erster Stunde: Meine Begegnung mit homosexuellen Gruppen und Zeitschriften nach 1945', *Capri: Zeitschrift für schwule Geschichte* 1 (1990), 33–51

Zentralrat der sozialistischen Kinderläden (ed.), *Für die Befreiung der kindlichen Sexualität* (Berlin, 1969)

Secondary literature

Albrecht, Clemens et al. (eds), *Die intellektuelle Gründung der Bundesrepublik: Eine Wirkungsgeschichte der Frankfurter Schule* (Frankfurt a.M., 2000)

Andresen, Knud, 'Linker Antisemitismus – Wandlungen in der Alternativbewegung', in *Das Alternative Milieu: Antibürgerlicher Lebensstil und linke Politik in der*

Bundesrepublik Deutschland und Europa 1968-1983, ed. by Sven Reichardt and Detlef Siegfried (Göttingen, 2010), 146–68

Angelides, Steven, *A History of Bisexuality* (Chicago, 2001)

Apor, Peter, Rebecca Clifford, and Nigel Townson, 'Faith', in *Europe's 1968, Voices of Revolt*, ed. by Robert Gildea et al. (Oxford, 2013), 211–38

Armstrong, Elizabeth and Suzanna Crage, 'Movements and Memory: The Making of the Stonewall Myth', *American Sociological Review* 71 (2006), 724–51

Balzer, Carsten, 'The Beauty and the Beast: Reflections about Socio-Historical and Subcultural Context of Drag Queens and "Tunten" in Berlin', *Journal of Homosexuality* 46 (2004), 55–71

Bauer, Heike, *The Hirschfeld Archives: Violence, Death and Modern Queer Culture* (Philadelphia, PA, 2017)

Bauman, Zygmunt, *Modernity and Ambivalence* (Ithaca, 1991)

Baumann, Cordia, Sebastian Gehrig, and Nicolas Büchse (eds), *Linksalternative Milieus und Neue Soziale Bewegungen in den 1970er Jahren* (Heidelberg, 2011)

Bayer, Ronald, *Homosexuality and American Psychiatry: The Politics of Diagnosis* (Princeton, 1987 [1981])

Beachy, Robert, *Gay Berlin: Birthplace of a Modern Identity* (New York, 2014)

Behrmann, Günter C., 'Kulturrevolution: Zwei Monate im Sommer 1967', in *Die intellektuelle Gründung der Bundesrepublik: Eine Wirkungsgeschichte der Frankfurter Schule*, ed. by Clemens Albrecht et al. (Frankfurt a.M., 2000), 312–85

Bernstein, Mary, 'The Strategic Uses of Identity by the Lesbian and Gay Movement', in *The Social Movements Reader: Cases and Concepts*, ed. by Jeff Goodwin and James M. Jasper (Oxford, 2003), 234–48

Biess, Frank, 'Die Sensibilisierung des Subjekts: Angst und "Neue Subjektivität" in den 1970er Jahren', *Werkstatt Geschichte* 49 (2008), 51–71

Bleuler, Eugen, 'Die Ambivalenz', in *Beiträge zur Schizophrenielehre der Züricher Psychiatrischen Universitätsklinik* Burghölzli (1902-1971), ed. by Manfred Bleuler (Darmstadt, 1979), 85–97

Bollas, Christopher, 'Cruising in the Homosexual Arena', in *Being a Character: Psychoanalysis and Self Experience* (London, 1994), 144–64

Bösch, Frank, 'Die Krise als Chance: Die Neuformierung der Christdemokraten in den siebziger Jahren' in *Das Ende der Zuversicht: Die siebziger Jahre als Geschichte*, ed. by Konrad Jarausch (Göttingen, 2008), 296–312

Bösch, Frank, 'Campaigning against "Red Public Television": Conservative Mobilization and the Invention of Private Television in West Germany', in *Inventing the Silent Majority in Western Europe and the United States: Conservatism in the 1960s and 1970s*, ed. by Anna von der Goltz and Britta Waldschmidt-Nelson (Cambridge, 2017), 275–94

Bourg, Julian, *From Revolution to Ethics: May 1968 and Contemporary French Thought* (Montreal, 2007)

Bourke, Joanna, *Fear: A Cultural History* (London, 2005)

Boyd, Nan Alamilla, 'Talking about Sex: Cheryl Gonzales and Rikki Streicher tell their Stories', in *Bodies of Evidence: The Practice of Queer Oral History*, ed. by Nan Alamilla Boyd and Horacio Roque Ramírez (New York, 2012), 95–112

Boyd, Nan Alamilla and Horacio Roque Ramírez (eds), *Bodies of Evidence: The Practice of Queer Oral History* (New York, 2012)

Braunthal, Gerard, *Political Loyalty and Public Service in West Germany: The 1972 Degree against Radicals and its Consequences* (Massachusetts, 1990)

Brown, Timothy, 'Music as a Weapon? *Ton Steine Scherben* and the Politics of Rock in Cold War Berlin', *German Studies Review* 32:1 (2009), 1–22

Brown, Timothy, *West Germany and the Global Sixties: The Antiauthoritarian Revolt, 1962–1978* (Cambridge, 2013)

Brown, Wendy, 'Wounded Attachments', *Political Theory* 21:3 (1993), 390–410

Brückweh, Kerstin, 'Fantasies of Violence. German Citizens Expressing Their Concepts of Violence and Ideas about Democracy in Letters Referring to the Case of the Serial Killer Jürgen Bartsch (1966–1971)', *Crime, Histoire & Sociétés/Crime, History & Societies* 10:2 (2006). Not paginated

Bruns, Claudia, 'Der homosexuelle Staatsfreund: Von der Konstruktion des erotischen Männerbunds bei Hans Blüher', in *Homosexualität und Staatsräson: Männlichkeit, Homophobie und Politik in Deutschland 1900–45*, ed. by Susanne zur Nieden (Frankfurt a.M., 2005), 100–17

Bude, Heinz, 'The German Kriegskinder: Origins and Impact of the Generation of 1968', in *Generations in Conflict: Youth Revolt and Generation Formation in Germany, 1770–1968*, ed. by Mark Roseman (Cambridge, 1995), 290–305

Callwood, Dan, 'Anxiety and Desire in France's Gay Pornographic Film Boom, 1974–1983,' *Journal of the History of Sexuality* 26 1 (2017), 26–52

Callwood, Dan, 'Re-evaluating the French Gay Liberation Moment 1968–1983' (unpublished doctoral thesis, Queen Mary University of London, 2017)

CheSchahShit: Die sechziger Jahre zwischen Cocktail und Molotov (Hamburg: Rowohlt, 1993)

Confino, Alan, *Germany as a Culture of Remembrance: Promises and Limits of Writing History* (Chapel Hill, 2006)

Cook, Matt, 'AIDS, Mass Observation, and the Fate of the Permissive Turn', *Journal of the History of Sexuality* 26:2 (2017), 239–72

Crouthamel, Jason, *An Intimate History of the Front* (New York, 2014)

Czubayko, Astrid, *Die Sprache von Studenten- und Alternativbewegung* (Aachen, 1997)

Dannecker, Martin, 'Der glühende Wunsch nach Anerkennung und die Affirmation der Differenz. Von den Homophilen der Nachkriegszeit zur Schwulenbewegung der 1970er Jahre', in *Ohnmacht und Aufbegehren: Homosexuelle Männer in der frühen Bundesrepublik*, ed. by Andreas Pretzel and Volker Weiß (Hamburg, 2010), 231–41

Davis, Belinda, 'New Leftists and West Germany: Fascism, Violence and the Public Sphere, 1967–1974', in *Coping with the Nazi Past: West German Debates on Nazism and Generational Conflict, 1955–1975*, ed. by Philipp Gassert and Alan Steinweis (Oxford, 2006), 210–37

D'Emilio, John, *Sexual Politics, Sexual Communities. The Making of a Homosexual Minority in the United States, 1940–1970* (Chicago, 1983)

Dennert, Gabriele, Christiane Leidinger, and Franziska Rauchut (eds), *In Bewegung bleiben: 100 Jahre Politik, Kultur und Geschichte von Lesben* (Berlin, 2007)

Dirke, Sabine von, *All Power to the Imagination! The West German Counterculture from the Student Movement to the Greens* (Lincoln, NE, 1997)

Doan, Laura, *Disturbing Practices: History, Sexuality and Women's Experience of Modern War* (Chicago, 2013)

Dobler, Jens, 'Schwule Lesben', in *Rosa Radikale: Die Schwulenbewegung der 1970er Jahre*, ed. by Andreas Pretzel and Volker Weiß (Hamburg, 2012), 113–23

Dobler, Jens and Harold Rimmele, 'Schwulenbewegung', in *Die Sozialen Bewegungen in Deutschland seit 1945: Ein Handbuch*, ed. by Roland Roth and Dieter Rucht (Frankfurt a. M., 2008), 541–56

Doering-Manteuffel, Anselm and Lutz Raphael, *Nach dem Boom: Perspektiven auf die Zeitgeschichte seit 1970* (Göttingen, 2010 [2008])

Downs, Jim, *Stand by Me: The Forgotten History of Gay Liberation* (New York, 2016)

Duberman, Martin, *Has the gay movement failed?* (Oakland, CA, 2018)

Ebner, Katharina, *Religion im Parlament: Homosexualität als Gegenstand parlamentarischer Debatten im Vereinigten Königreich und in der Bundesrepublik Deutschland (1945–1990)* (Göttingen, 2018)

Eckel, Jan, 'The Rebirth of Politics from the Spirit of Morality: Explaining the Human Rights Revolution of the 1970s', in *The Breakthrough: Human Rights in the 1970s*, ed. by Jan Eckel and Samuel Moyn (Philadelphia, 2014), 226–59

Eckel, Jan and Samuel Moyn (eds), *The Breakthrough: Human Rights in the 1970s* (Philadelphia, 2014)

Eley, Geoff, *Forging Democracy: The History of the Left in Europe, 1850–2000* (Oxford, 2002)

Elman, R. Amy, 'Triangles and Tribulations: The Politics of Nazi Symbols', *Journal of Homosexuality* 30 (1996), 1–11

Evans, Jennifer, 'Bahnhof Boys: Policing Male Prostitution in Post-Nazi Berlin', *Journal of the History of Sexuality*, 12 (2003), 605–36

Evans, Jennifer, 'Decriminalization, Seduction, and "Unnatural Desire" in East Germany', *Feminist Studies* 36 (2010), 553–77

Evans, Jennifer, 'Seeing Subjectivity: Erotic Photography and the Optics of Desire,' *American Historical Review* 18:2 (2013), 430–62

Evans, Jennifer, 'Why Queer German History?,' *German History* 34, 3 (2016), 371–84

Ewing, Christopher, '"Color Him Black": Erotic Representations and the Politics of Race in West German Homosexual Magazines, 1949–1974', *Sexuality and Culture* 21 (2017), 382–403

Ewing, Christopher, '"Toward a Better World for Gays": Race, Tourism, and the Internationalization of The West German Gay Rights Movement, 1969–1983', *Bulletin of the German Historical Institute* 61 (2017), 109–34

Faulenbach, Bernd, *Das sozialdemokratische Jahrzehnt. Von der Reformeuphorie zur neuen Unübersichtlichkeit. Die SPD 1969–1982* (Bonn, 2011)

Foucault, Michel, *The History of Sexuality. Volume One: An Introduction* (London, 1990 [1976])

Frank, Gillian, '"The Civil Rights of Parents": Race and Conservative Politics in Anita Bryant's Campaign Against Gay Rights in 1970s Florida', *Journal of the History of Sexuality* 22 (2013), 126–60

Fraser, Nancy, 'Rethinking the Public Sphere: A Contribution to the Critique of Actually Existing Democracy', in *Habermas and the Public Sphere*, ed. by Craig Calhoun (Cambridge, MA, 1992), 109–42

Frieling, Willi (ed.), *Schwule Regungen, Schwule Bewegungen: Ein Lesebuch* (Berlin, 1985)

Gabriel, Karl, 'Entkirchlichung und (neue) Religion', in *Auf dem Weg in eine neue Moderne? Die Bundesrepublik Deutschland in den siebziger und achtziger Jahren*, ed. by Thomas Raithel, Andreas Rödder, and Andreas Wirsching (Munich, 2009), 99–111

Gammerl, Benno, 'Frau Muskel-Typ. Herr Hexe und Fräulein Butch? Geschlechtlichkeiten und Homosexualitäten in der zweiten Hälfte des 20. Jahrhunderts,' in *Zeitgeschichte als Geschlechtsgeschichte: Neue Perspektiven auf die Bundesrepublik*, ed. by Julia Paulus et al. (Frankfurt a.M., 2012), 225–45

Gammerl, Benno, 'Mit von der Partie oder auf Abstand? Biografische Perspektiven schwuler Männer und lesbischer Frauen auf die Emanzipationsbewegungen der 1970er Jahre', in *Rosa Radikale: Die Schwulenbewegung der 1970er Jahre*, ed. by Andreas Pretzel and Volker Weiß (Hamburg, 2012), 160–76

Gammerl, Benno, 'Früher war mehr Lametta? Schwule Perspektiven auf die siebziger Jahre', paper presented at *Sonntagsclub*, Berlin (4 November 2013)

Gammerl, Benno, 'Ist frei sein normal? Männliche Homosexualitäten seit den 1960er Jahren zwischen Emanzipation und Normalisierung', in *Sexuelle Revolution? Zur Geschichte der Sexualität im deutschsprächigen Raum seit den 1960er Jahren*, ed. by Peter-Paul Bänziger et al. (Bielefeld, 2015), 223–43

Gassner, Frank, 'Wer war Heinz Heger? Klärung eines Pseudonyms', March 2011 <http://www.offener-buecherschrank.at/werwarheinzheger.pdf> [accessed 10 July 2016]

Gilcher-Holtey, Ingrid (ed.), *1968: Vom Ereignis zum Gegenstand der Geschichtswissenschaft* (Göttingen, 1998)

Gildea, Robert, James Mark, and Anette Warring (eds), *Europe's 1968, Voices of Revolt* (Oxford, 2013)

Giles, Geoffrey, 'The Denial of Homosexuality: Same-Sex Incidents in Himmler's SS and Police', *Journal of the History of Sexuality* 11 (2002), 256–90

Goltz, Anna von der, 'A Polarised Generation? Conservative Students and West Germanys "1968"', in *Talkin' 'bout My Generation'—Conflicts of Generation Building and Europe's '1968'*, ed. by Anna von der Goltz (Göttingen, 2011), 195–215

Goltz, Anna von der, 'A Vocal Minority: Student Activism of the Center-Right and West Germany's 1968', in *Inventing the Silent Majority in Western Europe and the United States: Conservatism in the 1960s and 1970s*, ed. by Anna von der Goltz and Britta Waldschmidt-Nelson (Cambridge, 2017), 82–104

Goltz, Anna von der (ed.), *Talkin' 'bout My Generation'—Conflicts of Generation Building and Europe's '1968'* (Göttingen, 2011)

Gotto, Bernhard, 'The Best Thing That Remained of '68? Experiences of Protest and Expectations on Change in the West German Women's Movement during the 1970s and 1980s', paper presented at *Social Movements after '68: Germany, Europe, and Beyond* conference at Rutgers University (9 November 2018)

Gould, Deborah, *Moving Politics: Emotion and ACT UP's Fight against AIDS* (Chicago, 2009)

Gould, Deborah, 'The Shame of Gay Pride in Early AIDS Activism', in *Gay Shame,* ed. by David Halperin and Valerie Traub (Chicago, 2009), 221–55

Gregg, Ronald, 'Fassbinder's Fox and His Friends and Gay Politics in the 1970s', in *A Companion to Rainer Werner Fassbinder*, ed. by Brigitte Peucker (Oxford, 2012), 542–63

Griffiths, Craig, 'The International Effects of the Stonewall Riots', in *Global Encyclopedia of Lesbian, Gay, Bisexual, Transgender, and Queer History*, ed. by Howard Chiang et al. (Farmington Hills, MI, 2019), 1549–55

Griffiths, Craig, 'Gay Activism in Modell Deutschland', *European Review of History* 22 (2015), 60–76

Griffiths, Craig, 'Sex, Shame and West German Gay Liberation', *German History* 34 (2016), 445–67

Grisard, Dominique, 'Zum Stellenwert der Farbe in der Schwulen- und Lesbenbewegung', in *Rosa Radikale: Die Schwulenbewegung der 1970er Jahre*, ed. by Andreas Pretzel and Volker Weiß (Hamburg, 2012), 177–98

Grühn, Gerhard, 'Troubles in Paradise. 30 Jahre Schwulen- und Lesbenzentren in Köln', *Invertito* 7 (2005), 37–64

Grumbach, Detlef (ed.), *Was heißt hier schwul? Politik und Identitäten im Wandel* (Hamburg, 1997)

Häberlen, Joachim C., 'Feeling Like a Child: Dreams and Practices of Sexuality in the West German Alternative Left during the Long 1970s', *Journal of the History of Sexuality* 25:2 (2016), 219–45

Häberlen, Joachim C., *The Emotional Politics of the Alternative Left: West Germany, 1968–1984* (Cambridge, 2018)

Häberlen, Joachim C. and Jake P. Smith, 'Struggling for Feelings: The Politics of Emotions in the Radical New Left in West Germany, c.1968–84', *Contemporary European History* 23 (2014), 615–37

Halle, Randall, 'Rainer, Rosa, and Werner: New Gay Film as Counter-Public', in *A Companion to Rainer Werner Fassbinder*, ed. by Brigitte Peucker (Oxford, 2012), 564–78

Halperin, David, *How to Be Gay* (Cambridge, MA, 2012)

Halperin, David and Valerie Traub (eds), *Gay Shame* (Chicago, 2009)

Harthauser, Wolfgang, 'Der Massenmord an Homosexuellen im Dritten Reich', in *Das große Tabu: Zeugnisse und Dokumente zum Problem der Homosexualität*, ed. by Willhart Schlegel (Munich, 1967), 7–37

Haunss, Sebastian, *Identität in Bewegung: Prozesse kollektiver Identität bei den Autonomen und in der Schwulenbewegung* (Wiesbaden, 2004)

Healey, Dan, *Homosexual Desire in Revolutionary Russia: The Regulation of Sexual and Gender Dissent* (Chicago, 2000)

Heichel, Stephan and Adrian Rinscheid, 'Ein klassischer Fall von Inkrementalismus: Die Liberalisierung der Regulierung von Homosexualität', in *Moralpolitik in Deutschland: Staatliche Regulierung gesellschaftlicher Wertekonflikte im historischen und internationalen Vergleich*, ed. by Christoph Knill et al. (Wiesbaden, 2015), 127–46

Heineman, Elizabeth, *Before Porn Was Legal: The Erotica Empire of Beate Uhse* (Chicago, 2011)

Henze, Patrick, *Schwule Emanzipation und ihre Konflikte: Zur westdeutschen Schwulenbewegung der 1970er Jahre* (Berlin, 2019)

Herbert, Ulrich (ed.), *Wandlungsprozesse in Westdeutschland: Belastung, Integration, Liberalisierung 1945–1980* (Göttingen, 2002)

Herzog, Dagmar, *Sex after Fascism: Memory and Morality in Twentieth-Century Germany* (Princeton, 2005)

Herzog, Dagmar, *Sexuality in Europe: A Twentieth-Century History* (Cambridge, 2011)

Herzog, Dagmar, *Cold War Freud: Psychoanalysis in an Age of Catastrophes* (Cambridge, 2017)

Hesford, Victoria, *Feeling Women's Liberation* (Durham, NC, 2013)

Hilderbrand, Lucas, 'A Suitcase Full of Vaseline, or Travels in the 1970s Gay World', *Journal of the History of Sexuality* 22 (2013), 373–402

Hillman, Betty Luther, '"The most profoundly revolutionary act a homosexual can engage in": Drag and the Politics of Gender Presentation in the San Francisco Gay Liberation Movement, 1964–1972', *Journal of the History of Sexuality* 20 (2011), 153–81

Hirsch, Marianne, *The Generation of Postmemory: Writing and Visual Culture After the Holocaust* (New York, 2012)

Hobson, Emily, *Lavender and Red: Liberation and Solidarity in the Gay and Lesbian Left* (Oakland, CA, 2016)

Hodenberg, Christina von, 'Konkurrierende Konzepte von "Öffentlichkeit" in der Orientierungskrise der 60er Jahre', in *Demokratisierung und gesellschaftlicher Aufbruch: Die sechziger Jahre als Wendezeit der Bundesrepublik*, ed. by Matthias Frese et al. (Paderborn, 2003), 205–26

Hodenberg, Christina von, *Konsens und Krise: Eine Geschichte der westdeutschen Medienöffentlichkeit 1945–1973* (Göttingen, 2006)

Hodenberg, Christina von, 'Mass Media and the Generation of Conflict: West Germany's Long Sixties and the Formation of a Critical Public Sphere', *Contemporary European History* 15 (2006), 367–95

Hodenberg, Christina von, *Televisions's Moment. Sitcom Audiences and the Sixties Cultural Revolution* (New York, 2015)

Hodenberg, Christina von, *Das andere Achtundsechzig: Gesellschaftsgeschichte einer Revolte* (Munich, 2018)

Hodenberg, Christina von, 'Writing Women's Agency into the History of the Federal Republic: "1968", Historians, and Gender', *Central European History* 52 (2019), 87–106

Holy, Michael, '"Macht euer Schwulsein öffentlich!" Zum Verhältnis von "privat" und "öffentlich" in der zweiten deutschen Homosexuellenbewegung', in *Schwule Regungen, Schwule Bewegungen: Ein Lesebuch*, ed. by Willi Frieling (Berlin, 1985), 37–46

Holy, Michael, 'Historischer Abriß der zweiten deutschen Schwulenbewegung 1969–1989', in *Neue Soziale Bewegungen in der Bundesrepublik Deutschland*, ed. by Roland Roth and Dieter Rucht (Bonn, 1991), 138–60

Holy, Michael, 'Der entliehene Rosa Winkel', in *Der Frankfurter Engel: Mahnmal Homosexuellenverfolgung*, ed. by Initiative Mahnmal Homosexuellenverfolgung (Frankfurt a.M., 1997), 74–87

Holy, Michael, 'Lange hieß es, Homosexualität sei gegen die Ordnung: Die westdeutsche Schwulenbewegung (1969-1980)', in *Dokumentation einer Vortragsreihe in der Akademie der Künste: 100 Jahre Schwulenbewegung*, ed. by Manfred Herzer (Berlin, 1998), 83–109

Holy, Michael, 'Jenseits von Stonewall – Rückblicke auf die Schwulenbewegung in der BRD 1969-1980', in *Rosa Radikale: Die Schwulenbewegung der 1970er Jahre*, ed. by Andreas Pretzel and Volker Weiß (Hamburg, 2012), 39–79

Holy, Michael, 'Bewegungsgeschichte und Sammelleidenschaft: Zur Entstehung der "Sammlung Holy",' in *Politiken in Bewegung: Die Emanzipation Homosexueller im 20. Jahrhundert*, ed. by Andreas Pretzel and Volker Weiss (Hamburg, 2017), 193–245

Horn, Gerd-Rainer, *The Spirit of '68: Rebellion in Western Europe and North America, 1956-1976* (Oxford, 2007)

Jackson, Julian, *Living in Arcadia: Homosexuality, Politics and Morality in France from the Liberation to AIDS* (Chicago, 2009)

Jarausch, Konrad, 'Verkannter Strukturwandel: Die siebziger Jahre als Vorgeschichte der Probleme der Gegenwart', in *Das Ende der Zuversicht? Die siebziger Jahre als Geschichte* (Göttingen, 2008), 10–26

Jensen, Erik N., 'The Pink Triangle and Political Consciousness: Gays, Lesbians, and the Memory of Nazi Persecution', *Journal of The History of Sexuality* 11 (2002), 319–49

Jessen, Ralph, 'Bewältigte Vergangenheit – blockierte Zukunft? Ein prospektiver Blick auf die bundesrepublikanische Gesellschaft am Ende der Nachkriegszeit', in *Das Ende der Zuversicht? Die siebziger Jahre als Geschichte*, ed. by Konrad Jarausch (Göttingen, 2008), 177–95

Johnson, David K., *The Lavender Scare: The Cold War Persecution of Gays and Lesbians in the Federal Government* (Chicago, 2004)

Jureit, Ulrike and Michael Wildt (eds), *Generationen: zur Relevanz eines wissenschaftlichen Grundbegriffs* (Hamburg, 2005)

Kandora, Michael, 'Homosexualität und Sittengesetz', in *Wandlungsprozesse in Westdeutschland: Belastung, Integration, Liberalisierung 1945-1980*, ed. by Ulrich Herbert (Göttingen, 2002), 379–401

Kennedy, Elizabeth Lapovsky, 'Telling Tales: Oral History and the Construction of Pre-Stonewall Lesbian History', *Radical History Review* 62 (1995), 58–79

Kennedy, Hubert, *The Ideal Gay Man: The Story of Der Kreis* (New York, 1999)

Kießling, Friedrich, and Bernhard Rieger (eds), *Mit dem Wandel Leben: Neuorientierung und Tradition in der Bundesrepublik der 1950er und 60er Jahre* (Cologne, 2011)

Kissack, Terence, 'Freaking Fag Revolutionaries: New York's Gay Liberation Front, 1969–1971', *Radical History Review* 62 (1995), 104–35

Klimke, Martin and Joachim Scharloth (eds), *1968 in Europe: a History of Protest and Activism, 1956–1977* (New York, 2008)

Knoch, Hanno (ed.), *Bürgersinn mit Weltgefühl: Politische Moral und solidarischer Protest in den sechziger und siebziger Jahren* (Göttingen, 2007)

Koenen, Gerd, *Das rote Jahrzehnt: Unsere kleine deutsche Kulturrevolution, 1967–1977* (Cologne, 2001)

Kogon, Eugen, *Der SS-Staat. Das System der deutschen Konzentrationslager* (Düsseldorf, 1946)

Kuckuc, Ina [pseudonym], *Der Kampf gegen Unterdrückung: Materialien aus der deutschen Lesbierinnenbewegung* (Munich, 1975)

Kühn, Andreas, *Stalins Enkel, Maos Söhne: die Lebenswelt der K-Gruppen in der Bundesrepublik der 70er Jahre* (Frankfurt a.M., 2005)

Kraushaar, Elmar, '"Nebenwidersprüche": Die neue Linke und die Schwulenfrage in der Bundesrepublik der siebziger und achtziger Jahre', in *Die Linke und das Laster: Schwule Emanzipation und linke Vorurteile*, ed. by Detlef Grumbach (Hamburg, 1995), 142–78

Kraushaar, Elmar, 'Höhenflug und Absturz - Von Homolulu am Main nach Bonn in die Beethoven-Halle', in *Rosa Radikale: Die Schwulenbewegung der 1970er Jahre*, ed. by Andreas Pretzel and Volker Weiß (Hamburg, 2012), 80–90

Laplache, Jean and Jean-Bertrand Pontalis, *The Language of Psycho-Analysis* (London, 1973)

Lautmann, Rüdiger, 'The Pink Triangle: The Persecution of Homosexual Males in Concentration Camps in Nazi Germany', *Journal of Homosexuality* 6 (1980), 141–60

Lautmann, Rüdiger, 'Homosexuelle in den Konzentrationslagern: Zum Stand der Forschung', *Homosexuelle in Konzentrationslagern*, ed. by Olaf Mussmann (Berlin, 2000), 31–8

Lautmann, Rüdiger (ed.), *Capricen: Momente schwuler Geschichte* (Hamburg, 2014)

Lautmann, Rüdiger, Winfried Grikschat, and Egbert Schmidt, 'Der rosa Winkel in den nationalsozialistischen Konzentrationslagern', in *Seminar: Gesellschaft und Homosexualität*, ed. by Rüdiger Lautmann (Frankfurt a.M., 1977), 325–65

Leidinger, Christiane, 'Gründungsmythen zur Geschichtsbemächtigung? Die erste autonome Schwulengruppe der BRD war eine Frau', *Invertito—Jahrbuch für die Geschichte der Homosexualitäten* 13 (2011), 9–39

Lenz, Ilse, 'Das Private ist politisch!? Zum Verhältnis von Frauenbewegung und alternativem Milieu', in *Das alternative Milieu: Antibürgerlicher Lebensstil und linke Politik in der Bundesrepublik Deutschland und Europa 1968–1983*, ed. by Sven Reichardt and Detlef Siegfried(Göttingen, 2010), 375–404

Love, Heather, *Feeling Backward: Loss and the Politics of Queer History* (Cambridge, 2007)

Lybeck, Marti, *Desiring Emancipation: New Women and Homosexuality in Germany, 1890–1933* (New York, 2014)

Marhoefer, Laurie, *Sex and the Weimar Republic: German Homosexual Emancipation and the Rise of the Nazis* (Toronto, 2015)

Markovits, Andrei and Philip Gorski, *The German Left: Red, Green and Beyond* (Cambridge, 1993)

Marwick, Arthur, *The Sixties: Cultural Revolution in Britain, France, Italy, and the United States, c. 1958–1974* (Oxford, 1998)

Mausbach, Wilfried, 'Wende um 360 Grad? Nationalsozialismus in der "zweiten Gründungsphase" der Bundesrepublik', in *Wo '1968' liegt: Reform und Revolte in der Geschichte der Bundesrepublik*, ed. by Christina von Hodenberg and Detlef Siegfried (Göttingen, 2006), 15–47

Mausbach, Wilfried, 'Americas Vietnam in Germany – Germany in America's Vietnam: On the Relocation of Spaces and the Appropriation of History', in *Changing the World, Changing Oneself: Political Protest and Collective Identities in West Germany and the U.S. in the 1960s and 1970s*, ed. by Belinda Davis et al. (New York, 2010), 41–64

März, Michael, *Linker Protest nach dem Deutschen Herbst: Eine Geschichte des linken Spektrums im Schatten des 'Starken Staates', 1977–1979* (Bielefeld, 2012)

McLellan, Josie, 'Glad to be Gay Behind the Wall: Gay and Lesbian Activism in 1970s East Germany', *History Workshop Journal* 74 (2012), 105–30

McLellan, Josie, *Love in the Time of Communism: Intimacy and Sexuality in the GDR* (Cambridge, 2011)

Meeker, Martin, *Contacts Desired: Gay and Lesbian Communications and Community, 1940s–1970s* (Chicago, 2006)

Merton, Robert and Elinor Barber, 'Sociological Ambivalence', in *Sociological Ambivalence and Other Essays*, ed. by Robert Merton (New York, 1976), 3–31

Micheler, Stefan, 'Heteronormativität, Homophobie und Sexualdenunziation in der deutschen Studierendenbewegung', *Invertito: Jahrbuch für die Geschichte der Homosexualitäten* 1 (1999), 70–101

Mildenberger, Florian G., *Die Münchner Schwulenbewegung 1969–1996: Eine Fallstudie über die zweite deutsche Schwulenbewegung* (Bochum, 1999)

Mildenberger, Florian G., 'Socialist Eugenics and Homosexuality in the GDR: The Case of Günter Dörner', in *After the History of Sexuality*, ed. by Scott Spector, Helmut Puff, and Dagmar Herzog (New York, 2012), 216–30

Milder, Stephen, *Greening Democracy: The Anti-Nuclear Movement and Political Environmentalism in West Germany and Beyond, 1968–1983* (Cambridge, 2017)

Moeller, Robert G., 'The Homosexual Man Is a "Man", the Homosexual Woman Is a "Woman": Sex, Society, and the Law in Postwar West Germany', *Journal of the History of Sexuality* 4 (1994), 395–429

Moeller, Robert G., *War Stories: The Search for a Usable Past in the Federal Republic of Germany* (Berkeley, 2003)

Moeller, Robert G., 'Private Acts, Public Anxieties, and the Fight to Decriminalize Male Homosexuality in West Germany', *Feminist Studies* 36 (2010), 528–52

Moses, Dirk, *German Intellectuals and the Nazi Past* (Cambridge, 2007)

Moyn, Samuel, *The Last Utopia: Human Rights in History* (Cambridge, MA, 2010)

Moyn, Samuel, 'Two Regimes of Memory', *American Historical Review* 103:4 (1998), 1182–6

Mücke, Detlef, 'Schwule und Schule: 11 Jahre Initiativen von schwulen Lehrergruppen', in *Schwule Regungen, Schwule Bewegungen: Ein Lesebuch*, ed. by Willi Frieling (Berlin, 1985)

Oosterhuis, Harry, 'The "Jews" of the Antifascist Left', *Journal of Homosexuality* 29:2–3 (1995), 227–57

Ording, Dominic, 'Intimate Fellows: Utopia and Chaos in the Early Post-Stonewall Gay Liberation Manifestos,' in *Anarchism and Utopianism*, ed. by Laurence Davis and Ruth Kinna (Manchester, 2009), 187–206

Papadogiannis, Nikos, *Militant Around the Clock?: Left-wing Youth Politics, Leisure, and Sexuality in Post-dictatorship Greece, 1974–1981* (New York, 2015)

Pareik, Andreas, 'Kampf um eine Identität. Entwicklung, Probleme, Perspektiven der neuen Homosexuellen-Emanzipationsbewegung am Beispiel der Homosexuelle Aktion Westberlin' (unpublished doctoral thesis, Berlin, 1977)

Passmore, Leith, 'The Art of Hunger: Self-Starvation in the Red Army Faction', *German History* 27 (2009), 32–59

Pater, Monica, '"Gegen geile Männerpresse – für lesbische Liebe". Der Andersen/Ihns-Prozess als Ausgangspunkt für das Coming-out von Lesben', *Invertito: Jahrbuch der Homosexualitäten*, 8 (2006), 143–68

Paternotte, David, 'The International (Lesbian and) Gay Association and the Question of Pedophilia: Tracking the Demise of Gay Liberation Ideals,' *Sexualities* 17 (2014), 121–38

Peña, Susana, 'Gender and Sexuality in Latina/o Miami: Documenting Latina Transsexual Activists', *Gender and History* 22 (2010), 755–72

Perincioli, Cristina, *Berlin wird feministisch: das Beste, was von der 68er Bewegung blieb* (Berlin, 2015)

Perinelli, Massimo, 'Longing, Lust, Violence, Liberation: Discourses on Sexuality on the Radical Left in West Germany, 1969–1972', in *After the History of Sexuality*, ed. by Scott Spector, Helmut Puff, and Dagmar Herzog (New York, 2012), 248–81

Plant, Richard, *The Pink Triangle: The Nazi War against Homosexuals* (New York, 1986)

Pretzel, Andreas, 'Aufbruch und Resignation: Zur Geschichte der Berliner "Gesellschaft für Reform des Sexualrechts e.V." 1948–1960', in *NS-Opfer unter Vorbehalt: Homosexuelle Männer in Berlin nach 1945*, ed. by Andreas Pretzel (Münster, 2002), 287–343

Pretzel, Andreas and Volker Weiß (eds), *Ohnmacht und Aufbegehren: Homosexuelle Männer in der frühen Bundesrepublik* (Hamburg, 2010)

Pretzel, Andreas and Volker Weiß (eds), *Rosa Radikale: Die Schwulenbewegung der 1970er Jahre* (Hamburg, 2012)

Probyn, Elspeth, *Blush: Faces of Shame* (Minneapolis, 2005)

Puff, Helmut, 'After the History of (Male) Homosexuality', in *After the History of Sexuality*, ed. by Scott Spector, Helmut Puff, and Dagmar Herzog (New York, 2012), 17–30

Raithel, Thomas, Andreas Rödder, and Andreas Wirsching (eds), *Auf dem Weg in eine neue Moderne? Die Bundesrepublik Deutschland in den siebziger und achtziger Jahren* (Munich, 2009)

Ramírez, Horacio N. Roque, 'Sharing Queer Authorities: Collaborating for Transgender Latina and Gay Latino Historical Meanings', in *Bodies of Evidence: The Practice of Queer Oral History*, ed. by Nan Alamilla Boyd and Horacio N. Roque Ramírez (Oxford, 2012), 184–201

Rehberg, Peter, 'Männer wie Du und Ich': Gay Magazines from the National to the Transnational', *German History* 34, 3 (2016), 468–85

Reichardt, Sven, 'Inszenierung und Authentizität. Zirkulation visueller Vorstellungen über den Typus des linksalternativen Körpers', in *Bürgersinn mit Weltgefühl: Politische Moral und solidarischer Protest in den sechziger und siebziger Jahren*, ed. by Hanno Knoch (Göttingen, 2007), 225–50

Reichardt, Sven, *Authentizität und Gemeinschaft: Linksalternatives Leben in den siebziger und frühen achtziger Jahren* (Berlin, 2014)

Reichardt, Sven and Detlef Siegfried (eds), *Das alternative Milieu: Antibürgerlicher Lebensstil und linke Politik in der Bundesrepublik Deutschland und Europa 1968–1983* (Göttingen, 2010)

Reiche, Reimut, 'Sexuelle Revolution – Erinnerung an einen Mythos', *Die Früchte der Revolte: Über die Veränderung der politischen Kultur durch die Studentenbewegung*, ed. by Lothar Baier et al. (Berlin, 1988), 45–71

Reimann, Aribert, *Dieter Kunzelmann: Avantgardist, Protestler, Radikaler* (Göttingen, 2009)

Reimann, Aribert, 'Zwischen Machismo und Coolness. Männlichkeit und Emotion in der westdeutschen "Kulturrevolution" der 1960er- und 1970er Jahren', in *Die Präsenz der Gefühle: Männlichkeit und Emotion in der Moderne*, ed. by Manuel Borutta and Nina Verheyen (Bielefeld, 2010), 229–54

Riechers, Burkhardt, 'Freundschaft und Anständigkeit. Leitbilder im Selbtsverständnis männlicher Homosexueller in der frühen Bundesrepublik', *Invertito: Jahrbuch für die Geschichte der Homosexualitäten* 1 (1999), 12–46

Robinson, Lucy, *Gay Men and the Left in Post-War Britain* (Manchester, 2007)

Rosa Geschichten (ed.), *Eine Tunte bist du auf jeden Fall: 20 Jahre Schwulenbewegung in Münster* (Münster, 1992)

Roseman, Mark (ed.), *Generations in Conflict: Youth Revolt and Generation Formation in Germany, 1770–1968* (Cambridge, 1995)

Rosenkranz, Bernhard and Gottfried Lorenz, *Hamburg auf anderen Wegen. Die Geschichte des schwulen Lebens in der Hansestadt* (Hamburg, 2005)

Roth, Roland and Dieter Rucht (eds), *Die sozialen Bewegungen in Deutschland seit 1945: Ein Handbuch* (Frankfurt a.M., 2008)

Rothberg, Michael, *Multidirectional Memory: Remembering the Holocaust in the Age of Decolonization* (Stanford, 2009)

Rucht, Dieter, 'Das alternative Milieu in der Bundesrepublik. Ursprünge, Infrastruktur und Nackwirkungen', in *Das alternative Milieu: Antibürgerlicher Lebensstil und linke Politik in der Bundesrepublik Deutschland und Europa 1968–1983*, ed. by Sven Reichardt and Detlef Siegfried (Göttingen, 2010), 61–88

Rupp, Leila, 'The Persistence of Transnational Organizing: The Case of the Homophile Movement', *American Historical Review* 116 (2011), 1014–39

Salmen, Andreas and Albert Eckert, *20 Jahre bundesdeutsche Schwulenbewegung 1969–1989* (Cologne, 1989)

Schäfer, Christine, *Zwischen Nachkriegsfrust und Aufbruchslust: Lesbisches Leben in München in den 1950er bis 1970er Jahren* (Munich, 2010)

Schappach, Beate, 'Geballte Faust, Doppelaxt, rosa Winkel: Gruppenkonstituierende Symbole der Frauen-, Lesben- und Schwulenbewegung', in *Linksalternative Milieus und Neue Soziale Bewegungen in den 1970er Jahren*, ed. by Cordia Baumann, Sebastian Gehrig, and Nicolas Büchse (Heidelberg, 2011), 259–83

Schiefelbein, Dieter, '". . . so wie die Juden"– Versuch, ein Mißverständnis zu verstehen', in *Der Frankfurter Engel: Mahnmal Homosexuellenverfolgung*, ed. by Initiative Mahnmal Homosexuellenverfolgung (Frankfurt a.M., 1997), 35–73

Schildt, Axel, '"Die Kräfte der Gegenreform sind auf breiter Front angetreten": Zur konservativen Tendenzwende in den Siebzigerjahren', *Archiv für Sozialgeschichte* 44 (2004), 449–79

Schulz, Kristina, *Der lange Atem der Provokation: Die Frauenbewegung in der Bundesrepublik und in Frankreich 1968–1976* (Frankfurt a.M., 2002)

Schwartz, Michael, 'Warum machen Sie sich für die Homos stark?' Homosexualität und Medienöffentlichkeit in der westdeutschen Reformzeit der 1960er und 1970er Jahre', *Jahrbuch Sexualitäten 2016*, ed. by Mari Borowski et al. (Göttingen, 2016), 51–93

Sedgwick, Eve Kosofsky, *Touching Feeling: Affect, Pedagogy, Performativity* (Durham, NC, 2003)

Sedgwick, Eve Kosofsky, *Epistemology of the Closet* (Berkeley, 2008 [1990])

Sedlmaier, Alexander, *Consumption and Violence: Radical Protest in Cold-War West Germany* (Ann Arbor, 2014)

Smith, Charles, 'The Evolution of the Gay Male Public Sphere in England and Wales, 1967–c.1983' (unpublished doctoral dissertation, Loughborough University, 2015)

Spector, Scott, Helmut Puff, and Dagmar Herzog (eds), *After the History of Sexuality* (New York, 2012)

Steakley, James D., *The Homosexual Emancipation Movement in Germany* (New York, 1975)

Steakley, James D., 'Selbstkritische Gedanken zur Mythologisierung der Homosexuellenverfolgung im Dritten Reich', in *Nationalsozialistischer Terror gegen Homosexuelle: verdrängt und ungesühnt*, ed. by Burkhard Jellonek and Rüdiger Lautmann (Paderborn, 2002), 55–70

Stedefeldt, Eike, *Schwule Macht. Oder, Die Emanzipation von der Emanzipation* (Berlin, 1998)

Stein, Marc, *City of Sisterly and Brotherly Loves: Lesbian and Gay Philadelphia, 1945–1972* (Chicago, 2000)

Stein, Marc, *Rethinking the Gay and Lesbian Movement* (New York, 2012)

Steinbacher, Sybille, *Wie der Sex nach Deutschland kam: Der Kampf um Sittlichkeit und Anstand in der frühen Bundesrepublik* (Munich, 2011)

Stümke, Hans-Georg, 'Demokratie ist abendfüllend. Die alte Coming-out-Bewegung ist tot. Wir brauchen eine politische Schwulenbewegung', in *Was heißt hier schwul?: Politik und Identitäten im Wandel*, ed. by Detlef Grumbach (Hamburg, 1997), 45–56

Sutton, Katie, *Sex between Body and Mind: Psychoanalysis and Sexology in the German-speaking World, 1890s–1930s* (Ann Arbor, MI, 2019)

Tändler, Maik, '"Psychoboom". Therapeutisierungsprozesse in Westdeutschland in den späten 1960er- und 1970er Jahren', in *Das beratene Selbst: Zur Genealogie der Therapeutisierung in den 'langen' Siebzigern*, ed. by Sabine Maasen et al. (Bielefeld, 2011), 59–94

Terhoeven, Petra, *Deutscher Herbst in Europa. Der Linksterrorismus der siebziger Jahre als transnationales Phänomen* (Munich, 2014)

Tobin, Robert Deam, *Peripheral Desires: The German Discovery of Sex* (Philadelphia, 2015)

Tomkins, Silvan, 'Shame-Humiliation and Contempt-Disgust', in *Shame and its Sisters: A Silvan Tomkins Reader*, ed. by Eve Sedgwick and Adam Frank (Durham, NC, 1995), 133–78

Tompkins, Andrew, *Better Active than Radioactive! Anti-Nuclear Protest in 1970s France and West Germany* (Oxford, 2016)

Tümmers, Henning, '"Heaven can Wait": Reaktionen auf die Aids-Bedrohung in Hamburg', *Zeitgeschichte in Hamburg* (2011), 13–30

Valentine, David, *Imagining Transgender: An Ethnography of a Category* (Durham, NC, 2007)

Valocchi, Steve, 'The Class-Inflected Nature of Gay Identity', *Social Problems* 46 (1999), 207–24

Valocchi, Stephen, '"Where Did Gender Go?" Same-Sex Desire and the Persistence of Gender in Gay Male Historiography', *GLQ: A Journal of Lesbian and Gay Studies* 18 (2012), 453–79

Varon, Jeremy, *Bringing the War Home: The Weather Underground, The Red Army Faction, and Revolutionary Violence in the 60s and 70s* (Berkeley, 2004)

Vider, Stephen, '"The Ultimate Extension of Gay Community": Communal Living and Gay Liberation in the 1970s', *Gender and History* 27 (2015), 865–81

Wachsmann, Nikolaus, *KL: A History of the Nazi Concentration Camps* (London, 2015)

Wackerfuss, Andrew, *Stormtrooper Families: Homosexuality and Community in the Early Nazi Movement* (New York, 2015)

Warner, Michael, *Publics and Counterpublics* (New York, 2002)

Waters, Chris, 'Distance and Desire in the New British Queer History', *GLQ: A Journal of Lesbian and Gay Studies* 14 (2008), 139–55

Waters, Chris, 'The Homosexual as a Social Being in Britain, 1945–1968', *Journal of British Studies* 51 (2012), 685–710

Weeks, Jeffrey, *Coming Out: Homosexual Politics in Britain from the Nineteenth Century to the Present* (London, 1990 [1977])

Whisnant, Clayton, *Male Homosexuality in West Germany: Between Persecution and Freedom 1945–1969* (New York, 2012)

Whisnant, Clayton, *Queer Identities and Politics in Germany: A History, 1880–1945* (New York, 2016)

Wilde, Harry, *Das Schicksal der Verfemten: Die Verfolgung der Homosexuellen im 'Dritten Reich' und ihre Stellung in der heutigen Gesellschaft* (Tübingen, 1969)

Wildenthal, Lora, *The Language of Human Rights in West Germany* (Philadelphia, 2013)

Winter, Jay, *War beyond Words: Languages of Remembrance from the Great War to the Present* (Cambridge, 2017)

Wolfert, Raimund, *Gegen Einsamkeit und 'Einsiedelei': Die Geschichte der Internationalen Homophilen Welt-Organisation* (Hamburg, 2009)

Index

Note: Figures are indicated by an italic "*f*", following the page number.

For the benefit of digital users, indexed terms that span two pages (e.g., 52–53) may, on occasion, appear on only one of those pages.